# Government in America

# GOVERNMENT

NEW YORK   HENRY HOLT AND COMPANY

# in America

**STEPHEN K. BAILEY**
Princeton University

**HOWARD D. SAMUEL**

**SIDNEY BALDWIN**
New York University

*Picture Credits*

TO

ELMER ERIC SCHATTSCHNEIDER
teacher, scholar, counsellor, friend;
defender of the democratic faith; and
master purveyor of the legends of man's
foibles, humors, and promise.

# Preface

This book is an attempt to tell in short compass the essential story of government in America. It is addressed particularly to the beginning student in college who wishes to understand his nation's federal, state, and local governments and his role as a citizen in them, but who is more often bewildered than enlightened by what Professor Schattschneider once called "vast compendia of free and equal facts."

Two of the three authors have spent much time in the past decade organizing, and teaching in, the introductory undergraduate course in American government. The perennial problem for us has been one of student motivation. Serious books on serious subjects are not meant to be entertaining; but learning is made unnecessarily difficult if material is not presented in a way that is both interesting to the student and somehow relatable to his own experience. Only a distinguished few textbooks in American government meet these criteria, and most of these are too long for a one semester course—or even for a year's course if supplementary reading is assigned.

Hence, this new, brief attempt at a most difficult object. Only other textbook writers know how difficult the object really is. No human mind —or three together—can encompass the sweep and moral grandeur as well as the art and artfulness of government in America.

Not only is American government dispersed and complex; but like all stories of man, it is a story of good and evil—sometimes between men, but mostly within men. As G. K. Chesterton has written

> The error of Diogenes lay in the fact that he omitted to notice that every man is both an honest and dishonest man. Diogenes looked for his honest man inside every crypt and cavern, but he never thought of looking inside the thief. And that is where the Founder of Christianity found the honest man. He found him on a gibbet and promised him paradise.[1]

It is this moral ambivalence particularly that makes a meaningful portrait difficult. And if the portrait painter is limited—as we are—to a wide brush and a small canvas, he is necessarily faced with a series of difficult choices. Not only must he decide what to include and exclude on the canvas; he must decide whether to dip his brush in the mud or in the rainbow.

This book frankly and openly resolves the ambiguities of man's nature in favor of his promise: his reason, his charity, his sense of injustice, his reverence. If this perspective seems on occasion to ignore the irrational, the cruel, the inequitable, and the selfish, it is not because of the authors' ignorance that these exist in American government and politics—as in all aspects of human life. All three of us have been rather deeply involved in public affairs. One of us has been mayor of a city of 30,000, and an administrative assistant to a United States Senator; one has served as a public relations lobbyist at the national level and as a political campaign manager at the local level; the third has served on the political staff of a Governor and has spent many months in a grim autopsy of a dead Washington agency. Our collective innocence can hardly be recaptured.

But we can and do affirm that the decency and creative wisdom of man are more than a match for his foibles and follies. If this optimism makes us nothing more than blind creatures of our culture, so be it. But we think it reflects more than this. Practical experience in government and politics has given us respect for the decency and charity of most people most of the time, and for the constitutional and institutional checks which exist in our society to contain man's intermittent depravity. The problem in American life is not a surfeit of positive evil, but a surfeit of bewilderment, indifference, and, occasionally, of cynicism.

This book attempts to cut away at these, and to suggest the vast sources of strength which abound—actually and potentially—in our political system.

The scheme of the book is relatively simple. It starts with a look at our value heritage, on the assumption that our political institutions ultimately reflect our moral inheritance—appetites and aspirations alike. This value heritage is then placed in the context of our expectations of constitutional government, and the policies and programs which these expectations have produced. Since well over sixty percent of our federal budget presently goes for military purposes in an explosive world, a nontraditional emphasis is given to the military in the chapter on the Common Defense.

The heart of the book deals with the political and governmental instruments available to us as we continue to struggle with the complexities about us and within us. The final section suggests some of our obligations as citizens—as beneficiaries of, and as key participants in, the American political system.

Our thanks go out to patient scholars and perceptive non-scholars alike, to other textbook writers, and to the following persons who have contributed especially to whatever is of merit in the following pages:

To Mrs. William Fairburn and Mr. and Mrs. Robert Fairburn, for a desk and a roof; to the Ross Gortners and to Charles S. Hyneman for encouragement when it was needed most; to Leo Byrnes for indispensable grubbing; to Professors Robert Lively, Harold Stein, Richard Frost, and William Beaney of Princeton University, to Professor Robert F. Cushman, of New York University; to Professor Charles P. Sohner of El Camino College; and to Dr. Evron Kirkpatrick, Reverend John Bodo, and Mrs. William Beaney, for catching mistakes of ignorance and oversight and for making valuable suggestions; to Doris Lake, for typing and retyping beyond the call of duty; and to our respective wives for a variety of goods and services too numerous to mention.

Since three can never assume responsibility for anything, the senior author assumes full responsibility for all errors and omissions.

Princeton, N. J.　　　　　　　　　　　　　　　　　S. K. B.
New York, N. Y.　　　　　　　　　　　　　　　　　H. D. S.
New York, N. Y.　　　　　　　　　　　　　　　　　S. B.
February 1, 1957

# Contents

# SECTION I

## Our Inherited Values

*T*o have faith in the dignity and worth of the individual man as an end in himself; to believe that it is better to be governed by persuasion than by coercion; to believe that fraternal goodwill is more worthy than a selfish and contentious spirit; to believe that in the long run all values are inseparable from the love of truth and the disinterested search for it; to believe that knowledge and the power it confers should be used to promote the welfare and happiness of all men rather than to serve the interests of those individuals and classes whom fortune and intelligence endow with temporary advantage—these are the values which are affirmed by the traditional democratic ideology. . . . They are the values which since the time of Buddha and Confucius, Solomon and Zoroaster, Plato and Aristotle, Socrates and Jesus, men have commonly employed to measure the advance or decline of civilization, the values they have celebrated in the saints and sages whom they have agreed to canonize. They are the values that readily lend themselves to rational justification, yet need no justification.

—Carl Becker

## CHAPTER 1

# The Wilderness

A SURPRISINGLY LARGE area of the North American continent still looks much as it did to the Indian savage. Actually, parts of this book were written in a pastel wilderness of western Maine which has changed little since the days of the early American settler. A hundred miles to the East, the surf—as it has for millennia—pounds on the reefs and shoals of Penobscot. Directly to the West, the ageless Presidential range of the White Mountains rises to its symbolic peak, Mt. Washington. In the immediate foreground birch and pine arch over fern and moss and lichen. The sounds are wilderness sounds: the wind in the leaves, the lapping of water on the lake shore, the scamper of small animals in the underbrush, the song and cry of the birds.

What better place to reflect upon government in America? For this is the way it began—in the wilderness—and the wilderness has been a powerful force in the shaping of American values, and consequently of American political institutions.


## THE CONQUEST OF THE WILDERNESS

The conquest of the wilderness and its transformation into a continental dynamo of unsurpassed power and wealth has been a story of epic proportions. It is not just an American epic; it is a world epic. For America has been peopled by men and women of almost every conceivable racial, religious, and nationality background who for over four centuries have come from the far reaches of the earth to search for opportunities and values they were unable to realize at home.

If we, their descendants, fail to understand why they came, what they brought with them, and what they learned from the wilderness they conquered—and from each other—we shall never understand ourselves or the institutions of free government which they created and which we have gratefully inherited.

3

# WHY THEY CAME

There is no easy way to recapture the emotions of sixteenth-century Europeans who suddenly learned that a vast new continent had been discovered beyond the western seas. Perhaps the closest modern analogy is the released imagination of youngsters who follow the rocket in its upward flight and who refuse to turn back when it does. Suppose that the planet Mars really could sustain human life. Suppose the journey through space were rough but possible. Suppose the planet had a few hostile "red" men and a severe climate, but unlimited resources for food, shelter, clothing, and eventual economic comfort. What an invitation to the restless, the adventuresome, the greedy, the oppressed, and the peculiar. What a race would be on among the nations of the world to stake out claims and to corner Martian continents. What a stimulus to scientists and explorers to master the perils of space and to test the viability of other planets and galaxies.

## The Explorers

The call of the wild is heard first by the explorer. He may rationalize that he is after money or fame but like the men who climbed Mt. Everest because "it was there," the explorer explores because he cannot help it. So it was in the "Age of Discovery."

At first it was by ocean-going ships under men like Columbus, Vespucius, the Cabots, and Hudson. There were occasional forays and temporary settlements ashore, but for the most part the explorers stood on the deck and watched with wonder as their ridiculously tiny vessels nosed into unknown harbors, river mouths, and desolate bays. Even if the distant call of the Indies and its riches had not been present, who could doubt that the process would have gone on anyway?

From ships the explorers turned to small boats, rafts, and canoes, pursuing the narrowing course of rivers to their head waters in the mountains or to the great inland lakes. And long before Boone or Lewis or Crockett, there were explorers and adventurers who walked and rode as well as sailed and paddled. Every colonial settlement on the Eastern seaboard was by-passed by new immigrants

This colonization circular for Virginia was the precursor of thousands of similar ads which for three centuries were nailed to the trees and buildings of Europe, inducing families to leave their homes and try their fortunes in a new world.

or had its own restless few who pushed west—first on foot, then by horse, then by wagon—following Indian trails or blazing new ones. As hunters and trappers and finally settlers caught up, the explorers bid them good day and pushed on again to the next range, the next river, the next winter.

## The Missionaries

We sometimes forget that the wilderness had people. To a special group of sixteenth- and seventeenth-century Europeans, the American Indian rather than the wilderness was the real frontier. The newly formed Jesuit Order, for example, saw in the American Indian and in the hardships of the New World an ideal mission for the expression of Jesuit militancy and Catholic zeal. Some of the most heroic chapters in the early years of American exploration were written by Jesuit priests.

As the forests were cleared and white settlements established, the example of the early Jesuits was carried on both by other Catholics and by missionary preachers of the proliferating Protestant sects. From Marquette and Joliet through Roger Williams and William Penn through John Eliot and the Wesleys to contemporary clergy, the evangelical strain in American history has been an ever-present force. Indians, Negro slaves, hardy and greedy exploiters of the frontier, materialists, doubters, and cynics—all have heard the voice of redemption. That many remained unconvinced, that others turned the Gospel message into an instrument of bigotry and self-righteousness, that the kindness of the priest was sometimes followed by the ruthlessness of the exploiter, cannot be denied. But the evangelical spirit has been and remains an important part of the American heritage.

## The Search for Wealth

The call of the American wilderness appealed not only to man's curiosity and missionary zeal. It appealed to his appetite. The search for wealth has been a constant theme in the American epic. What Veblen called "the acquisitive instinct" is a powerful drive. It leads men to almost superhuman effort; it results in the conquest and harnessing of resources; but historically it has often meant ruthless exploitation, lawlessness, and war.

The scramble of individuals and nations for gold in early America was awesome and terrifying. It involved almost constant warfare among the leading sea powers of Europe: England, France, Holland, and Spain. Frantic men like Pizzaro and Cortez indulged in excesses of cruelty almost beyond belief, and their counterparts were to be found in the north among the Dutch, the English, and the French.

The resources to be exploited were endless. After the first few years, gold by itself became almost incidental. A continent of forests, furs, fish, and agricultural and mineral wealth lay there for the picking—granted that the picking took at times almost superhuman effort. The picking increased in tempo as colonial settlements created new markets. After the break with England, a combination of forces fostered an economic explosion unrivaled in world history. Among the most important of these forces were (1) the revolution in transportation and industry; (2) the development of lush agricultural, mineral, and grazing lands in the South and West; and (3) incessant immigration. In the middle of the nineteenth century, the discovery of gold in California stimulated the final conquest of the Rockies and the Sierras, and presaged the linkage of the Atlantic and the Pacific by rail.

America today boasts the greatest production of material wealth that mankind has ever known. That wealth has been fashioned by the creative energy of men and women who found in America a land of opportunity and of unparalleled plenty, and, in capitalism—often stimulated by government largess—a dynamic system of incentives. If the exploitation has at times been ruthless, if money and materialism have at times seemed dominant passions of our national character, America has not been alone in these excesses. Fortunately, the crasser aspects of man's struggle for wealth have been ultimately checked at most points of serious abuse by conscience, competition, or democratic law. Even when, as in the case of the American Indian and the American Negro, fantastic damage was done, genuine attempts have been and are being made to make up for a shoddy past—although such problems are by no means behind us.

## The Search for Economic Opportunity

For millions of Europeans who came to America in droves as the nineteenth century wore on, the abundance of this country was a promise not of unlimited wealth, but of simple economic opportunity. The overwhelming majority of immigrants were not wild-cat entrepreneurs, but thrifty and hard-working men and women who saw a chance in this vast and expanding nation to achieve through their own efforts a reasonably decent living for themselves and their families. That this growing nation provided a better living for more people than had ever before been true in the world is a tribute not only to fabulous resources and a free market, but to the activities of governments which from the very beginning considered one of their major jobs to be that of keeping the population "in contact with the sources of wealth." Both encouraged and regulated by government, our mixed capitalistic economy has been, and is, the envy of much of the rest of mankind.

## The Victims of Oppression

Even if the economic largess of the American continent had been substantially less, the wilderness would still have attracted a vast number of people from across the oceans. For the frontier meant freedom as well as economic opportunity: political freedom, social freedom, and above all, religious freedom.

The sixteenth and seventeenth centuries in Europe were centuries of fanatical religious strife and persecution. The struggle was not limited to Catholics against Protestants or Christians against Muslims. Protestants set up their own orthodoxies and persecuted those who refused to conform. The story of colonial settlement in America is in no small measure the story of escape from religious oppression.

First came the Pilgrims. Forced by Anglican persecution to Holland, these early Protestant Separatists, fearing the renewal of religious war between Holland and Spain, sailed for the New World in 1620 seeking a haven for religious liberty.

From 1627 to 1631, for both religious and economic reasons, the Puritans left England in substantial numbers and settled in the Massachusetts Bay area just north of the Pilgrims.

In 1633, under Lord Baltimore, persecuted Catholics settled in what is now Maryland.

In the third quarter of that bitter century, the most severely persecuted of all Protestant sects, the Quakers, left England and ranged from Rhode Island to North Carolina, sinking their deepest roots in Pennsylvania.

The Baptists came to Virginia and Rhode Island.

From Germany, where they had suffered persecution both by Catholics and Lutherans, the Moravians accepted William Penn's invitation and settled in Pennsylvania.

---

The strong men keep coming on.
They go down shot, hanged, sick, broken.
They live on fighting, singing, lucky as plungers.
The strong mothers pulling them on . . .
The strong mothers pulling them from a dark sea,
    a great prairie, a long mountain.

—Carl Sandburg

Presbyterians were driven from Scotland to Ireland and from there to the western fringes of every English colony in the New World. And so the story went.

Unfortunately, the persecution did not end on the Eastern seaboard of the American colonies. The virus of religious intolerance was carried in the very ships of freedom. Almost every colonial settlement along the seaboard, whether Protestant or Catholic, set up rigid standards of religious conformity. The only real exceptions were the colonies established by Roger Williams in Rhode Island and by William Penn in Pennsylvania. The group search for religious freedom was not generally accompanied by the acceptance of religious toleration for individuals—or for other groups. The westward movement in American history was due in part to this lack of tolerance in the East. Witness the epic story of the Mormons in their trek from New York to Illinois to Utah.

Even though religious tolerance increased markedly as time went on, the legacy of intolerance is evident in extremist literature, religious discrimination, and anachronistic "blue laws" even today. That these expressions of intolerance are relatively scarce is due in no small measure to the influence of the wilderness which served as a haven for more than three centuries for those who thought otherwise.

## THE IMPACT OF THE WILDERNESS

Explorers, missionaries, seekers after wealth or opportunity, fugitives from oppression or intolerance—these were the ones who discovered, cleared, and developed the American wilderness.

But what did the wilderness teach them?

It is not easy to separate those values and principles which our ancestors brought with them from those which they developed after they arrived. Certainly there was constant interaction between the old and the new, and even the new ideas were fertilized in part by the contributions of later arrivals who brought with them the changing values of a changing European society. The great American historian, Frederick Jackson Turner, perhaps attributed too much to the frontier itself. But the fact remains that the frontier has been a major force in shaping the mind, behavior, and political expectations of the American people. At least five major tenets of the American faith can be assigned in part to the influence of the wilderness:

A clearing in the wilderness that shows the beginnings of a home surrounded by hardship. This is the way America grew. Taken in the Pacific Northwest in 1890, this picture with minor changes could be seen in sections of Alaska today.

pragmatism, equalitarianism, individualism, cooperation, and optimism.

## Pragmatism

Frontiers are hostile to tradition. Rigid theories of social organization and pat political doctrines find rough sledding in a wilderness environment. When the key problem is the struggle for survival, inventiveness and adaptation become paramount considerations. During the French and Indian Wars, General Braddock suffered crushing defeats because he attempted to use traditional British army formations in hostile forest country. American history is filled with myriad analogous examples in the fields of economics, politics, social organization, and art forms. The reason we can now talk with meaningful pride of a unique American civilization is that the frontier caused ceaseless adaptation of old skills, habits, and ideas.

As we shall note later in more detail, our Constitution was a supreme act of invention. Ideas came from a variety of sources, but the final product was the result of the efforts of a number of talented practical men who were trying to fashion a useful political instrument for a new nation. This instrument has since been amended twenty-two times, and has been adapted to new circumstance by thousands of implementing laws and Supreme Court decisions. These laws and decisions have reflected the needs of a rapidly changing society and have had little relevance to abstract theories of politics and government. Perhaps one reason that America now has so much difficulty in developing a "theory of democracy" for export to countries now flooded with Communist propaganda is that we have never been able to form a consistent ideological package from our amorphous mass of experimentation. It is not accident that great American philosophers like William James and John Dewey centered their philosophies around pragmatism: around the idea that concepts have value only in terms of action, and that results are the sole test of the truth of one's belief. American government today is the product of pragmatic adaptation—the adaptation of those who, through frontier experience, were not afraid of the unprecedented.

## Equalitarianism

Not only was the frontier hostile to doctrinaire precedent, it was especially hostile to class distinctions and claims of hereditary superiority. In the difficult task of clearing the wilderness, a man's worth was judged by his physical capacity and his intellectual ingenuity. Past titles, reputations, even wealth were lost in the solvent of frontier life. Only on the frontier plantations of the South were aristocratic pretensions allowed to gain form and relative substance, and even there the story was mixed. Andrew Jackson, perhaps the most militantly equalitarian President in our history, was a slave owner.

As we shall see, the concept of human equality has roots deep in the religious, ethical, and political substratum of Western civilization. But the frontier provided a unique environment for the realization of that ideal and helped release the influence of equalitarianism with explosive force. Our political and economic history is pockmarked with the shell holes of equalitarian attack and counterattack: the frontier revolts against the power of royal colonial governors and of seaboard wealth, the supremacy of popularly elected legislatures during the Revolution, the prohibition against titles of nobility in our Constitution, the Bill of Rights, the Jeffersonian attacks on the aristocratic presumptions of the Federalists, the Jacksonian contempt for John Quincy Adams and the "Eastern bankers."

As the nineteenth century wore on and industrialization started a relentless drift of population toward the city, urban ugliness and poverty reinforced frontier pressures against stultifying privilege. After the Civil War, urban and agricultural forces—sometimes in combination, sometimes alone—sought redress through political action against the abuse of economic power. The Granger movement against the railroads; the Populist revolt of the 1890's; the Progressive movements of the early twentieth century; the growth of provisions for the initiative, referendum, and recall in state and local governments (see page 406) ; the New and Fair Deals—all these reflected in part the equalitarian pressures of a society whose memories of frontier equality were still vivid.

Equalitarianism has produced its excesses and its crudenesses, but by and large it has been a liberating and dynamic force in our history. The frontier had a major catalytic effect in releasing this force in American life.

### Individualism

Long before Herbert Hoover popularized the expression, America was known as a land of "rugged individualists." The equality of the frontier was not the equality of a prison. It was the equality of *individual* opportunity. Horatio Alger stories and the literary expression of the "log-cabin-to-the-White House" theme in American life were stories of individual success through thrift and hard work. Given more than half a chance by the fabulous resources placed at his disposal by friendly instruments of government, the individual trapper, planter, farmer, ranger, speculator, inventor, financier, worker, or manufacturer could, and often did, rise to unbelievable pinnacles of material success.

On the positive side, this individualism created a fluid and dynamic society. Individual initiative and free enterprise have been watch-words of our culture. Imagination and self-reliance have brought returns not only to the individual but to society as a whole. America was not built like the pyramids, by the autocratic mobilization of slave labor. It was built, in large measure, by frontier entrepreneurs who, with the help and encouragement of government, mastered the skill of turning nature into wealth.

On the negative side, individualism has sometimes meant exploitation of men as well as nature. In a real sense the basic dilemma of American government has been how to perpetuate the dynamics and wealth-producing effect of individual initiative without suffering the social cost of unrestrained ambition. America has not been alone in this dilemma, but the frontier heightened the drama, and when the geographical frontier ended with the close of the nineteenth century the clash between the entrepreneur and democratic regulation became increasingly severe.

Working together was an imperative of the frontier. Individualism and cooperation, therefore, became complementary American characteristics.

The struggle still goes on to find a workable synthesis of individualism and social responsibility.

## Cooperation

If individualism was the privilege of the frontier, cooperation was
its necessity. Mutual defense and mutual aid were the conditions of
individual survival. In one sense this is the story of the entire human
race, and of many species of animals, birds, insects, and even plants.
What distinguished frontier life was the necessity of spontaneous and
creative cooperation beyond the limits of formal government. Men
cooperated, not because they were ordered to, but because they had
to or wanted to. If cattle rustlers appeared, a citizen's posse was
formed. If the Indians attacked, everyone manned the stockade. If a
neighbor's barn burned down, the community rebuilt it. If flood,
drought, or tornado struck, everyone banded together to salvage
what could be salvaged and to help the suffering.

This heritage of spontaneous cooperation is one of the most pervasive and magnificent gifts of the frontier. Its influence can be seen
today in every community in America: community chests, volunteer fire departments, district nurse associations, subscription-built
YMCA's and hospitals, service clubs, ladies' aid societies, libraries,

and all the other current manifestations of cooperative community endeavor.

Although a now largely urbanized society has placed limits upon the effectiveness of dealing with all social problems by voluntary cooperation, the spirit of barn-raising is still with us. It affects almost every aspect of our domestic life and carries over into our policies and attitudes toward other nations. No country on earth, for example, has shown more generosity toward victims of disaster and misfortune in other nations than ours. There is scarcely a part of the civilized globe which in time of disaster has not received help in the form of money, food, clothing, medicine, goods, or technical assistance from the American people.

It will be a sorry day for America and for the world if this frontier spirit of mutual aid and generosity ever disappears.

## Optimism

Finally, the promise of the wilderness made Americans optimistic people. Beyond the blue horizon was the pot of gold. If the Rockies could be licked, what could not be. The wilderness was hostile, but conquerable. Defeat was not defeat, but a temporary setback.

This faith in the future has occasionally been shaken by depressions, wars, and the threat of wars. At times it has manifested itself in quixotic ways. But it has always been the most basic faith of the American people. Faith in the future has woven a hundred nationalities and a thousand creeds into a single tapestry. It has been the core faith of our staggering productivity. It shines through the hydrogen thunderhead on the present horizon. It has caught the imagination of peoples all over the world who until yesterday knew nothing but the dismal repetition of birth, subsistence, and death.

This belief that there is nothing impossible, that God and man in partnership can conquer the traditional hostilities of nature and savagery with resulting wealth and happiness—this is without question the most dynamic legacy of the American wilderness.

# CONCLUSION

## Synopsis

The wilderness must be listed among the major factors which have shaped the attitudes and behavior of the American people. For over four hundred years America has been explored, settled, and developed by people from the far ends of the earth who saw in the New World both a stimulus and an opportunity to seek a variety of goals: adventure, salvation, wealth, security, and freedom. In pursuing these goals, the American people were profoundly conditioned by the frontier itself. Today, if giant institutions—public and private— seem to have substituted the "organization man" for the "rugged individualist" as the American prototype, it should not be forgotten that we are children of revolt against blind tradition. Equal justice, opportunity, cooperation, individualism, optimism—these legacies of the wilderness will continue to haunt the "organization man" until he constructs institutions which more perfectly permit of their expression.

### Significance

Governments, and what governments do, are important manifestations of the habits and goals of a society. If America had never had the wilderness as a safety valve and as an almost limitless source of wealth, it is doubtful that our crazy-quilt pattern of government and politics could have survived—or, for that matter, would have been formed in the first place. The fact that we have been, in David Potter's words, a "people of plenty," has had a profound impact upon our economic and social, and, consequently, upon our political behavior. What follows in this book takes on meaning only in this context.

### Prospectus

But if the wilderness helped to mold our national character, it was not the only force at work. From across the oceans our ancestors brought ancient knowledge, skills, tools, and values, all of which were alien to the New World. The real story of America is the story of the reciprocal impact of the old and the new. We have examined the new; we now turn to the old.

## CHAPTER 2

# Our Religious and
# Ethical Heritage

CLEARING A FOREST wilderness does not by itself produce attitudes
and institutions of freedom.

In all societies it is what Harold Sprout has called "the interaction
between *man* and milieu" which is determinative. The real story of
America is that of the reciprocal impact of the old and the new.

This is especially true of government in America in all its myriad
forms. For even before the trees had been felled and the land cleared,
the early settlers had to contain the primeval in themselves; had to
order their relationships with each other; had to organize for defense
against the attacks of hostile savages and the winter's wind. And if,
as we have seen, the wilderness frontier challenged political im-
aginations, nurtured individual talent, and stimulated spontaneous
cooperative energies, it did so in men and women whose lives had
already been conditioned by church and law and by the struggle
against oppression in distant lands.

All the political documents in our history, all our governmental
instruments, stem from ideas whose roots are deep in the moral,
spiritual, and political experience of Western man.

## THIS NATION UNDER GOD

In 1620, the Mayflower Pilgrims began their solemn compact with
the words, "In the name of God, Amen."

In 1954, the United States Congress added the phrase, "under
God," to the pledge of allegiance to the American flag.

These widely separated events reflect a simple historic truth: the
idea of God has been an integral part of America's political history.

17

All of our important political values have either derived from, or have been justified by, an ancestral belief that above, behind, and beyond man there is a Divine Being upon whose will, judgment, intelligence, and compassion man's fate ultimately depends.

So widespread is divine symbolism in our national life that it is taken for granted.

On every American coin is the national motto: "In God We Trust." On the back of every dollar bill is the symbolism of an unfinished pyramid under the all-seeing eye of God. Daily sessions of our major legislative bodies at the state and national level open with prayer. Scarcely a major political speech is delivered today which does not refer to God or Divine Providence. All our national anthems refer directly to God. The third verse of the *Star-Spangled Banner* reads in part, "And this be our motto, In God is our trust." The final verse of *America* ends, "Great God our King." *America the Beautiful* refers to God in every stanza. Our whole culture reflects a deeply theological past.

### The Link Between Religion and Politics

America, of course, is not unique in this respect. From earliest times religion and politics have been inextricably linked. Anthropologists tell us that in most primitive forms of government religious authority and political authority are indistinguishable. All major civilizations and most minor ones have had their god or gods, and these deities have more often than not been appealed to by and through, or with the sanction of, the instruments of government.

The special impact of the idea of God upon American history and government derives from the peculiar characteristics which our ancestors assigned to Him—or discovered in Him. The God of our fathers was not a mischievous Loki of Norse legend, an embalmed pharaoh, or a deified commissar. The nature of the God of our fathers is a complex one. It unfolds in the most important book in Western history, the Bible, and in the interpretations which theologians, priests, ministers, statesmen, and lay citizens have subsequently made of the Biblical God.

### The God of the Bible

The Old Testament is the story of the moral and religious development of an ancient and remarkable people, the Israelites, who lived in the second and first millennia before Christ in the lands bordering the eastern Mediterranean Sea.

Under the tribulations of slavery, exile, nomadic wanderings, war, pestilence, hunger, and persecution, the Israelites evolved theories of God which have subsequently influenced the philosophy, culture, and politics of the entire Western world.

Beginning as a jealous, wrathful, and fickle tribal deity, the God of the Old Testament gradually changes as the Bible story unfolds. He becomes a God of law and justice. He becomes the creator, sustainer, and protector of life. He becomes both a personal and a universal God. He becomes, for the psalmist, a God of cosmic majesty and righteousness. Through prophets like Isaiah and Amos, He judges evil rulers and demands government in the interest of the many. Through Hosea and Micah, He becomes a God of mercy and compassion.

In the New Testament, God becomes all-embracing love—to the point of suffering and self-sacrifice. Man's obligation becomes simple but supremely difficult: to love God and neighbor, with neighbor defined to include enemies. Every human being, as a creature of God, assumes a potentially imperishable dignity. In the teachings of Jesus, the least is as important as the greatest.

Contemporary American concepts of law, justice, human rights, government by consent, equality, and freedom can never be fully understood apart from this Biblical heritage. It is true that this heritage was reinforced by Greek philosophy and Roman and British jurisprudence, by economic and political forces in medieval and modern Europe pressing for liberation, and by our own colonial and frontier experience. It is also true that the Biblical God suffered historically the ambiguities of His evolving nature. But in a search for the origins of our political values, great importance must be assigned to the Biblical concept of a moral and omnipotent God.

## The Roman Church

How this Biblical God came to America is an integral part of the story of Western civilization. Unfortunately, it is not a simple story of doctrinal consistency and spiritual evolution. Like the Bible itself, the story of Western man since Biblical times is a saga of the admixture of moral and spiritual aspirations and doctrine, on the one hand, and of the crass struggle for power, wealth, and advantage on the other. It is the story of wars between men and wars within men.

All that can be said is that the story would have been profoundly different had it not been for the fact that Christianity, between the second and fourth centuries A.D., gradually became the prevailing religion of that great imperial melting pot of those distant times: the Roman Empire. By the year A.D. 300, with our Bible as its source and guide, Christianity was effectively planted in all parts of the then civilized Western world.

For the next twelve hundred years, through the Barbarian conquest of Rome, the Dark Ages, the rise of militant Islam, the violence of heresies and crusades, the rise and fall of feudalism, the struggle between church and state for ultimate power in Christendom, and the emergence of the nation state in its modern form, the great legacy of Constantine's conversion—the Catholic Church—survived and grew as the religious monopoly of the West. And with it, in monasteries, in universities, and in men's hearts survived the religious and ethical principles, and the very text, of our Bible.

### The God of the Reformation

But the Bible which the pilgrim William Bradford brought in his hands to Plymouth in 1620 represented a break with the religious monopoly of the Church of Rome. That break had begun, in earnest, a hundred years earlier. America is peculiarly a child of that vast economic, political, social, and religious hurricane which swept Europe during the sixteenth and seventeenth centuries: the Protestant Reformation.

The Reformation—although it had profound economic and polit-

---

When one rules justly over men ruling in the fear of God, he dawns on them like the morning light . . .       —II Samuel 23:3–4

Learn to do good; seek justice, correct oppression; defend the fatherless, plead for the widow.       —Isaiah 1:17

But let justice roll down like waters, and righteousness like an overflowing stream.       —Amos 5:24

ical aspects—was ostensibly a revolt against the abuses and power of the Catholic Church. In spite of its long record of saints of humility and learning, the Roman Church, after its spiritual zenith in the thirteenth century, had gradually become secular and corrupt. By the latter part of the fifteenth century, at the time when explorers were first touching the coast of the New World, popes and clergy were often indistinguishable in morals or politics from the cruel and cynical lay rulers of feudal baronies and of the rising city and nation states.

Although there had been rumblings earlier, the real break with the Church of Rome came in the sixteenth century with the rise of two powerful theologians, Martin Luther and John Calvin.

Luther, a Doctor of Theology at Wittenberg, Germany, broke with the church over the corrupted practice of selling Papal assurances of eternal salvation called indulgences. He drew up ninety-five theses attacking this money-raising practice and was promptly tried for heresy and asked to recant. In the famous Diet of Worms in 1521, Luther refused to change his mind or lessen his attack.

Unless I am convinced, [he said], by the testimony of the Scripture or by evident reason . . . I neither can nor will revoke anything, seeing it is not safe or right to act against conscience. God help me, Amen.

In this simple statement we have the basic idea that has governed Protestants to this day: the Bible takes precedence over the laws of the church. Conscience, as the voice of God, is man's ultimate judge.

So whatever you wish that men would do to you, do so to them; for this is the law and the prophets.                    —Matthew 7:12

And he made from one every nation of men to live on all the face of the earth. . . . he is not far from each one of us. . . . we are indeed his offspring.                    —Acts 17:26–28

Live as free men, yet without using your freedom as a pretext for evil; but live as servants of God.                    —I Peter 2:16

John Calvin of Geneva reacted against the abuses of the Church of Rome with equal vigor and with a more systematic theology. According to Calvin, all lives were predestined, and neither the church, nor petitions for grace nor even good works, could have the slightest effect upon man's ultimate salvation. God identified the "elect," and those not "chosen" could do nothing about it. The "elect" had an obligation to rule and to enforce a narrowly defined morality to contain the innate depravity in man. As one writer put it, "The Ten Commandments provided the framework of this code, and the Bible was searched for texts which limited every natural weakness or worldly indulgence, from the recognized crimes of thievery and violence to gambling, avarice, dancing, theatre-going, drunkenness, unchastity, immodesty, pride, and vanity. Assuming the form of rules imposed by the will of God, Calvinistic ethics was legalistic and authoritarian." [1]

## The Reformation and the Renaissance

No one knows what the legacy of Calvinism would have been by itself. We have hints in Calvin's own Geneva dictatorship, in the early Puritan theocracy in Massachusetts, and in the various "blue laws" which at various times have cluttered the statute books of state and local governments in America. But the Protestant revolt took place in a Europe of bewildering social, economic, and political change. The relatively stable and diffused society of feudalism, which had dominated Europe for five hundred years, was dying. New political entities, city and nation states, were coming into being. Greek and Roman learning was being rediscovered outside the context of church theology. A class of venturesome artisans and traders were planting the early seeds of urban and commercial capitalism, and were acquiring wealth for themselves and their new rulers at an unprecedented rate. New worlds were being discovered beyond the seas by explorers and in the skies by scientists. Inquisitive and acquisitive men appeared in such numbers that ancient fortresses of conformity, class, and feudal contract could not contain them. A vast awakening—a renaissance—was under way.

The revolt was on against traditional authority in all its forms. And even though much of early Protestantism was itself authoritarian in implication, the Reformation started and shared a process of challenge of orthodoxies which had far reaching political as well as religious effects. Within a hundred and fifty years of Calvin and Luther, liberal Protestant sects like the Quakers, Anabaptists, and Congregationalists, were hurling quiet defiance at Papists, Anglicans, and Presbyterians alike. In the New World, men and women like Roger Williams, Anne Hutchinson, William Penn, and John Wise worked to free men's consciences and established their dignity through democratic forms of both church and politics.

In the eighteenth century, the humanistic forces released by the Renaissance and by the growth of science culminated in a new kind of religion—an almost non-theological theology: deism. Deism combined the mechanics of Newtonian science with the optimism and humanitarianism of the New Testament. God had so ordered the universe that all man had to do to achieve salvation was to discover and follow the laws of nature. Reason and benevolence were the touchstones of unlimited progress.

Deism combined with low-church, democratic, liberal Protestantism set ideas in motion which were a far cry from Calvinist tenets of original sin, Old Testament legalisms, and antidemocratic forms of church and government.

### Calvinism, Deism, and Liberal Protestantism

The fact is that America inherited both the pessimistic and suspicious puritanism of Calvin and the explosive optimism of humanism and liberal Protestantism. Our religious, cultural, and political history is in no small measure the story of the conflict and adjustment of these rival views of man and society. The Bible which our colonial ancestors brought with them to the wilderness of America was an ambivalent symbol of authority and revolt against authority.

Our federal Constitution was drawn up by men like James Madison who shared this ambivalent heritage. Deism and liberal Protestantism are most clearly reflected in Jefferson's Declaration of Independence and in the Bill of Rights. These two instruments of free and aspiring men bracket historically the Constitution which itself reflects a lingering Calvinist orthodoxy in which "original sin" and "human depravity" must needs be checked. Hence our "separation of powers" and our "checks and balances."

The greatness and permanence of our early constitutional and political documents stem in part from the fact that, together, they

## CHURCH MEMBERSHIP: CURRENT AND ADJUSTED ESTIMATES

| The Major Bodies | Current Reported Figures membership | Church-affiliated Totals | |
|---|---|---|---|
| | | membership constituency | communicants age 13 and over |
| PROTESTANT | 58,448,567 | 84,000,000 | 56,000,000 |
| ROMAN CATHOLIC | 33,396,647 | 34,000,000 | 20,000,000 |
| JEWISH | 5,500,000 | 5,500,000 | 3,600,000 |
| EASTERN ORTHODOX | 2,386,945 | 2,500,000 | 1,600,000 |
| | | ⬆ (estimated, Oct. '56) ⬇ | |
| ROMAN CATHOLIC | 33,396,647 | 34,000,000 | 20,000,000 |
| THE METHODIST | 9,292,046 | 14,100,000 | 9,400,000 |
| SO. BAPTIST | 8,467,439 | 12,750,000 | 8,500,000 |
| NAT'L BAPTIST USA | 4,557,416 | 7,000,000 | 4,600,000 |
| PRESBYTERIAN USA | 2,645,745 | 4,600,000 | 2,750,000 |
| NAT'L BAPTIST, AM. | 2,610,774 | 4,000,000 | 2,650,000 |
| DISCIPLES OF CHRIST | 1,897,736 | 3,000,000 | 2,000,000 |
| PROT. EPISCOPAL | 2,757,944 | 2,800,000 | 1,900,000 |
| UNITED LUTHERAN | 2,175,726 | 2,250,000 | 1,500,000 |
| LUTHERAN-MO. SYNOD | 2,004,110 | 2,100,000 | 1,400,000 |
| CHRIST UNITY SCIENCE | 1,581,286 | 2,400,000 | 1,600,000 |
| AMERICAN BAPTIST | 1,513,697 | 2,300,000 | 1,550,000 |
| CHURCHES OF CHRIST | 1,600,000 | 2,400,000 | 1,600,000 |
| CONGREG.-CHRISTIAN | 1,342,045 | 2,000,000 | 1,350,000 |
| AF. METH. EPISC. | 1,166,301 | 1,800,000 | 1,200,000 |

This table of church membership in the United States gives evidence of the vast number of Americans who today associate themselves with the ethical precepts of our Judaeo-Christian heritage. (*Presbyterian Life,* Nov. 10, 1956, p. 17.)

took account both of the possibilities of good and the realities of evil in man.

Today there are around 100,000,000, church members in almost 300,000 separate congregations in the United States. The beliefs of these congregations run the gamut of theology and religious philosophy. But underlying all of them, Catholic, Protestant, and Jewish, is a single religious heritage—a heritage which places both individuals and corporate societies under the judgment of a moral, just, and omnipotent God. American character and American government are unintelligible if approached apart from this heritage.

## THE RULE OF LAW

Important as the Judaeo-Christian theological heritage has been in shaping the social and political values of Western man, it has not been the only influence at work. As we have noted, the spiritual heritage of the Near East fused early in the Christian era with the philosophical heritage of Greece and Rome. The greatest contribution of Graeco-Roman philosophy to the subsequent politics of the West was the idea of the rule of law.

The rule of law is an ethical proposition which can be stated quite simply: in any free society both subjects and rulers must act under the restraints of commonly accepted rules which neither is free, by whim, to disobey or to change.

So important is this idea that some writers and philosophers claim it is equivalent with the word "civilization." Whether accepted as a mandate from heaven, or as a felicitous man-made myth, the idea of the rule of law is unquestionably one of the most remarkable expressions we know of man's long climb out of the pit of his animal beginnings.

The most important single source of this idea in the Western world was in the philosophy and experience of ancient Greece and Rome. As George Sabine has pointed out, the ideal of free citizenship in the Greek city state "was founded on the conviction that there is an ineradicable moral distinction between subjection to the law and subjection to the will of another human being, even though that other be a wise and benevolent despot. The difference is that the first is compatible with a sense of freedom and dignity while the second is not." [2]

The idea of supremacy of law fitted perfectly into the practical needs of the far-flung Roman Empire. On the basis of this idea a vast civil law was established for effectuating stable government within the empire, and a law of nations was created, a *jus gentium,* which regulated commercial disputes between Roman citizens and non-Romans.

Since the time of its codification by Justinian in the sixth century A.D., Roman law has served as the basis of the legal systems of most of western and southern Europe, and of the colonial settlements which emanated therefrom.

---

True law is right reason, harmonious with nature, diffused among all, constant, eternal. . . . It is a sacred obligation not to attempt to legislate in contradition to this law. . . . Nor is it one law at Rome and another at Athens; one now and another at a later time; but one eternal and unchangeable law binding all nations through all time . . ."

—Cicero

Rome did more than codify its own laws, however; it gave special currency to the idea that above man-made law was a "natural law" —a law of "right reason," a "higher law" to which lesser laws must conform in order to be equitable. From Cicero through the church fathers of the Middle Ages, through various political theorists and jurists of fifteenth- and sixteenth-century Europe, this idea of a "higher law" came eventually to America and became a point of reference justifying independence, and later, justifying the suprem-

A Declaration by the Representatives of the UNITED STATES OF AMERICA, in General Congress assembled.

When in the course of human events it becomes necessary for one people to dissolve the political bands which have connected them with another, and to [assume among the powers of the earth the] separate and equal station to which the laws of nature & of nature's god entitle them, a decent respect to the opinions of mankind requires that they should declare the causes which impel them to the separation.

We hold these truths to be self-evident; that all men are created equal; that they are endowed by their creator with inherent & inalienable rights, that among these are life, liberty, & the pursuit of happiness, that to secure these rights, governments are instituted among men, deriving their just powers from the consent of the governed; that whenever any form of government becomes destructive of these ends, it is the right of the people to alter or to abolish it, & to institute new government, laying it's foundation on such principles & organising it's powers in such form, as to them shall seem most likely to effect their safety & happiness. prudence indeed will dictate that governments long established should not be changed for light & transient causes: and accordingly all experience hath shewn that mankind are more disposed to suffer while evils are sufferable, than to right themselves by abolishing the forms to which they are accustomed but when a long train of abuses & usurpations [begun at a distinguished period & pursuing invariably the same object, evinces a design to reduce

This rough draft of the Declaration of Independence serves to remind us that the great documents in our history were painstakingly drafted by mortal men who held "a decent respect to the opinions of mankind."

acy of constitutional law over all other forms of law in our society.

Although our American civil and criminal law (law in Louisiana excepted) inherited more from British common law and equity (see Chapter 5) than it did from the Roman code, the Graeco-Roman idea of the rule of law—especially of a higher law—was a major antecedent of American constitutional principles and practices.

Today the traditions of civility, which as Walter Lippmann has pointed out are the fruits of the rule of law, are deeply engrained in American government and society. When that tradition has been violated, the prestige and social health of the nation has declined precipitously.

## HUMAN RIGHTS

We hold these truths to be self-evident, that all men are created equal, that they are endowed by their creator with certain inalienable Rights, that among these are life, liberty, and the pursuit of Happiness. That to secure these rights, Governments are instituted among Men, deriving their just powers from the consent of the governed.

This eloquent and oft-quoted passage from the Declaration of Independence possibly comes closer to summarizing the value premises of government in America than any other statement in our political literature.

Unfortunately, these truths have not been self-evident in most times and places in human history. That America was founded at a time in the history of the Western world when these truths were considered to be self-evident is a fortuitous blessing.

Where did these ideas come from? Why were they "self-evident" to Thomas Jefferson?

Some of the roots we have already traced in the soil of America's religious heritage and of the frontier. The rule of law implies rights and a legal equality of individuals. But the rights alluded to in the Declaration, and spelled out in detail in our state and federal constitutions, were peculiarly the legacy of British experience and political philosophy.

In one sense, the British struggle for individual liberty can be traced back to Magna Charta in A.D. 1215, and to the early beginnings of parliamentary restraints upon the royal discretion in the fourteenth century. These distant origins were, however, less important in themselves than as points of reference for a later age. The real struggle in England for individual rights and for government by consent of the governed came in the seventeenth century at the very time that the New World was first being settled.

## The Seventeenth-Century Struggle in England

The causes of the seventeenth-century struggle in England for Parliamentary supremacy over the King and for human rights were complex. They were partly economic: the pressure of a rising commercial middle class against certain forms of royal taxation and economic control. They were partly religious: the resistance of radical Protestant sects to the alleged Catholic sympathies of the Stuart kings, and to the Anglican orthodoxy of the Church of England. They were partly political: the reaction of those who had experienced a tempering of the royal prerogative under Elizabeth, and who resented the attempts of the Stuart kings to reassert in theory and practice the "divine right of kings."

In any case, commercial, religious, and political forces combined to challenge the arbitrary actions and attitudes of the monarchy. For the first three quarters of the seventeenth century, England was torn by tension and civil strife. In its most violent period in the 1640's and 1650's, the struggle laid bare the English countryside and substituted the Puritan dictatorship of the intransigent Cromwell for the cavalier rule of King Charles I, who was beheaded.

After a brief period of relaxation, following the Restoration of Charles II in 1660, the struggle rose to a bloodless climax with the forced abdication of King James II in 1688. William of Orange was brought over from Holland to become England's first truly constitutional monarch, subservient to Parliament and limited by a bill of rights.

It is not surprising that a century of constitutional tension and strife should have produced a varied and exciting political literature. Tracts were written justifying royal authority on religious and secular grounds. Other tracts were written justifying revolt against the royal power and proclaiming basic human rights. Biblical texts, classical texts, medieval texts, legal precedents, and continental philosophies were searched by partisans on both sides, and were used to buttress opposing positions.

Although the struggle was won by a conservative, propertied, middle class, the language of liberty unleashed in the course of the struggle had no logical stopping place short of universal application. John Locke, the great philosophical justifier of the "Glorious Revolution of 1688," may have stressed the rights of "life, liberty, and property," but before a hundred years had passed Jefferson had substituted the more inclusive "pursuit of happiness" for the less inclusive "property."

## Bills of Rights

Seventeenth-century British experience and philosophy became an integral part of the value system of British colonials in America, and of their more independent descendants. The bills of rights in our state constitutions and the first eight amendments to our federal Constitution were taken almost directly from two British constitutional documents of the seventeenth century: the Petition of Rights, drafted in 1628, and the Bill of Rights of 1688. These guaranteed the "ancient liberties" of all Englishmen: freedom of speech and of the press, freedom of religion, freedom from arbitrary imprisonment, the right of assembly, the right to petition against grievances, certain protections against martial law, and procedural rights in the course of criminal prosecution such as the right to bail and trial by jury (see Chapters 5 and 22).

In addition, the seventeenth-century struggle reinforced the idea that governments were under God and the law, and that government itself was a sacred and solemn compact between ruler and ruled. When rulers ceased to rule justly and by consent, the "social contract" was broken, and the people had a right to revolution. The reason why the conservative Edmund Burke could in good conscience on the floor of Parliament defend the American Revolution was because he felt that the colonists were acting in full conformity with accepted British political theory.

---

The ways of nature require peace: The ways of peace require obedience to the laws: Laws in England cannot be made but by Parliaments: Parliaments in England are come to be mere popular assemblies: The laws made by popular assemblies . . . must be popular laws; and the sum of popular laws must amount to a commonwealth.

—James Harrington

This church and war memorial on a New England village green together suggest that our inherited values have not been maintained without cost.

## Democratic Thought

Finally, the seventeenth century in England left a legacy of radical, democratic, political thought which found its way, almost inevitably, into the minds and consciences of American frontiersmen and small farmers, the urban poor, and the humanitarian defenders of the common man. On the "left wing" of the Cromwellian revolt was a small group of unusual men called Levellers. Their enemies caricatured their philosophical position to mean abolition of private property and the levelling of all social differences. Actually, as Sabine has pointed out,

. . . the equality sought was before the law and equality of political rights, especially for the class of small property owners. Indeed, the Levellers appear to have grasped with remarkable clearness the point of view of radical democratic liberalism, individualist rather than socialist in its philosophy and political rather than economic in its aims.[3]

One of the clearest and most picturesque statements ever made of the right of every individual to vote and participate in government was produced by the Levellers:

Really I think that the poorest he that is in England has a life to live as the richest he; and therefore truly, Sir, I think it's clear, that every man that is to live under a government ought first by his own consent to put himself under that government; and I do think that the poorest man in England is not at all bound in a strict sense to that government that he has not had a voice to put himself under.[4]

In the seventeenth century, the fire of the Levellers was only a tiny spark. But the spark, fed by religious, economic, and social pressures in America and Europe alike, was to grow until it became the guiding light of political democracy in America, and in the entire Western world.

# CONCLUSION

## Synopsis

Our most familiar and significant political ideas have roots deep in the moral, spiritual, and political experience and prophetic insights of Western man. Three great streams of moral speculation and political experience flowed into America in its formative centuries: Judeo-Christian, Graeco-Roman, and British. The confluence of these three streams left a rich spiritual deposit in the soil of the New World: ideas such as the dignity and worth of the individual; the responsibility of governments to rule in the interests of the many, and by their consent; freedom; the rule of law, and equality under it; and human rights.

## Significance

This ethical and religious heritage, fused with the lessons of the wilderness, gave our eighteenth-century ancestors words with which to declare independence and to fashion constitutions for a new nation. But its impact was not limited to our formative years as a nation. We as a people judge the value of our contemporary institutions and relationships in terms of their relevance to these inherited values. There is some danger, in view of the explosive changes and diffusions of modern life, that we may forget where these values have come from, and how important they have been in creating our "way of life." There is some danger also that in our wealth and power we may forget that it is God rather than man that is omnipotent.

## Prospectus

Fortunately, the illusion of omnipotence is not encouraged by our institutions of government. These institutions were fashioned on the basis of complex and flexible constitutional blueprints which in turn were drawn by men of political experience, moral insight, and considerable learning. To the most important of these blueprints, the United States Constitution, we now turn.

## CHAPTER 3

# Our Constitutional
# Heritage

WE NOW COME to a third factor which has influenced profoundly the character of American government. To the wilderness and the value legacy of the Western world must be added our particular constitutional heritage.

Although the American constitutions—federal and state—are written documents, they stem from a series of unwritten practices originally developed as part of the pragmatic struggles of the English people for order and liberty in their home communities. As Wallace Notestein has demonstrated in his fascinating account of *England on the Eve of Colonization 1605–1630,* the institutions of the Justice of the Peace, Sheriff, Constable, Mayor, Court Sessions, Selectmen, and Churchwardens combined to form the images of governing institutions which our colonial ancestors brought with them to the small wilderness communities of the New World; just as the manor, the plantation, and various kinds of trading charters in the New World reflected common economic arrangements and practices in the Old.

Even though the facts of the wilderness and of colonialism changed many of these institutions radically, recent historical scholarship assigns a rich role to these colonial and English antecedents of our constitutional system. The relative independence of the County Court in colonial Virginia, for example (an independence which dates back to English practices under the Tudors), may have given the American people a taste of "federalism" long before the Federal Constitution was written or signed. Certainly the ultimate colonial appeal to the Privy Council on matters of high law is related to the later American practice of judicial review. And, the peculiar compromises between executive control through a royal governor and legislative control through partly popular chambers were important experiential underpinnings of the doctrine of Separation of Powers.

Of course, written constitutions themselves were nothing new. The ancient Greek philosopher, Aristotle, spent a great deal of time collecting and analyzing the various kinds of written constitutions used in the city states of the eastern Mediterranean area in the fourth century B.C.

But of all the nations presently in existence, the United States boasts the oldest written constitutions in continuous operation. It is true that certain "constitutional documents" in Great Britian are older; but the British have no single legal instrument which sets forth the basic framework of government, and they have no law of the land which is above Parliament.

A written constitution does not guarantee a free society—as we know from Soviet experience. Nor does a nation need a written constitution in order to be free—as we know from British experience. But the written federal and state constitutions of the United States constitute a unique contribution to the politics and government of the modern world. They have been widely copied.

## The Function of Constitutions

Constitutions as we know them are basic legal documents which attempt to set forth: (1) the general powers of government; (2) the division of powers among various levels, branches, or officials; (3) the ways in which officials are to be elected or selected, and for what periods of time they are to serve; (4) the limits within which these officials must operate in their exercise of power.

In America, the idea of a supreme law of this kind is taken for granted. It is well to remember, however, that for most of human history governmental power has been exercised by despots who have known no real restraints except the threat of counterforce. Constitutionalism, in the sense of recognized legal restraints upon the power to govern, is a remarkable manifestation of man's capacity to impose upon himself and upon his rulers the disciplines necessary for freedom.

## The American Tradition of a Basic Written Document

It is not surprising that our Founding Fathers decided upon written documents of supreme law at both the state and the national level. We have already noted the "higher law" background of eighteenth-century thinking. As British colonists our ancestors had been used to mercantile, proprietary, and colonial charters which set forth the

FIRST MEETING OF THE ASSEMBLY IN VIRGINIA.

The year 1619 saw the first representative assembly in America—the Virginia House of Burgesses. The House of Burgesses was made up of planters sent by the plantations to help the governor and council (both appointees of the London Company) to redraft the laws of the colony. By 1621 the House of Burgesses had been made a permanent feature of Virginia colonial government under a permanent constitution provided by the London Company.

framework and source of authority for civil government in the several colonies. And when the struggle with Great Britain became intense, the charge that king and Parliament were acting "unconstitutionally" stemmed in part from the feeling of informed colonists that the spirit of Britain's major "constitutional documents" (like Magna Charta and the seventeenth-century Bills of Rights) was being violated.

By the time the Founding Fathers met in Philadelphia in 1787, of course, most Americans had lived for a decade or more with written state constitutions and with the Articles of Confederation under which the several states had banded together during the war against the mother country.

We shall have reason later on to refer to the early state constitutions and their implications for contemporary state government (see Chapter 20). In this present chapter we are concerned with the United States Constitution, for it is primarily from this single document that our proud constitutional heritage stems. Scores of nations the world over—nations that have come into being in the past century and a half—have attempted to imitate part or all of America's basic written document.

# CONSTITUTION OF THE UNITED STATES: A VERY HUMAN DOCUMENT

There have been times in our history when the United States Constitution has been romanticized as a "sacred document" struck off by almost superhuman political prophets working under divine inspiration.

If our Founding Fathers were alive today, they would be the first to disclaim this interpretation. Alexander Hamilton thought privately that the Constitution was such a "frail and worthless fabric" it would not last a generation. Among the original drafters no one was very happy with the finished product. The aged Benjamin Franklin urged its adoption in spite of a series of misgivings about particular parts of the document. Months of bitter debate, artful salesmanship, and shrewd tactics were necessary before the instrument was finally ratified by the necessary nine states.

## A Compromise

The Constitution, in short, was the product of compromise, and was forged and finally ratified in the furnace of free debate and rough-and-tumble politics. And herein lies its strength. Had it been more systematic, more rigid, more dogmatic, it is doubtful whether it ever could have been successfully adapted to the cyclonic changes which have taken place on the American continent and in the world since 1787.

The word "compromise" is frequently heard in connection with modern politics and government—and usually in an unfavorable context. It is well to remember that without compromise there would have been no Constitution. The great moments in the Constitutional Convention in 1787 were those when forward movement was made possible by the willingness of two opposing factions to accommodate themselves to a solution in which no one got everything but everyone got something. Compromise was necessary, for example, over the issue of representation (whether the national Congress should represent "states" or "people"); over the issue of slavery (whether slaves should be counted for purposes of representation and taxes); over treaty-making powers (whether one section of the country might subordinate another section through the device of commercial treaties with foreign countries).

Most important, the Constitution was in general a great philosophic compromise between those who feared democracy and those who did not. In the overworked and imprecise language of politics, the Constitution was a compromise between aristocrats and democrats, conservatives and liberals, the claims of the few and the claims of the many. That in 1787 the balance fell initially on the conservative, or antidemocratic, side is one of the fortuitous events of history. For the result was that as democratic forces expanded in the nineteenth and twentieth centuries, the excesses traditionally associated with unbridled popular governments were contained, ordered, and governed by our conservative constitutional framework. The Constitution, by and large, has acted like a well-functioning steam boiler— releasing the energies of a democratic society without undue dissipation and, excepting the Civil War, without explosions.

### The Background of the Constitution

Why the Constitution was a necessary compromise, why the balance fell initially on the conservative side, cannot be undersotod apart from the history of America at the time of the Revolution.

*Anglo-Colonial Friendship.* In spite of occasional tensions, colonial attitudes toward England from 1620 to 1763 were on the whole remarkably friendly. Especially in the first half of the eighteenth century, the more settled and prosperous portions of the Eastern seaboard enjoyed many British imperial advantages and, except on paper, suffered few imperial restrictions. By and large, there was far more hostility between the rich colonial merchants and plantation owners on the seaboard and their poorer cousins on the small farms on the inland frontier than there was between colonists and England. In fact, the dominant clash between colonial legislatures and royal

Nothing has excited more admiration in the world than the manner in which free governments have been established in America; for it was the first instance, from the creation of the world . . . that free inhabitants have been seen deliberating on a form of government, and selecting such of their citizens as possessed their confidence, to determine upon and give effect to it.

—James Madison

governors was often overshadowed by the struggle between the underrepresented and populous small farmers and woodsmen of the West, and the British-oriented, aristocratic, propertied, commercial, and landed classes of the East.

*Origins of Democracy.* What changed this configuration of interests, what forced the merchants and the landed aristocracy to join with the small farmers, small tradesmen, and the voteless lower classes of the seaboard towns and cities, was a sudden change in British colonial policy after 1763. The tightening up of colonial administration and the imposition and reimposition of colonial taxes is too familiar a story to Americans to need repetition here. It is sufficient to point out that the language of liberty, natural rights, "taxation without representation," and finally, independence, which the commercial and landed gentry found expedient to use against the restrictive actions of the mother country, aroused the democratic passions and aspirations of the smaller farmers and of the disenfranchised lower classes of the colonial towns and villages.

The American Revolution was a social and political revolution within the colonies as well as a political and commercial break with England. The incendiary pamphlets of Tom Paine and the opening paragraphs of the Declaration of Independence were the peak literary expressions of this domestic revolution. The new state constitutions, with their emphasis upon human rights and upon the supremacy of more popularly elected legislatures, were further evidence of the profound democratic forces which the Revolution unleashed.

*Fears of Men of Substance.* During the period of the Articles of Confederation, from 1781 to 1788, the state legislatures under their new constitutions moved further and further in the direction of economic legislation favorable to the small farmers and the other segments of the population most sorely pressed by the postwar depression. The Congress of the Confederation, with only a slowly evolving executive system and no taxing power of its own, was of course powerless to stop what creditors in the various states believed to be legislation inimical to their interests. When Shay's Rebellion erupted in Massachusetts in 1786 as an armed debtor protest, the "men of substance" of America became deeply alarmed—even though the rebellion was quashed in short order.

The majority of men who came to Philadelphia to "revise" the Articles of Confederation in 1787 unquestionably felt that they had suffered direct economic hardship at the hands of the diffused, popular governments of the new states. The feelings of the drafters and supporters of the new federal Constitution toward the growing forces of democracy in the land were not hidden.

Elbridge Gerry, confessing that he "had been too republican heretofore," declared that "the evils we experience flow from the excess of democracy." Alexander Hamilton denounced the masses as "turbulent and changing; they seldom judge or determine right," and ventured the opinion that the British form of Government was "the best in the world." Like Gerry, Edmund Randolph believed that the evils of the country had their origin "in the turbulence and follies of democracy." Gouverneur Morris held that there was no more reason to entrust the vote to "the ignorant and the dependent" than to children. Roger Sherman thought that the people directly "should have as little to do as may be about the government." [1]

As Arthur Schlesinger, Sr., and other leading modern historians have pointed out, "The Constitution as it was framed by the Convention was well calculated to keep the plain people in a subordinate place and to assure political power to the men of substance and quality." [2]

This was a far cry from the ringing words of the Declaration of Independence that "all men are created equal" and that "governments derive their just powers from the consent of the governed." But it was an understandable reaction of an upper middle class society to the amorphous and disordered impact of new democratic forces upon its fortunes and traditions which had already been disrupted by an extended war for independence.

It would be unfair to leave the story here, however. If some of our Founding Fathers were by and large hostile to the new forces of democracy, they were also hostile to the monarchical presumptions, imperial centralization, and lush parasitic court life of the Old World. Hamilton's abortive intent to make Washington a constitutional monarch represented the viewpoint of only a tiny minority. Most of the Founding Fathers wished a government by the propertied and well-born, but without monarchical or even aristocratic trappings.

## Achievements of Articles of Confederation

They wished something else. They wished an orderly, national, constitutional government, capable of managing the common affairs of a people only recently independent and beset with the strains and uncertainties of postwar economic and political problems. It is true that the need for interstate cooperation had been recognized prior to and during the Revolution. This need was reflected in the First and Second Continental Congresses, and from 1781 to 1789 in the Articles of Confederation. It is also true that the Articles of Confederation have been much maligned. In view of the nonenforceable quality of state participation in the Confederation, and in view of the fact that the Congress under the Confederation had power neither to tax nor to regulate interstate commerce, the accomplishments of this experimental cooperation were truly astounding. The Confederation somehow weathered the most serious financial problems of the immediate postwar years, and in the Northwest Ordinance of 1787 it created one of the most remarkable political documents in world history: an imaginative and practical set of regulations for the development and eventual political and economic integration of the entire American continent.

It is of course true that the lack of a strong central government created diplomatic, commerical, financial, and interstate problems which were difficult to solve under the limited authority of the Articles of Confederation. But in view of what we now know of the returning prosperity in the two years just prior to the Constitutional Convention, it is debatable whether the men of substance among our Founding Fathers wished a strong national government because the Confederation was failing, or because in fact the democratic forces in some of the states were succeeding too well.

However, none of this speculation should blind us to the fact that among the statesmen of that day there existed a disinterested concern for effective and orderly government as a guarantor of civility, liberty, prosperity, and peace in the life of the people as a whole. *Noblesse oblige* is not ignoble.

## The Answer in Philadelphia

During the hot summer of 1787, then, the men drawn to Philadelphia for the limited purpose of "revising the Articles of Confederation," were confronted with the question of how to build an effective national government which would (1) have the dangers neither of a centralized monarchy nor of a decentralized democracy; (2) be strong enough to provide for the orderly regulation and promotion of economic life on terms which in general would be recognized with approval by men of substance; (3) and be weak enough to stand some chance of being ratified by the increasingly democratically-inclined population of the several states.

This was no easy task. Our pride in the political genius of our

Founding Fathers is justified. In the short space of three months, a small group of personally interested but politically dedicated men shaped a document which gradually gathered a life and meaning of its own and withstood and channeled the buffeting winds and waves of cyclonic change.

A review of the Constitution itself (see Appendix 556) is sufficient to identify the major provisions which have stood the test of time: a Congress made up of a Senate and a House of Representatives; a single chief executive in the person of the President; an independent Federal court system; and, after 1791, a Bill of Rights. All these will be discussed in detail in later chapters.

At this point, however, there are three constitutional propositions which deserve particular attention. They may be categorized under interrelated headings: federalism, separation of powers, and peaceful change.

## FEDERALISM

Federalism is technically a constitutional division of power between two or more levels of government within a single area. In the literature of political science, federalism is contrasted with both a unitary form of government, where all power derives from one central government, and a confederation where all power derives from sovereign participating units. England and France, for example, operate under a unitary form of government. The United Nations is a modern example of a confederation.

At the Constitutional Convention of 1787, a unitary form of government was unthinkable. The American people had memories of intermittently applied centralized authority going back a century and a half. The Founding Fathers had no intention of fashioning

---

*COMMONLY CONFUSED CONSTITUTIONAL POWERS*

*Express, Enumerated,* or *Delegated:* Powers specifically mentioned in the U.S. Constitution;

*Implied:* Powers deducible from, and needed for the effectuation of, express powers. (See Article I, end of Section 8);

*Inherent:* Powers not clearly denied which exist as elemental attributes of government;

*Reserved:* Powers not delegated; reserved to states or people.

an American counterpart of British imperial centralization, especially since in some of the colonies a kind of state-local "federal" system had been comfortably enjoyed for decades.

On the other hand, a loose confederation of individual states was causing a number of American leaders considerable consternation.

In a supreme act of invention, the drafters assigned certain direct powers to the new national government, provided for the sharing of certain powers by both the Federal government and the state governments, and reserved all other governmental powers to the individual states or "to the people." This was accomplished both by positive grants of power and by specified restrictions upon the exercise of power.

For example, among other things the national government was given unique authority to:

1. Make war
2. Negotiate treaties with foreign countries
3. Regulate commerce among the several states
4. Establish post offices
5. Issue patents
6. Support and maintain an army and navy
7. Coin money

The national government was allowed to share with the individual states such powers as the right to:

1. Tax
2. Use the state militias
3. Build roads
4. Acquire land by eminent domain

But the Federal government was specifically prohibited from such practices as:

1. Suspending the writ of habeas corpus * (except under conditions of dire emergency)
2. Passing bills of attainder * or ex post facto laws *
3. Giving preferential commercial treatment to one state as against another
4. Granting titles of nobility

And the individual states, among other things, were specifically denied the right to:

1. Enter into any treaty, alliance, or confederation
2. Coin money
3. Pass any law impairing the obligation of a contract

* For definitions, see Chap. 5.

The amendments to the Constitution, of course, contain a wide variety of other restrictions upon both federal and state action, especially where basic human rights are concerned. And the Tenth Amendment reads, "The powers not delegated to the United States by the Constitution, nor prohibited by it to the States, are reserved to the States respectively, or to the people." Since the time of the great controversy between Jefferson and Hamilton, however, the precise limits of the powers of the national government—express and implied—has been a key subject of constitutional and political debate. For federalism is not a simple form of government. In some ways it is a highly unstable form of government. Conflicts of interest are almost bound to appear between state power and national power. Our own Civil War was a critical test of the federal system. The Supreme Court has been kept busy as the arbiter of federal disputes. Every session of Congress has witnessed a struggle between those who prefer "states' rights" and those who favor federal authority. Such present issues as segregation, discrimination, resource conservation, labor-management relations, and education are enmeshed in federal questions of primary and proper jurisdiction.

There are some people who would claim today that there is almost nothing left of our original federal system; that the Federal government has, to all intents and purposes, become a unitary, central authority which has ridden roughshod over the constitutional prerogatives of the states. There are others who would claim that state governments still have far too much power, and that they stand in the way of national progress.

That national necessity, growth, and experience have changed the relative positions of the states and the Federal government in the control of public policy cannot be denied. But a division of power still remains, and it is doubtful if the vast and complicated American experiment could have survived at all had it not been for the flexibilities and ambiguities which are implicit in a federal charter. By and large, Americans have adjusted the guide lines of federalism to suit their needs. They will undoubtedly continue to do so.


# SEPARATION OF POWERS

For 150 years prior to the American Revolution, the American colonies had lived under a system of divided powers. Certain colonial powers were exercised by the royal governors; certain powers were in the hands of locally elected colonial legislatures; and certain powers were lodged in the king's courts and the Privy Council.

The state constitutions which were created during the Revolutionary War departed from this heritage. In the revolt against British authority, the colonists had an understandable desire to contain those functions and prerogatives of government which had traditionally been exercised by the crown. In the state constitutions, therefore, the executive and judicial functions were made subservient to legislative control. It was this very legislative supremacy in the states, however, which most bothered the drafters of the federal Constitution. They associated legislative supremacy with democratic passions and legislation hostile to the rights of property. On the other hand, the Founding Fathers had just lived through a war which had been fought against monarchical power. The need they saw was for an executive power stronger than that permitted either by the state constitutions or by the Articles of Confederation; but not so strong as that exercised by an eighteenth-century British monarch— George III—who enjoyed subverting seventeenth-century parliamentary checks by artifices of patronage and politics.

## The "Middle Way"

Taking their cue from earlier colonial experience, from the necessary compromises within the convention itself, and from the writings of Roman, English, and French theorists like Polybius, Harrington, Locke, and Montesquieu, the Founding Fathers wrote into the Constitution a "middle way." The middle way provided for a division of class interests between the House of Representatives on the one hand and the Senate and the President on the other, and for a division of powers between branches of government—executive, legislative, and judicial. It also provided for chesslike internal checks— but without a checkmate.

This complex system was designed to prohibit the growth of arbitrary power at either the democratic or aristocratic extremes of the political spectrum, and to perpetuate the safeties of institutional competition in the actual conduct of government.

The complexity of the design is apparent in every Article of the Constitution:

Legislative power is vested in the Congress, but the Congress is divided in two, and both halves must agree before a law can be passed. Furthermore, the law can be vetoed by the Executive. However, the Congress by a two-thirds vote in both Houses can override the President's veto.

The President can negotiate treaties and make certain executive and judicial appointments; but in each case, the Senate must concur. If the expenditure of money is involved (as it usually is today), the House of Representatives must initiate appropriations.

The Supreme Court can decide issues arising under the Constitution, but it cannot enforce its own decisions. If the President refuses to enforce the decisions of the Supreme Court, he can be impeached —not by the Supreme Court but by the Congress.

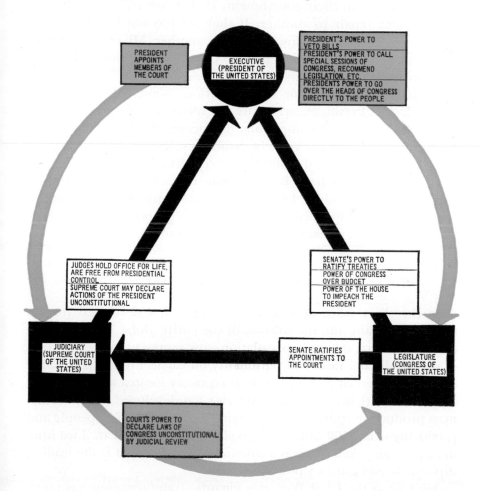

The above is a graphic presentation of the system of divided powers and checks and balances which characterizes our form of government and distinguishes it from the *parliamentary* system in which the legislature is supreme.

## Checks and Balances

Like federalism, there is nothing neat about a separation of powers, checks and balances, form of government. At its worst it permits irresponsibility, buck-passing, and stalemates—sometimes to a critical degree. But at its best, it not only does what it was intended to do—checks the growth of arbitrary power—it provides for a healthy variety of pressure points for the diverse interests of a vast and complicated nation. The aggrieved have a number of points of access to their government. If they are frozen out by one branch, they repair to another. If they get too much redress from one branch, they are cut down to size by another. Mixed government is a kind of flywheel which regulates the tensions, intermittences, and torques of competing social pressures.

In the course of five or six generations, some roles have been reversed. The President, originally the ultimate conservative check, has become the first line of popular democracy. The House of Representatives, originally the voice of democracy, has become, along with the state governments, the first line of conservatism. The Senate and the Supreme Court have both become more reflective of popular will than the Founding Fathers anticipated. But the fundamental pattern, modified to a degree by the rise of a generally unanticipated two-party system, remains—to worry us and to bless us.

# PEACEFUL CHANGE

In the short space of 165 years America has developed from a struggling infant into the colossus of the entire globe. Cosmopolitan even in colonial days, the population now represents a cross section of every religion, race, and nationality on earth. From a reasonably simple commercial and agricultural economy located on a marginal strip of the Atlantic seaboard, America has developed a continental mass production technology employing nearly 70,000,000 people and producing over $400 billions of goods and services a year. Two hundred years ago, America was a colonial pawn. Today it is the leading diplomatic and military power on earth.

Aside from the Civil War, this gigantic transformation has taken place with almost no domestic bloodshed and with a remarkable degree of internal harmony and personal freedom. The frontier itself was of course a safety valve for the release of social and economic tensions. The very size of the American continent permitted geographic and social mobility. But full tribute must also be paid to the Constitution, both for what it *provided* and for what it *permitted*.

The Constitution provided for peaceful change in three ways: by insisting upon civilian supremacy over the military; by establishing fixed terms for elected officials; and by building into itself orderly devices for amendment.

## Civilian Supremacy

The pages of world history are filled with stories of military domination of civilian life. In times of social and political chaos, military supremacy has often been welcomed as the only guarantor of internal order. But by and large, domination of civilian life by the military has spelled tyranny, insecurity, rigidity, and fear for the nations concerned. It is true that America has had a number of generals in the White House, from Washington to Eisenhower. But these generals have all dropped their uniforms and have adopted the garb and the mind-set of constitutionally limited civilians whose job it was not to enthrone military power but to control it. Until the exigencies of international tension and global strife forced the issue, America refused to permit peacetime conscription of a large standing army. Even today, the Congress still struggles with the implications and details of this issue.

By making the President of the United States the Commander-in-Chief of our military forces; by insisting upon senatorial confirmation of officer appointments; by following the British tradition of limiting all military pay bills to no longer than two years; by maintaining a dispersed state militia; by prohibiting the quartering of soldiers in private houses during peacetime; and by leaving the maintenance of public order for the most part to state and local magistrates, the Constitution has systematically abetted the doctrine of civilian supremacy. The consequence has been that all through our national history we as a people have been spared the experience, so common to so many other countries, of seeing change enforced or prohibited by entrenched military might.

## Fixed Terms

Even the entrenchment of civilian power is curbed by the Constitution. Lifetime appointments in our government are permitted only in the judicial branch, and then, only on condition of "good behavior." "Bad" behavior can result in impeachment. The President is elected for four years and, as a result of the Twenty-second Amendment, can only serve for two terms. Members of the House of Representatives must face election every two years, and members of the Senate every six years. Even with the limited franchise permitted in the early years of the Republic, and even with the essentially undemocratic provisions for electing the President and the United States Senate found in the original document, the constitutional provisions for periodic elections established a representative form of government which could and did reflect the changing needs and demands of a growing society.

## Amendments

Finally, the Constitution provided for its own amendment. The first ten amendments, which include our prized Bill of Rights, were passed by popular demand as early as 1791. Most of the remaining twelve have served either to extend democratic rights and privileges or to modernize the powers and procedures of the national govern-

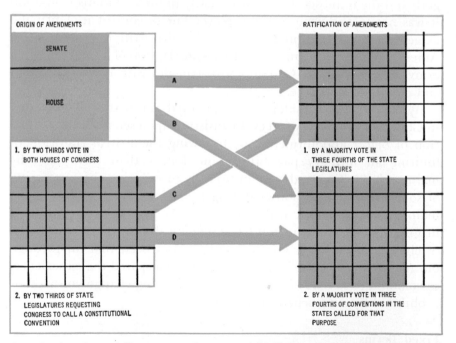

Constitutional amendments must be *proposed* (1) by a two-thirds majority of both Houses of Congress, or (2) by a national convention called by the legislatures of at least two thirds of the states; and must be *ratified* (1) by the legislatures of three fourths of the states, or (2) by special conventions in three fourths of the states. (Adapted from "Congress at Work," *Senior Scholastic,* Vol. 58, No. 2, Feb. 14, 1951, Part II, p. 9.)

ment. That resort to amendment has been necessary so infrequently is an amazing fact in itself. The fact can be explained only by noting what the Constitution *permitted* in addition to what it *provided.*

# NONCONSTITUTIONAL "CONSTITUTIONAL" FACTORS

The two most important nonconstitutional factors in guaranteeing peaceful change in our hisory have been judicial review and the rise of political parties. Both came early in our national history; both were tacitly permitted (some would say, made inevitable) by our Constitution; and yet, neither is specifically referred to.

## Judicial Review

Judicial review in its broadest context is the self-appointed right of the courts to pass upon the constitutionality of legislative and of executive actions—state and federal. Although some of our Founding Fathers assumed that the courts would have this right, although the idea of a "higher law" had roots deep in our political heritage, and although the "supremacy" clause of the Constitution set the federal document clearly above all the other laws, no explicit and authoritative statement of the power of judicial review appeared until Chief Justice John Marshall, in the famous case of *Marbury vs. Madison,* pronounced the right by judicial fiat. Originating as a rearguard weapon of conservative Federalists, judicial review has since 1803 given constitutional sanction alternately to some of the most profound forces of change, and resistance to change, in our national life. This is true even though the power has been exercised infrequently over the years. The possibility that it may be invoked has been an influential factor in the deliberations of Congress and in the actions of the President. It has not been a consistent instrument of liberalism or conservatism, national power or state power. In general, in Mr. Dooley's felicitous phrase, the Courts have "followed the election returns." But judicial review has slowed, sobered, and by and large dignified the process of state and national adaptation to new conditions. In certain areas, notably in its review of segregation and discrimination laws affecting Negroes, the Supreme Court has at last hastened change long overdue.

By exercising the power of judicial review, the courts have made our basic document a living instrument—responsive, even if with intermittent delays, to the needs of each new generation. (For a further discussion see Chapter 19.)

### Political Parties

As supreme instruments of peaceful change, however, highest tribute must be paid our political parties. The most significant difference between the United States and the Soviet Union is not in their written constitutions, but in their party systems. Russia has one party. We have at least two.

Political parties have had a bad press in our history. Our Founding Fathers were bitterly hostile to what they called factions. President George Washington in his Farewell Address warned the people against the growing menace of factionalism. Fortunately, however, Washington's Farewell Address was itself a "factional" speech—aimed at the new democratic cells of Jeffersonian Republicanism which were springing up all over the country.

Before our nation was out of swaddling clothes it was up to its ears in partisan politics. The constitutional provisions for periodic elections, and the fundamental guarantees of freedom in the First Amendment, made political parties inevitable.

Political parties are still evolving as responsible instruments of government, but even in the highly diffuse and pluralistic form which they have assumed during most of our history, they have been extenders of democracy, guarantors of freedom, and supreme instruments of peaceful change. They have placed alternative candidates and multitudinous issues before the American public. They have frequently bridged the gulf between the President and Congress and between disparate regional and economic interests. If, at times, the partisan struggle has been bitter and obstructive, it has been preferable by far to open rebellion, tyranny, or perpetual civil war.

Our political parties have thus become an integral part of our constitutional heritage—buttressed by our constitutional guarantees of freedom of speech, press, assembly, and religion; operating through the buffers and baffles of federalism, separation of powers, and judicial review; and moderated and transcended by our ethical and religious heritage.

# CONCLUSION

### Synopsis

Our constitutional heritage, although traceable to ideas deep in Western thought, stems particularly from British tradition, from colonial experience, from experience under the two Continental Congresses and the Articles of Confederation, and from the compromises of men of wisdom who gathered in 1787 to fashion a written instrument for a new nation. Through provisions for a *federal* system of government, for *separation of powers* and *checks and balances* among the various branches, and for *peaceful change* through *civilian supremacy, fixed terms for elected officials,* and *constitutional amendment,* the Constitution became a complex but flexible framework of government for a freedom-loving people. *Judicial review* and *political parties,* although not specifically mentioned in the Constitution, have become valued additions to our constitutional heritage.

### Significance

The wilderness, our ethical and religious heritage, and our constitutional heritage combined in the latter part of the eighteenth century to set the value and institutional framework for a self-conscious and institutionally insecure new nation. The wonder is that the nation lasted. It almost did not! Even after it learned the art of steady flight in the early years of the nineteenth century, it almost crashed from the wild turbulence of civil war in 1861. Since that time, however, it has prospered increasingly within the flexible framework of our constitutional heritage. This is particularly remarkable granted the cyclonic changes which have occurred in the past century: in technology, in population, and in international affairs. Fortunately, ours has been a land of plenty; and our Founding Fathers drafted well.

### Prospectus

In Section I we have reviewed our value inheritance as a people. Many of these inherited values—particularly those referred to in Chapters 1 and 2—are, of course, reflected in the total folkways and mores of American life—in the family, in the content of television programs, in the means and places of religious worship, in books and pamphlets and newspapers, and in all our business, professional, and social activities. But these values are particularly reflected in our expectations of government. What we expect from government and how government in America has responded to these expectations is the theme of the following section.

# SECTION II

# Our Expectations of Government

We the people of the United States, in Order to form a more perfect Union, establish Justice, insure domestic Tranquillity, provide for the common defense, promote the general Welfare, and secure the blessings of Liberty to ourselves and our Posterity, do ordain and establish this Constitution for the United States of America.

—Preamble to the U.S. Constitution

## CHAPTER 4

# A More Perfect Union

THE PREAMBLE to the United States Constitution is more than a literary flourish. In fifty-two words the high expectations of the American people about the functions of government are epitomized. One constitutional scholar has gone so far as to suggest that the Preamble was meant to be the most important part of the Constitution—that all other sections of our basic document should be read in the Preamble's conditioning light. Even if this suggestion is still being subjected to the parries and thrusts of scholarly debate, the fact remains that the Preamble sets up a series of expectations of constitutional government which are as meaningful today as when they were first written.

An exposition and analysis of these categories of expectation should help us understand our constitutional system more fully. But it should do more. It should give us some appreciation of the vital role which government plays in our individual lives. Justice Oliver Wendell Holmes once said, "When I pay taxes, I buy civilization." The Preamble to the Constitution suggests what the word "civilization" includes. In fact, it would be hard to find a more comprehensive definition of the basic values of a civilized society. If a society is reasonably united on fundamentals, if it is just, if it is protected against domestic violence and alien domination, if it is committed to securing the general welfare without sacrificing the blessings of liberty, who can doubt that it has the right to be called civilized?

## TO FORM A MORE PERFECT UNION

If we begin where the Constitution begins, with the value of "a more perfect union," we have a right to ask what the phrase can possibly mean in tangible twentieth-century terms. We have already noted that our Founding Fathers wanted and designed an improved constitutional instrument for managing the common affairs of a new nation. It was natural for them to talk about "a more perfect union."

But that was more than a century and a half ago. Once the Constitution was adopted and ratified was not the obligation to form a more perfect union discharged?

The answer, of course, is No. No union of diverse groups of people is ever perfect. Interests shift. New problems, new goals, new tensions arise within a complex and dynamic society, and these must be settled and adjusted. James Madison in the tenth *Federalist* pointed out that

A landed interest, a manufacturing interest, a mercantile interest, a monied interest, and many lesser interests, grow up of necessity in civilized nations, and divide them into different classes, actuated by different sentiments and views. The regulation of these various and interfering interests forms the principal task of modern legislation, and involves the spirit of party and faction in the necessary and ordinary operations of government.

A society would not be free without parties and factions; but if a fundamental unity did not underlie these divergencies the society would be torn asunder. The greatest constitutional crisis in our history, the Civil War, developed around the question of the preservation of the Union. America has always known factional struggles: economic, racial, religious, political, social, and regional.

Fortunately, however, these disintegrative forces have been countered by equally powerful integrative forces during most of our history. One of the pervasive themes in American life has been the struggles of peoples for a sense of belonging. This hunger for belonging motivated every settlement and territory in the westward movement during the nineteenth century and is still present in the statehood aspirations of Alaska and Hawaii. The fondest hopes of the millions who came to this country in great waves of immigration during the nineteenth and early twentieth centuries were centered on the single goal: to become—not a Texan or a New Yorker—but an American, with the dignity and opportunity which this connotes. And under constitutional provisions of state and nation, governments in America have taken positive steps to foster a greater sense of economic, political, and social unity among the citizenry.

## The United States Postal Service

No greater contribution has been made to the development of common bonds of unity in American life than the creation of the postal service. That a safe and inexpensive means of transmitting written and printed information was fundamental to any kind of collective purpose was recognized even before the Constitution.

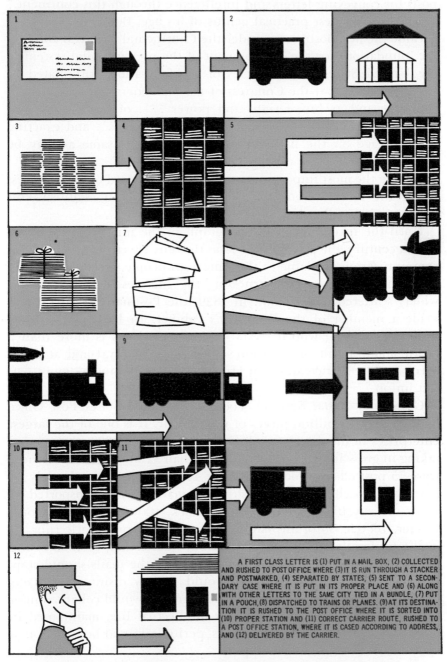

The Post Office handles 150,000,000 pieces of mail a day, 55 billion pieces a year. ("The Story of a Letter," Washington, D. C.: U. S. Post Office Department. Submitted by Frank Farley, Postmaster, New Orleans, La.)

The journals of the Continental Congress in 1775 report the establishment of a postal system as "the best means of establishing posts for conveying letters and intelligence through this continent." Probably the ablest practical genius of his age, Benjamin Franklin, became the first postmaster under the Continental Congress and laid the foundations for the development of the present postal system of the United States. The Articles of Confederation, formulated in 1777, provided that the Congress of the Confederation should have "the sole and exclusive right and power . . . of establishing and regulating post offices from one state to another . . . and exacting such postage on the papers passing through the same as may be requisite to defray the expenses of said office. . . ."

Among the most important specific powers granted to the Congress under the federal Constitution is the power "To establish Post Offices and post Roads."

Until the invention of the telegraph in the middle of the nineteenth century, the postal service was the only effective instrument of communication available to the American people. So important did this function become in harnessing the energies of a diverse and widely scattered nation that, in 1829, the Postmaster General was made a member of the President's cabinet. In back of the blue-uniformed official who delivers mail to our doors is more than a century and a half of tradition—a tradition of loyal and at times heroic public service aimed at creating and sustaining a "more perfect union."

*Growth of Postal Service.* Today the United States Post Office handles over 50 billion pieces of mail a year. It is one of the largest enterprises in the world, employing more than 500,000 workers and taking in gross annual receipts of more than $2 billion. In 1789 there were 75 post offices. Today there are 40,000. Once carried solely by horseback, coach, or coastwise ship, the mail today is transported by every conceivable kind of vehicle: truck, train, bus, auto, motor scooter, bicycle, ship, airplane, helicopter, and pneumatic tube. It facilitates family and social integration, intellectual, economic, and political integration. If suddenly, tomorrow, the mails should stop, our economic and political life would rapidly disintegrate. Telegraph, telephone, radio, and television services would collapse under the weight of panic. Our common intellectual life, maintained in large part by the shipment of papers, periodicals, and books through the mails, would quickly disappear.

We should not take the mails for granted. Our postal service is

One of the continuing jobs of the Federal government is to keep knowledge about the physical aspects of the United States up-to-date and as complete as possible. Here a map-maker in the Department of the Interior works on a new master map of the United States. Maps are instruments of unity.

our single most important artery of communication. Without it the national organism could hardly survive.

## Highways and Transportation

The postal service, however, could not operate without roads and vehicles of transportation. Neither could our complex economy. Even simple community life would be made supremely difficult without connecting arteries of travel.

In the early days of our republic, road building and maintenance was generally a function of local government or of private enterprise. Even today, most local authorities in the United States spend more tax money on roads than on any other single item except education. From its beginnings in intermittencies and mud, the road and highway system of America has grown to the point where it now interlaces the entire country. As the needs increased, progressively higher and more inclusive levels of government assumed responsibility: from settlement to township; from township to county and city; from county and city to state; from state to interstate authorities and finally to the Federal government.

The great revolution in highway construction came, of course, after the turn of the twentieth century with the advent of the automobile. The dusty or muddy post roads, state roads, county roads, and local roads of the nineteenth century were totally inadequate to the demands of the internal combustion engine. Virtually the entire hard-surface network of the United States has been built in the past fifty years. Today, the investment in state highways alone is estimated at more than $50 billion. Currently, the Federal government is spending hundreds of millions of dollars annually through its Bureau of Public Roads in a $50 billion long-range program to perfect the grid of federal highways and to help state and local governments carry a financial burden which is rapidly becoming intolerable. And, even so, no one pretends that government has kept pace with the ever increasing need for safer and more convenient highways and roads in America.

## Waterways and Railroads

Roads and highways have only been part of the story, however. Almost from the beginning of our national existence, Federal and state governments cooperated in the development of a system of internal waterways—linking seacoast, rivers, and lakes with a network of canals. Until the advent of the railroad, this system of internal waterways carried more people and goods than all the interstate roads of the country combined.

The advent of the railroad was a major turning point in the history of internal transportation. During the nineteenth century, no other single factor contributed more to the geographical unity of the American continent. Both the Federal and the state governments became inextricably involved in the extension and regulation of the railroads. Hundreds of millions of acres of public lands were given to private railroad companies as rights of way. Special legislation gave the companies tax concessions and special legal benefits. After the Civil War, and the linking of the Atlantic and Pacific, some of the railroad companies became so powerful, greedy, and ruthless that popular indignation and the need for economic stability in the industry itself forced public regulation. Early state regulation broke down because of the interstate character of railroad operation and management; but in 1887, with the passage of the Interstate Commerce Act, federal regulation was imposed and has remained to this day.

By 1960, commercial jets will be commonplace, and will negotiate the distance between San Francisco International Airport (shown above) and the east coast in four hours or less. This projected speed is causing the CAB to review the entire air traffic control pattern in the United States.

The Interstate Commerce Commission, the agency established by the Interstate Commerce Act to regulate railroad rates and practices, now has residual control over almost every aspect of railroad management and operation in the entire country.

Through subsequent legislation, the Commission has been granted authority to regulate interstate buses and trucks, as well as water carriers operating coastwise, and upon inland waterways.

Similar authority over intrastate transportation is exercised in a number of states by public utility commissions. And, of course, many transit systems are municipally operated or regulated.

## Air Transportation

In 1903, the Wright brothers fulfilled man's age-old ambition to conquer the air. The discovery of the airplane brought with it a series of governmental and intergovernmental problems, the magnitude of which we are only now beginning to realize. Like the railroad before it, the airplane has become a powerful force in promoting national unity. The once long and arduous journey from coast to coast, which a hundred years ago had to be reckoned in months, is now accomplished between lunch and dinner.

Although state and local governments have been concerned with the growth of air travel—notably in terms of the location, construction, and use of airports—the major burden of promotion and regulation of air transportation has understandably fallen upon the Federal government. Attempts of individual states or private enterprise to regulate air travel would have resulted, not in a "more perfect union," but in unbelievable chaos.

The Federal government has aided and abetted the air age by postal subsidies, military purchase, federally sponsored research, the provision of air navigation facilities, the establishment of interstate airways and mandatory levels of flight, the working out of international air agreements, the promotion and inspection of safety devices, and in a host of other ways. Today, the Civil Aeronautics Administration, the Civil Aeronautics Board, the air arms of the Department of Defense, and the Air Coordinating Committee constitute the basic administrative and operational instruments for the federal promotion and regulation of aviation.

## Wired and Wireless Communication

With all the prescience of our Founding Fathers, they could not have been expected to foresee the harnessing of electricity for purposes of verbal and visual communication. The telegraph, the telephone, the radio, and television allow almost instantaneous communication—and permit, potentially, a more perfect union than man has ever experienced in his long history.

Although telegraph and telephone services were subject to various kinds of state regulation before the turn of the twentieth century, and for a time, to limited federal regulation by the Interstate Commerce Commission, the rise of wireless communication in the 1920's made strict federal control of all telecommunications imperative. The first Federal Radio Commission was established in 1926.

In 1934, the Congress established the Federal Communications Commission for the purpose of "regulating interstate and foreign commerce in communication by wire and radio so as to make available, so far as possible, to all people of the United States a rapid, efficient, nationwide, and worldwide wire and radio communication service. . . ."

A moment's thought is sufficient to suggest what would happen to radio and television service in the United States without federal regulation. With a limited number of frequencies, either the receiving sets would emit a babel of competing sounds and pictures, or the enterpriser with the largest wattage would dominate what the American people heard and saw. In a nation where unity is the orderly framework for individual diversity, private control over airwaves is unthinkable. To ensure orderliness in transmission and reception, and to protect the American people against programmatic monopoly, the F.C.C. has been given wide powers of regulation. Every technological advance in the vast telecommunications industry brings new problems which the Federal Communications Commission must somehow solve if we are to have a more perfect union.

## Currency, Banking, and Standards

Anyone who has ever traveled in Europe has experienced the problems of having to deal in a multitude of currencies. Francs must be exchanged for pounds, pounds for liras, liras for marks, marks for crowns. A common currency is one indication of political unity. It is no accident that of the first six powers enumerated under Section 8 of Article I of the United States Constitution, three involve the coinage and use of money. The currency problem in America before the drafting of the federal Constitution was more complicated and unstable by far than that in modern Europe.

The fact that today a dime is just as acceptable a medium of exchange in San Diego, California, as it is in Eastport, Maine, stems from the federal monopoly over the coinage of money.

At the present time, the Bureau of Engraving and Printing and the Bureau of the Mint of the Treasury Department supervise the issuance of billions of dollars worth of coin and paper money annually.

But hard money and paper money constitute only one small part of the exchange needs of a complex economy. Most financial transactions are handled through banks. Bank transfers are unquestionably America's most important instruments of economic unity.

Although federal banks were part of the experimentation and controversy of our early history, the National Bank Act passed by Congress in 1863 was the first really successful attempt of the Federal government to introduce order into a highly diffuse and disorganized banking and currency system. In the short space of fifty years, however, even the national bank system proved inadequate.

In 1913, the Federal Reserve System was established to provide a series of regional "bankers' banks" under the general control of a semi-autonomous board of governors in Washington, D. C. Strengthened by depression-born banking acts and by the establishment of the Federal Deposit Insurance Corporation in the 1930s, the interlocking Federal Reserve and national bank systems constitute today the primary instruments of banking stability and flexibility in America. These federal instruments are aided by state banking departments and commissions which regulate the operations of savings and commercial banks within the respective states. The economic unity of our people would be an impossibility without these governmentally operated or regulated media of financial exchange.

Unity would be impossible, also, without enforced standards of weights and measures. If a yard were 34 inches in Utah and 36 inches in North Carolina, if a pound were 16 ounces in Maine and 12 ounces in Louisiana, or if the butchers' scales approximated no standard norms, science, industry, and economic life generally would be chaotic.

The federal Bureau of Standards in Washington, similar state agencies, and hundreds of local sealers of weights and measures combine to provide standards and services which ensure common quantitative denominators in our national life.

## Fact-Gathering

The development of an orderly collective life in a highly complex society would be next to impossible without the central collection, compilation, and analysis of social and economic facts.

Every department of the Federal government and most governmental departments at the state and local level gather facts which give some kind of statistical picture of the entire American community, or important segments thereof. These facts are used as a basis for taxation, as indices of social and economic problems and tensions, as clews to change, as bases for voting, as measurements of resources and of community health, and in a host of other ways.

No single volume of information tells us more about ourselves as a nation, for example, than the *Statistical Abstract* of the United States Bureau of the Census. Stemming from the constitutional provision for a periodic enumeration of population for tax purposes and for purposes of political representation, the census has become an impressive comprehensive survey of social and economic data in the forty-eight states.

There are of course thousands of private fact-gathering agencies in America, but most of the important information developed by these private sources is ultimately incorporated in the reports and summaries of government bureaus and agencies. The most comprehensive information we have, not only about the American people, but about the physical characteristics of the American continent, is to be found in the files and reports of government offices.

## Parks, Monuments, and Symbols

The provision of common facilities for the relaxation and recreation of our citizens is one of the happiest expressions of governmental intent to "form a more perfect union." Spotted over our land are thousands of public squares, playgrounds, beaches, and state and national parks and forests—all owned and managed by units of government. Even if local facilities are excepted, the public use of these common recreational areas is staggering. Every year fifty million citizens from all over the country visit our national parks. Forty million visit our national forests. State parks are hosts to nearly 170 million visitors annually.

Not only do these public facilities provide a common meeting place for people from different geographic regions; they serve as points of contact between the various religions, races, creeds, and occupations which form the rich tapestry of our national life. These public facilities are symbols of our collective unity, and are catalytic agents of a developing sense of community.

In many of our public places are statues, monuments, and shrines commemorating wars, historical events, or the lives of famous Americans. Many of these symbols were originally erected by public subscription or were the gifts of private groups. But most of them are today maintained by units of government as reminders of our common heritage and of the people who shaped it. Our nation's capital, with its impressive collection of monuments, memorials, statues, museums, and public buildings, is visited annually by millions of Americans who wish to share the symbols of a common history.

In Washington, also, are the guardians of our written experience: the National Archives and the Library of Congress. Not only do these agencies house the great basic documents of our government, like the Declaration of Independence and the Constitution; here also countless millions of books, newspapers, periodicals, and government records are preserved and made available to scholars and to the general public. Similar official and unofficial documents are housed at the state and local level in state and community libraries, in state capitols, and in town halls.

In relation to the cost of most other activities of government, the preservation of community symbols and historical documents is a miniscule budgetary item. But the appropriations for this purpose reflect a fundamental expectation of constitutional government. When we pledge allegiance to the flag, or remove our hat during the playing of the *Star Spangled Banner,* the extent to which we share

## 1. HOW CITIZENSHIP MAY BE ACQUIRED
### (a) By birth:

In virtually every country of the world, citizenship is acquired by birth or naturalization. Citizenship by birth is determined generally in the civilized world either by rule of *jus sanguinis* (law of blood or parentage) or by the rule of *jus soli* (law of soil or place). All persons born in the United States are citizens even if the parents are aliens and are themselves ineligible to become citizens. However, the place of birth must be subject to American jurisdiction, and therefore children born to foreign diplomats stationed in this country are not citizens. On the other hand, children born to American parents outside the United States can also claim citizenship by birth if both parents are citizens and one of them has lived in the United States prior to the birth of the child concerned or if one parent is a citizen and has lived in this country for at least 10 years (five of which must be after attaining age 16) prior to the birth. In this latter case, the child must be brought to this country before he reaches age 23 and live here for five years between the ages of 14 and 28.

### (b) By naturalization:

American citizenship may also be acquired by naturalization, that is, by some kind of established legal process. Naturalization may be either collective or individual. Typically, collective naturalization is accomplished by an act or treaty extending citizenship to the people of an area acquired by purchase or conquest. . . . .

The immigrant to the United States may achieve citizenship by individual naturalization.

## 2. PROCEDURE OF NATURALIZATION

The procedure for individual naturalization involves two main steps:

First step:  Filing of a petition to an appropriate court containing sworn evidence designed to support the qualifications of the applicant alien. These qualifications include:

American citizenship is a sober privilege. The steps leading to it are not designed to be speedily and easily negotiated.

a common imagery depends in large measure upon the symbols of community maintained by our governments.

## The Melting Pot

No public monument has greater symbolic significance for Americans than the Statue of Liberty, maintained by the National Park Service of the Department of the Interior. A gift from the people of France to the people of the United States in 1886, the 300-foot statue

---

*(a)* an understanding of the English language, including the ability to write, read, and speak it;

---

*(b)* an understanding of the "fundamentals of the history, and of the principles and form of government, of the United States";

---

*(c)* an attainment of 18 years of age;

---

*(d)* an absence of advocacy of subversive ideas or of association with individuals or groups who advocate them within the 10 years preceding the prospective naturalization.

---

The petitioner must, furthermore, demonstrate that he has been lawfully admitted to this country, that he has lived here continuously since admission and for at least five years, that he is of good moral character, and that he is "attached to the principles of the Constitution of the United States and well disposed to the good order and happiness of the United States."

---

Investigation of alien applicant to determine truthfulness of his assertions and affidavits is made by agents of Immigration and Naturalization Service. Court is supplied with their evidence and recommendations. Since 1926, much of the work of examining applicants and evidence has been borne by hearing examiners of the Service who then report their findings and recommendations to the court. The Service, since 1943, has also conducted a central review of the examiners's findings and recommendations and the results of this central review are also presented to the court.

---

Second Step: Final hearing and examination in open court at end of which the judge administers the oath (in oath the person renounces all allegiance to any foreign nation or state and promises to support government of the United States.) and authorizes issuance of letters of citizenship (final papers). This step may not occur until at least 30 days after filing of the petition.

rests on tiny Bedloe's Island in the middle of New York harbor. Inscribed on the pedestal are the following words, addressed to the continent of Europe:

> . . . Give me your tired, your poor,
> Your huddled masses yearning to breathe free,
> The wretched refuse of your teeming shore.
> Send these, the homeless, tempest-tossed to me,
> I lift my lamp beside the golden door.

The poetry seems maudlin today. But to the men, women, and children who came to the United States from across the Atlantic Ocean during the nineteenth and early twentieth centuries in search of a new life, the statue and the words on the pedestal conveyed meaning almost unbearably poignant. Between 1820 and 1920, 35 million Europeans found a new chance in a new world. America meant to them—our ancestors—what it presently means to millions the world over whose fondest dreams would be realized if they could leave their present locations and settle in the United States. The Hungarians who have come to America after escaping from Soviet tanks in the autumn of 1956 are but the latest of a vast horde of human beings who have found safety and opportunity in this nation.

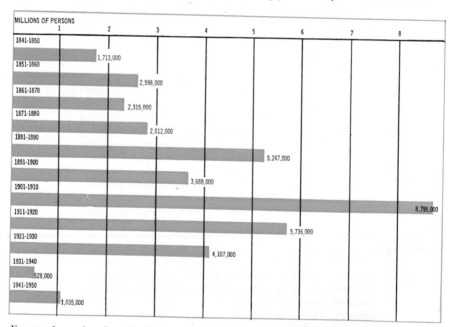

Except for a few hundred thousand American Indians, all Americans are either immigrants or descendants of immigrants. (*The American Workers' Fact Book,* Washington: U. S. Department of Labor, 1956, pp. 2–3.)

The banner is the Hungarian flag, placed there at the time of the tragic heroic rebellion of Hungarian patriots against the Russians in Budapest, Hungary, November 1956.

As recently as the years just prior to World War I, new settlers were arriving from abroad at the rate of over a million a year. Since 1920, however, under various quota and exclusion laws, immigration has been cut to less than a quarter of that figure. The atrocious indignity of Oriental exclusion has been removed from the books, although our quota system is still discriminatory.

Through public as well as private language and citizenship schools and welfare agencies, through our educational system generally, and through the instrumentalities of an expanding capitalism and an inclusive politics, people of every color, race, creed, and nationality background have in a remarkably short space of time developed the sense and the reality of "a more perfect union." This is the rich mixture which has given America its strength and vitality.

And to many of the millions who presently compose this mixture, and to their parents and grandparents, the first sight of the Statue of Liberty was the initial and most moving symbol of their sense of identity with the free institutions and the free people of America.

## Other Roads to Unity

The few illustrations given above scarcely scratch the surface. We shall have reason in the chapters ahead to discuss such topics as education, race relations, our military establishment, and our political parties. Each one of these has either a direct or a powerful indirect impact upon the state of the *union*. So do constitutional instruments of power like a President. But perhaps the activities of government described above are sufficient to suggest that the constitutional mandate "to form a more perfect union" is still taken seriously by our public officials.

Unfortunately for our peace of mind the problem has now become world-wide.

## TOWARD A MORE PERFECT INTERNATIONAL UNION

We are raised to consider our allegiance to the nation our terminal loyalty. There are many historical as well as currently practical reasons why this is so. But the revolution in technology and communications which has knit our forty-eight states more tightly together has had a similar effect in our relations with other people the world around. Questions of national defense are only part of the picture. In scores of different ways we are linked to our neighbors abroad. The links have been forged of necessity, convenience, and a sense of common humanity.

Ruling out strictly defense agreements, America participates, both inside and outside the framework of the United Nations, in a bewildering variety of international agencies. The following list is merely suggestive:

> Caribbean Commission
> Food and Agriculture Organization of the United Nations
> Intergovernmental Committee for European Migration
> International Bank for Reconstruction and Development
> International Civil Aviation Organization
> International Labor Organization
> International Monetary Fund
> International Telecommunication Union
> Pan American Railway Congress Association
> Pan American Sanitary Organization
> South Pacific Commission
> United Nations Educational, Scientific, and Cultural Organization
> Universal Postal Union
> World Health Organization
> World Meteorological Organization
> American International Institute for the Protection of Childhood
> Inter-American Commission of Women

Inter-American Indian Institute
Inter-American Institute of Agricultural Sciences
Central International Office for the Control of Liquor Traffic in Africa
Consultative Committee on Economic Development in South and Southeast Asia
International Bureau of Weights and Measures
International Commission for Northwest Atlantic Fisheries
International Council of Scientific Unions, and 8 Associated Unions

The very titles of these agencies suggest the diversity of connections which necessarily exist between the United States and other nations.

It is misleading to draw too close an analogy between the world as it is today and the American colonies just after independence. The fact remains, however, that the world today suffers from many of the ills which beset our Founding Fathers. And the urgency for solution is even greater.

If, in these apocalyptic days, a series of nuclear explosions should suddenly destroy all human life it is small comfort to recognize that the rest of the material universe would remain almost totally unchanged. Astronomers may comfort themselves with the thought that distant stars would still hurtle down the dark corridors of space; that the sun would continue to light the barren craters of the moon.

But in one small eddy of the cosmos, there would be no one left to ponder or to care. There would be no love, no poetry, no art, no science, no beauty, no feeling. One of the experiments of nature's God would have ceased to exist. A tiny island of warmth would have been submerged in an impersonal sea heaved by a desolate wind.

Whereas saints and heroes have frequently denied that their own individual lives were of ultimate value, they have consciously sacrificed themselves so that others might live—and live more abundantly. Few would deny that the life of the human race as a whole is an ultimate concern of mankind. And for the first time in history, that ultimate concern is an immediate issue.

Perhaps from the storehouse of experience of America's experimental past, the peoples of the world can draw hints of how to form a more perfect union. It is not that America has conquered all its problems. We have a long way to go, for example, before our vast and sprawling metropolitan areas overcome their kaleidoscopic character. Many a businessman has been frustrated by the lack of uniformity in the commercial and corporation laws of the several states. Thousands of American mayors have spent sleepless nights trying to

Eighty nations attempt through the United Nations to identify the causes of war and misery the world around, and to substitute talk, compromise, and co-operative action for bullets and guided missiles. As yet an imperfect instrument, the UN is still the world's best hope for international peace and justice.

figure ways and means of accomplishing an efficient consolidation of local fire departments or school districts. But with all these reservations and failures, America is the outstanding example in the world of a nation which has woven a reasonably unified tapestry from hundreds of separate threads and designs.

Today, *E Pluribus Unum* is more than a national motto. It is the condition of man's very survival on this turbulent globe.

# CONCLUSION

**Synopsis**

A more perfect union is not just a phrase to describe the results of the Constitutional Convention of 1787 or the outcome of the tragic War Between the States four score and seven years later. A more perfect union is fostered by the postal service; by highways; by various means of transportation and communication; by parks and playgrounds and monuments; by libraries and archives; by stable media of exchange; and in innumerable other ways. Government is necessarily involved in all of these activities. One of the tasks of this generation is to create a more perfect union with other peoples. If we fail in this task, civilization as we know it will not survive.

## Significance

"One nation, indivisible" does not just happen. Our Founding Fathers took the giant step in creating the Constitution. But all government at all levels of American society, and in every generation, exists to form a more perfect union. We must remember, however, that *union* is not the same as *uniformity*. Actually, union can be justified only insofar as it creates the framework for individual and group diversity. The job of government is not to make us all alike, but in Acton's words to make us "so fundamentally at one that we can safely afford to bicker."

## Prospectus

If a more perfect union is one of our expectations of government, it is far from the only one. We expect government to establish justice —equal justice under law. This expectation is deeply ingrained in our common heritage. We now turn to the kinds of law and the principles of justice which protect our rights as free citizens of a free commonwealth.

## CHAPTER 5

# Justice

JUSTICE HAS MANY sides. Justice concerns the complaint of a home-owner whose neighbor picked apples on the wrong side of a stone wall, or whose contractor used inferior materials in building a porch. It involves a driver who failed to stop at a red light, a giant corporation which forced its suppliers to give it preferential price treatment, or a labor union which condoned violence during a strike. A wife seeks justice in divorcing an unfaithful husband, and so does a Negro who was denied a job because of his race, or a worker who has been fired for union activity.

Most justice is evolved in the courts, and it is one of the fundamental expectations of constitutional government that our courts will settle disputes between people, between people and government, and between governments, equitably and according to due process of law. But justice is also made outside the courts. Much of the agenda of modern legislation and administration is concerned with what the British call fair shares—to ensure that each citizen shall have equal opportunity to obtain an education, earn a decent living, and in general fulfill his own capabilities.

Achieving these goals involves not only protecting the individual's rights but also providing necessary facilities and opportunities. Not only must children have the right to attend school; the schools and teachers and textbooks must be provided in the first place. Justice for the worker involves not only the right to bargain collectively through a union of his own choice; it also involves the right to a decent wage, which in turn requires enough job opportunities for all who need them. Justice for the farmer is meaningless if he is unable to obtain a fair price for his products. Justice is a mockery to the businessman who is destroyed by the ruthlessness of a rival.

Justice, therefore, concerns the relationship of people to each other and to their environment on a broad front: social, political, and economical. One major expectation of constitutional government is that it should sort out conflicting claims of individuals and

75

groups in our society and see to it that a just and equitable balance of interests is maintained.

Many of these conflicts and adjustments involve economic justice and other matters which more logically fall within the scope of Chapter 8, The General Welfare. Others have to do with the *substantive* rights of individuals and groups, especially of minorities, and these shall be described in Chapter 9, The Blessings of Liberty. In this chapter we shall confine our discussion to the place of justice and law in our governmental system generally, and to the *procedural* rights to which American citizens are entitled by the Constitution.

## WHAT IS LAW?

Much of our daily life is conducted within a framework of man's "sense of injustice." The desirability of fair and equitable relations with others is accepted by most people without question. Since earliest times, however, civilized man has sought greater certainty and predictability in these relationships, and so has turned to written forms of law. Today in the United States we are guided by several different kinds of written law.

1. *Common Law.* Common law evolved out of the daily decisions of the judges of early England. Its highest development was reached in the centuries after the Norman conquest when judges traveled around the shires and towns hearing and settling cases on commission of the kings. Based upon a combination of custom, church teachings, and common sense, common law was addressed to disputes which were not covered by statutes. Who, for example, should inherit the father's estate? Does an unwritten promise to buy a plot of land constitute a legal sale? What are the obligations of a wife? What action may a community take against a person whose behavior constitutes a breach of the peace?

Over the years a body of law developed which was said to be derived from the "common custom of the realm." This body of rules was composed of judge-made rather than statutory law. This judge-made law was gradually codified in written form, and subsequent judges were guided by such common law rules as the following:

  (1) The eldest son is heir to the estate of the father;
  (2) Property may be acquired and transferred only in writing;
  (3) A deed is of no validity unless sealed and delivered;
  (4) Wills should be interpreted liberally and deeds strictly;

(5) Breaking the public peace and quiet is an offense and is punishable by fine and imprisonment; and

(6) A citizen is guaranteed the right to "due process of law," that is, he has the right to a fair hearing by an impartial court.

Today common law regulates many of our everyday affairs, such as wills, contracts, debts, and much of our criminal law. Although common law in America originates at the state level, federal judges, in settling cases between citizens of different states, have the necessary privilege of interpreting lower court decisions. As a result, a national common law has also developed.

The law of one state, Louisiana, is based not on common law but on civil law, which depends more upon statutory codes (see below) than on judge-made common law. Over the years, however, even in Louisiana the common law has been mingled to a large extent with the civil codes by which Louisiana is guided.

2. *Equity.* As common law hardened over the centuries, it became difficult to obtain relief from injustice occurring under changing circumstances. Especially in civil suits, involving such matters as property rights, a new form of law, equity, was developed as a supplement to common law. Today equity and common law are often difficult to distinguish in practice, and courts deal with both kinds of law interchangeably.

3. *Precedent.* To endow common law and equity with continuity and permanence, much of their development has been governed by the principle of *stare decisis,* or precedent. Once a judge has made a decision, it is deemed to establish a precedent for other judges to follow when they encounter the same type of case. But precedents are many, and sometimes conflicting. As conditions change precedent is either broken or selectively replaced when judges find it necessary to reverse a previous decision. If the principle of *stare decisis* was not occasionally broken or bent, it could become a major obstacle to necessary social, economic, and political responses to change.

4. *Constitutional and Statutory Law.* Other kinds of law governing our relationships are constitutional and statutory law. In this country, constitutional law, as written into our federal Constitution and into the forty-eight state constitutions, establishes the broad framework within which our government operates. One function of statutory law (legislative law) has been to change the boundaries of common law to fit modern conceptions of social and economic relationships. Under common law, for example, workers seeking to band together to bargain collectively with their employers were

given short shrift in the courts. As our social philosophy changed, statutory law, such as the Anti-Injunction Act and the National Labor Relations Act, gave legal recognition to union organization.

Statutory law, which is written by the legislative branch of government, is superior to judge-made common law; but since judges have the responsibility of interpreting and applying both, the two kinds of law have become inextricably mixed and often the statutory law receives a common-law cast.

# WHEN JUDGES MAKE LAW

It is obvious from what has been said that neither common law nor statutory law nor equity exists in a vacuum. Laws by their very nature must be drafted in broad and inclusive terms, and in most cases the general phrases of a law must be interpreted and applied by a judge. A violation of the constitutional amendment forbidding more than two terms to the President of the United States would be fairly easy for a judge to distinguish. But few laws are so specific. It might take the wisdom of Solomon to decide a case under the constitutional injunction against "excessive" bail, or to determine when an alleged violation of the free speech privilege is a "clear and present danger" to the community. The law is full of such flexible words as "undue," and in many cases there may be conflicting precedents to confuse the judge still further.

Flexibility in law is a necessary concommitant to our flexible society, where new inventions and new ideas propel man along new paths. If the law were a series of immutable edicts, it would become a straitjacket on society. Men must constantly write new law, and judges must constantly interpret it in the light of still newer developments.

In its role of law-maker, the court also has a special function in guarding the separation of powers in our government and in protecting our heritage of individual liberty. As we shall note in Chapter 9, our rights as individuals are often difficult to define. It normally falls to the courts to draw the line between license and liberty. In addition, through judicial review—the power of the courts to apply the constitutional yardstick to statutory law (see page 378) — judges also have a special role to play in guarding minority groups and unpopular causes until the "sober second thoughts" of the majority can catch up.

# WHAT HAPPENS IN COURTS

Judges do not reach out and bring cases in for judgment. Our court system goes into action only when it is presented with a case, either by an individual who seeks a remedy for injustice or by an agent of the government, such as the district attorney, who seeks to enforce the law. Most cases brought by private persons never reach the judge; opposing lawyers confer and more often than not the case is settled out of court.

There are two broad categories cutting across the various kinds of law described above. *Civil law* involves crimes against individuals rather than against the state—although government on occasion is involved in civil law cases. *Criminal law* involves transgressions which are defined as "public wrongs," and they are prosecuted by the government, not by the victim.

*Civil Law.* There are several classes of civil law. *Property rights* cases involve questions regarding ownership of real or personal property. *Contract* law involves the obligations assumed by the parties to a contract. *Torts,* a word which means "wrongs," involve such transgressions as libel and slander, false imprisonment or arrest, family disturbances, trespass, or negligence leading to injury or death. *Domestic relations* involves the legal relationships of husband, wife, and offspring. *Inheritance* cases involve disputes over wills and estates.

Examples of civil issues include the following:

(1) A citizen's automobile, for no apparent reason, breaks away on a steep hill and damages a neighbor's property;

(2) A tenant in an apartment house refuses to pay his landlord the month's rent;

(3) A passenger riding in a taxicab is killed or injured in a collision, through no fault of the drivers;

(4) A citizen who is partly deaf plays his "hi-fi" record so loudly at night that his neighbors complain;

(5) A group of boys playing baseball in a sandlot accidentally break an expensive picture-frame window in a nearby house; and

(6) A widow contests her late husband's will.

In civil cases, the law provides remedies for wrongs committed, but the state will take no action unless the wronged person brings the case to court through a suit. The aggrieved person is the *plaintiff,* the alleged wrongdoer is the *defendant,* and the state is the *judge.* The deaf music-lover, for example, would be the defendant, the angry neighbor the plaintiff, and the local court the judge. If the defendant loses, he may be required to pay money damages, or, if it has been a case in equity, he may be ordered to do or not to do or to stop doing whatever has been the subject of the complaint. If the defendant fails to comply, he can be cited for contempt of court and fined or jailed.

*Criminal Law.* Criminal law involves what are called public wrongs. These wrongs must be defined statutorily (or constitutionally). There are basically three different kinds of crime:

1. *Treason,* defined by the United States Constitution as consisting only in levying war against the United States or in adhering to the nation's enemies, giving them aid and comfort. The Constitution goes on to say that "No Person shall be convicted of Treason unless on the Testimony of two Witnesses to the same overt Act, or on Confession in open Court."

2. *Felonies,* which include serious crimes like murder, rape, kidnapping, arson, perjury, forgery, and embezzlement.

3. *Misdemeanors,* which include such offenses as defacing public property, exhibiting indecent pictures, illegal driving or parking of an automobile, disturbing the peace, keeping disorderly establishments, maintaining nuisances (such as dogs that bite) or using profane or blasphemous language.

Three terms which are often confused are *burglary,* which is breaking and entering with intent to commit a crime; *robbery,* which is a hold-up (in the victim's presence); and *larceny,* which is stealing by any means. The value of the articles stolen determine whether it is grand larceny (a *felony*)—or petty larceny (a *misdemeanor*).

Attempted crimes, as well as those actually committed, are often punishable, and accomplices to a crime are just as guilty as the chief malefactor. However, in all cases of crimes, it must be proved that the wrong doer had criminal intent, which prevents prosecution of minors and the insane, who are assumed not to be responsible for their actions.

Under criminal law, the court need not wait until the offender is brought before the court by a wronged person. Instead, if a crime has been allegedly committed, the prosecutor may initiate criminal action, in which case the alleged wrongdoer is the *defendant,* while the state is both *plaintiff* and *judge.* Thus, if a teenager commits a misdemeanor by breaking the windows in a public school or by uttering profane language on a public street, the local prosecutor may initiate action against him in the court.

Procedures under criminal law afford ample right for the accused to defend himself.

*Arrest.* An officer of the law may make an arrest without a warrant if he sees a violation or an attempted violation of the law, or if a felony has been committed and the officer has reason to believe that the accused person committed it. In most cases, arrests are made under a judicial warrant, which is an order signed by a magistrate or judge specifying the crime and the probable culprit and directing the officer to make an arrest.

Immediately after arrest, the accused must be informed of the charge and a record of the arrest is reported in the "arrest book." This process is known as being "booked." Without unnecessary delay, the accused must also be arraigned before a magistrate or justice of the peace for a preliminary hearing. The accused has the right to have counsel and may ask for a postponement in order to secure a lawyer. If the crime is not a serious one, bail is set by the hearing judge.

In minor crimes, the hearing judge may be able to decide the case directly. In more serious offenses, the prosecuting attorney presents the case to a grand jury for an indictment, or files an "information" with the court itself.

Subsequent steps include the accused's option of a plea, guilty or not guilty, and if the latter, the trial and sentencing.

In almost every case it is possible for the guilty party to file an appeal, and when federal matters are involved, especially in regard to the due process of law, the appeal may be taken through the courts to the United States Supreme Court. Periodically there are complaints about the multiplicity of appeals, but in view of our reluctance as a people to risk convicting the innocent, it would be difficult to restrict the right to appeal.

## THE APPELLATE COURTS

The procedures described above concern only courts of original jurisdiction—places where suits and crimes are brought to the bar of justice for the first time. Above these courts, in both the nation and the states, are a series of higher courts called appellate courts.

Appellate courts not only may give a second hearing to the accused, but have the broader function of making law uniform throughout an area. In the federal court system and in every state some kind of supreme court stands at the top of all the courts below. In hearing appeals from lower courts, the superior court provides a single source of justice where the varied standards of inferior courts are made uniform. This function is fulfilled to a certain extent even when an appeal does not reach the highest court, because most judges are deterred from making partisan or eccentric decisions by the fear of reversal in an appellate court.

It is obvious that every case could not be brought to the highest appellate court; the latter would be swamped. Certain minor cases, therefore, usually cannot be appealed, and in common law cases, the appellate courts are often limited to reviewing questions of law, not of fact. In other words, the appellate court will not review the evidence produced to prove that the defendant was guilty, but only whether the defendant's arrest and trial and the judge's conduct were proper in every respect.

## THE ROLE OF THE EXECUTIVE BRANCH

The effectiveness of justice is in large part measured by the vigor with which the law is enforced, which is a function not of the courts but of the executive branch of government. Although there is little formal connection between the courts and the executive branch (see page 378 for a discussion of the relationship at the federal level), the executive branch plays an important role in the establishment of justice.

In all criminal cases and in some civil cases, it is the executive branch which initiates litigation in the courts. At the local level, the responsibility belongs to the prosecuting attorney, also known as the district attorney, while at the state and federal level it belongs to the attorney general. At the federal level, United States attorneys are located in each judicial district to supervise the local work of the Department of Justice. United States marshals in each district arrest offenders of federal law and assist in the administration of law.

Besides enforcing the law, the United States Attorney General also serves as legal advisor to the government, providing opinions on request, and the Department of Justice represents the government when the latter is party to a suit.

# JUSTICE UNDER LAW

A basic function of our government is to provide equal justice under law, to assure all persons the same kind of treatment before the courts, and to provide courts in which cases shall be judged impartially on their merits.

To help obtain this climate of justice, certain safeguards have become part of our expectations of justice. Accused persons, for example, are considered innocent until they are proved guilty. Their guilt must be proved beyond a reasonable doubt, and the burden is on the prosecution to establish guilt, not on the defendant to establish innocence. No man may be found guilty merely because of his association with wrongdoers; each defendant must be tried individually and found personally guilty of a crime.

## Specific Guarantees

These protections are reinforced by specific guarantees, written into our Constitution, which are binding on Federal courts and, where the Supreme Court has so ruled, upon state courts as well.

1. There shall be no "unreasonable searches and seizures," and warrants for arrest may be issued only for good reason and for a specified crime and person. This is designed to prevent unwarranted harassment by the police. This is the provision, for example, which is relevant to the ticklish question of the legality of wiretapping. The Supreme Court's earliest decision on this subject, in 1928, held that wiretapping was not prohibited by this constitutional guarantee, but the decision has been outlasted in national memory by a famous minority opinion, by Justice Holmes, in which he called wiretapping "dirty business." Wiretapping has been the subject of subsequent decisions in courts and of legislation by Congress. At the present time, the use in courts of evidence obtained through wiretapping is sharply restricted by legislation, but the problem is far from settled. Standards have yet to be established which will on the one hand permit our crime-detection and counterespionage agents to have the advantage of modern technology in combating threats to the public safety and, on the other hand, assure a measure of privacy to the average American. (Fourth Amendment)

2. No excessive bail may be imposed on defendants. (Eighth Amendment)

# THE SUPREME COURT DEFINES PROCEDURAL RIGHTS
## (Five Representative Cases)

| Case | Situation | Majority Opinion | Decision | Minority Opinion |
|---|---|---|---|---|
| Hurtado v. California 110 U.S.516(1884) | Hurtado was examined and committed by a magistrate; tried, convicted, and sentenced to be hanged for murder. Claimed his rights were denied by court's failure to indict by Grand Jury. | Grand Jury indictment is not the only due process procedure. New methods, such as prosecution by information as provided in California Constitution, equally acceptable. | Judgment of California court affirmed. [7-1] | Legal tradition supports view that criminal prosecution not based upon Grand Jury indictment is denial of constitutionally guranteed due process of law. |
| Betts v. Brady 316 U.S.455(1942) | Betts, in trial for robbery, could not afford counsel, and state refused to provide it. He claimed this was denial of counsel and thus violation of due process. | State's refusal to furnish counsel did not cause unfair trial. Due process of law does not require that legal counsel be provided for a poor man in every case. | Judgment of lower court affirmed. [6-3] | There was denial of legal counsel and it did produce unfair trial. Right to counsel is requisite of due process of law. |
| Ashcraft v. Tennessee 322 U.S.143 (1944) | Ashcraft was found guilty of murdering wife. Conviction based on confession which he claimed had been extracted from him by involuntary methods. | Procedures employed by police in questioning Ashcraft amounted to "third degree." Conviction by means of coerced confession is violation of due process. | Judgment by Supreme Court of Tennessee affirming Ashcraft's conviction reversed. [6-3] | There is no evidence that Ashcraft was forced to confess against his will, and, furthermore, Supreme Court of United States has no right to supervise rules of evidence in state courts. |

| Case | Facts | Issue | Decision | Opinion |
|---|---|---|---|---|
| **Harris** v. **United States** 331 U.S.145 (1947) | FBI agents, with valid arrest warrants but no search warrant, arrested Harris for mail fraud and then searched apartment. Found nothing connecting him with mail fraud but found selective service registration cards later used as evidence in charging him with unlawful possession, concealment, and alteration of cards. | Dangers resulting from excesses of law enforcement officials are not illusory, but search of Harris' apartment did not violate individual rights. Fourth Amendment does not require that every valid search and seizure be effected under authority of search warrant. | Decision of lower court affirmed. [5-4] | Evidence found and used against Harris was secured through illegal search and seizure. Majority decision errs in concluding that illegal methods are legalized by finding evidence of crime. An arrest warrant is not in itself sufficient to justify unlimited search of man's home. |
| **Rochin** v. **California** 342 U.S.165 (1951) | California deputy sheriffs, believing that Rochin was selling narcotics, broke into his home. To conceal incriminating evidence, Rochin swallowed two morphine capsules. Involuntarily, his stomach was pumped and capsules were retrieved and used as evidence in his conviction for violating narcotic laws of California. | Interpreting meaning of due process in terms of "community sense of justice," Court concluded that sheriff's methods offended popular sensibilities and thus violated due process. | Decision of lower court reversed. [8-1] | Court majority errs in holding that due process clause empowers court to nullify any state law if its application "shocks public conscience." Due process should be defined on basis of judges' reasoning and legal tradition rather than evanescent standards of "community sense of justice." |

3. In the case of major crimes, defendants must be indicted by a grand jury. Under this provision which prevents trials based on trumped-up charges, prosecuting attorneys must first present an outline of the case to a grand jury before a trial can be ordered. However, grand jury indictments are used only in serious cases, and as the need for this kind of protection has diminished, it has been replaced in many states by other procedures (see below). (Fifth Amendment)

4. The right of habeas corpus prevents arrest without charges or imprisonment without trial. The "corpus" in this case refers not to the victim of homicide, but to a defendant, who must be set free by his jailors if a court decides that he was arbitrarily arrested or imprisoned without cause. Habeas corpus can be suspended in time of "rebellion or invasion," but this has been tried only twice in our national history: once during the Civil War, and in Hawaii and on the West Coast during the early days of World War II. Most legal scholars are convinced that its suspension even on these occasions was a tragic and needless error. (Article I, Section 9)

5. Every defendant in any kind of case has the right to a trial by jury, although he may waive the right and request the judge to make the decision without benefit of jury. Especially in civil cases, juries have come under serious criticism, particularly because of their tendency to be swayed more by emotion or sentiment than by the facts, and they are increasingly being dispensed with. (Article III, Section 2; Sixth and Seventh Amendments)

6. Every defendant has the right to the assistance of legal counsel. In the case of a major crime, if a defendant cannot afford to hire a lawyer, the court must make one available to him. (Sixth Amendment)

7. Every defendant has the right to confront the witnesses in his case, and the further right to compel the appearance of witnesses for his own defense. (Sixth Amendment)

8. Defendants are protected from self-incrimination; they do not have to answer questions regarding an alleged crime. Originally the provision against self-incrimination was designed to prevent confessions obtained under torture. Today it has come under considerable criticism because of the use of the right by witnesses in Congressional hearings. Some legal authorities believe that defendants should be required to answer limited, reasonable questions; others claim that any dilution of the privilege would destroy it. Congress recently sought to circumvent it by passing legislation of-

## The Recording Angels

fering Congressional witnesses immunity from prosecution based on their testimony. (Fifth Amendment)

9. No person may be tried for the same crime twice (but a defendant may be tried in both federal and state court if he is accused of an act violating both federal and state laws). (Fifth Amendment)

10. Guilty persons shall not receive unusual punishment, a right which has the effect of forbidding torture. (Eighth Amendment)

11. No person shall be subject to a bill of attainder, which is a legislative act inflicting punishment on specified people. This right guarantees that every person must be found guilty by a court, not by a legislative body. The Supreme Court has ruled, for example, that Congress cannot exert control over public officials by cutting

their salaries out of the appropriation for their department. (Article I, Sections 9, 10)

12. No person may be convicted under an *ex post facto* law—in other words, under a law which establishes a crime after it has been committed. If what a person does today is legal, nothing the legislature does tomorrow shall make today's action illegal. (Article I, Sections 9, 10)

13. The crime of treason is limited by the Constitution to an act committed in war, and it must be witnessed by two people. The crime of treason is frequently a weapon utilized by dictators anxious to dispose of political enemies; in this country few people have been prosecuted for treason. However, laws covering similar crimes, not necessarily committed in wartime, have been passed under other names, such as subversive activities, espionage, and sabotage. (Article III, Section 3)

14. Every act of government shall be conducted under due process of law. This requirement regulates to a certain degree the actions of the executive and legislative branches as well as of the courts, and applies to legislative measures on a broad front of human activities. In its broadest sense, due process has been subject to sharply varying judicial opinion over the years; at one time it was used to strike down, as unconstitutional, legislation establishing minimum wages. Today its use in the legislative field is more restricted. In judicial proceedings it governs not only procedures and rules, but also the conduct of the judge and even manifestations of public opinion in the surrounding area. (Fifth and Fourteenth Amendments)

# CONCLUSION

## Synopsis

Justice is one of our major expectations of government. It involves virtually all relationships between the individual and authority. Over the years, as a result of our British heritage, this nation has erected an imposing legal edifice to insure that all of our citizens shall be equal under the law. The procedural guarantees written into our Constitution provide a towering fortress for our system of justice.

## Significance

The ends of justice are to protect the individual against society and to protect society against the individual. Winston Churchill has contended that the root protection of the individual against society is the writ of habeas corpus. But justice involves more than habeas corpus; it involves procedural guarantees at every step in the judicial process. It depends ultimately, of course, upon the application of a just and humane conscience to the controversies, foibles, and malevolences of mankind.

## Prospectus

Justice is of particular importance when placed along side of our next expectation of government: the insurance of domestic tranquility. Justice to the accused is not necessarily incompatible with the safety of the community; but there have been times when the "police power" of the state and the Bill of Rights have come into conflict. This does not mean that either the goal of order, or the goal of liberty is wrong. It simply means that justice, among other things, involves balancing the claims of both.

# Domestic Tranquillity

THERE IS ONLY one political experience more intolerable than tyranny. That experience is anarchy. Human history is dotted with illustrations. Time and again men have rushed from the storms of chaos to the stifling shelter of despotism. Governments cannot ensure happiness, but they can ensure order without which happiness or even a tolerable existence would be impossible. The great seventeenth-century British political philosopher, Thomas Hobbes, rested his entire theory upon the elemental obligation of governments to preserve order.

Domestic tranquillity can be interrupted by a variety of forces: crime, fire, war, revolutions, natural disasters like floods or storms, uncontrolled disease, mobs, maniacs, or simply the confused reactions of people who lack rules of social convenience. Certainly no single expectation of constitutional government is more basic than the assurance of domestic tranquillity. In this and in the following chapter we shall examine some of the things that governments in America do toward this end.

## THE POLICE

Without laws to protect persons and property against criminal attack, and without designated officers to enforce laws, civilized life would be an impossibility.

### Local Police

The overwhelming burden of responsibility for discouraging, discovering, and apprehending lawbreakers and criminals rests with local police forces. These range in size from a single constable to metropolitan departments consisting of thousands of patrolmen, detectives, and officers. In many nations of the world, the word "police" has a sinister connotation. In American municipalities, in spite of the occasional officiousness of frequently underpaid "cops," the policeman is a valued instrument of domestic tranquillity. A series of images come immediately to mind: the protective figure at the school crossing; the signs of relief on the face of a pedestrian who sees a policeman quietly patrolling a dark street at night; the sense of assurance of the merchant who knows that his shop will be checked two or three times between dusk and dawn; the disappearance of panic when the cruiser arrives at the scene of an accident; the thrilling release of tension when the siren is heard down the street after a homeowner has called to report unusual noises in the basement.

Modern police activities are conducted with the aid of a wide variety of the instruments of modern technology. The bicycle and the billy have been replaced by the cruiser and the tommy gun. The magnifying glass has been replaced by the microscope. Cross-examinations are subject to the verifications of chemical analyses and fingerprints. Radar is rapidly replacing the motorcycle. State and interstate telecommunications networks have kept pace with the increase in criminal mobility occasioned by modern means of transportation. Largely as the result of this growing technology, police work is becoming increasingly professionalized. Training schools and merit systems are now commonplace. And with this increased professionalization there has come a greater public respect for the responsibilities and problems of our local police. It is only to be hoped that this growing respect will increasingly be translated into higher salaries and better working conditions for America's most important guardians of domestic tranquillity. They have rarely received the pay they deserve.

## State Police

Supplementary to the work of the local police is the work of state police. Although some romantic historians trace the idea of a state police back to the days of the Texas Rangers in the early nineteenth century, present state police organizations are a product of the past fifty years. Today, every state in the union has a police force of its own. Collectively, the states spend well over $100 million a year on this vital function. In addition to patrolling state highways, the state police assist local police departments in a variety of ways and actually perform local police functions in areas where local law enforcement has broken down or is inadequate.

## The FBI

Vital police functions are, of course, performed at the national level—especially by the Federal Bureau of Investigation (FBI) and by various agents and inspectors of the Treasury and Post Office departments.

Established in 1908, the FBI is a bureau of the Department of Justice. Under the colorful leadership of J. Edgar Hoover, the FBI has grown in the last quarter century from a tiny investigating arm of an executive department into a national police force with over fifty regional offices. Today it investigates alleged violations of approximately 140 federal statutes, including such laws as the National Bank Act, federal kidnapping statute, the White-slave-traffic Act, and the Atomic Energy Act of 1946. It also has charge of investigating matters pertaining to internal security, such as threats to our national life through sabotage or espionage.

The FBI agents are the most highly trained police officers in the United States. Through example and cooperation, and through the provision of training facilities, the FBI has been an important instrument for inducing state and local police organizations to increase their technical proficiency and to raise their standards of performance.

## T-men

The Treasury Department has two main police bureaus: the United States Secret Service, and the Bureau of Narcotics. The former is responsible for tracking down counterfeiters, forgers, embezzlers, and other persons committing offenses against the laws of the United States relating to banking and currency. It also is responsible for protecting the persons of the President and the Vice-President. The work of the Bureau of Narcotics is implicit in its

Time after time I have seen law enforcement betrayed . . . by one of these factors: . . . by the resignation of intelligent, fearless, and honest police officers who simply could not and would not make law enforcement a career at such low wages and long hours; by poor morale caused by lack of civic respect, and the treatment of the police department as the "lost duckling" of government, deprived of funds, equipment, and interest. . . .

—J. Edgar Hoover

title. Other police functions in the Treasury are conducted by customs officials and internal revenue agents.

### Postal Inspectors

Little known, but highly important in the insurance of domestic tranquillity, are the United States postal inspectors. Established to investigate violations of the postal laws, the postal inspectors prohibit attempts to use the mails for purposes of extortion, lotteries, or fraud; or to ship by mail such things as explosives, poisons, firearms, intoxicants, or scurrilous or obscene literature.

Working separately and working together, backed by public prosecutors and by our entire court system, law-enforcement officers at the federal, state, and local levels give American citizens a degree of civil protection without which domestic tranquillity would be impossible.

# DISASTER

The word "disaster" usually refers to an event of violence which either devastates a sizable area or involves a relatively large number of people, or both: a school fire, with a considerable loss of life; a tornado which cuts its way through a thickly populated area; floods, hurricanes, and earthquakes; blizzards and droughts.

The earth has had its inhospitable aspects ever since man first appeared. From earliest times, natural disasters have been an integral and unpredictable part of man's existence. And today man manufactures disasters of his own.

### Fire

Losses from fire in the United States exceed a billion dollars a year. Every year millions of acres of forest land go up in smoke. Every year thousands of American citizens lose their lives through burning or asphyxiation. Tragic as these totals are, they would be infinitely greater if it were not for the efficient action of the fire-fighting and fire-prevention activities of agencies of government. It is true, of course, that in many rural areas and in many small towns and cities volunteer fire companies carry the major responsibility of fire fighting, but even these volunteer agencies are not immune to governmental influences, direct and indirect financial support, and various types of regulation.

In August 1955, one of the most destructive floods in American history struck six Northeastern states. Nearly two hundred deaths resulted and property damage totalled approximately two billion dollars.

Fire prevention is partly a matter of adequate and rigorously enforced laws, partly a matter of continuous education. Every state and most local authorities have a wide variety of statutes and ordinances aimed at preventing and controlling fires: regulations governing the disposal of inflammable material, the condition of electrical circuits, ventilation, the installation of heating systems, the sale of fireworks, the location of hydrants and water holes, smoking in public buildings, exit signs, automatic sprinkler systems, and so on. These regulations, many of them sponsored by private insurance and underwriting companies, are enforced by state and local fire marshals or by the police. Many fire marshals are also charged with inspecting fire alarm networks and with investigating fires after they have happened.

In spite of these precautions, and in spite of educational campaigns conducted by radio, television, posters, demonstrations, and through the school systems, fires continue to happen. Most of them start as a result of human carelessness. Only a relatively few are caused by lightning or other natural phenomena.

Once a serious fire has broken out, paid and volunteer firemen go to work. Modern fire-fighting equipment is complex and expensive. A modern pumper truck costs upward of $20,000. A fully rigged hook and ladder may cost upward of $50,000. Modern firemen must not only master the intricacies of this equipment, they must be skilled in handling people in conditions of panic. Every fire involves risk to the fire fighter. Anyone who has ever seen a forest fire can only wonder at the courage and skill of the men who undertake to subdue it.

Federal and state forest rangers, paid and unpaid firemen at the local level, and many unsung individual citizens risk their lives every day in the year to maintain domestic tranquillity for those threatened with injury, death, or property loss by fire.

## Civil Defense

In order to establish prior warnings of possible disaster, and in order to minimize the loss of life and property caused by disaster, governments in the United States have more highly organized disaster control units today than ever before in our history. Most communities of any size no longer rely solely upon the police, the fire department, or upon semiprivate agencies like the Red Cross. These traditional agencies are increasingly being integrated into civil defense organizations which have as their objective the mobilization of all community resources in case of disaster.

Organized primarily to deal with wartime devastation, civil defense units have already proved their value in handling situations caused by natural disasters. A notable example was their work in the Worcester, Massachusetts, region a few years ago when, with almost no warning, a tornado ripped through a heavily populated area.

Civil defense is a nation-wide phenomenon. Federal responsibility is lodged in the Federal Civil Defense Administration which was created by an Act of Congress in 1951. In 1953, the President assigned to the Civil Defense Administration the responsibility of coordinating the activities of all federal agencies in natural disaster relief. The main function of the FCDA is to aid and coordinate the activities of civil defense units created at the state and local levels, with special reference to the possibility of nuclear attack. Under federal and state supervision, many urban communities have now developed highly integrated civil defense organizations ready to go to work at a moment's notice if nuclear or natural disaster threatens. Not only are police, auxiliary police, firemen, doctors, local National Guard personnel, Red Cross workers, nurses, truckers, telecommunications experts, and a host of other specialists trained and alerted to their respective functions, but service and facility agreements and communication networks are sponsored among neighboring communities and neighboring states.

It is devoutly to be hoped that civil defense organizations will never have to fulfill the mission for which they have been primarily established. But the threat of nuclear war has had one beneficent effect. It has stimulated the development of coordinated disaster units. The consequence is that in many parts of the nation we are now better prepared than ever before to combat the wild and often unpredictable forces of nature which have interrupted man's tranquillity since time immemorial. Unfortunately, our national civil defense program is not efficiently organized in all areas of the country.

### Weather Bureau

No discussion of protection against natural disasters would be complete without reference to the United States Weather Bureau and its allies in the Civil Aeronautics Administration, the Coast Guard, and the air weather services of the military establishments.

The national weather service was first established in the Signal Corps of the Army in 1870. Since then, through a series of executive branch reorganizations, it has had its responsibilities greatly increased. It is now a bureau of the Department of Commerce. To have complete coverage of developing weather patterns, the Bureau maintains over 300 local offices manned by full-time personnel. In addition, there are over 10,000 part-time Weather Bureau stations. Weather forecasts, emanating from fourteen district forecast centers, are normally issued four times a day and are disseminated to the public through radio, television, telephone, and newspaper reports. In case of serious storms, such as hurricanes or tornadoes, the Weather Bureau issues emergency bulletins as often as necessary or possible. An increasingly sophisticated mapping of hurricane paths is now possible through the assistance of the Air Weather Service and Navy Aerology which send instrument-laden planes at frequent intervals into the eye of threatening storms. Coast Guard stations, of course, hoist storm warnings along our seacoasts, and perform other meteorological services.

The Weather Bureau cannot prevent storms from happening; but with the help of other government agencies it can and does provide warning services which give people time to protect themselves and their property in advance of the onslaught.

# DISEASE

It is difficult for modern Americans to appreciate the fact that for most of human history epidemic disease has been one of the most constant and terrifying threats to mankind's search for domestic tranquillity. Even today, in vast areas of the world, epidemic disease is a constant menace, although its incidence is rapidly being reduced by the work of the World Health Organization of the United Nations, and by the quiet, heroic efforts of the Rockefeller Foundation.

The fact that America is not subject to the ravages of traditional scourges like typhus, cholera, bubonic plague, diphtheria, typhoid, and malaria is due not only to the progress of private medicine and medical research, but to the rapid development of public health laws, inspections, and services at every level of government.

At the state and local levels, statute books are loaded with regulations governing the handling of food; the disposal of human, animal, and industrial waste; the sale of drugs; the control of disease-bearing insects and animals; the condition of drinking water; the pasteurization of milk; the use of chemicals in preserving food; food containers; meat inspection; swimming facilities; and so on. In addition, state and local health authorities are frequently given wide discretionary powers to take whatever action seems warranted in the identification, prevention, and control of disease. Elaborate inspection and reporting systems are in operation all over the country so that public health authorities will be made instantly aware of disease-producing conditions or of the outbreak of any disease which might become epidemic. In many parts of the country, school children receive periodic health examinations and a variety of inoculations at public expense.

## Public Health Service

At the federal level, a number of agencies are involved in the fight against disease. The primary responsibility falls upon the Public Health Service of the Department of Health, Education, and Welfare. Tracing its origins back to the Merchant Seamen's Hospital Act of 1798, the Public Health Service operates today under a comprehensive statute passed by Congress in 1944. Under this statute, the Public Health Service conducts and sponsors research; gathers national health statistics; provides advisory and technical services to state and local health departments; cooperates with congressionally sponsored national advisory councils such as the Cancer Council, the Heart Council, the Mental Health Council,

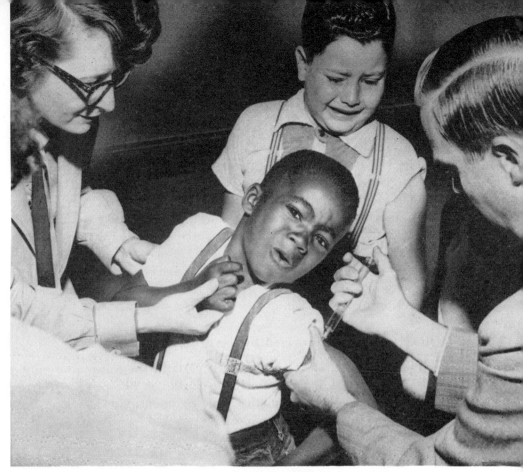

Every year through the cooperation of public and private health agencies, millions of school children are protected against diseases—notably smallpox, diphtheria, and poliomyelitis—which once took a frightful toll of young lives.

and the Blindness Council; and enforces foreign quarantine regulations covering sea, land, and air traffic.

## Food and Drug Administration

Other divisions of the Department of Health, Education, and Welfare are also vitally concerned with protecting the public's health. The Food and Drug Administration, for example, enforces the Federal Food and Drugs Act of 1906 and a variety of subsequent statutes in such fields as cosmetics, milk, caustic poisoning, and tea importation. It establishes controls over and issues licenses for the manufacturing of new drugs. It has elaborate research facilities for bacteriological and pharmacological testing. For enforcement purposes, the Food and Drug Administration maintains sixteen regional headquarters each with its chemists, inspectors, and laboratories. Citizens rarely think of the protection afforded them by the activities of this single agency of government.

## Meat Inspectors

The Department of Agriculture has a number of responsibilities affecting the health of the American people. The Meat Inspection Branch, for example, insures the wholesomeness of all domestic and imported meat and meat products. It also checks the purity of a variety of agricultural products covered in the Farm Products Inspection Act and in acts relating to the processing and sale of consumable fats. In its crop-research and insect-control activities, the Department of Agriculture gives both indirect and direct health protection to the citizen.

## Other Protections Provided by the Federal Government

The Federal Trade Commission safeguards the consuming public by preventing the dissemination of false or deceptive advertisements of food, drugs, cosmetics, and therapeutic devices.

Here an inspector from the United States Department of Agriculture puts the government's stamp of approval on a side of beef—a routine activity for the health protection of Americans.

The Atomic Energy Commission is charged with the safe disposal of radioactive waste materials.

The Fish and Wildlife Service of the Department of the Interior carries on control work against rabid wild animals.

And so the story goes. In fact, it is difficult to think of a department of the Federal government which is not in some way concerned with the protection of domestic tranquillity through the control of disease.

# SAFETY

Closely related to the control of disease is the prevention of accidents. Accidents cause in the neighborhood of 100,000 deaths a year, and nearly 10,000,000 injuries. Although much accident prevention work is carried on by private agencies such as the National Safety Council, industrial associations, labor unions, farm organizations, and women's groups, governments play a major role in this area. Not only does the National Safety Council itself operate under a federal charter, but the statute books at every level of government carry a variety of laws designed to reduce hazards which lead to accidents. Furthermore, a number of administrative agencies at the federal, state, and local levels have educational and regulatory programs in the accident prevention field.

## Industrial Accidents

Industrial accidents have long been a concern of government. In the latter part of the nineteenth century, state legislatures began to enact a series of laws and to establish inspection and enforcement agencies to protect factory workers against industrial hazards. Since 1934, the Bureau of Labor Standards of the Department of Labor has performed advisory functions in this area. That the job is not finished is evidenced by the fact that as late as 1954 President Eisenhower felt compelled to call a three-day conference in Washington, D. C., on industrial safety. Work accident fatalities still total nearly 15,000 a year.

## Mine Safety

Many states have laws and inspection services regulating mine safety. The Federal government has also assumed jurisdiction in this field. The Bureau of Mines of the Department of the Interior has wide research, advisory, and regulatory powers to help prevent mine disasters. The Bureau studies the explosion hazards of dusts, fumes, and gases; determines the safety of electrical equipment to

HERBLOCK
©1954 THE WASHINGTON POST

**"We Must Stop This Federal Interference!"**

be used in mines; analyzes atmospheric contaminants; tests respiratory protective devices; trains mine workers and officials in accident prevention, first aid, and mine rescue and recovery work; and helps arrange local, state, and national first-aid and mine rescue contests. Federal coal mine inspectors are empowered to issue safety orders to mine owners and operators, although these orders are subject to review by the recently established Federal Coal Mine Safety Board of Review.

## Other Safety Activities of Government

Farm safety is a continuing responsibility of the extension services of the Department of Agriculture, and of most state agricultural agencies. Over thirty states have special farm safety committees.

The Interstate Commerce Commission has extensive powers to prevent accidents on rail and motor carriers.

The Civil Aeronautics Board has similar powers over air carriers.

Safety at sea is promoted both by the regulatory authority of the Federal Maritime Board and by the varied operations of the United States Coast Guard.

Home accidents, which account for 30,000 deaths a year, are an increasing concern of state and local health departments.

Although the American Red Cross is supported by and large by voluntary contributions, it is a creature of the United States Congress and has a quasi-public status. No agency, public or private, approaches the success of the Red Cross in providing educational and training services for safety in swimming—although water safety is also taught by many local recreation departments and by most schools. And, of course, the Red Cross responds in force to any disaster—natural or man-made.

## Traffic Safety

No problem looms larger in the accident field, however, than traffic safety. Auto accidents claim 40,000 lives every year. Property damage and injuries reach a staggering total. Prevention is the concern of a variety of government as well as private agencies: highway departments, police departments, motor vehicle departments, schools, courts, special traffic safety committees, and health authorities. With the help of insurance companies, automotive manufacturers, automobile associations, private safety councils, and the press, radio, and television industries, these governmental agencies promote safety legislation and educational drives to reduce the fearful toll of highway accidents.

The technological miracles of the present age have brought many blessings to the American people. But these blessings have been accompanied by a frightening increase in accidental deaths and injuries. If, at times, the statute books seem overloaded with regulations, and some of our communities overrun by inspectors, it is only because accidents can violently interrupt domestic tranquillity, and because domestic tranquillity is one of the fundamental obligations of constitutional government.

# CUSTODY

No enlightened person would pretend that the sole purpose of penal and mental institutions is custodial. There is no doubt, however, that domestic tranquillity would be seriously threatened if criminals, aggressive alcoholics, and the violently insane were allowed to roam the streets of our communities at will.

Custody of criminals and other "disturbers of the peace" is a responsibility of every level of government. The initial burden, of course, falls upon local and county jails where most alleged violators of the law are held pending trial or release on bail, or for short sentences. Serious offenses against society are punished by incarceration in state or federal prisons, reformatories, juvenile institutions, correctional institutions, camps, or hospitals.

## Complexity of Problem

The magnitude of the problem can be judged from a few statistics. State and federal institutions now house in the neighborhood of 180,000 adult offenders. Five individual state prisons have populations in excess of 3,000. There is hardly a county jail in America which is not overcrowded, and the condition of many of our county jails is deplorable. A recent federal survey disclosed that 82 percent of county jails inspected could not meet standards established for housing federal prisoners. Each year sees a number of prison riots, most of which are due to the failure of governments to appropriate sufficient funds for decent facilities, programs, and personnel. A few years ago a riot broke out in the Missouri State prison which ended in four deaths and damage estimated up to $5 million. At the time of the riot, the average pay for prison guards was $145 per month.

Unfortunately, traditional penal policy has done almost as much to upset domestic tranquillity as it has to protect it. Every year thousands of prisoners are released to hopelessly overburdened parole officers only to revert to antisocial behavior—perhaps of a more sophisticated kind than before their terms in prison. Chronic alcoholics, who account for more than 50 percent of the inmates of county jails, generally head for the first bar after their release. A startlingly high proportion of the juvenile delinquents, who have spent time in correctional institutions, end up in adult prisons. Some of the most savage crimes in recent annals have been committed by criminally insane who have been prematurely released from mental hospitals.

It is becoming increasingly obvious that penal reform is long overdue in the United States.

# CONCLUSION

## Synopsis

Domestic tranquillity is a requisite of any civilized society. Government in America insures domestic tranquillity in a number of ways: by recruiting and training police officers, Treasury agents, and postal inspectors; by providing fire equipment, and the firemen needed to use and maintain it; by establishing a nation-wide civil defense system organized to combat both man-made and natural disasters; by maintaining weather stations, public health services, and food, drug, meat, and other inspectors; by adopting regulations and programs designed to reduce various kinds of accidents; and by providing custody for the violent.

## Significance

If government cannot maintain order it is not government. We must remember, however, that the preservation of order is not the sole objective of government. Order, as we shall have reason to note more fully in Chapter 9, is not only the precondition of liberty; it is liberty's potential enemy. This is a paradox which should never be forgotten. What are known as the "police powers" of the state—the elemental powers of duly constituted authorities to preserve domestic tranquillity—are absolutely necessary if society is to exist at all. But these powers must be exercised with restraint, and in conformity to law, if society is to remain free.

## Prospectus

In the twentieth century, the most horrendous disruption of domestic tranquillity would come, not from within, but from without— from nuclear war. What government in America does to provide for the common defense is the subject to which we now turn.

## CHAPTER 7

# The Common Defense

WHEN OUR NATION was founded, the new Constitution wisely provided that defense against external attack was to be the prerogative solely of the national government. Actually, this function was judged to be so important that half the enumerated powers of Congress in Article I, Section 8, refer to matters relating to the common defense. Congress among other things is empowered to raise and support armies and navies, to declare war, to call out the state militias for purposes of repelling invasion, and to make rules governing and regulating all military forces.

In Article II, the Constitution makes the President of the United States the Commander-in-Chief of all military personnel called into national service, and gives the President the initiative in the conduct of diplomatic relations with other countries (see Chapter 16).

## THE STRANGE WORLD OF YESTERDAY

Without minimizing the eighteenth- and nineteenth-century dangers to the new American Republic from the imperial rivalries of the leading European powers, it is fair to say that by modern standards the defense problems of our ancestors were unbelievably simple. A three-thousand-mile moat—the Atlantic Ocean—protected them from the possibility of massive attack by hostile armies. The defeat of professional Hessians by amateur "Minute Men" during the Revolution had proved that even if limited armies could be landed and deployed, they could be successfully dealt with by those who were more familiar with the logistics and techniques of wilderness fighting. It is true that naval blockades and forays could occasion considerable inconvenience along the Atlantic seaboard. But we were then a seafaring people. Our ships were as good as those of possible attackers. And we were infinitely closer to sources of naval equipment, supplies, and maintenance than any real or potential adversary.

Furthermore, after the War of 1812, British imperial interests fell on our side, and for the rest of the nineteenth century the British Navy became the main umbrella for American policies of hemispheric isolation and supremacy. Until World War I, the Army was a small, volunteer force used mainly for territorial patrols against the Indians.

In fact, until the twentieth century, the constitutional mandate to provide for the common defense was one of the simpler problems of American government. Diplomatic posts were frequently sinecures. Military and naval forces were tiny, dispersed, and only sporadically employed. The Civil War was costly and terrible; but it was an insurrection, not an invasion. The Mexican and Spanish-American Wars were limited engagements which had no perceptible impact upon the national economy or upon civilian life generally, and they were fought on our continental periphery—or beyond.

## THE TWENTIETH CENTURY

How distant, strange, and tranquil these bygone years now seem. At times we are haunted by an understandable nostalgia which blurs the fact that we have fought two global wars and one Far Eastern war in less than a half century, and that today the sun never sets on American military graves. The fact is that "the common defense" today necessarily involves worldwide commitments as well as the possible mobilization of our total available resources at home. Air power, nuclear energy, and electronics have hurtled us into a new age. Traditional concepts of fixed battle lines are almost totally outmoded. So are traditional distinctions between civilian and military activity. Foreign policy and domestic policy are the warp and woof of a single cloth. Detroit is as vulnerable today as Warsaw was in World War II.

Astride the world sit two military giants: the United States and the U.S.S.R., both equipped with hydrogen weapons, both supported by allies—some of whom are unstable, and both struggling to extend their influence at the expense of the other.

But here the similarity stops. America's world-wide interests have virtually been forced upon her. The Washingtonian dream of a sovereign nation free of entangling alliances was challenged by World War I, disrupted by World War II, and destroyed by the Korean crisis. Americans have learned in this century that if aggressive totalitarianism—whether Prussian or Japanese militarism, Nazism,

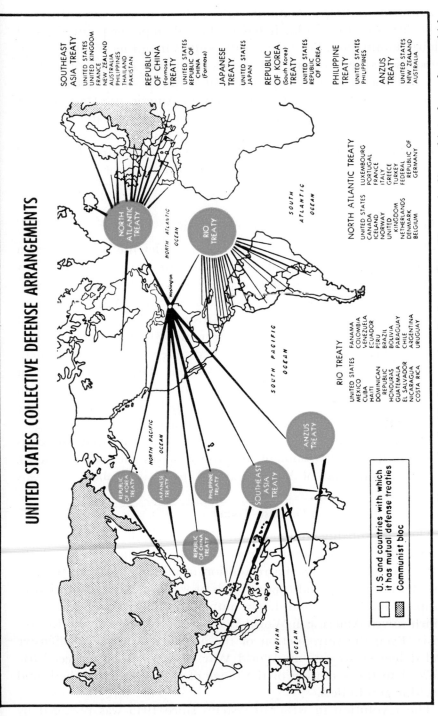

# UNITED STATES COLLECTIVE DEFENSE ARRANGEMENTS

**SOUTHEAST ASIA TREATY**
UNITED STATES
UNITED KINGDOM
FRANCE
NEW ZEALAND
AUSTRALIA
PHILIPPINES
THAILAND
PAKISTAN

**REPUBLIC OF CHINA (Formosa) TREATY**
UNITED STATES
REPUBLIC OF CHINA (Formosa)

**JAPANESE TREATY**
UNITED STATES
JAPAN

**REPUBLIC OF KOREA (South Korea) TREATY**
UNITED STATES
REPUBLIC OF KOREA

**PHILIPPINE TREATY**
UNITED STATES
PHILIPPINES

**ANZUS TREATY**
UNITED STATES
NEW ZEALAND
AUSTRALIA

**NORTH ATLANTIC TREATY**
UNITED STATES      LUXEMBOURG
CANADA             PORTUGAL
ICELAND            FRANCE
NORWAY             ITALY
UNITED             GREECE
KINGDOM            TURKEY
NETHERLANDS        FEDERAL
DENMARK            REPUBLIC OF
BELGIUM            GERMANY

**RIO TREATY**
UNITED STATES      PANAMA
MEXICO             COLOMBIA
CUBA               VENEZUELA
HAITI              ECUADOR
DOMINICAN          PERU
REPUBLIC           BRAZIL
HONDURAS           BOLIVIA
GUATEMALA          PARAGUAY
EL SALVADOR        CHILE
NICARAGUA          ARGENTINA
COSTA RICA         URUGUAY

☐ U. S. and countries with which it has mutual defense treaties

▨ Communist bloc

Today American security is inextricably entwined with the security of other nations. Hence, the lines of interdependence which lead us to treaty commitments across the face of the globe. (Report to Congress on the Mutual Security Program.)

Fascism, or militant Communism—starts to march successfully in other parts of the world, it has no logical stopping point short of global domination. Freedom to talk politics in our local barber shops depends upon the extent of freedom in the rest of the world. Freedom cannot be imposed by force, but it can be destroyed by force.

These lessons have not come easily to Americans. Many of our ancestors came to this country to escape from the wars and threats of wars which have plagued so much of the rest of the world for so long. But the twentieth century has taught us a bitter lesson and with explosive speed has pushed us into a position of leadership in the free world.

### The Impact upon the Federal Government

The growing importance of "the common defense" on the agenda of our national government during the past forty years can easily be traced. The most startingly visible index has been architectural. Prior to World War I, the departments of State, Army, and Navy were all housed in one gloomy monstrosity situated on the corner of Pennsylvania Avenue and 17th Street, next to the White House. Today, this one building is devoted solely to the constituent units of the Executive Office of the President. The State Department now occupies a sizable office building on Virginia Avenue, and is presently building a vast extension due to be ready in 1960. The military departments have their central headquarters in the gargantuan Pentagon Building across the Potomac in Virginia; but parts of the military establishment are strewn across the map of metropolitan Washington, of America, and of the entire globe.

### Problems of Common Defense Today

There is probably no time in our history when the question of how to provide for the common defense has been so difficult. The twentieth century has witnessed a revolution in military weapons without parallel in the long and tragic annals of warfare. This revolution in weapons has almost completely outmoded the kinds of war plans which served America in World War II and throughout the Korean crisis. Even the introduction of the airplane as a major offensive and defensive weapon in World War II seems in retrospect little more than the extension of the range of sizable artillery shells and machine-gun bullets.

The revolution in weapons systems since 1945 was presaged by three developments during the Second World War: The German V-1 and V-2 rockets, the perfection of radar and other electronic systems, and, of course, atomic energy. We now live in a military world of "atomics, electronics, and supersonics." Science fiction of only a few years ago has been outdistanced.

## ICBM

Perhaps there is no ultimate weapon, but both America and Russia are on the verge of perfecting a weapon so ghastly in its impersonality and destructive power, so easily concealed, so swift in its execution, and so difficult to counter that it must be considered as being as close to an ultimate weapon as man has ever conceived. This weapon is the ICBM—or intercontinental ballistic missile. Essentially the ICBM is a rocket with a nuclear warhead which can be electronically guided and which can travel from Moscow to Chicago over the polar cap in 30 minutes. Even with our so-called DEW (Distant Early Warning) line of radar screens along the Arctic Circle, we should at best have only 15 minutes warning. We could, of course, retaliate—but in the meantime we might lose half or better of our population if 100 ICBM's landed on our key metropolitan centers. Electronically controlled interceptors may be developed, but it would be fanciful to make plans solely on the basis of this possibility.

When the ICBM is perfected (shorter range missiles have of course been operational for some time) it may create a stalemate between the United States and the U.S.S.R. which could open up long vistas of peace—what Winston Churchill has called "a balance of terror." This is possible; but again it is by no means certain. Stalemate might lead to its own undoing. It might turn the world into a tinder box of international intrigue, guerrilla actions, and small adventures any one of which might lead eventually to someone's pressing the apocalyptic button. With big forces immobilized, the little forces might move to create dangerous injustices or tyrannies which could eventually spread so that the ideal goal of the Communists, world Communism in this century without a major war, might come close to being realized. Even without ICBM, the threat of hydrogen-bomb destruction delivered by long-range bombers may be presently sufficient to preclude anyone's deliberately starting a "big" war. The problem of the common defense, therefore, may already have become one of maneuver within the narrow limits set by the possible use of extreme weapons.

It would be wonderful if the world and human nature were in such shape that no force of any kind would ever have to be used again. But the world and human nature are not in such shape. Among the possible causes of continuing violence on a scale larger than that capable of being handled by domestic police, are the following:

1. The blind search for power on the part of an irrational adventurer. The twentieth century has had a number of examples of this phenomenon already, and it may have more.

2. The struggle of subject peoples for independence from colonial status, or from other forms of external control.

3. Religious or racial hatreds, perhaps expressed in conjunction with national aspirations.

4. Attempts at peripheral extensions of big power holdings (as in Korea and Indochina).

5. Unpremeditated wars between unfriendly neighbors who react emotionally to an "incident."

6. Police or defensive actions undertaken by a powerful nation or nations to protect economic or political interests somehow threatened by anarchic or calculated violence in other countries.

The ICBM is not equipped to deal with these continuing troubles; but the continuing troubles may inadvertently set off a chain reaction which could end with ICBM.

For this reason there is not a brush fire anywhere on earth that is not watched with care by our diplomatic and military leaders. For this reason our military budget is continuing at close to $40 billion a year. For this reason, the United States maintains a bewildering variety of weapons and supplies which can be adjusted to any scale war in any medium—land, sea, or air. The debate is bound to continue as to how much of what is needed, when, and where; and how much our economy can stand. But only an ostrich could pretend that in the foreseeable future our military budget and our budget for a multifaceted diplomacy could be reduced to the lower pre-World War II levels.

What, then, in the face of these complex issues does the Federal government do today to provide for the common defense? The activities are necessarily vast. Well over two thirds of the federal budget is devoted to this function. Nearly half of all federal civilian employees have duties directly tied to problems of the nation's security. Perhaps the easiest way to visualize the scope of our defense ac-

The quest for peace is the stateman's most exacting duty. . . . Practical progress toward lasting peace is his fondest hope. Yet in pursuit of his hope he must not betray the trust placed in him as guardian of the people's security. A sound peace . . . *can* be achieved, but only by patiently and thoughtfully following a hard and sure and tested road.

—Dwight D. Eisenhower

tivities is to summarize briefly a few of the activities of some of the major agencies concerned.

# DEPARTMENT OF DEFENSE

As a result of the lessons learned in World War II, the Congress passed in 1947 a National Security Act which placed all armed forces of the United States within a single "National Military Establishment." The 1947 Act also created within the new Military Establishment a Department of Air separate from the Army and the Navy. In 1949, a series of amendments to the National Security Act of 1947 strengthened the powers of the new Establishment, changed its name to the Department of Defense, and provided for tighter reins of control over the three armed services.

The major job of the Department of Defense is to foster teamwork among its various components and to present to the President, the Congress, and the people an integrated military program to provide for the common defense. Advising the Secretary of Defense are the Secretaries of the three service departments: Army, Navy, and Air; a number of Assistant Secretaries of Defense assigned to fields in which coordination among the several armed services is particularly important; and, perhaps most important, the Joint Chiefs of Staff.

## Joint Chiefs of Staff

The Joint Chiefs of Staff consists of a chairman; the Chief of Staff, United States Army; the Chief of Naval Operations; and the Chief of Staff, United States Air Force. The Commandant of the Marine Corps sits as a coequal of the other members of the Joint Chiefs when Marine Corps matters are being discussed.

Among the harrowing, continuing responsibilities of the Joint Chiefs are the following:

1. To prepare strategic plans and provide for the strategic direction of the military forces

2. To prepare joint logistics (materiel support) plans and assign to the military services responsibilities in accordance with such plans

3. To establish unified commands in strategic areas

4. To review major material and personnel requirements of the military forces in accordance with strategic and logistic plans

5. To formulate policies for the joint training of the military forces

6. To formulate policies for coordinating the military education of members of the military forces

7. To provide the United States representation on the Military Staff Committee of the United Nations in accordance with the provisions of the Charter of the United Nations.

Over the regular military forces of the United States, then, is a Department of Defense whose officials are charged with the responsibility of seeing our military problems as a whole.


## Department of the Army

The Army is the largest and the oldest of our military services. One of the first acts of our first Congress in 1789 was to establish a Department of War. Under this title the Army was managed until the National Security Act of 1947.

Today, the Army has over 1,000,000 men in uniform and by 1960 should have a ready reserve of nearly 3,000,000, including the state militia (National Guard).

Today's "foot" soldier is a far cry from yesterday's. Because of the radius of devastation of nuclear weapons, the idea of large armies massed in the field is outmoded. The new stress is upon armies broken into small, highly mobile units with tremendous fire power per unit. Transported by air or by swift amphibious or overland vehicles, the modern G.I. carries a rifle which can fire twenty rounds in less than two seconds. His artillery support includes atomic cannon. He is prepared to fight in any climate over any kind of terrain. He can carry a two-way radio in his helmet.

For our defense, the Army has six major Continental Armies blanketing the United States; four Territorial Army Commands (Hawaii, Panama Canal Zone, Puerto Rico–Virgin Islands, and

Alaska); and a series of overseas commands organized in conformity with mutual defense alliances such as NATO (North Atlantic Treaty Organization), or on the basis of bilateral agreements with allies.

Questions of how large an army we should have in view of the rapid changes in military technology will continue to plague our military and civilian leaders. There are some people who believe that the day of the foot soldier, no matter how mobile, is through; that push-button warfare and nuclear weapons have eliminated the necessity for the G.I.—slogging or airborne. There are others, however, who still side with the comedian Bob Hope who said during World War II, "After the navy has bombarded the beaches, and the air force has strafed and bombed the interior, there is really nothing left for the army to do—except wade in and do all the fighting."

## Department of the Navy

The United States has the largest navy in the world. In the single category of submarines, the Soviet Union is quantitatively superior; but in over-all balanced strength, no fleet in the world approaches that of the United States in size or quality.

The Department of the Navy was created in 1798. Prior to that, during the first decade of our national existence, naval forces were under the authority of the War Department.

A paragraph from a recent Year Book of the *Encyclopedia Britannica* is worth quoting in full to indicate what is happening to the United States Navy under the impact of the revolution in military technology:

Three giant aircraft carriers of 60,000 tons were being built, the "Independence," "Ranger" and "Saratoga" and a fifth ship of this "Forrestal" class, the "Kitty Hawk," was projected. Fifteen aircraft carriers of the "Midway" and "Oriskany" ("Essex") classes were being converted with the new angled deck and the enclosed bow. The heavy cruisers, "Boston," "Camberra," and "Los Angeles" were converted to guided missile ships. Eleven large destroyers were under construction and seven more were projected. Four destroyer escorts were completed or being built and nine more were projected. Another six nuclear-powered submarines and four large submarines of conventional design were projected.[1]

In this single paragraph there is to be found indication of the Navy's new emphasis upon speed, maneuverability, air power, missiles, and atomic energy. The battleship, once the king of the ocean, is not even mentioned.

In addition to the construction, operation, and maintenance of

The *Nautilus* is the Navy's first atomic-powered submarine. The only practical limit to its underwater range is the endurance of its crew.

battle fleets and military sea transport systems, the Navy has developed a superb air arm which operates both from carriers and from land bases. And, of course, the Navy has under its aegis the toughest shock-utility troops among our land forces—the United States Marine Corps. During wartime, or when the President directs, the Navy also takes charge of the United States Coast Guard, which normally is under the Treasury Department.

The debate will rage for some years as to how vulnerable surface vessels—particularly large aircraft carriers of the *Forrestal* class—have become in this world of "atomics, electronics, and supersonics." The Navy has two basic answers: one, if nuclear war should come, floating air bases are still harder to locate and knock out than set land bases; and two, if big war does not come, and America is forced into a series of brush-fire actions, the traditional roles of the Navy and the Marine Corps will be more important than ever.

### Department of the Air Force

Created by the National Security Act of 1947, the Department of the Air Force is the newest and most powerful military department in the United States.

For combat purposes the Air Force is divided into a series of commands, the most important of which are SAC (Strategic Air Command), which has the responsibility for long-range instantaneous "massive retaliation"; TAC (Tactical Air Command), which provides for direct air force support of land, naval, and various amphibious forces; and the Air Defense Command which provides for the air defense of the United States itself.

SAC bases gird the globe. They constitute a fantastic retaliatory threat. At a moment's notice, huge jet bombers like the B-52 and the new B-58 can become airborne and can deliver nuclear bombs to enemy targets half around the globe. SAC bases have seemed a kind of terminal and ultimate protection. With the development of medium-range and long-range guided missiles, particularly the Atlas (ICBM), however, questions are inevitably being raised about the continuing utility of overseas SAC bases. If pilotless missiles hidden in the Rocky Mountains or in the dismal wasteland of the Canadian tundra can pinpoint targets 5,000 miles away, why should expensive, vulnerable, and often locally resented air bases be maintained in Turkey or Pakistan? This question has diplomatic and military implications which need the most careful thought.

Recognizing that potential enemies of the United States also have long-range aircraft and nuclear bombs, and are working on an ICBM, the Air Defense Command of the Air Force has a particularly harrowing job of planning for a battery of manned and unmanned interceptors capable of protecting the continental United States. The first step, of course, is provision for adequate warning. The Distant Early Warning (radar) line in North Canada is being supplemented by a second line in central Canada, and a third line at the Canadian border. Ocean towers and specially equipped radar ships and planes give increasing assurance of warning if enemy planes should attack over the sea. But the question remains, Given a few minutes' warning, how can interceptors be dispatched with a speed and an accuracy which is sufficiently deadly to preclude calamitous devastation of our industries and our centers of population—especially since nuclear attack might well come for enemy submarines launching missiles a few miles off our shores.

# INTELLIGENCE, SCIENCE, INDUSTRY, AND DIPLOMACY

It is becoming increasingly obvious that no country can "win" a major war. In a fundamental sense, therefore, important as our armed forces are in providing for our national security, they no longer constitute our "first line" of defense. Increasingly, the responsible officials of government have come to realize that our ability to protect ourselves in a dangerous world depends upon the quality of our intelligence, science, industry, and diplomacy.

## Intelligence

Prior to World War II, the United States had no intelligence service worthy of the name. Both the Army and the Navy had intelligence branches, but they were uncoordinated and largely ineffectual—witness the surprise Japanese attack on Pearl Harbor which triggered America's entry into World War II.

Largely as the result of the promptings of General William Donovan, President Roosevelt established during World War II an Office of Strategic Services, one of whose functions it was to gather and analyze secret intelligence.

Today, a large Central Intelligence Agency exists in the Federal government to gather information about the intentions and capabilities of other nations, and to analyze that information for the benefit of the National Security Council (see pages 341–42) and other policy-making arms of the President. The CIA is of course not the sole or even the primary collector of information about other countries; but it has the responsibility for piecing together information derived from a wide variety of sources, and it has the primary responsibility for learning things about the intentions and capabilities of foreign powers which those foreign powers do not wish us to know. In the kind of world we live in, the existence of such an agency—no matter how distasteful to our sensibilities—is imperative.

## Science

Never before in our history has the common defense depended to such a marked extent upon the quality and productivity of American scientists. The real battle with the Communist world at this time is a battle of intellects: a struggle on their part to catch up with our scientific lead; a struggle on our part to maintain that lead.

Only since 1940 has the Federal government taken seriously the role of science in national defense. Fortunately, progress since then has been swift. All three services now have vast research and development staffs. In the Department of Defense there is an Assistant Secretary for Research and Development whose official responsibilities include developing policies for assuring that the nation's best scientific and technical talents are applied to the planning and prosecution of military research and development programs, and that research and development information is efficiently assigned and interchanged among the military departments.

*National Science Foundation.* Knowing that the struggle for scientific supremacy would be a long and drawn-out affair, in 1950 Congress established the National Science Foundation to develop a national policy for the promotion of basic research and education in the sciences; to initiate and support basic scientific research; to initiate and support defense-related scientific research activities (at the request of the Secretary of Defense); to provide a central clearinghouse for information covering scientific and technical personnel; to award scholarships and graduate fellowships in the sciences; and to perform a variety of related functions.

There is scarcely a major university or industry in the United States that is not somehow tied into the scientific research functions which have grown out of the Federal government's recognition of the place of science in providing for the common defense.

In this connection, the elaborate research activities of the Atomic Energy Commission must be recognized. Established in 1946 as a separate agency of the Federal government, and under civilian control, the AEC works on both the wartime and peacetime uses of atomic energy. Important as the production and engineering aspects of the AEC's activities are, however, the true measure of our lead over the Soviet Union is not in production or engineering but in the number and quality of our scientists. In view of present educational drives in the Soviet Union for the production of scientists, we have no reason to be sanguine.

## Industry

America's industrial production is perhaps the key factor in our national power. It is American industry and labor working in close cooperation with government officials which turns dollars into guns, ships, missiles, tanks, and radar. In case of another war, the ability to use effectively our industrial and manpower resources might well be decisive.

It is for this reason that there exists in the Executive Office of the President an agency called the Office of Defense Mobilization. Its

"And What's New with You?"

present functions derive both from provisions of the National Security Act and from a series of mobilization instruments created
before and during the Korean War. The present responsibilities of
the director of ODM are staggering in their complexity. Here are
some of them: [2]

1. Develop policies concerning industrial and civilian mobilization to ensure the most effective mobilization and maximum uti-
lization of the nation's manpower in the event of war.

2. Prepare programs for the effective use in time of war of the
nation's natural and industrial resources for military and civilian

needs, for the maintenance and stabilization of the civilian economy in time of war, and for the adjustment of our economy to war needs and conditions.

3. Develop policies for unifying, in time of war, the activities of federal agencies and departments engaged in or concerned with production, procurement, distribution, or transportation of military or civilian supplies, materials, and products.

4. Plot the relationship between potential supplies of, and potential requirements for, manpower, resources, and productive facilities in time of war.

5. Establish policies for ensuring adequate reserves of strategic and critical materials, and for the conservation of these reserves.

6. Plot the strategic relocation of industries, services, government and economic activities, the continuous operation of which is essential to the nation's security.

7. Coordinate the development of telecommunications policies and standards as these might impinge upon national security problems.

These are impossible responsibilities; and yet survival in some meaningful sense may depend upon the application of wisdom gained by government officials who are paid to wrestle with such questions.

## Diplomacy

If our international goals of a peaceful and free world are to be achieved, if big wars are to be avoided, if small wars are to be prevented or contained—the attainment of these goals depends upon the skill, breadth of vision, and imagination of our diplomacy; also upon our capacity to construct institutions, national and international, which are capable of adjusting differences and solving problems without violence.

Diplomacy is a term which conjures up unhappy images of striped trousers, duplicity, guile, and effetism. Actually, successful diplomacy is nothing but the achievement of goals without war. Needless to say, the umbrella of massive military strength is a prime ingredient of successful diplomacy; but it is far from being the sole ingredient, and unless properly used it can result in widespread hostility. As Macauley once said, "It is the spirit we are of, not the machinery we employ, which binds us to others."

*United States Foreign Service.* The day to day burden of formal diplomatic activity falls upon the Foreign Service of the United States. Established as a career service by the Rogers Act in 1924, the Foreign Service today has nearly 15,000 men and women, the core of whom are the Foreign Service officers. An increasing number of ambassadors, other chiefs of mission, and top State Department officials are career Foreign Service officers, as are thousands of subordinate diplomatic personnel. These men and women are spread all over the globe. Many of them live for years in uncomfortable climates and dangerous surroundings. Their job is to protect American interests and citizens abroad, to pick up signs of trouble before the trouble occurs, to advise superiors, and to negotiate (or assist their superiors in negotiating) with leaders of foreign nations on matters of vital concern to the security and common defense of the United States.

*Special Programs.* Traditional diplomatic activities have been supplemented in recent years by special programs of our national government designed to strengthen the free world through military, financial, economic, and technical aid. In 1947, for example, the so-called Truman Doctrine ("support to free peoples who are resisting attempted subjugation by armed minorities or by outside pressures") was announced and implemented by a $400 million grant to Greece and Turkey. The following year, the Marshall Plan of economic aid to our allies, particularly those which had been devastated by World War II, was put into effect. Since then, America has appropriated tens of billions of dollars to shore up the economies and military establishments of allies the world around.

As in the case of military superiority, money is a double-edged sword. Real friends cannot be bought. But if proffered with the proper spirit, a helping hand to our friends abroad in their struggle to achieve their own goals of freedom and independence and a rising standard of living, can be a powerful guarantor of our own long-range security. More important in an ethical sense, it can demonstrate to the rest of the world our understanding of the brotherhood of man, and our sense of obligation to use some of our unparalleled wealth to make life worth living for others.

*United Nations.* One of the most significant dividends of our participation in the United Nations is the heightened appreciation which such membership gives us of the common problems and aspirations of mankind. Founded in 1945, its headquarters presently in New York City, the United Nations is man's second major attempt in this century to build an international institution which can identify and relieve the social, economic, and political tensions of mankind without resort to war. With its Security Council, its General Assembly, and its various specialized agencies in such fields as health, trade, cultural exchange, and dependencies, the UN has a potentially powerful influence on the diplomatic affairs of the world. The rapid creation of a UN "Police Force" during the Suez crisis of 1956 may have been one of the great institutional innovations in the history of international relations.

*Regional Alliances.* In accord with the Charter of the United Nations, the United States in recent years has entered into a series of regional diplomatic alliances with non-Communist nations the world around (see page 109). These, and unilateral pledges or demonstrations of military aid to areas threatened by Communist aggression (e.g., Korea, the Middle East), have made the United States the keystone of free-world security. Increasingly our government is recognizing, in the words of President Eisenhower in his Second Inaugural Address, that "to counter the threat of those who seek to rule by force, we must pay the costs of our own needed military strength and help to build the security of others."

*Effect of Americans Abroad.* But modern diplomacy is not something which can be delegated exclusively to instruments of government. Our formal diplomats and our top policy makers act of necessity within tolerances set by the attitudes and behavior of American citizens at home and abroad. In this connection, the following observations are worthy of consideration:

1. America presently has hundreds of thousands of military personnel and private citizens stationed or residing in foreign countries. The behavior of these officers, enlisted men, and civilians can have a vast effect upon our long-range diplomatic relations with these countries.

2. America, directly and through the United Nations, sends many kinds of technical missions abroad. In the long run, the "human" and "institutional" success of these missions may be infinitely more important than their "technical" success.

3. Thousands of American commercial and industrial establishments have interests abroad. Some of these firms such as the oil, rubber, fruit, and manufacturing companies, have tremendous economic, and consequently political, power in certain areas like the Middle East, Central and South America, and sections of Africa. The policies of these companies, the social behavior of company executives and their wives in foreign countries, the skill and understanding with

"Shall We Say Grace?"

which home offices recruit and train for overseas positions are matters which cannot help but affect our diplomatic position the world around.

4. Every year millions of American tourists, students, and professional people visit other countries. Each one of these tourists—for good or ill—is a representative of the United States.

5. Most of mankind does not have white skin. This is particularly true of those sections of the human race which are just now coming into positions of national independence in Asia and Africa. The behavior of white Americans toward colored people, at home and abroad, will have a profound effect upon the future of our security in the world.

6. America is rich, and most of the world is poor. How we use our private as well as public economic strength in relation to other nations of the earth is of great diplomatic significance. At this point, the common defense merges with our value heritage. Enlightened self-interest and genuine altruism become fortuitously wedded.

# CONCLUSION

## Synopsis

In our early years as a nation, the common defense was a relatively limited task of the national government. Today, the common defense involves us in global commitments. In an age of "atomics, electronics, and supersonics," our vast military establishment is faced with problems of unprecedented magnitude and complexity. Important as it is to maintain our military strength, our first line of defense increasingly is the quality of our intelligence, science, industry, and diplomacy.

## Significance

Judged in terms of money alone, the common defense is the national government's most important function in the middle of the twentieth century. Our ultimate national interest is a decent and civilized existence for ourselves and our neighbors. We have learned the hard lesson in this century that this national interest cannot be achieved without power in a lawless world. The object of that power, however, must be increasingly to serve as an umbrella under which institutions can grow which will make the world less lawless, until the time comes when the umbrella itself will no longer be necessary.

## Prospectus

If war and the threat of war have been one great torrent of anguish in our time, another torrent has been the threat and reality of economic insecurity. This second torrent has forced government in America—as elsewhere—into actions and activities once considered beyond the pale of public policy. How government attempts to promote the general welfare in an increasingly interdependent, urbanized society is the theme of the following chapter.

## CHAPTER 8

# The General Welfare

WELFARE is more than an economic concept. All of the activities of government traced in the preceding chapters have had the welfare of the citizen as their ultimate objective.

But if one subsumes domestic tranquillity and the machinery for achieving justice, then it is in man's economic life that questions of the general welfare have their most extensive and intimate meaning. From the very beginning of the American republic it was assumed that governments had an obligation to intervene in the economy (1) to keep the people in touch with sources of wealth; (2) to regulate and control media of exchange, contracts, and other instruments of economic growth and stability; (3) to subsidize and foster particular groups within the economy (for example, baby industries through the device of the protective tariff).

In actual fact, the issue has never been whether government should join in attempting to promote the general welfare. The issue has been one of definition: for whose welfare should the government intervene, and in what form.

Our system of "free enterprise" or "capitalism," as it is called, has been shaped by the partnership of government and private initiative. The incentives of capitalism unleashed private energies with explosive force; but if it had not been for government action in the form of turnpikes, canals, roads, subsidies to railroads and to mineral speculators, and the giving away of millions of acres of free land to those pushing west, the story of America would have been far different from what it actually has been.

It is true, however, that government played a much smaller direct role in the lives of the majority of citizens in the eighteenth and nineteenth centuries than it does today.

The small tradesman of the 1790's, for example, could open a shop for business without fear of government intervention in regard to his trade practices, his manufacturing standards, or his income. If his business failed, no one was concerned except his creditors. If he flourished, and sought to employ others to help, his only guide in establishing wages and working conditions was his conscience and the prevailing demand for satisfactory workers. If one of his workers was injured or too old to work, it was up to the worker to find his own resources to meet the emergency.

And America had growing space. If a farmer worked his soil indiscriminately until it gave out, he could pull up stakes and move north, south, or west, to find new land. The history of the first one hundred years of our nation is the story of a population in motion, seeking security and prosperity in new lands and new communities.

America was rural. The great metropolises of the 1790's were small in comparison to our smaller cities today, and most people lived and worked beyond the city limits. Living off the land, people were relatively self-sufficient. Wealth was not measured so much in cash income, which was necessary only for a few necessities such as salt or cloth or nails, but in the amount of produce grown for food. The towns and cities themselves were relatively self-sufficient, depending on surrounding farm areas for food which was bought in exchange for the products made by local artisans in their homes and shops.

In this kind of a society, government had limited, although important, functions. It set the prices and conditions under which public land was acquired. It sponsored a postal system and protected patents. It fixed customs duties from time to time. It levied minor taxes on certain articles. At the local level, government took care of the needy and repaired the roads. In a nation endowed with great empty spaces and a small population, extensive government activity to promote the general welfare was vitally necessary as a catalytic agent for expansion; but its day-to-day involvements with the citizenry—particularly the sedentary citizenry—were sporadic.

## THE NATION CHANGES

Today America is a vastly different nation. The frontier is gone, and gone with it is the opportunity to carve a new life out of virgin land. Our population is huge and still growing, and most of us live in urban areas, jammed against our neighbors and jostling for elbow room.

The most significant change has been in our role as producers. The smith who used to turn out horseshoes in a shed next to his home has been replaced by a tire company employing thousands of workers in several widely scattered factories. The local general

# Economic Growth in the United States

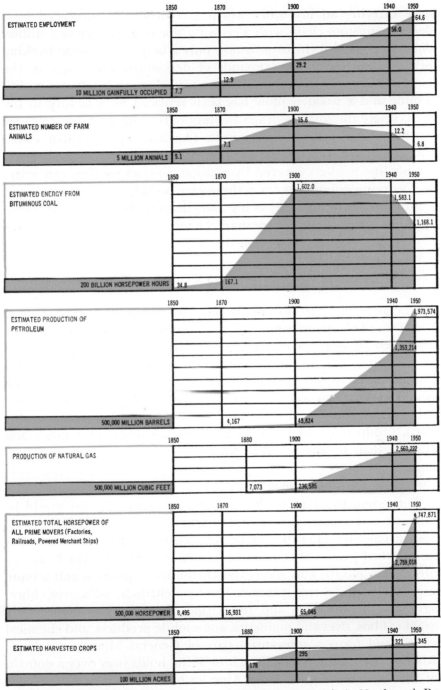

Adapted from J. Frederic Dewhurst and Associates, *America's Needs and Resources,* New York: Twentieth Century Fund, 1955, 1. p. 1073; 2. p. 1108; 3. p. 1111; 4. p. 1111; 5. p. 1112; 6. p. 1117; 7. p. 809.

store carrying an inventory worth $250 has been succeeded by a department-store chain with a gross income of a quarter of a billion dollars. The old town bank is now only a branch of a huge banking network, with tens of thousands of depositors, and assets in the hundreds of millions. The lonely farmer clearing his 40 acres with a mule and a wooden plow has been replaced by a factory in the field, where the soil is worked by hundreds of hands using complex machinery and gallons of chemicals. The skilled journeyman selling his services for a day's pay has been succeeded by thousands of assembly-line workers covered by a union contract spelling out wages and working conditions for a three-year period.

In short, America today is big and complex. Size is not the whole story, however. Two concomitant factors play a part—the concentration of economic power and the interdependence of people.

# CONCENTRATION OF POWER

The growth of our productive facilities was an obvious answer to the needs of the population, but for a number of reasons growth has also been accompanied by a concentration of productive facilities in a relatively few hands. One reason was the competitive quest for profits: early in our history it was found that larger production would usually lead to larger profits. Another reason was technological progress, particularly the discovery that by using interchangeable parts, products could be turned out on assembly lines faster and cheaper than by any previous way.

## Concentration and Bigness

The extent to which capital resources are concentrated would be fantastic to a factory owner of 150 years ago. The Bell Telephone System employs 745,629 people. The General Motors Corporation in 1955 had profits after taxes of $1,189,480,000. The Du Pont empire makes electro and industrial chemicals, explosives and ammunition, coated fabrics, plastics, finishes, enamels, adhesives, films, agricultural fungicides and insecticides, X-ray screens and photographic films, dyes and pigments, automobile products, and chemical yarns—and owns a substantial part of General Motors and U. S. Rubber as well. The King Ranch in Texas holds sway over a domain of 940,000 acres. The Bank of America has 6,037,663 depositors and assets of $9,669,145,972. The AFL-CIO has a combined membership of 14 million workers.

Is bigness bad? Some observers insist that giant corporations or unions necessarily contain the seeds of antisocial conduct; others defend size as a necessary condition to the development of new products, and to efficiency in production leading to lower prices to the consumer and higher wages to the workers. The latter, in turn, must be represented by unions with sufficient strength and resources to deal on equal terms with a huge corporate enterprise. Actually the answer lies somewhere in the middle: giants have undoubtedly tended to throw their weight around with some damage to the crockery and antiques, but they have also made possible some of our most remarkable material progress.

Concentration of economic power, however, has led to two unfortunate practices: abuse of the consumer and elimination of competition. The former has included everything from adulteration of food and misleading advertising to fraudulent manipulation of stock and unnecessary strikes. Abuses such as these were never a universal practice, but they have been widespread enough, and they have claimed enough victims, to warrant more than private concern.

*Competition versus Monopoly.* Competition is not necessarily a natural function of a free economy; our history has demonstrated that competition is often one of the chief victims of an unregulated economy. The tendency of economic power in most industries is to expand through concentration, the final result being either monopoly or collusive agreement between ostensible competitors. Monopoly is not inevitably antisocial, but its results are frequently undesirable for society as a whole and for the consumer in particular. In the early stages, before monopoly control is complete, other businesses in the industry suffer from ruinous competition; later the public suffers from the lack of competition. In effect, therefore, regulation of monopoly practices is aimed not at limiting freedom of enterprise but at ensuring it. Not the least of the results of regulation is to prevent complete government ownership of industry—socialism— to which an outraged population might turn as a last resort.

# INTERDEPENDENCE OF PEOPLE

As the nation grew, people and communities generally became more dependent on each other. The growth of cities and increasing concentration and specialization in business accelerated the process. As our economic edifice grew larger and more complex, it also became more vulnerable to the failure of one of its components. If many people, because of illness or old age or unemployment, were unable to earn a living, they became a dead weight on the community, or, even worse, they pulled down the community with them. If farm income began to slide, farmers were unable to buy farm machinery, which reduced the income of factory workers in the agricultural implement industry. When factory workers were laid off, they were unable to buy groceries or pay their rent, thus affecting the retailer and the landlord, sending farm prices even lower and forcing lay-offs in other industries.

Interdependence also meant that the individual no longer exercised the same degree of control over his own destiny. Talent might go unrewarded, ability unnoticed, if there were no jobs to be had for anyone. The individual could be as rugged and self-reliant as his distant ancestors, but personal qualities alone were no assurance of success.

# GOVERNMENT AND ECONOMIC WELFARE

Government has always had a stake in our economic welfare. But the concentration of economic power and our increasing interdependence has, over the years, sketched the government's role in new dimensions. These new terms involved not only what government should do, but who should do it—what level or branch of government, in other words, should bear the responsibility.

*What Should Government Do?* The answer to the first question began to evolve toward the end of the last century, and one of the earliest notable signposts was the passage of the Sherman Antitrust Act in 1890. As the years passed, as business abuses multiplied and competition faltered, government expanded its role. Antimonopoly control was strengthened, manufacturing processes were put under stricter regulation, workers were given a helping hand in time of injury. In the past twenty years the government's role in promoting the general welfare has increased to cover every part of the population. The businessman is ringed with regulations and supported by subsidies; workers together are encouraged to bargain collectively but their relationships with management are carefully controlled; workers individually are protected by minimum wages and compensation for injury and insurance against unemployment and old age;

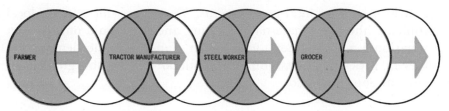

In an interdependent economy it is impossible to affect seriously the income of one segment of the population without affecting all segments.

. . . the Congress hereby declares that it is the continuing responsibility of the federal government . . . to coordinate and utilize all its plans, functions, and resources for the purpose of creating and maintaining . . . maximum employment, production, and purchasing power.

—Employment Act of 1946

farmers float on a sea of assistance—and controls. Veterans get free schooling, slum dwellers get new housing, the disabled get vocational rehabilitation. The roll call could go on for pages.

Perhaps the culmination of the process was the passage of the Employment Act of 1946, by which government accepted the responsibility for the health of the economy as a whole and for the economic well-being of virtually everyone in the community. If the Act is too imprecise to represent much more than a philosophical commitment, nevertheless the philosophy alone is a powerful influence on the government and the governed.

*Who Should Do It?* Much of the burden of promoting the general welfare has traditionally been assumed by state and local governments, and they still retain many of their powers in this area. Corporations are chartered, education is provided, and the needy are assisted under state and local laws.

The great revolution in human welfare activities, however, coincided with the entry of the Federal government into the field. This revolution, which occurred less than thirty years ago, was prompted in large part by the inability of state and local governments and private organizations to cope with the problems of economic depression. Our economy had become so huge and so complex that nothing less than a national program could meet the demands. Farm problems, urban poverty, the control of monopoly, could not be confined within local or state borders, or solved by the erratic efforts of various state or local governments. They were not state or local problems; they were national problems, and they could only be met by national action. Unemployment in Kansas cut the demand for shoes in Brockton, Massachusetts. Monopoly in Pittsburgh affected prices in San Francisco.

## Tailoring Philosophy to Practice

The revolution in the government's role in the economic field was attended by considerable modification of traditional beliefs and ideals. Living in an era when man was largely self-sufficient, our forefathers clung staunchly to the idea that the least government was the best government, that our economic relationships were most effectively regulated by the allegedly automatic process of supply and demand, that the individual was entitled to the measure of prosperity which he could win through his own ability or talent. They believed many of these things, of course, in the face of a variety of powerful public measures designed to aid various segments of the economy during the nineteenth century. It has taken us a long time to admit in the open that the average individual might not have complete influence over his own destiny; that competition is elusive and supply and demand subject to human manipulation; that rigid government disinterest in times of distress can lead the nation to the brink of disaster. It has taken a long time for our old ideals to be modified, and for much of the nation it took the immense impact of the depression of 1929 to destroy illusions cherished for more than a century. The lessons of the depression could not be shrugged off.

Many people are still not reconciled to the full sweep of government activity in promoting the general welfare. Some groups are striving desperately to turn back to the states or to eliminate entirely many of the Federal government's present obligations.

Indications are that their efforts are largely doomed to failure. The size and scope of our private economy cannot be reversed; national needs cannot be compressed. In recent years, our commitments for defense at home and abroad have ballooned to such an extent that our general welfare is inevitably affected by government spending and government taxing. Furthermore, the prosperity of other nations depends on the state of our economy. If government were to take the position of a disinterested spectator at a time when a depression loomed, we could bring down with us the economic underpinnings of the entire free world. Promoting the general welfare, in short, has become a concomitant to diplomacy and national defense.

Undoubtedly the nationalization of welfare programs and the extension of federal regulation have led to waste and inefficiency, encouraged the evils of bureaucracy, offended certain regional prejudices, upset many of our traditions, and tended to restrict the authority of local government. But despite the pains of change, and the obvious inefficiencies and danger of big bureaucracies, federal responsibility to promote the general welfare is here to stay.

### Welfare in the Courts

Possibly the last major barrier to intervention of the national government in our economic life was the United States Supreme Court. As guardians of property, the Justices fought a rear-guard action against both political parties for more than forty years. The Court's principal weapon was the privilege of judicial review, and over the years it was repeatedly used to strike down legislation designed to assist and to regulate. President Franklin D. Roosevelt was faced with the same challenge during his terms in office, but by that time the Court's power to delay was ebbing away. Shortly after the introduction of Roosevelt's "court-packing" bill (see page 380), the Court began to reverse itself. The commerce clause of Article I, the due process clauses of the Fifth and Fourteenth Amendments, began to take on new meanings. Today, the federal courts are often ahead of the other branches of government in interpreting the role of government in promoting the general welfare.

### Pragmatism and Compromise

Despite our broad commitment to government activity in the field of welfare, the nation has never lost its heart to political control of our economic system. As a result, the growth of government programs has been haphazard, depending more on the expressed needs of a temporarily aggrieved people than on advance planning. Each program has been the result of an accommodation of conflicting needs and desires, a compromise between different groups in the community.

Partly this is due to our pragmatic heritage (see page 10) ; partly, the result of our reluctance to allow government interference in our private affairs until the need is critical. Our aversion to planning has

# THE SUPREME COURT DEFINES THE POWER TO GOVERN
## (Five Representative Cases)

| Case | Situation | Majority Opinion | Decision | Minority Opinion |
|---|---|---|---|---|
| Gibbons v. Ogden 9 Wheaton 1 (1824) | Both Ogden and Gibbons claimed exclusive rights to operate steamboats between same two points. Gibbons, operating under federal license, ordered to discontinue by New York court in favor of Ogden's | Operation of steamboats is commerce and may be regulated. Regardless of whether commerce was exclusive or concurrent power of national government, law of Congress is superior to law of state. | Injunction issued by New York court annuled. National supremacy over commerce affirmed. [6-1] | Decision was proper, but power of Congress over interstate commerce was intended to be wholly exclusive. |
| Cooley v. Board of Wardens of the Port of Philadelphia 12 Howard 299 (1851) | Cooley claimed exemption from payment of state authorized pilotage fees, demanded under state law of Pennsylvania, because law was unconstitutional. | While no state may invade federal commerce power if subject demands uniform national policy, state may regulate a subject of commerce if consequences of regulation are local and not in conflict with national commerce. | State regulation affirmed. [7-2] | Commerce power exclusively federal. Decision would empower states to void acts of Congress. |
| United States v. Butler 297 U.S. 1 (1936) | Payments to farmers for crop acreage reduction was to come, under 1933 Agricultural Adjustment Act, from tax on processors of commodities, Butler the receiver for a processor, refused to pay tax. | The Constitution and the entire plan of our government negative any such use of the power to tax and to spend as the Act undertakes to authorize. | AAA unconstitutional. [6-3] | Supreme Court has no business deciding on wisdom of laws passed by Congress, only with the power of Congress to legislate. |

| Case | Facts | Opinion | Decision | Dissent |
|---|---|---|---|---|
| National Labor Relations Board v. Jones & Laughlin Steel Corporation 301 U.S.1 (1937) | National Labor Relations Board charged Jones & Laughlin Steel Corporation with violation of National Labor Relations Act of 1935 because Corporation discriminated against union members with regard to terms of employment. Board issued cease and desist order against Corporation but order invalidated by circuit court as beyond range of federal power. | Commerce power broadened to include regulation of activities having "such a close and substantial relation to interstate commerce that their control is essential or appropriate to protect that commerce from burdens and obstructions." | National Labor Relations Act and order of Board valid Decision of lower court reversed. [5-4] | National Labor Relations Act puts into hands of a board power of control over industry that exceeds constitutional bounds. |
| Charles C. Steward Machine Co. v. Davis 301 U.S.548 (1937) | Company refused to pay social security tax, maintaining that purposes for which tax was collected were not supported by Constitution. | Federal taxing and spending powers not restricted to carrying out powers directly granted by Constitution. Broader social purposes may be attained constitutionally through these means. | Decision of lower court affirmed. Social Security Act valid. [5-4] | Social Security Act unconstitutional. Administrative provisions of Act invade powers reserved to states by 10th Amendment. |

sometimes led to failure and inadequacy, to too little and too late, but it has also helped to maintain our democratic control over government. Despite the size and complexity of government programs, in the last analysis the hand on the tiller is not that of the planning expert, the economist, or the scientist, but of the people themselves.

### Government Fiscal Policy

The government collects and spends more than $70 billion a year, a sum which represents about a quarter of the total national income. Such a budget will obviously have a major influence on the state of the economy. If $1 billion is spent on new roads, for example, the construction, cement, and allied industries will benefit. If the billion is spent instead for military aircraft, the airplane and allied industries will benefit. If the same billion is spent instead to buy grain for shipment to underdeveloped nations, a large segment of agriculture, grain processors, and the shipping industry will benefit. Thus every dollar spent by government has an effect on the welfare of some segment of the economy.

*Power over Inflation and Deflation.* The government's over-all influence on the national economy is far more purposeful than this, however. Various agencies of the executive branch and the Congress have a number of tools which can be used directly for regulating our general economic health. In a time of impending depression, government can spend more money (e.g., spending a billion for each purpose described above), reduce taxes, and encourage borrowing. The first puts more money into circulation, which leads to higher employment and more capital investment by industry. The second leaves more money in the hands of consumers for spending on the products of private industry. The third makes it easier for consumers and businessmen to obtain loans for purposes of purchase or capital investment.

During an inflationary period, government can dry up credit, raise taxes, and—if international tensions permit—reduce government spending. In an emergency, it might even impose rationing and price controls. All these courses of action are designed for the opposite purposes than those described above: they reduce the circulation of money, cut down consumer purchasing power and capital investment, and may even affect employment, driving out women and students and others who are on the margin of the labor force.

The use of these governmental tools is one of the most controversial areas of governmental activity. When government reduces taxes and spends more money during a recession, any housewife faced with declining income and greater demands on the family budget could surmise that something is going to break. Actually, government solves the dilemma by borrowing, but this leads in turn to an increase in the national debt. The battle over the national debt has raged for twenty years, with no end in sight. Many authorities now agree, however, that there does not seem to be any actuarial limit to the national debt; the only limit is set by the confidence of the people, especially of the banking and business community, and the ability of the government to pay interest on the debt without prohibitive taxation or the curtailment of necessary government programs.

*Power over Credit.* Equally controversial is the government's influence over credit. It is partly the responsibility of the Federal Reserve Board, which holds sway over the regional network of Federal Reserve banks. These, as we have seen, were established by act of Congress in 1913 to act as bankers' banks; commercial banks are obliged to deposit in the Federal Reserve bank a certain percentage of the money they have available for loans to their clients. Through their power to reduce or increase this percentage, and by other means, the Federal Reserve can influence the amount of money which banks have available for loans. The Treasury Department also can control the money available for loans by raising or lowering the interest rates on its own bonds. If the interest rate is raised, people and businesses will put their money into government bonds instead of into banks. The result: less money available for loans and higher costs for those who borrow.

This governmental power over credit can have a vital effect on many segments of the economy. When the government raises interest rates, perhaps to cope with inflation, it makes it harder for the worker to buy his new car on time, or a home builder to find mortgage money. When it lowers interest rates, it stimulates the forces of inflation, which play hob with the pensioner or teacher on a fixed income. The question here is not whether government should possess this powerful weapon over our economy, but when and how government should use it.

*Power to Tax.* Finally, the power to tax, as any history student knows, is also the power to destroy. Our economic thinking has advanced beyond the time when taxation was regarded as purely a money-raising function: today it is fairly well accepted that taxes are a fit weapon with which to regulate the economy. It is also generally agreed that taxes should be levied according to ability to pay.

But within the boundaries of agreement there still remains a large area of dispute. In time of recession, for example, should government lower taxes on moderate income groups, in order to stimulate consumer purchasing power, or on business, in order to encourage capital investment and employment? The same question, for opposite purposes, is raised during an inflationary period. Another recurring issue is the sales tax. When business, real estate, and home owner groups look for relief from high local taxes, they turn to the sales tax, which falls heaviest on low income groups and is opposed by labor. And at all times some interest groups are on the prowl for special advantages, like the oil industry with its allowance system for the depletion of oil reserves, while other groups seek special relief, like the music industry's effort to reduce the excise tax on cabarets.

Many volumes would be necessary to give the full story of government's involvement in our economy, but perhaps these few broad strokes give an indication of how our political economy works.

Today, the power to tax and to spend and to regulate can affect every individual and every endeavor to an extent unequaled before. It is incumbent on us to use these powers well, because our safety and security, and the security of much of the world, depend on it.

# AREAS OF GOVERNMENTAL ACTIVITY

In fulfilling its responsibility for promoting the general welfare, government supplements its broad influence over the economy as a whole with myriad specific programs designed to regulate and assist the three main producing sectors: business, agriculture and labor.

### Assisting Business

In assisting business, the Federal government has frequently gone far beyond its constitutional obligations to establish laws of bankruptcy, protection for patents and copyrights, and uniform standards for weights and measures. Over the years, government has given untold billions worth of dollars and property in direct subsidies to business and industry. The chief beneficiaries have been the various kinds of transportation industries, starting with inland water carriers in the 1820's and ending with the airlines today. In the 1820's, government built canals. Later the government turned over millions of acres of land to the railroads to encourage the extension of rail transportation. In the twentieth century government began building roads to accommodate not only private cars but also buses and trucks.

Many ocean shipping concerns receive loans and direct subsidies to stimulate the construction of ships—which can be converted into troop carriers in time of war. The airlines use government-built airports and weather reporting facilities and receive substantial subsidies through mail contracts.

A different kind of subsidy is extended to publishers, who benefit through low postage rates on periodicals and books.

One of the functions of the Commerce Department is to serve as a link between government and business. Its remarkably extensive research activities into every aspect of commerce and industry represent a service which could hardly be duplicated by a private agency.

One of the major arms of government help for business is the tariff. The first customs duties were only intended to raise money. As various industries and regions began to feel the effects of competition from abroad, however, government initiated the long series of protective tariffs, which, down through the years, have been one of the most durably controversial issues between North and South, East and West, Democrat and Republican. Early high-tariff laws were passed for the ostensible purpose of protecting so-called infant industries. Today the demands for protective tariffs may come from different quarters including workers and farmers, but behind the demands is the same search for protection against competition from abroad. To this problem we shall return in Chapter 16.

*Regulating Business.* The passage of the Sherman Antitrust Act in 1890 put the government specifically into the business of regulating business monopoly. It was not an auspicious beginning; efforts at antitrust regulation were limited by the courts. Supplementary laws have been passed, but techniques to minimize competition evolved by ingenious entrepeneurs have usually been a few steps ahead of the legislative barriers. Government itself has not always been overly enthusiastic about curbing such practices. Finally, the penalties imposed on companies convicted of illegal practices have been ludicrously mild. Despite its inadequacy, however, antitrust regulation is a pillar of the government's power to promote the general welfare.

Some monopolies have been deemed necessary and desirable, such as in the area of public utilities, transportation, and communications. In return for their monopoly privileges, however, electric companies, municipal bus lines, airlines, railroads, the telephone company, and many others must also submit to close regulation of their rates and service. Regulation over banks, which stand at the heart of our business community, is effected through the Federal

Reserve System, described above, as well as through state banking departments. The stock market is regulated through the Securities and Exchange Commission, which has powers over trading practices and the issuance of new securities.

The Federal Trade Commission devotes most of its energies to refereeing advertising practices, although it also has broad powers to prevent price-fixing and other practices aimed at limiting competition.

## Government and Agriculture

Farmers are subject to a major factor over which they have no control: weather. In recent years the problem of climate has been aggravated by what appears to be a chronic state of overproduction, which is actually caused by inadequate distribution. Thus if the nation's and the world's consumers had the income to buy enough food and fiber, they would soon eat up or wear out what appears to be surplus production. Unfortunately, technological progress in the form of better soil practices, improved seed and fertilizers, and the extension of farm machinery have normally pushed farm production above what the nation could afford to consume. International trade has occasionally drained off the balance, but international trade has been erratic and undependable. As a result, the farmer's income has always been below the income of the industrial worker, and the farm economy as a whole has lagged far behind the industrial economy.

Government assistance to the farmer spans a broad field. The principal method has been through government programs designed to maintain prices at the level of parity, which is an ideal relationship of farm and nonfarm prices based on a past period of farm prosperity. Under one program the government encourages restriction of acreage through payments to farmers and marketing agreements. Under another program, if prices fall below parity, the farmer has the privilege of turning over his products to the government, which will put them into storage and pay the farmer the parity price.

*The Problem of Parity.* The main point of controversy is whether the government should seek to maintain full parity, or less than full, or a sliding scale. The problem is complicated by the huge surpluses of food and fiber which government piles up under the support program. If these surpluses are disposed of at cut rates

The government helps the farmer to help himself by bringing to his attention the latest scientific knowledge and reliable technical advice.

abroad, or through a food stamp plan to the needy in this country, farm prices may plunge even lower, thus reinforcing the vicious circle.

The most recent attempt to break the impasse was incorporated in the so-called soil bank program of 1956, under which farmers are paid to put part of their land into crops which will be used only to improve the soil. Time will tell whether the result will be better soil and an amelioration of overproduction (which is caused in part by the extravagant use of marginal land), or merely a gigantic government bonus for agriculture.

Farmers also receive government help in the form of farm credit, payments for certain soil conservation practices, and agricultural guidance made available through the county agents of the Department of Agriculture.

Perhaps our greatest failure has been in our inability to evolve a satisfactory government program which would solve the problem of farm income without restricting production. In seeking to raise farm income, we have constantly taken the alternative of maintaining high prices through the restriction of production, rather than of fostering abundance and reimbursing farmers when prices fall to natural levels. Complex political and economic reasons lie behind our acceptance of this philosophy of scarcity, but it is probable that no solution to the so-called farm problem will be found until we develop a program based on abundance.

## The Nation's Resources

The United States is one of the world's greatest treasure houses of natural resources—vast acres of fertile lands, tens of thousands of miles of inland rivers, great tracts of forests, and fabulous mineral deposits underground. Actually, although our resources are vast, they are far from limitless, and we have already found to our pained surprise that reckless exploitation can eat up our resources faster than they can be replenished.

For more than fifty years, in recognition of our dependence on our natural resources, the federal and the various state governments have played a part in protecting and cultivating under careful safeguards our natural wealth. Government has attempted:

(1) To serve as a mediator among conflicting groups interested in the same resource, but for different purposes—a river, for example, whose waters might be developed for navigation, or turned to hydroelectric power, or run off in irrigation ditches.

(2) To guard against the waste that frequently accompanies private exploitation—overgrazing of lands or the overcutting of forests, for example, which denudes the soil of its recuperative power.

(3) To take over the development of resources so huge that no single private organization could do the job properly—as in the Tennessee Valley or the Missouri Valley.

## Range of Activities

Since most of our resource development involves more than one state, or is too costly for state treasuries, it is the Federal government which is the chief participant in this area of public policy. Today the government, principally through the Departments of Interior and Agriculture, the Corps of Engineers of the Army, and the Atomic Energy Commission, is active in a wide range of resource development projects: improving beaches and harbors; developing sources of hydroelectric power; furthering navigation on inland waterways; providing public parks and recreation areas; protecting fish and wild life; preventing and controlling floods; providing irrigation for parched lands; conserving soil and forest; developing atomic energy; and managing publicly owned lands, which amount to more than 50 percent of the total area of the eleven Western states.

## The TVA

One of the most dramatic of the government's achievements is the Tennessee Valley Authority's twenty-year record in the five-state area affected by the Tennessee River and its tributaries. Thirty major dams and reservoirs and miles of electric transmission lines have converted what was once one of the most backward areas in the nation into one of the most prosperous. Floods have been prevented, the river has become a major artery of navigation, cheap electricity has stimulated the introduction of modern farm practices, water pollution and malaria have almost disappeared, recreation opportunities have been provided for everyone. As a result, new industry has moved in and old marginal farm lands have become productive. For the residents of the Tennessee Valley, it has meant virtually a new life.

For the nation as a whole, the power generated at TVA installations took on new meaning during World War II, when we needed ample reserves of electric power to build the atomic bomb. It was not by chance that the Army located its first atomic reactor at Oak Ridge, Tennessee, in the heart of the Tennessee Valley.

## Major Controversies

In light of the wealth at stake, it is not surprising that over the years every step taken by the government in developing public resources has been attended by bitter controversy. Our national goal has been to utilize our natural wealth efficiently and with maximum benefit, but still within the framework of our private enterprise system. The principal areas of disagreement are threefold:

(1) Some people believe that certain major areas in the nation, notably the great river valleys, might best be developed through single, over-all, multi-purpose public authorities. The expressed need for such planning bumps squarely against a widely held objection to extensive government planning or government interference with what are felt to be private and local prerogatives. Interagency disputes within the federal government have not helped to resolve this issue.

(2) There is a constant pulling and hauling over the use of the public lands in the West: Cattle raisers want more extensive grazing rights; recreation enthusiasts want more land reserved for national parks; lumber companies want to cut down more trees for wood and paper; mining companies want to dig for minerals. The federal government is fortunately, but uncomfortably, in the middle.

The most bitter battles arise over the complex problems of public versus private power. Should the government develop the sources of hydroelectric power, or can private companies do the job? Once the government steps in, should it sell power on a priority basis to co-operatives and municipally-owned companies for distribution, or should it be first come, first served? Does cheap public power constitute unfair competition to private companies, and is it paid for in the long run out of the pockets of ordinary taxpayers? These controversies flare up with each new dam, but so far no pattern of answers has evolved. During the administrations of Presidents Roosevelt and Truman public power advocates held the upper hand; under President Eisenhower, the pendulum is swinging the other way. Presumably this question, like so many others in the field of public policy, will continue to be settled on a pragmatic, case-to-case basis rather than on the basis of "right-wing" or "left-wing" doctrinaire theory.

## Government Regulation of Labor

Until recently, government and business were allied in a common antagonism against labor unions. In the 1930's, public attitudes began to change, and with the rise of a new leadership in labor, largely through the Congress of Industrial Organizations (CIO), organized labor became a strong factor in the economy. Between 1932 and 1938, new laws, such as the Norris-LaGuardia Anti-Injunction Act, the short-lived National Industrial Recovery Act (administered by the NRA), the National Labor Relations Act (named the Wagner Act) and the Fair Labor Standards Act (establishing minimum wages and maximum hours), encouraged collective bargaining and protected union efforts to organize the unorganized. As a result, labor unions grew fivefold in a decade, from 3 million members to 15 million.

As unions grew in size and strength, however, the strike and the picket line began to cause increasing discomfort to the general public. Big unions, like big business, had a tendency to throw their weight around. This the government sought to control through the Taft-Hartley law, passed in 1947. T-H is one of the lengthiest and most complex nonfiscal pieces of legislation on the books, and is the subject of continuing and occasionally violent controversy. Its broad effect is to put government into the field of labor-management relations to a hitherto undreamed-of extent. Much of the law is beyond dispute and suggested amendments would touch only a few provisions.

In the meantime, the law has encouraged unions to take action themselves to end certain abuses, and in the long run mature unions and enlightened management will learn to live in mutual trust and benefit, as has already happened in a number of industries. The question today is whether the injection of government into the field of labor-management relations will speed the day when the two parties learn to live in peace, or rather tend to perpetuate border warfare, especially in some areas, like the South, where unions are striving to increase their strength.

## Government Assists the Worker

Government programs to protect the individual worker exist at the national, state, and municipal levels. Child labor is restricted and regulated; the employment of women is subject to controls in many states; national minimum-wage levels protect workers in many industries and are supplemented by similar laws in most states.

The establishment of workmen's compensation laws in all states ended the worker's obligation to sue his employer for negligence after an injury incurred on the job. Employers are required to carry insurance and workers are paid according to the severity of their injury. Four states have also established disability insurance, under which the worker receives a small weekly sum to tide him over when sickness or accident prevents him from working.

Unemployment compensation, which provides the worker with payments during temporary periods of unemployment, is a state responsibility, discharged under the eye and with the help of the Federal government. Employers pay their tax to a state fund, which is partly subsidized and regulated by the Federal government, but states have full power to set the level and duration of benefits. To supplement this program, all states have established employment offices, also subsidized and supervised by the Federal government, to help workers locate jobs.

## Government and Social Security

The one piece of federal legislation which most clearly signalizes the government's responsibility for the general welfare is the Social Security Act of 1935. The broad provisions of this law effect virtually every person at some point in his life. Under the old age and survivors insurance program, approximately 92 percent of all those working for a living are entitled to pension payments when they retire (not before age sixty-five for men, sixty-two for women) and their dependent spouses to similar payments on the death of the family breadwinner. The most recent amendment to the law also provides benefits starting at age fifty to those who suffer total and permanent disability. The fund is financed by a tax on workers and employers; benefits are scaled to the worker's income level.

The Social Security Act also provides federal subsidies to state programs for the needy, the blind, and for maternal care and child health services. The unemployment insurance program, which is also a part of the Act, was described in the section above.

Many other groups in our society receive government assistance in time of need under several specialized government programs. Chief among these groups are the veterans of our wars, who are

**"Here I Am, Mister"**

entitled to receive compensation for disabilities suffered in the service, retirement benefits supplementary to the social security benefits, low cost insurance and loans, education benefits, and, perhaps of greatest importance, extensive medical treatment and hospital care for injuries or sickness regardless of whether they were incurred during military service. Today there are 22,539,000 veterans in this country, and the Veterans' Administration, paying out nearly $5.0 billion a year in benefits, is one of the largest agencies in our government.

## Government and the Nation's Health

One of the most startling advances in the field of medicine, although perhaps one not so well publicized as the discovery of a new miracle drug or disease-combating vaccine, is our realization that the individual's health is a matter of importance to all of society. This belief is founded not only on our recognition of the danger of contagious diseases, but also on an awareness that the nation's health is one of our most vital and irreplaceable resources. At no time was this fact brought home with more impact than during World War II, when the nation lost the services of approximately one third of its military manpower through bad health.

Today all levels of government are concerned with the people's health, to the extent that seven out of ten hospital beds in the United States are maintained by some branch of government. Government is the largest sponsor of research into the cause and prevention of disease, both through its own facilities and through grants to universities and other research organizations. Government medical care is available for millions of civic workers, for veterans, and for other groups. The only aspect of health for which government has so far refused to assume responsibility is health insurance. Many of the health insurance needs of the people, of course, are increasingly being met by private insurance programs and by labor union plans.

## Government and Education and Housing

In any discussion of the general welfare some mention must be made of education and housing. Public education is more than a hundred years old and today most of the responsibility in this area rests with state and local government. At present the Federal government assists education largely through grants for vocational training

The present and foreseeable shortages of educational facilities and teachers is one of the two or three most critical domestic problems facing our country. Every level of government will necessarily be involved in meeting the crisis in our schools. Rare indeed is the classroom similar to that depicted above—with vacant seats.

and for research. Aroused by our current and increasing shortages of teachers and schools, however, there has been growing pressure on the Federal government to step in with its larger resources to supplement the efforts of states and local communities. In the past few years the traditional opposition of those who feared the injection of the Federal government into a traditionally local responsibility has begun to ebb, and it is likely that within the forseeable future Washington will assume a new obligation, that of ensuring the ability of state and local governments to fulfill their responsibilities for public education.

The government's concern for housing is a more recent development, evolving out of the needs exposed by the Great Depression. Today an extensive federal program includes mortgage aid for private builders, slum clearance subsidies to local communities, grants to cities and states for low-rent housing, and loans for farm housing to individuals. At the present time some 422,000 families are living in houses or apartments built in whole or part with federal funds, and many more have benefited from grants from states or municipalities.

# CONCLUSION

## Synopsis

From a tiny fringe of largely rural civilization hugging the Eastern seaboard, America has grown into an immense nation spanning a continent. The process of growth and rapid technological change was attended by inevitable dislocations in our economy and in our social life. In the last few decades we have turned increasingly to the national government to solve many of the problems caused by these dislocations. Today the government's role in promoting the general welfare—in curbing the abuses of economic power and guaranteeing a measure of prosperity for our vast population—is one of its biggest jobs and extends into every aspect of our lives.

## Significance

The growth of America has put many strains on our Constitutional and philosophical inheritance, but few so severe as the need for governmental activity in the field of the general welfare. It is a tribute to our pragmatic philosophy that we have been able to adjust our theories peaceably and reasonably rapidly, and to our flexible Constitution that our government has had the power and the instruments with which to cope with vast new obligations.

## Prospectus

The general welfare and personal liberty have often been treated as philosophical antagonists. Together, American capitalism and America's pragmatic political heritage have come close to making this forbidding proposition look ridiculous. Even a cursory glance around the world indicates that welfare and liberty—however incompatible in the minds of nostalgic reactionaries or impatient radicals at home and abroad—are in practice happily married in most free nations. What liberty is and what it means in our society, is the subject of the following chapter.

## CHAPTER 9

# The Blessings of
# Liberty

ON THE EVE of the American Revolution, the patriot Patrick Henry shouted words now familiar to every school child, "Give me liberty or give me death!" The phrase is a stirring one and deserves the immortality it has received. Furthermore, in the context in which it was delivered, the phrase had a reasonably precise meaning: death was preferable to the alleged tyranny of British colonial policy.

Today, however "liberty" is one of the words we live by, but find it extraordinarily difficult to define. Most Americans would agree that "liberty" is what our "way of life" is all about; but few Americans could give the word a clear-cut definition, and no American could draft a definition which would be acceptable to all other Americans. This last is true, of course, because our nation was conceived in liberty. Liberty, among other things, means the right to disagree about the meaning of "liberty."

If we accept the fact, however, that liberty is one of the key expectations of constitutional government, it is crucial that we give the word some intellectual content. For if "liberty" remains solely in the realm of the emotions, anyone who pronounces the word forcefully and dramatically may at some critical date in the future command our allegiance—to our lasting sorrow. Many Fascist and Communist regimes in this century have ridden into being on a brutal steed cynically called Liberty.

## LIBERTY AND AUTHORITY

Perhaps the first thing that needs to be said about liberty is that it is not synonymous with the phrase, "I can do whatever I want to." No one is "at liberty" to drive 80 miles an hour down the left-hand side of a crowded boulevard—even if this were possible. No one, as Justice Holmes once said, is free to indulge his whim by shouting "fire" in a crowded theater when the theater is not actually on fire. Certainly, outside of cowboy movies, no one is "at liberty" to shoot an erstwhile partner because "his eyes ain't fray-endly."

A primary tension in all free societies comes from the disturbing paradox that authority is both the precondition and the potential enemy of liberty. *Without* government, there would be social chaos —hardly a condition of liberty; *with* government, liberty is contingent upon the ability of the people to keep government in its proper place.

The problem is made more complicated by the fact that government is not the only creator of limits within which individuality makes its claims in our society. We speak meaningfully of *economic* liberty, *political* liberty, *social* liberty, *individual* liberty, and *civil* liberty. The employment of these various adjectives suggests that there are a variety of forces or conditions in society which can limit the freedom of the individual. A hungry, sick, persecuted, or fearful person does not enjoy the "blessings of liberty" no matter how benign and restrained the government. As the great Italian philosopher, Benedetto Croce, once put it, "When we go to the rescue of a person who is ill, and quiet or lessen his pain, we are striving, in effect, to restore a source of activity, in other words a source of freedom to society." [1]

*Freedom—Everyone's Business.* Freedom, then, or liberty—since we are using the words interchangeably—is everyone's business; and if the concept cannot be defined precisely, perhaps its major dividend can be described: negatively, as the feeling of not being followed and of not being pushed around; positively, as the chance to achieve one's highest potential as a creative, moral, and rational being.

Any barrier to this feeling and this opportunity—whether the barrier comes from government, from business, from labor, from neighbors, from illness, from impersonal economic forces, or from the threat or reality of aggression from abroad—is a limitation upon the "blessings of liberty."

In this sense, of course, all of our social relationships and all of our constitutional expectations involve liberty. Certainly liberty is one of the fruits of "justice," of "domestic tranquillity," of the "common defense." Certainly liberty is the ultimate goal of measures taken in the name of the "general welfare."

But since, as we have pointed out, liberty lives on the horns of the dilemma that authority is both its necessity and its enemy, the continuing debate in any free society is how far instruments of authority can go in demolishing barriers to individual freedom without in the process setting up new and equally frightening barriers.

There are many who believe that this problem will never get out of hand as long as both people and governments take seriously the procedural and substantive rights guaranteed in the Constitution— and especially in the first ten amendments. Experience confirms that "liberty is secreted in the interstices of procedure." But our constitutional guarantees are not only procedural; they are substantive. They not only tell us what our rights are when we are arrested, they suggest the types of acts for which we cannot be arrested at all, and the privileges we enjoy as citizens of the United States.

## THE BILL OF RIGHTS

Few documents have meant so much to so many as the Bill of Rights.

The First Amendment guarantees the freedom of religion, speech, press, assembly, and petition. The Second and Third amendments, of less importance today, uphold the citizen's right to bear arms and enjoin the quartering of soldiers in private homes. As we have seen in Chapter 5, the Fourth, Fifth, Sixth, Seventh, and Eighth amendments erect a barrier of protection around judicial procedures. The Ninth and Tenth amendments limit the power of the Federal government still further by emphasizing the ultimate and residual powers of the several states and of the people themselves.

Following the Civil War, three additional amendments were passed, largely to guarantee individual freedom against encroachment by the states. The Thirteenth Amendment prohibits slavery or involuntary servitude; the Fifteenth Amendment guarantees the right to vote regardless of race or color. The Fourteenth Amendment, although somewhat cryptic, has been interpreted by the courts to mean that most of the rights guaranteed to the people in the first eight amendments cannot be infringed by state action.

### Who Protects Our Liberties?

The courts are usually considered to be our principal instrument for the defense of liberty. It should not be forgotten, however, that

# THE SUPREME COURT DEFINES SUBSTANTIVE RIGHTS
## (Six Representative Cases)

| Case | Situation | Majority Opinion | Decision | Minority Opinion |
|---|---|---|---|---|
| **Schenck v. United States** 249 U.S. 47 (1919) | Schenck, during World War I, printed and distributed leaflets urging men, in passionate language, to resist draft. Schenck found guilty of conspiring to violate Espionage Act, causing insubordination, and obstructing recruitment and enlistment. Schenck claimed protection of First Amendment forbidding abridgment of free speech and press. | Schenck's actions constitute criminal violations, even though they failed to secure their aims. Freedom of speech does not imply license to incitement of violence. However, question in every case is whether inflammatory words are used so "as to create clear and present danger." | Decision of lower court affirmed. Schenck guilty. [9-0] | |
| **Near v. Minnesota** 283 U.S. 697 (1931) | A newspaper in Minneapolis, in a series of articles, charged local law-enforcement officials with neglect of duty, graft, illicit relations with criminals, and other offenses. Supreme Court of Minnesota, upholding constitutionality of state law against "malicious, scandalous and defamatory" publications, issued injunction against newspaper. | Liberty of speech and press is within liberty safeguarded by due process clause of 14th Amendment. Minnesota state law clearly violated these liberties. | Decision of lower court reversed. Minnesota law unconstitutional. [5-4] | Majority decision of Court renders states incapable of restraining malicious, scandalous, and defamatory publications. Gives press undue license. |
| **Minersville School District v. Gobitis** 310 U.S. 586 (1940) | Two children obeying their church (Jehovah's Witnesses) refused to salute American flag in school. Children expelled. School regulation requiring the salute challenged by children's father as unconstitutional violation of freedom of religion. | Right of religious freedom not absolute. Designed to promote common end; flag salute requirement not sufficiently unreasonable to warrant being called unconstitutional. | Flag salute requirement constitutional. [8-1] | Religious belief an absolute. If individual considers salute of flag a religious rather than political act, and salute violates religious principle, he should not be forced to submit. |

| Case | Facts | Decision | Result | Opinion |
|---|---|---|---|---|
| West Virginia State Board of Education v. Barnette 319 U.S.624 (1943) | Board of Education adopted resolution requiring flag salute in public schools. Children refusing to salute were expelled. Failure to attend school made them subject to delinquency proceedings. Parents subject to jail and fine. Jehovah's Witnesses protested this as denial of religious liberty. | Refusal to salute flag did not involve collision with rights of others and did not present clear and present danger. Uniformity of sentiment cannot be produced by coercion. Compulsion not permissible means for achievement of national unity. | 'Gobitis rule' reversed, and West Virginia regulation found unconstitutional. [6-3] | Court should practice self-restraint in judging unwise laws. Flag salute regulation of state lies beyond Court's power of review. |
| Terminiello v. Chicago 337 U.S.1 (1949) | Father Terminiello, a Catholic priest, delivered inflammatory address in auditorium that stirred up protesting crowds outside. A riot followed. Terminiello convicted of violating Chicago "breech of peace" ordinance. He claimed this violated freedom of speech. | A function of free speech under American system is to invite dispute. It may best serve its high purpose when it induces a condition of unrest. | Decision of lower court reversed Chicago ordinance unconstitutional. [5-4] | Majority decision dealt with abstractions rather than realities. Circumstances of Father Terminiello's address warranted stern legal action. His efforts to incite mob violence seriously endangered the peace without which liberty cannot survive. |
| Dennis v. United States 341 U.S.494 (1951) | Eleven leaders of Communist party in United States convicted of violating Smith Act of 1940, which makes it criminal to "conspire to commit" certain subversive acts. Specifically charged with conspiring to organize Communist party for purpose of advocating forcible overthrow of government of United States, the eleven claimed Smith Act violated First Amendment. | Smith Act is legitimate governmental measure of self-protection. Doctrine of clear and present danger should not paralyze government. Conviction of Communist leaders justified. | Decision of lower court affirmed. Communist leaders guilty. [6-2] | Trial failed to introduce any evidence of seditious conduct. Restraint on free speech must be based on more than fear. Advocacy of Communism did not constitute clear and present danger. Circumstances underlying case did not warrant restriction on free speech. |

the legislative and executive branches of our various governments also share in this responsibility. Ultimately, of course, the responsibility is ours as citizens of a free nation.

Over the years, the stark declarations of the First Amendment have been endowed with flesh and blood through countless court decisions on almost every aspect of human freedom. Some of the decisions have been contradictory; precedent has been met with counterprecedent as ideas and circumstances have changed. But our last resort has remained the courts, and the last resort within our judicial system has been the United States Supreme Court.

It is interesting to note that the executive and legislative branches of our national government have been less of a threat to civil liberty than state and local authorities. The Supreme Court has never voided federal legislation in the field of the First Amendment, but it has served as a bastion against the excesses of state and local police power—especially as exercised against unpopular minorities.

Many violations of liberty occur, of course, beyond the boundaries of the law and cannot be prosecuted in the courts. In these cases, some of which will be described below, the responsibility for preserving civil liberty belongs to the people themselves. Even more than our other democratic privileges, the preservation of freedom depends in the long run on the pleasure of the people. If the citizenry grows lax and apathetic, neither the legislature nor the administration nor the Supreme Court will assume the defense of liberty in our place. No big brother or supreme leader stands watch over our liberties; only we ourselves.

# WHERE WE STAND NOW

### Freedom of Expression

Neither speech nor publications can be subject to prior censorship by federal or state authorities: this is the basic principle involved in the Constitutional guarantee of freedom of expression. Movie censorship remains in five states, but this practice is steadily declining under the impact of Supreme Court decisions limiting the scope of censorship. Radio and television, by legislative mandate, are subject only to the control of the Federal Communications Commission, but this agency has no right of censorship. Its chief weapon against the abuse of the airwaves is its power to refrain from renewing a license to operate a station.

A wide variety of federal and state laws protect us against abuses of this freedom of expression. The states have used their police power to legislate against obscenity. The Federal government has the power to control the importation of published materials, and to regulate materials circulated through the mails. Individuals can sue for slander or libel to protect themselves against defamation. (Cases such as these are rarely criminal cases; the usual remedy is damage payments.)

Many of the state laws and federal and local executive activities limiting the freedom of expression have found their way into the Supreme Court. The burden of the Court's decisions has been to insist that laws must be precise and that the violation must be substantial. A book, for example, cannot be made subject to vague or ill-defined standards of obscenity and cannot be judged on the basis of a few sentences.

*Principle of "Clear and Present Danger."* Until recently, many of the Court's decisions had been guided by the principle of "clear and present danger." First enunciated in 1919, this criterion has been applied both to laws limiting freedom of expression and to specific cases under the laws. Under its terms, expression could be limited only if it posed an obvious and immediate threat to the safety or welfare of others. However, this has often proved to be a difficult principle to put into practice, and recently it has been modified (see below).

Neither the First nor the Fourteenth Amendment afford protection against private interference with the freedom of expression: such interference can be prosecuted in the courts only if it leads to disorderly conduct or to the committal of a tort. Several organizations, often with laudable motives, are especially active in propagandizing against obscenity, sacrilege, or un-Americanism. No matter how sincere or well-motivated their restrictive practices, these private censors often pose a distinct threat to the liberty of the individual, and to the freedom of ideas to win acceptance (or suffer defeat) in the market place of opinion. In most cases where private censorship has been exercised, existing laws actually offered society ample protection against obscenity or potential sedition. Unfortunately, there are few remedies in law against private censorship; it can best be met by counterpressures exerted by other organizations, and by the courage of outspoken individuals—men and women who prefer not to be told what they can see or read and are willing to stand up and say so.

## GREAT STATEMENTS OF LIBERTY

And proclaim liberty throughout the land to all its inhabitants.
—Leviticus 25:10

There is no exclusiveness in our public life, and in our private intercourse we are not suspicious of one another, nor angry with our neighbor if he does what he likes. . . . While we are thus unconstrained in our private intercourse, a spirit of reverence pervades our public acts; we are prevented from doing wrong by respect for the authorities and for the laws. . . .

—Pericles

And ye shall know the truth and the truth shall make you free.
—John 8:32

The human race is in the best condition when it has the greatest degree of liberty.

—Dante

Give me the liberty to know, to utter, and to argue freely according to conscience, above all liberties.

—John Milton

The political liberty of the subject is a tranquillity of mind arising from the opinion each person has of his safety. In order to have this liberty, it is requisite that government be so constituted as one man need not be afraid of another.

—Montesquieu

A Bill of Rights is what the people are entitled to against every government on earth, general or particular, and what no just government should refuse, or rest on inference.

—Thomas Jefferson

# IN OUR ETHICAL HERITAGE

Not the violent conflict between parts of the truth, but the quiet suppression of half of it is the formidable evil; there is always hope when people are forced to listen to both sides; it is when they attend only to one that error hardens into prejudices, and truth itself ceases to have the effect of truth, by being exaggerated into falsehood.

—John Stuart Mill

. . . If there is any principle of the Constitution that more imperatively calls for attachment than any other, it is the principle of free thought—not free thought of those who agree with us but freedom for the thought that we hate. . . . The best test of truth is the power of the thought to get itself accepted in the competition of the market. . . .

—Justice Holmes

The world is slowly learning that because two men think differently neither need be wicked.

—Sir Wilfred Grenfell

If I am to say what are "the principles of civil liberties and human rights," I answer that they lie in habits, customs—conventions if you will—that tolerate dissent, and can live without irrefragable certainties; that are ready to overhaul existing assumptions; that recognize that we never see save through a glass darkly; and that at long last we shall succeed only so far as we can continue to undertake "the intolerable labor of thought"—that most distasteful of all our activities. If such a habit and such a temper pervade a society, it will not need institutions to protect its "civil liberties and human rights"; so far as they do not, I venture to doubt how far anything else can protect them: whether it be Bills of Rights or courts that must in the name of interpretation read their meaning into them. . . .

—Judge Learned Hand

### Freedom of Religion

Individuals are guaranteed the right to practice their religious beliefs without interference by government. This privilege is limited only if it leads to antisocial conduct, such as polygamy or a refusal to observe health requirements. Conscientious objectors, who refuse to bear arms because of religious conviction, are given special consideration in the armed forces.

The First Amendment also forbids government to "establish" a religion, which guarantees the separation of church and state in our society. Where the line should be drawn, however, is not made clear in the Constitution. Governments, for example, have enforced laws regarding the observance of Sunday as a Christian day of rest; provided chaplains for the armed forces; and paid for bus services and hot lunches to parochial school children on the basis that such assistance was of primary aid to children, not to religion.

A bitter current controversy revolves around the relationship of public education and religious instruction. The Supreme Court has ruled that public school property cannot be used for religious instruction, but that children can be released from school for a special period to obtain religious instruction. In some areas, where there are no public schools, sectarian schools are supported by public taxes. This practice is usually forbidden, however, when it is brought to the attention of the courts.

### Freedom of Assembly and Petition

Assembly and petition are often merged with the right to free speech. The special problem of public assembly is that some meetings may possibly provoke disorder or riot. Local authorities have police power to curb disorder, but the courts have made it difficult to ban a meeting before it occurs. The issue is further complicated by the right of public authorities to ban the use of public facilities, such as a school auditorium. In several cases this right has been utilized to prevent meetings of "controversial" organizations, a dangerous practice (since liberty and controversy are inseparable) which has not yet received any extensive judicial regulation.

The right to petition government has been seriously questioned mainly in the efforts of Congress to restrict lobbying practices.

**Academic Freedom**

Although the Constitution does not mention the privileges of teachers or of schools, it has been widely recognized that the academic community is especially sensitive to the state of liberty. Over the years it has become accepted practice that teachers should have the freedom to do research, to speak freely in class and out, to choose their own textbooks and prepare their own curriculum without interference from nonacademic authorities. With these privileges goes the obligation of teachers to seek the truth wherever it may lead, without subservience to current doctrine or to foreign or domestic political dogma.

# THE PROBLEM OF LIBERTY AND SECURITY

Crisis has served to sharpen the problem of liberty by posing it against the demands of security. In times of tranquillity we have usually accepted the right of those with whom we disagree to talk and to persuade to their heart's content, so long as they did not act or incite others to act to destroy internal peace or our democratic forms of government. In times of crisis, however, especially in wartime, pressures mount to forego some of the luxuries of liberty in order to preserve our society.

Unfortunately, crisis provokes tension, and the result of tension is frequently a mild form of hysteria. There have been periods in our history when the problem of reconciling liberty and security have been approached in a spirit of fear. The needs of security have been exaggerated and the threat to our national safety has been overdrawn; individual liberty has been the chief victim. Perhaps the worst characteristic of crisis psychology has been the setting loose of forces of both radicalism and reaction, which have exploited the national anxiety for pathological and selfish ends.

**Sedition Laws**

The earliest expression of crisis-caused hysteria was the Alien and Sedition legislation passed by the Federalist administration in 1798. As a pretense of protection against possible French aggressiveness,

Congress made it a crime to discredit government or excite public contempt of the administration. Eventually public reaction to the laws helped bring down the Federalist government.

World War I inspired several sedition laws, which were loosely drawn and loosely applied. Their effect was felt for only a brief period. More lasting was the effect of war fever on public morale and trust; for several years organized vigilanteism roamed sections of the land, violating individual rights with impunity. The most notorious group was the infamous Ku Klux Klan.

## Laws and Investigations

Three major laws in the area of civil liberty have been passed since 1939. In 1940, Congress passed the Alien Registration Act, known as the Smith Act, which penalizes advocating the overthrow of government by force or violence. Its provisions apply equally to individuals acting alone or as members of organizations. The Smith Act has been upheld by the Supreme Court in a split decision which effectively read the time element out of the "clear and present" danger test and substituted "possible or probable" for "present."

The Internal Security Act, known as the McCarran Act, was passed in 1950 over a presidential veto. It requires the registration of Communists, of the Communist party, and of so-called Communist-front organizations. Following registration, individuals and groups are subject to certain limits on their normal privileges, such as the right to a passport or to a job in a defense industry. In time of war, they

. . . new objective perils do not *ipso facto* call for suppression of ideas. Foreign attack is a matter for generals, and spies can be handled, like other regular criminals, by trained federal and state police. There has been no authoritative statement that we are helpless to combat such dangers unless we create new political crimes. . . .

—Zechariah Chafee, Jr.

can be interned by the express order of the Attorney General.

The Communist Control Act of 1954 outlaws the Communist party and deprives it of the usual rights of a political party.

Legislation in the field of civil liberties has been supplemented by the work of legislative investigating committees. Since the establishment of the Un-American Activities Committee in the House of Representatives in 1938, a host of federal and state committees have sprung up with the purpose of exposing actual and potential subversion, sedition, and espionage. Much of their work has been accomplished through the medium of well-publicized hearings, some of them covered by television and newsreel cameras. These committees have fulfilled at least part of their purpose by inspiring the passage of legislation, including the McCarran and Communist Control acts described above.

## Loyalty Programs

The third major field of government action in this period has been the loyalty and security programs involving government employees. The first federal loyalty program was established by President Truman in 1947 in order to screen out government employees on the basis of "reasonable doubt" of their loyalty to the United States. In 1953 President Eisenhower expanded the program to cover employees of doubtful security, such as homosexuals, who, despite loyalty to the government might be forced through blackmail to reveal governmental secrets. Investigation by security officers and hearings before boards of review are included in the administration of the

A disloyalty trial is the most crucial event in the life of a public servant. If condemned, he is branded for life as a person unworthy of trust or confidence. To make that condemnation without meticulous regard for the decenies of a fair trial is abhorrent to fundamental justice. . . .

—Justice Douglas

program. In the states, the counterpart to the federal program is the loyalty test oath, which extends not only to government employees but also to teachers, to authors and publishers of textbooks (Texas), to persons eligible for unemployment compensation (Ohio), to wrestlers and prizefighters (Indiana), and to people and organizations who enjoy exemption from taxes, which includes churches (California).

### Are Civil Liberties Endangered?

Laws, investigations, and loyalty programs have been the subject of deep-seated controversy in the past few years. Are these measures necessary tools in our battle to protect ourselves against external and internal enemies? Or are they unnecessary weapons whose doleful, if unwitting impact, is to do nothing but limit individual liberty? Let us examine the charges.

*They Are too Vague.* Vague laws, especially in the field of liberty, are subject to abuse. Critics of the Internal Security Act attack its generalized standards under which Communists and Communist-front organizations could be compelled to register and thereby lose many of their privileges under the law. The Un-American Activities Committee, and its many imitators, have been criticized for their vague mission: *un-American* has no legal meaning and could extend to anyone, even to those who oppose the activities of the committee. Under the loose language of loyalty and security programs, much of the decision-making power has been left to security officers, who are often untrained in their work. In the past few years the inclusion of security as a criterion has made matters worse; an employee discharged not for disloyalty but as a security risk might find that there is no distinction between the two in the public mind—particularly in the mind of a prospective employer.

*They Have Encouraged Guilt by Association.* One of the cornerstones of our system of justice has been that crime is personal. No one can be convicted merely because of association with a criminal. According to their critics, congressional investigating committees have encouraged the practice of guilt by association by branding all members equally responsible for an organization's alleged acts. The Smith Act, its critics point out, enshrines the principle of guilt by association by making all Communist party members guilty of the party's revolutionary designs, regardless of the degree of their responsibility or attachment. Guilt by association has frequently been employed in the loyalty program; sons have been victimized because of their continued relationships with their parents.

*They Have Violated Procedural Rights.* Investigating committees have been widely criticized for their failure to afford witnesses certain elementary procedural rights, such as the right to counsel. Defenders have pointed out that legislative hearings need not be bound by customary judicial safeguards because legislative committees do not have the privilege of imposing punishment. However, it has been questioned whether a witness held up to scorn and exposure, leading to loss of job and ostracism, has been any less punished than a criminal sentenced to a jail term.

Some critics have pointed out that in seeking to expose crime, legislative committees are violating the constitutional separation of powers by impinging on the power of the judiciary.

Government loyalty programs have been attacked for the fact that the accused have no right to know the charges against them or to confront their accusers. Government officials have defended these practices as necessary to protect informers, who would lose their value if exposed, but some observers believe that the practices have mainly encouraged nameless whispering and anonymous slander.

The loyalty and security program rests in part on the Attorney General's list of subversive organizations. This list was not prepared under judicial safeguards—organizations were not allowed to testify before they were included—and was originally intended to represent only partial evidence against the accused. In practice, however, the Attorney General's list has been abused by security officers, who have often considered membership in one of the listed organizations as prima facie evidence of disloyalty.

*They Are Not Effective.* All aspects of the security program have been criticized for their lack of effectiveness in meeting possible danger of espionage or subversion. Committee investigations may actually interfere with the delicate administrative work of such agencies as the Federal Bureau of Investigation. Administered by untrained men, the government programs have been accused of having been exploited for political purposes.

The Communist Control Act, it is claimed, will only serve to drive the Communist party underground. Its defenders point out, however, that effective operation of the party has long been hidden from public view. Finally, the loyalty test oath, according to its critics, is valueless in rooting out subversives, who would have no compunction against swearing falsely.

## Nongovernmental Activity

Although governments have assumed the task of combatting subversion, certain private organizations have turned their zeal in the same direction. At one time or another, veterans' organizations, women's clubs, fraternal societies, nationality clubs, and a variety of self-appointed "patriotic" groups have spied on their fellow citizens, boycotted movies, censored libraries, and attacked teachers and school administrators for their choice of textbooks. All this may have been done with the highest of motives, but the fact remains that private censorship and boycotting inevitably poison the mutual trust and respect which are necessary to a free society. Many private activities in this unhappy area are technically legal, and can only be combated by other private organizations and by alert and courageous individuals.

One of the most distasteful practices has been "blacklisting," particularly in the entertainment industries. An actor may find himself unable to find employment, not because he lacks talent, but because his name appears on a private "blacklist." Although it is difficult to get a legal foothold against blacklisting, one authority has warned that it can "very easily degenerate into vigilante activity, which cannot be defended in a community based upon law and order. Private justice is irresponsible justice, which, in essence, is injustice." [2]

## The Critical Division

The questions of those who defend the restrictions upon liberty which governments and private groups have imposed in recent years cannot be lightly dismissed. When national survival may be the issue at stake, how much liberty can be granted to those who would take liberty with our liberties? If all agencies in our society, public and private, are not vigilant against those who would destroy us, will we not in truth be destroyed?

These questions reflect genuine fears and genuine dangers. But their logic is not clear. On one side sit the fearful and the suspicious who face the terrors of our age by flailing blindly about them—destroying everything but the object of their wrath. On the other side sit those who are conscious of the great affirmations and the historical experience of our society and our civilization, and who therefore realize that the demands of liberty and of security are not

contradictory; that basic civil liberties need not be violated to preserve our defenses; that it is not necessary to burn down the barn to
catch the rats, or to spread an indiscriminate dragnet in order to
jail a handful of spies.

"Fire!"

Surely it is possible to write laws carefully; to grant judicial safeguards to witnesses at congressional hearings; to evaluate unproved
charges with due consideration for the accused. These things are
possible, and in many cases they have been done. In the long run,
this is the only effective way to preserve democracy. If anything is
clear it is that the edifice of democracy is not protected by destroying
those basic principles which distinguish us from our enemies.

As in times past, the spirit of controversy—the spirit of liberty—is reasserting itself. The pressures for conformity which but a few years ago were doing real and potential damage to the quality of our universities, our diplomatic corps, and many other of our most valued and necessary free institutions are gradually letting up. The American people, with their usual resiliency, are recovering their former equilibrium and courage.

# LIBERTY AND EQUALITY

Liberty has little meaning if it is not accompanied by equality. All men, of course, are not equal in talent or ability or knowledge, but in a democratic society men must be equal under the law (see Chapter 5) and must have equal opportunity to develop spiritually and materially as fully as they can.

The overwhelming majority of Americans are white Protestants. For white Protestants, all doors are usually open; they are judged only as individuals. But this is not true of many men and women, who are frequently faced by an extra barrier of race or religion or nationality. In our history, Indians, Negroes, Catholics, Jews, deviant Protestant sects, Orientals, and a wide diversity of nationality groups have all felt the intermittent lash of discrimination. The sorry and sordid story has not ended, but substantial progress has been made in recent years and the enlightened conscience of the majority of American citizens is increasingly being manifested in the policies of government.

### The American Indian

It is of symbolic importance that the Bureau of Indian Affairs, which was created in the War Department in 1824, was transferred to the Department of the Interior upon the latter's establishment in 1849. Military engagements with the Indians continued sporadically for another quarter century, but the transfer of departmental jurisdiction in 1849 reflected a changed emphasis in public policy. The Indians, who for centuries had been hunted, hounded, dispossessed, and pushed by the white men, were at long last to receive the protection of a government bureau specifically established to look after their claims to just treatment.

In the hundred years which have passed since the transfer of the Bureau of Indian Affairs from the War Department to the Department of the Interior, there has been a gradual evolution of government policy. In the early period, the emphasis was placed upon protection against undue exploitation and upon the establishment of tribal reservations. More recently, the Bureau of Indian Affairs has concentrated upon helping the Indians make more effective use of their lands and other resources, and upon providing public health, welfare, and educational services not available to the Indians from other agencies.

Today, the policy of the Bureau may be summed up in its own words:

The ultimate goal of the Bureau is to abolish the need for its own existence. This involves (1) guidance and assistance for those Indians who wish to leave their ancestral homes and enter normal channels of American economic and social life, and (2) collaboration with the Indian people (both tribally and individually) in the development of programs leading toward full-fledged Indian responsibility for the management of their own property and affairs as well as the gradual transfer of public service responsibilities from the Bureau of Indian Affairs to the agencies which normally provide these services to non-Indian citizens.[3]

## The American Negro

Like the Indian, the American Negro has had a difficult role in American history. Imported from Africa during colonial days, Negro slaves accounted for more than a sixth of the American population at the time of the Declaration of Independence. During the drafting of the federal Constitution, the question of slaves and slavery was an ever-present consideration. The question arose in a number of contexts but notably in connection with the development of state formulas for federal taxation and representation. On the basis of present ethical conceptions, the single most degrading and inequitable provision of the Constitution was the sentence in Section 2 of Article I, which read:

Representatives and Direct Taxes shall be apportioned among the several States which may be included within this Union, according to their respective Numbers, which shall be determined by adding to the whole number of free Persons, including those bound to Service for a Term of Years, *and excluding Indians not taxed, three fifths of all other Persons.*

It took a Civil War to end the institution of slavery and to permit amendments to the Constitution ending the indignities of the original document.

## SUPREME COURT DEFINES EQUAL PROTECTION OF THE LAWS
### (Five Representative Cases)

| Case | Situation | Majority Opinion | Decision | Minority Opinion |
|---|---|---|---|---|
| Plessy v. Ferguson 163 U.S. 537 (1896) | Plessy, one-eighth Negro, occupied vacant seat in railway coach for white passengers, on trip in Louisiana. State statute required railroads to provide "equal but separate" rail accomodations, and imposed twenty-five dollar fine on Negroes violating law. Statute attacked as unconstitutional. | State laws separating races in public conveyances and in public schools are not unreasonable or in violation of constitutional requirements for equal protection of laws. Interracial understanding cannot be legislated. Legislation is powerless to eradicate racial differences. | State statute held valid. [7-1] | Common knowledge that statue was designed, not to exclude whites from cars occupied by Negroes, but to exclude Negroes from cars assigned to whites. Statute interferes with personal freedom of citizens. American Constitution knows no castes or classes; it is color-blind. |
| Oyama v. California 332 U.S. 633 (1948) | California alien land law forbade aliens ineligible for American citizenship to hold or derive benefits from agricultural land. Agricultural land purchased in name of Oyama, young American citizen of Japanese parentage, but paid for by Oyama's father. State law denied to either. State law attacked as denial of Oyama's claim to equal protection under law. | State law, as applied in this case, did deprive the Oyamas of equal protection of laws and of their constitutional privileges. State law discriminated against young Oyama solely on basis of parents' country of origin. Law saddled children of Japanese ancestry in California with onerous burdens. When state's right to formulate policy of landholding within its boundaries conflicts with right of American citizens to own land anywhere in United States, right of citizen may not be subordinated merely because of father's country of origin. | State law not unconstitutional, but application to Oyama is. [6-3] | Particular set of land transactions made illegal by California. Anyone, not matter what his racial origin, would be equally governed by law. Any burdens borne by Oyama were caused not by Japanese origin, but because he had been party to transaction challenged by state as illegal under law. Discrimination in sense of placing more burdens upon some than others not in itself unconstitutional. If all types of discrimination were unconstitutional, society would be incapable of legislating upon many important and vital questions. |

| Case | Facts | Opinion | Ruling |
|---|---|---|---|
| McLaurin v. Oklahoma State Regents 339. U.S.637(1950) | Negro citizen of Oklahoma, possessing Master's degree, was admitted to Graduate School of state-supported university in Oklahoma. Permitted to use same classroom, library, and cafeteria as white students, McLaurin was assigned to special seat in classroom, special desk in library, and special table in cafeteria. McLaurin charged that these conditions were denial of equal protection of laws guaranteed by Amendment. | Such restrictions impair and inhibit ability to study, engage in discussion, exchange views with other students, and learn his profession. Removal of state restrictions would not necessarily change group predilictions, prejudices, and choices, but removal of restrictions would give McLaurin opportunity to secure acceptance by fellow students on own merits. Conditions imposed upon him violate equal protection of laws. 14th Amendment forbids differences of treatment by state on basis of race. | Decision of federal district court reversed. McLaurin's rights upheld. [9-0] |
| Brown v. Topeka 347 U.S.483(1954) | Negro children in four states forbidden to attend public school on non-segregated basis. Counsel contended that segregated public schools were not "equal," and could not be made "equal," and that the children were thus deprived of equal protection of the laws. | In field of public education, doctrine of "separate but equal," enunciated in Plessy case, has no place and violates 14th Amendment's requirement of equal protection of laws. Separation of children on basis of race generates sense of inferiority and insecurity and causes irreparable damage to children. "Separate but equal" doctrine repudiated. | State statutes violate Constitution. [9-0] |
| Gayle v. Browder 1 Led. 2d 114 (1956) | Four Negro women in Montgomery, Ala., arrested and fined for refusal to comply with local and state segregation laws governing local buses, challenged constitutionality of city code and state law. Federal circuit court held statutes unconstitutional. Ala. Public Service Commission and Montgomery Board of Commissioners appleaied to Supreme Court for ruling. | Principles expressed in Brown case, relative to public schools, extended to public conveyances. Without hearing argument, on motion and without opinion, Court declared that state or city cannot compel segregation of races on local buses. | Segregation on local buses violates 14th Amendment. [9-0] |

*"Separate But Equal," and After.* One of the amendments, the Fifteenth, provided that all the people, regardless of race, were entitled to the equal protection of the law. At the end of the nineteenth century, in an effort to keep the rising Negro populace subservient socially, politically, and economically, southern and border states attempted to sidestep the Fifteenth Amendment by passing segregation laws (known as Jim Crow laws) providing "separate but equal" facilities in many areas of life. In 1896, in the *Plessy* vs. *Ferguson* decision, the Supreme Court ruled that segregation laws fell within the letter of the Fifteenth Amendment. The fallacy of the Supreme Court decision was twofold: separate facilities, whether on trains or in education, were in fact not equal for Negroes, and the mere separation of the races inevitably placed a stigma on the minority group. The dissenting opinion of Justice Harlan rings true today: "Our Constitution is color-blind."

The segregation laws of the states were supplemented by private action, usually lawless, to limit the freedom of Negroes. The most infamous of these activities, which was limited to a few southern states, was the practice of lynching, which took the lives of scores of human beings annually for many years.

In recent years, however, private forces and government action have been working to protect and restore Negro rights. Little progress was made in Congress because of the veto power exercised by Southern senators through the use of the filibuster. But in a number of northern cities and states legislation was passed to guarantee to minorities equality of opportunity in employment, in housing, and in the use of transportation and recreation facilities. Through enlightened administrative action, discrimination in our military services also is fast on its way out.

*Higher Standards after World War II.* Much of the progress of the Negro has been due to the generally higher economic standards enjoyed by the nation as a whole during and after World War II. Housing, welfare, and social security legislation raised the standards of both white and black. High employment levels opened job opportunities for Negroes in industries which formerly were restricted to white workers. (This pressure for Negro workers led to the national wartime Fair Employment Practices Commission, which prohibited job discrimination in companies working on war contracts.)

Negroes in the North have also benefited by the increasing use of their political franchise. In many areas, Negro voters are widely believed to hold the balance of power in a close election.

### School Bell

*Supreme Court Bars Segregation.* In 1954 the legacy of *Plessy* vs. *Ferguson* was finally overthrown by an historic, unanimous Supreme Court decision barring segregated public schools. The revolution this decision wrought will take many years to work itself out. But there is no doubt that we are passing through an upheaval in the history of minority rights in this country. Progress toward full equality may be slowed but it cannot be halted by the frenzied efforts of bigoted and backward-looking men to prevent the application of the spirit and letter of the law.

In this area of minority rights, the question is often raised, How can the government outlaw prejudice? What useful role can the courts play in ending discrimination? Perhaps the final answer must await the progress of compliance with the Supreme Court's decision outlawing segregation in public schools; but in the meantime, it should be acknowledged that the Court has an obligation to enjoin legalized prejudice where it interferes with our constitutional guarantees of equality and liberty. Underlying these laws of prejudice may be a deep-seated conviction, which can ultimately be eradicated only through the slower processes of education. But until the legal outcroppings of this conviction are pruned, until the practices of prejudice lose their legal authority and sanction, the processes of education cannot even begin.

*Justice for the Negro.* The establishment of justice for the Negro is no longer a purely domestic issue. In a world in which over two thirds of the population is nonwhite, our treatment of colored people is of prime international importance. No American fault has been more widely or successfully exploited by international Communism than the failure of American whites to treat colored people as equals.

It will be many years before the Negro wins full equality of opportunity—economically, politically and socially—in the North as well as in the South. The key battle over law has finally been decided; more skirmishes remain to be won, but now the principal job is for the people themselves. Prejudice leading to discrimination is still widespread at every level of society. Future battles, therefore, must be won not in the courts alone but in the classrooms, in the churches, and in the homes, so that future generations are brought up as color-blind as our Constitution, and all human beings can be judged by the common standard of individual merit.

---

No one expects laws to reform the hearts of people, and this is not their purpose. They can, however, and do, according to the venerable Judge Learned Hand, control the disorderly, even at times at the risk of making them angry.

—Charles S. Johnson

. . . nor shall any state . . . deny to any person within its jurisdiction the equal protection of the laws.—U. S. Constitution, 14th Amendment, Section I.

## Other Minorities

Aside from the American Indian and the Negro, the story of injustices to minority groups has been sporadic and intermittent. The legend of hope at the base of the Statue of Liberty has not been a mockery. By and large, and in spite of invidious distinctions written into some of our immigration laws, persecuted sects from all over the world have found America receptive to their claims for liberty and justice. Almost every public or private attempt to discriminate against individuals or groups because of race, color, or creed has been, and is being, ultimately checked by the corrective of a liberal and humane conscience operating through both private and public channels. Mormons, Jews, Catholics, and scores of other religious groups, which at one time or another have suffered both overt and subtle injustices, are today almost fully integrated in the American culture. The same is true of nationality groups. The liberty reflected in the phrase "equality of opportunity" is increasingly being realized in American life.

No small part of this progress has been due to American politics and government which have not only helped to create and enforce instruments of equality, but which have themselves served as occupational vehicles for the upward mobility of minority groups. The Catholic or Jew or Italian or Negro who a few years ago could not, for reasons of "social acceptability" become president of the local bank, could become mayor of the city, judge of common pleas, governor of the state, even a justice of the United States Supreme Court.

Government in America has helped to keep alive the expectation of every free country: that channels will exist to insure that the natural aristocracy of brains and character—not the artificial aristocracy of birth or money—will rise to top positions of leadership as symbols and protectors of man's liberty.

> For what avail the plow, or sail,
> Or land or life, if freedom fail?

# CONCLUSION

## Synopsis

The protection of liberty, which the Bill of Rights weaves into the fabric of our governmental obligations, is one of the most basic responsibilities of a democratic society. Despite the difficulty of drawing an unwavering line between the privilges of liberty and the necessities of authority, and despite our occasional backsliding in times of tension, government in America has fostered and helped maintain a free and open society. In the special field of minority rights, the present generation is trying to correct some of the sorriest mistakes of our past, and to exorcise some of the most serious irrationalities of the present.

## Significance

Protecting liberty and extending equality of opportunity depend both on the mood of the people and the fortitude of government. There are few areas in which leadership in government is so necessary to elevate public morality, and in which the natural decency of most people is such a vital precondition of strong governmental leadership. In few areas is our court system of greater significance.

**Prospectus**

In Section II, we have examined what government in America is all about: what we as citizens expect of it, and how it has responded to these expectations. Since this is a democracy—which means that ultimately public officials are answerable to the public—our most direct instruments of control over policies and events which affect us are *political*. Section III is devoted to an analysis of these political instruments.

# SECTION III

## Our Political Instruments

*A* landed interest, a manufacturing interest, a mercantile interest, a monied interest, and many lesser interests, grow up of necessity in civilized nations, and divide them into different classes, actuated by different sentiments and views. The regulation of these various and interfering interests forms the principle task of modern legislation, and involves the spirit of party and faction in the necessary and ordinary operations of government.

—James Madison

## CHAPTER 10

# Public Opinion

IN A NATION of 170 million people living in an area of some 3 million square miles, most individuals are considerably removed from the policy-making centers of government.

Under these circumstances there arises a genuine problem of how the expectations of the public are to be discovered—let alone interpreted. The problem exists both with the government and with the individual: with the former in the attempt of representative officials to know what the people think and want; and with the latter in his attempt to make his thoughts known to his chosen representatives at the various levels and in the various branches of government which affect him.

## Communication and Democracy

This question of communications is, in one sense, at the heart of democracy. Politics, like nature, abhors a vacuum; and if the public at large has no means of registering its value goals and its expectations of constitutional government with responsible political officials, policies and programs may frequently be adopted which have the interests of the few, not the many, as their objective. If this happens consistently, a nation has no right to call itself democratic, for the word means literally "government by the people."

The necessary two-way communication between public servants and sovereign citizens is worked out in our democracy in a number of ways, none very exact; some positively misleading. The total impact of this variety of instruments of communication, however, is to produce a series of policies and programs year in and year out which are actively or passively accepted by all but a fraction of our vast population. This is a kind of miracle. Our public officials may at times distort the true image of the people; they may at times listen to "Johnnie drunk" rather than "Johnnie sober," "Johnnie selfish" rather than "Johnnie disinterested." But the ultimate faith of a votary of democracy is not that democratic government will always mirror the public image perfectly; but that it will generally mirror the enlightened interests of the many more accurately than any other form of government.

### Responsibility of Public Officials

This does not mean that the mirror is exact. In some policy areas, the public at large creates no meaningful image. The Secretary of State, for example, would not be particularly helped by the advice of the proverbial "man leaning against the barber pole" on the subject of a desirable policy of the United States government toward Indonesian currency problems.

T. Swann Harding has pointed out that in recent years it has been up to congressional committees and then to the Congress as a whole to grasp and decide upon the justice of appropriations for such projects as:

The use of endocrine to increase egg production; the role of Johne's disease; coccidiosis and worm parasites in cattle production; the production of riboflavin from milk by-products; spot treatment with soil fumigants for the control of root-knot nematode on melons; the use of mass releases of *Macrocentrus ancylivorous* to control oriental fruit moth injury; and the conversion of lactose into methyl acrylate to be polymerized with butadiene for the production of synthetic rubber.[1]

The public—as public—is not able to give legislators or executives much help on issues of this kind. In Paul Appleby's formulation, the higher the level of power, the more general should be the decision. Since, in a democracy, the people as a whole are sovereign, the people as a whole are capable of giving only the most general guidance to their servants in public office. Those who believe that a democracy can or should decide the detailed issues of government by means of popular referenda or public opinion polls misunderstand the nature of our political system and ignore the necessities imposed upon our governments by the complex world in which we live.

To the conscientious public official, the results of a public poll may not serve to guide his future policies, but to quicken his efforts to attempt to change the public's mind.

In the chapters below an attempt will be made to show how *public opinion, pressure groups, parties,* and *elections* contribute to the process of communication between the citizens of America and their various governments. For these are the major political instruments at our disposal to make our wishes known and to articulate our political goals.

# WHAT IS PUBLIC OPINION?

Two initial problems stand in the way of an understanding and evaluation of public opinion. One is the problem of deciding who is the public; the other is the problem of finding out its opinion.

### Individuals Are Complex

If each voter had but one interest and one loyalty in life, it would merely be a matter of adding up the columns and following the result. Unfortunately for orderly government, every individual has numerous and often mutually contradictory opinions, and the only figure that will stand up under close scrutiny is that there are about 170 million individuals in this vast country.

The reader of this volume, for example, may attend a co-educational college, where he is a member of a fraternity, a moderately agile tennis player, and interested particularly in civil engineering. At the same time, he is a communicant of the Presbyterian Church, and a resident of a city of 75,000 population in a Middle Western state. His father is in the sales department of a company manufacturing engine parts, his mother is a former schoolteacher, and a brother is finishing law school.

Each one of these relationships, interests, and affiliations—and the list could be much longer—involves a different set of opinions, and some of them are not particularly homogeneous. For example, his church sponsors missions abroad, while prevailing opinion in his home town leans toward noninvolvement in the affairs of other nations. He joined his fraternity knowing that under its by-laws it admitted only white Caucasians, but his mother had taught him to evaluate each person as an individual, not as a member of a racial, religious, or nationality group.

It would be relatively easy to evaluate public opinion if it could be assumed that every member of a taxpayers association favored fewer governmental expenditures, and every member of the Automobile Association wanted more government spending for roads. But how does the public official tabulate the opinions of the uncounted number of citizens who belong to both?

## Origins of Opinion

If it is difficult to determine who is the public, it is not much easier to discover the genesis of opinion. Through the learning process, through emotion or reason, and under the influence of family, friends, job, avocations, religion, and a host of other forces, the individual forms opinions in an unending stream. One man's opinion becomes public opinion when a number of others reach the same conclusion at approximately the same time. But how does this happen?

*Influence of Peers.* The most important influences on the individual come from personal contact with his peers. Sociologists and students of public opinion have discovered that the individual usually conforms to some degree to the view of his associates, at least to the degree that the individual seeks to maintain their respect. What the individual might prize as his own opinion, privately arrived at, may, more than the individual realizes, actually result from contact with others. Experiments also disclose that within any group, whether of friends or co-workers or neighbors, opinions tend to follow a definite pattern of flow. Usually such an opinion is introduced, or at least endorsed, by the leader of the group before it is generally accepted. Such a leader may never be elected or even acknowledged, but in every group of individuals, the student of mass behavior can usually discern some person who exercises leadership functions. Each group leans to some extent on such a leader, chosen—often invisibly and unwittingly—from within its own ranks.

In tracking down the source of public opinion, therefore, the first steps must be taken among small groups of individuals, who come to share the same goals and desires, and who are generally following the example set by one of their own number.

The next steps must be taken in a broader field, among the mass shapers of public opinion—newspapers, periodicals, books, movies, radio-television, and political leaders themselves. Day in and day out, everything the individual reads, sees, or hears adds to his store of inclinations and eventually builds up into an opinion. Even in this field, however, the sociologists have found a tendency toward what they call the two-step flow of communication. In other words, ideas and opinions tend to flow from the mass media to the opinion leaders of groups, and from them are disseminated to less active members of the group.

# HOW DO WE DISCOVER PUBLIC OPINION?

For much of the world's history public opinion has remained effectively unknown. This is partly because in past eras, and in some nations today, few governments have pretended to rest on the foundation of the will of the people. Until recently, even democratic governments—including our own—have had to rely solely upon indirect indices for expressions of public concern about particular issues.

In the past several decades in the United States, however, this has changed. At some point in his normal career, virtually every citizen is tapped on the shoulder, or called to the telephone, to answer a few questions for the public opinion poll-taker. The usual question will revolve around the citizen's taste in breakfast coffee or preference in laundry soaps or television programs, for it is in the field of market research that poll-taking agencies devote most of their energies and earn most of their income.

## Public Opinion Polls

Several major organizations, however, have dedicated much of their energies to uncovering public opinion in the field of government. During the year they evaluate attitudes on issues of current interest; at election time they seek to find out the result before the votes are cast. The four best known organizations are the American Institute of Public Opinion, headed by Dr. George Gallup; Elmo Roper and associates; the National Opinion Research Center at the University of Chicago; and the Survey Research Center at the University of Michigan. Behind these groups are ranged hundreds of other poll-takers, including newspapers, political parties, candidates for public office, governmental agencies, and scholars, some of whom regard poll-taking as a science and some as a game.

*Methods.* The method of the poll-taker is first to develop a cross-section of each segment of the population, representing such factors as income level, educational background, nationality, religion, and area, and then to question a small sample of each section.

The size of the sample varies with each organization; mere numbers are no guarantee that the sample accurately represents the population as a whole. (The disastrous *Literary Digest* poll before the 1936 election, was based on a sample of two million people; the Gallup poll, which allows itself only a 4 percent margin of error, uses a sample ranging from 1,500 to 10,000.) Once having established an accurate sample, the poll-taker must then develop a set of questions which will elicit unbiased answers. To take an extreme case as an example, the answers to a question phrased like this:

Do you agree with the President that if we are to maintain peace we must continue supporting the efforts of our democratic allies abroad?

might be quite different if the question were phrased like this:

In regard to the current controversy on foreign economic aid, do you believe that we should give more, the same, less, or none at all?

Although the representativeness of the sample and even the interviewer's appearance and attitude are important, experts agree that misleading questions are the principal cause of misleading results.

*Forecasts.* Pre-election forecasting in recent years has become a great American game, despite some notable failures which might have put a damper on the practice. One of the most notable was the *Literary Digest* poll alluded to above, which so misled the editors that they predicted the election would be won by Alf Landon. Their margin of error was 20 percent, which reflected the inaccuracy of their sample; but even the Gallup poll allows a margin of error of 4 percent. In 1948, when every major agency predicted an electoral victory by Thomas E. Dewey over President Harry S. Truman, two of the largest organizations missed by less than 5 percent. Predicting an election, however, is the most unaccountable of the poll-taker's arts; in some elections a prediction will be correct despite a substantial margin of error; in others a minute margin of error may result in a wrong prediction. For the poll-taker, as well as the candidate, a miss is as good as a mile.

In 1948, grim-faced poll-takers sat around the hot stove after the election and agreed that among the reasons for their error was their failure to evaluate correctly the eventual votes of respondents who said "Don't know" at the time they were asked their preference, and the lighter-than-expected total vote, caused by large numbers of Republican voters who did not vote at all or at least not for the candidates for national office.

In 1956, the pollsters recouped much of their prestige. Their pre-election forecasts were amazingly accurate. But does this mean that the pollsters have perfected their science? They would be the first to answer, No.

Here special interviewers from the Gallup Poll carry on a "depth interview" with the help of a wire recorder. The depth interview is generally long and attempts to get at such difficult factors as "intensity of feeling."

*Difficulties.* Basically the problem with polls is people. As one observer has commented, "Their opinions are too mercurial, often too contradictory, and their frames of reference too varied to make for completely reliable statistics." Putting this problem of timing, and the allied problem of quality (how deeply people may feel) in the form of an example, this same observer has written:

Dr. Gallup recently solicited opinions on the "ideal" number of children per family. Asked on a lonely summer day, with the kids away at camp, a mother may fondly answer three or four, or even more. But put the question to her on a late winter afternoon, with the same blessings tearing up the floorboards, and the answer may not only be different but unprintable.[2]

*Influence of Polls.* Polls exist not only to titillate the politician and amuse the student of current affairs, but also to guide the conscientious legislator and policy-making administrator. Many agencies of government, including most notably the Department of Agriculture, use poll-taking regularly. The Army worked out its discharge point system, following the end of World War II, on the basis of soldier preferences expressed through a poll of a selected sample and the result was widely praised.

More important, reputable polls can occasionally offset the frantic efforts of private interest groups who might, by intensive activity, hope to persuade the government that they represent the public at large. Polls played a part in the death of the Townsend plan in the late 1930's when, despite the pressure tactics of the Townsend organization, it was disclosed that relatively few people favored the plan. In 1941, when Congress was debating the extension of Selective Service, 90 percent of the mail flooding Capitol Hill and the White House opposed extension, but polls showed that a majority of the people favored it.

Despite the problems and the inaccuracies, public opinion polls have found a secure place in our national scheme, and as they continue to develop into a more dependable science, they will do much to give public opinion a growing influence in our democracy.

# IS PUBLIC OPINION A RELIABLE GUIDE FOR DEMOCRATIC GOVERNMENT?

But should public opinion as measured by the pollsters be the ultimate resource of democratic policy-making? The answer of course is, No. The average citizen finds many complex and far-reaching issues beyond his comprehension, or, more important, beyond the level of his interest.

It is fortunate, therefore, that we are not a direct democracy, but a representative democracy. Actually, we place great faith in our leaders not to mislead us, to take enlightened actions on matters which are frequently too complex or too technical for us to understand, and to straighten out kinks in our thinking caused by misinformation. If our leaders make mistakes, we can ultimately vote them out of power; but while they are in office they necessarily act with considerable discretion—a discretion usually untutored by opinion polls or by public opinion of any measurable sort. The internal self-restraints, "world views," and leadership abilities of our chosen officials, commingled with the special claims of organized interests in our society, are generally more significant determinants of particular public policies than public opinion—no matter how carefully measured or transmitted.

## Importance of Public Opinion

This is not to say, however, that public opinion is unimportant. Public opinion sets the ethical and sometimes the programmatic tolerances within which decision-makers and group pressures contend. If public opinion sets narrow tolerances, or reflects distorted images of reality, representative political leaders may feel constrained to adopt public policies which have no observable relationship to the long-range interest of the public. This suggests that one of leadership's greatest tasks in a democratic society is to educate the citizenry to the real issues of our time in language which is both honest and understandable.

# MASS COMMUNICATION MEDIA

This inevitably directs our attention to America's media of mass communications through which citizens receive many of their impressions and ideas from political, and other opinion, leaders.

### Press, Radio, Television

Among the principal media of mass communication, of course, are the daily press and radio-television. How fair and objective are these media? Do they give the citizen a clear image of what is

Only the miracle of modern printing makes it possible for daily newspapers to reach over 55 million readers every 24 hours. Here a pressman for the *New York Times* changes a roller plate.

going on and of the important political, social, and economic issues with which modern political leadership must deal? Ideally,
every citizen should have the opportunity to read several newspapers, or at least to have a choice of one among several, all of
which would do a reasonably complete and unbiased job of pre-
senting the news—or would, at least, be frank about their biases.
It has been charged that this ideal state of affairs is offset by two
factors: monopoly and hidden bias.

## Monopoly

The figures tell the story of monopoly. More than a thousand
cities have only one daily newspaper, and in ten states there are
no cities with more than one newspaper. Fourteen companies control one quarter of the circulation of daily newspapers. Few newspapers can afford large reportorial staffs of their own, and as a
result most of them depend on one or more of the three major
news-gathering organizations for their national and international
news. These three organizations are major factors in the task of
bringing news to the American people: the United Press, owned
by the Scripps-Howard Company; the Associated Press, a cooperative organization owned by the newspapers it serves; and the **International** News Service, owned by the Hearst interests.

## Bias

The criticism of bias in the press is largely centered on the fact
that owning a newspaper is a big business, and the industry is
dominated by a relatively small number of big businessmen who
share the generally conservative interests of big businessmen in
other industries. Other factors may also play a part in some newspapers. To avoid offending certain groups of readers, such as a
powerful religious group, a newspaper editor may block off, bury,
or distort the reporting of controversial views. Advertisers occasionally bring pressure on a newspaper to refrain from dealing
with a strike at a department store or an antitrust indictment of
a large company.

In the field of politics, monopoly and bias were at the root of
the charge of a "one-party press," raised by Democratic candidate
Adlai Stevenson during the presidential campaign of 1952. However, Stevenson failed to indicate whether he was referring to the

editorial position taken by newspapers or to the coverage of political news, and there is an important difference.

A substantial majority of the daily press of the United States undoubtedly favors the Republican party and has so declared itself repeatedly in columns on the editorial page at election time. This appears to have had less than an overwhelming effect on the nation. If the election results are worth-while indicators, few readers, it seems, turn to the editorial page, and if they do, they discount most of what they read. In thirty-seven presidential elections before 1952, the majority of the press supported the winner eighteen times and the loser nineteen times. President Roosevelt received support from only 40 percent of the press in 1932, 36 percent in 1936, 20 percent in 1940, and 17 percent in 1944, yet he won all four elections.

If the editorial support of newspapers cannot assure victory for a candidate, it undoubtedly plays some role in determining attitudes. More important than editorial support, however, is the coverage and handling of news events, for it is the day-to-day presentation of news and headlines which may add up to a vital force in determining public opinion in public affairs. In this field, no completely reliable methods have yet been evolved to determine whether the press slants the news. (Following the 1952 presidential election, one analysis of the content of thirty-five representative newspapers indicated that only a minority of newspapers demonstrated partiality in their coverage of the campaign, and partiality was extended to both major candidates.) [3]

Is there, then, significant monopoly and bias in the press? If so, is this a serious threat to our political health?

On both issues there is little agreement. Some people claim that the three major wire services—the A.P., U.P., and I.N.S.,—are so objective that they are colorless; that local newspaper monopolies are offset by the existence of other types of mass media like radio and television; that the professional ethics of newspaper men, particularly in the large metropolitan dailies, is generally high; and that Americans get news straighter and faster than the citizens of any other nation.

On the other hand, some critics of mass media see nation-wide "thought-control" just around the corner.

The evidence to date is meager and conflicting. If newspaper editors, by and large, reflect in their editorials and in their handling of news stories the economic and political philosophies of their publishers and advertisers, the fact remains that there is still considerable opportunity for the reading, seeing, and hearing of a sufficient variety of points of view on matters of public concern to insure the continuation of controversy and debate in our society.

This is especially true because radio and television appear to have more influence in determining public opinion than newspapers—and under law, and through a measure of self-regulation, the airwaves have been comparatively free of bias. Under federal law, the air is considered public property and all owners of broadcasting stations must be licensed. Owners cannot use time to disseminate their own opinions, and all candidates for public office must be given equal opportunity either to buy time for broadcasts or to appear on the air on time donated by the station as a public service. Theoretically this is admirable, but in practice "equal opportunity" may have only grim irony for the candidate who, facing a saturation campaign by his opponent, cannot afford to pay the high rates to respond.

## Censorship

Bias and monopoly in mass communication media, to the degree to which they exist, constitute one barrier to the operation of a free market place of ideas—even if, at times, this barrier is exaggerated. Far more serious is censorship. Under the First Amendment, government cannot establish a regular censorship at the source, that is, require newspapers or magazines to receive official approval before publication. But censorship at the source can be effectuated merely by withholding information from the public. A certain degree of this kind of censorship will always be necessary, especially in times of emergency, for reasons of security against espionage. But the practice of withholding information, sometimes accomplished by classifying information as secret, can be misused by government agencies wishing to protect themselves from public criticism. In 1955, for example, the Department of Defense publicly established a policy of releasing information only if "publication of material would constitute a constructive contribution to the primary mission of the Department of Defense." Many conscientious newsmen complained that this policy, which was adopted by other agencies on a less official basis, was inspired by political, not security reasons. There is no official punishment for the ambitious reporter who manages to penetrate this informal curtain of secrecy, but every reporter is aware that important officials have various informal penalties at their command to deter such zealousness.

# PROPAGANDA, PUBLIC RELATIONS, AND THE PUBLIC

## Propaganda

Surely one of the most disturbing but inevitable influences on the dissemination of information is the gentle art of propaganda. Basically, propaganda is the dissemination of trimmed, padded, or warped information with the goal of controlling the thought or action of other people. Propaganda may be true or false or a mixture of both, it may be rational or emotional or a little of each, but whatever its form, it aims to influence. (Education is also designed to influence, but its methods are controlled to a greater extent by professionally recognized standards of truth and reason.) Today propaganda is so pervasive that as a term it has become almost useless. Anyone who pays dues to an organization or is interested in public affairs plays a part in the processes of propaganda, and what is one man's propaganda is another man's education.

Americans are accustomed to propaganda. In this country propaganda has reached a peak of perfection, subtlety, and saturation through the American art of advertising. Every newspaper reader or bus rider or radio listener is acquainted with the techniques developed to influence people: the "name-calling" or the "glittering generality" technique (condemning or approving a subject by labeling it, without the use of supporting evidence); the "transfer" or "testimonial" technique (condemning or approving through association); "plain folks" and "band-wagon" appeals (association with the public at large, usually connoting broad public approval); card-stacking (a judicious selection of facts); repetition, repetition, repetition.

## Public Relations

Today the techniques of propaganda are not restricted to advertising or politics but, masquerading under the name of public relations, pervade every area of life. The use of public relations as a handmaiden to industrial management became widespread after the turn of the century, principally to counteract attacks on industry and commerce by the muckrakers and to offset mounting government concern over trusts and other business practices. The government itself turned to public relations during World War I when George Creel's Committee on Public Information helped to sell America on the reasons for American intervention. In the early days of the New Deal, the National Recovery Administration achieved much of its short-lived success through intensive advertising and publicity.

Today most large business firms, labor unions, and public organizations of all kinds boast publicity departments, the effort costing hundreds of millions of dollars. Publicity no longer concerns itself merely with the dissemination of information but also with the policies and goals of the organization itself. As an example, the Bell Telephone Company has evolved one of the most elaborate public relations patterns in the world. Besides using the standard media of information dissemination, such as publications, advertising, and press relations, it encourages its employees to join civic and fraternal groups in their local communities, often reimbursing employees for their dues.

### Lobbying

Much industrial public relations is frankly aimed at political goals. In the 1920's new records for ingenuity and expense were set by the private utilities in this country, largely to counter state and federal efforts to regulate them and to develop public power facilities. Hundreds of millions of dollars were spent in a relatively few years, and the techniques included examining high-school and college textbooks and suggesting revisions, giving col-

Our major problem comes from the modern development of the mass media of communication. These media are expensive and grow more so with time . . . (they involve) new advertising techniques, requiring professional skills that are also expensive. . . . If present tendencies continue, our federal elections will increasingly become contests not between candidates but between great advertising firms.

—Neil Staebler, Chairman of Michigan's Democratic Party

lege students summer jobs, and arranging tours for school children. In some ways, public relations not only supplements lobbying but even replaces it. In the words of one of the leading practitioners of the art, ". . . if you have a sound enough case to convince the folks back home, you don't have to buttonhole the Senator. He will hear from home, and he is prone to respect very highly the opinions he gets from that quarter." [4] At the present time, many organizations—business, farm, labor, and veterans'—that were originally designed to lobby in the halls of the legislatures, spend most of their time and money in public relations efforts (see page 210).

## Public Relations and Politics

The effect of public relations on political campaigns has been equally revolutionary. Until recently, campaign public relations was limited to press-agentry—handing out the texts of speeches to reporters, arranging for photographs, and managing press conferences. Following Alfred E. Smith's defeat by Herbert Hoover in 1928, the Democratic party instituted a full-time public relations department in the person of a former newspaper reporter named Charles Michelson, who promptly initiated an elaborate campaign against the Hoover Administration. Coining slogans, writing speeches for Democratic notables, even developing key issues, Michelson was perhaps the first exponent of modern-day public relations techniques in politics. Another outstanding exploiter of public relations techniques was Wendell Willkie, whose pre-convention campaign in 1940, although designed to give the impression of a spontaneous grass-roots upheaval, was actually a carefully developed build-up directed by leading experts in the field. Willkie himself, through his long association with utility compa-

*The Engineering of Consent*

(1) Define your objectives. (2) Research your publics. (3) modify your objectives to reach goals that research shows are obtainable. (4) Decide on your strategy. (5) Set up your themes, symbols, and appeals. (6) Blueprint an effective organization to carry on activity. (7) Chart your plan for both timing and tactics. (8) Carry out your tactics.

—Edward L. Bernays

nies, was aware of the potentialities of public relations and propaganda.

Today the public relations expert is an integral part of every political campaign, at least at the national and state levels, and responsibility for directing the campaign may rest more in the public relations expert than in the candidate himself or his official campaign manager.

## Public Relations in a Campaign

As a political campaign develops, certain public relations techniques may be immediately evident. The public relations expert always attacks, in the belief that defensive campaigns cannot win. To assure public attention in the face of competition from sporting events, radio murder mysteries, and TV comedy, the expert seeks a gimmick or novelty approach which will give public issues an entertainment value. To lend an appearance of momentum, the public relations director starts a campaign slowly and builds up to a climax during the last few weeks.

What does a public relations campaign involve in actual materials? In a campaign for a referendum issue in California some years ago, the firm of Whitaker and Baxter, which has brought political public relations to their fullest flower, prepared the following materials: 10 million pamphlets and leaflets, 4½ million postcards, 50,000 letters, 70,000 inches of display advertising in 700 daily and weekly newspapers, theater slides and trailers in 160 theaters playing to 2 million people each week, 3,000 radio spots on 109 stations, 12 fifteen-minute network radio shows, 1,000 large billboards, 20,000 posters. Thousands of speeches, sound trucks, and intensive press relations rounded out the picture, and this all in the pretelevision era!

# THE EFFECT OF MASS ADVERTISING TECHNIQUES

It is perhaps too early to evaluate the effect of mass advertising techniques in our political life. Some view the calculated use of modern propaganda and public relations machinery for political purposes as a dire threat to our democracy. Those with the most money and the cleverest public relations specialists, it is claimed, will eventually control the entire country. The contention is that

—Baltimore Sun

*Progress Of Politics . . . Former Presidents Didn't Have*
*To Contend With Problems Of National Networks.*

total control, as in George Orwell's chilling novel *1984,* will eventually be lodged in the hands of "Big Brother" who will rule
ruthlessly and quietly as a result of his command of all media of
propaganda and electronic surveillance.

No one who has watched a modern totalitarian state at close
range can doubt that the skilled propagandist is capable of being
diabolical and effective. There are always dangers in the unprin-
cipled uses of manipulative arts directed toward controlling human
behavior. America may not be immune to such dangers despite the
fact that we have built up more resistance to this sort of thing than
any other people on earth. Certainly Americans have been inoculated
with sufficient doses of the virus of radio, TV, and journal advertising
to have built up considerable immunity to the clever "gimmick" and
the subtle "pitch." Standing as a massive barrier between the American people and the easy virtue and seductive glances of the political
manipulator is the capacity of the average American to spot a

"phoney" no matter how "sincere" the "pitch." The house of freedom will not be blown down merely by the huffing and puffing of the slick artists of persuasion. But they certainly represent a threat to the rational discussion and understanding of public issues that lie at the foundation of our democracy.

# CONCLUSION

### Synopsis

Public opinion plays a more important role in government today than ever before. Persons in positions of leadership in the community must be prepared to defer to public opinion; but in a representative democracy they must lead it as well. In previous eras, perhaps the greatest danger to a democracy came from a single leader, or coterie of leaders, who sought to exploit government and limit freedom by backstage manipulation without reference to a moral image of the public interest. This kind of activity could be rationalized on the grounds that public opinion was either dormant or indecipherable. As education has spread and as government services have been experienced by more and more people, the citizen has found an increasing number of ways of expressing himself. Public opinion polls are one of these ways. Today the danger is the demagogue who is willing to employ the techniques of advertising and public relations to manipulate public opinion.

### Significance

The answer to any possible misuse of public relations is not alone an *actively* interested citizenry, but an *intelligently* interested citizenry. Our greatest security against the "manipulator" is the educated individual and the dedicated public servant, appreciative of our heritage and eager to "tune out" the false prophets when the "pitch" begins.

### Prospectus

It is often difficult for the conscientious representative to sort out the various "publics" from which he hears. Most of the "opinion" which flows over his desk or hums along his telephone wires is backed by a sufficiently small clientele to warrant its being called, not public opinion, but private opinion. Private opinion—that is, interest group opinion—is frequently a powerful force in policy making. Properly used, private opinion is one of our most valued instruments of self-government. Why this is so, and how such opinion makes its weight felt, is the subject of the following chapter.

## CHAPTER 11

# Interest Groups

PRIVATE INTEREST GROUPS, otherwise known as pressure groups, have existed in this nation since before the beginnings of our national government. As one observer has pointed out, "The first pressure group in this country to attain immortality was that little gang of painted-up merchants who pushed the British tea into the salt water of Boston Harbor." [1] The successors to those Boston merchants, instead of dressing in loin cloths and feathers, now pay dues to a national tea council and hire a full-time staff to handle their pressure work for them.

## Pressure Groups in a Democracy

Despite the occasionally unhappy connotation of the term "pressure groups," private interest organizations are an inevitable part of democratic government. In the past, as our population rose, individuals interested in some phase of government found it necessary to organize into groups in order to exercise enough power to achieve their goals. The perfection of communication media made it possible for similar groups in various parts of the nation to join hands in a common effort. As the life of the community grew more complex, individual congressional and other election districts began to include conflicting groups, and the legislator no longer could be counted on to represent any single group with uninterrupted concentration. Finally, government itself became more and more involved in economic life, stimulating group interest in government affairs.

For example, when our nation was young, the cotton grower in Virginia had little need to approach his government, and when he did he could be confident that his legislative representative would help him achieve his goals. The district in which the cotton grower lived was entirely devoted to cotton growing, and chances were that the representative owned a plantation, too.

## Development of Organized Pressure Groups

As the nation grew, however, other crops or industries began to be found in the district. Perhaps it was apple orchards, or a spinning mill; today it might be beef cattle in the country and half a dozen industries in the cities and towns. The congressman now represents a number of possible conflicting interests; the cotton grower is only one of his many constituents. The government itself has grown from a handful of administrators to the nation's largest industry, and the voice of one lonely cotton grower can barely be heard. Finally, especially in the last two decades, government has acquired a number of functions, ranging from setting and collecting income taxes to determining acreage allotments, which have had a vital effect on cotton growing, as well as on every other human endeavor.

Over the years, therefore, the cotton grower banded together with other cotton growers, first in Virginia, and later throughout the nation, and formed an organization. The final development was hiring an executive secretary in Washington to keep tabs on officials in the Department of Agriculture and to stay in touch with Congress, especially with members of the House and Senate agriculture and appropriations committees.

# INTEREST GROUPS, A TO Z

Judged by the newspaper headlines they receive and the expenditures they dispense, the most effective interest groups are a few giants of industry, labor, agriculture, veterans, and the professions which embrace thousands of organizations and millions of individual members and interest themselves in every major governmental field. With their ample treasuries and widespread memberships, these organizations undoubtedly can and do exercise a sizable influence. They can hire skilled lobbyists and public relations experts; their top officers may be well-known public figures; they can dramatize the issues on a national scale. But their very size may also handicap them, for among their membership internal differences arise to sap the strength of the organization. Their interests may be so heterogeneous that the average member cannot be counted as an automatic vote when it comes time to support or oppose candidates for public office or any particular issue.

Symbolic of the weakness of even the greatest pressure group when it disperses its interests is the comment of a Congressman friendly to both farmer and worker, who was somewhat puzzled when he was requested by William Green, late president of the AFL, to vote for a controversial farm bill: "I have always followed Mr. Green on labor bills. But this is not a labor bill. This is a farm bill. On this bill I follow the farm leaders." [2]

When organized labor and the National Association of Real Estate Boards clash over public housing legislation, for example, the former, despite its larger membership, operates at a distinct disadvantage. Union members have many interests, while realtors are principally concerned with housing. When the two forces clash, the impartial legislator is aware that union members probably will overlook his vote on public housing when they judge his over-all record come election time, but the realtor will look at nothing else.

### Industrial and Labor Groups

On the industrial and business front, the two largest interest groups are the National Association of Manufacturers and the Chamber of Commerce. The former represents 16,000 manufacturing firms; the latter is a federation of 400 trade associations and 1,000 local chambers of commerce. Since the merger of the two major federations of labor, the American Federation of Labor-Congress of Industrial Organizations represents most of the nation's 16 million union members.

### Agricultural Groups

Three organizations speak for most of the farmers in America: The National Grange (also known as the Patrons of Husbandry), the American Farm Bureau Federation, and the Farmers' Union. Founded in 1867, the Grange was once a rebellious, progressive group, but today its 750,000 members are among the most conservative of farmers. The Farm Bureau was organized early in this century around the county agents of the Department of Agriculture and still retains a semigovernmental status in many areas. Most of its million or more members live in the Middle West farm belt. The Farmers' Union is a smaller organization representing smaller farm owners. Its greatest strength is in the Missouri River valley and it is considerably more liberal than its competitors.

## Veterans and Professional Groups

Two organizations dominate the veterans' interests: the American Legion with more than three million members, and the Veterans of Foreign Wars, with a little over two million. The American Bar Association, representing most lawyers, has a semigovernmental status (see page 447). The American Medical Association, which embraces virtually all medical doctors through state and local Medical Associations, has enormous influence in policy areas of direct concern to its membership.

## Smaller Pressure Groups

*Economic Groups.* More typical of interest groups are smaller organizations, with a more limited membership and narrower goals. They may not carry much weight on the national scene, but they often are more influential within their restricted field of interest, precisely because their energies are concentrated. If their interests are limited, however, their membership may benefit from widespread geographical location. Although only 3 percent of the nation's farmers grow sugar cane or sugar beets, and only 25,000 people are employed in the processing of sugar, they are spread through 19 states, and thus they can approach with some familiarity a total of 38 Senators.[3]

Some of these groups, although relatively small in size, compare favorably with better known associations in resources and influence. Among these are the major industry and commodity organizations, such as the National Association of Real Estate Boards, the National Retail Dry Goods Association, the Edison Electric Institute (representing private utilities), the National Cotton Council, and similar associations representing the steel industry, railroads, wool growers, milk dealers, and many others.

One industry is so powerful that it defies all classification. The petroleum and natural gas industry, wealthy beyond all reckoning, favored by special treatment in the income-tax laws, dominating a number of states which are represented by particularly influential congressmen, is in a position of power today which can only be compared with the influence wielded by the railroads eighty years ago.

Ranking under the giants of the industry and commodity associations are some 2,000 other trade associations and 3,000 local business groups. Further down the ladder are individual companies, labor unions, and local farm cooperatives and marketing groups.

Besides the Bar Association and its affiliates and the AMA, there are 400 professional organizations. College teachers, for example, may belong to the National Education Association or the American Association of University Professors.

*National and Racial Groups.* As late as 1944 there were 23 organizations representing people of German extraction, 18 for those of Slavic origin, and 22 for Polish-Americans. Altogether there are in America more than 150 nationality groups with some 3,000,000 members. In several states and many congressional districts they exercise substantial influence. The Irish, for example, used to dominate Boston; the Germans and Scandinavians play a large role in the North Central states, as do the French Canadians in Maine and the Spanish Americans in New Mexico. The Italians have a rising political influence in New York City and other northern cities.

The two best known of the Negro groups are the National Association for the Advancement of Colored People (NAACP), which directs its efforts against discrimination, and the National Urban League, which stresses job and housing opportunities.

A few private interest organizations are primarily ideological in purpose, such as the Committee for Constitutional Government on the far right or Americans for Democratic Action, an anti-Communist liberal group. The CCG, and other splinter groups like it, round up much of their support from industrialists; ADA is made up largely of intellectuals and works closely with sections of organized labor.

*Educational Groups.* Most of the groups mentioned above have a direct economic or political impulse behind their activity. Some organizations, however, have a relatively disinterested community orientation directed toward such causes as better education, improved health facilities, or more responsible government. Perhaps the best known is the League of Women Voters, which annually chooses several public issues for study and action. Unlike most other organizations, groups such as these gain little from their efforts except a sense of satisfaction in a worth-while accomplishment.

*Religious Groups.* Finally, 100 million Americans are affiliated with churches, and many church groups, partly out of private interest but more importantly out of a desire to give concrete meaning to their ethical principles, are active on the political scene.

# HOW INTEREST GROUPS WORK

Private interest groups perform a wide variety of services for their membership, but in the context of a study of government their principal importance lies at the point where they touch governmental processes through lobbying. (In the trade the lobbyist is more likely to be known as a legislative representative.)

## Lobbying

"Lobbying" is a much maligned term which merely means the use of influence by a private person or group to obtain relief through government. The purposes for which men lobby run the gamut from the minuscule, such as paving on a country road, to the spectacular, such as turning over federal offshore petroleum deposits to the states. The results may be highly beneficial to the national welfare, such as a federal appropriation for medical research, or they might benefit only a very few, such as an amendment adding a loophole to a tax law.

*Techniques.* The techniques of lobbying include research, preparation of speeches and testimony, rounding up witnesses for legislative hearings, drafting bills and amendments, writing committee reports, arousing support from a Congressman's constituents, obtaining endorsements from other private interest groups, lining up congressional votes, and, although it no longer is of much importance, wining and dining relevant public officials. Outright bribery of legislators, at least on the national level, is rarely practiced, although occasionally a private group favors a friendly legislator by giving some legal or insurance business to his firm back home, or by paying him expenses and an honorarium for a speech at its annual convention.

*Lobbyists in Washington.* There are more than a thousand lobbyists in Washington, D. C. The average lobbyist is apt to be a practicing attorney who watches a few bills, keeps in touch with a few administration officials, and generally runs errands for a private interest group which has its headquarters elsewhere. A few of the larger organizations have staffs of research and publicity experts headed by highly paid and highly experienced full-time legislative representatives, a few of whom are better paid and more secure in their position in life than the average United States Senator.

Lobbying is found in the executive departments as much as on Capitol Hill, for most of the government's business is conducted by officials in the departments and agencies. Many lobbyists have close relationships with administrative personnel. Indeed lobbyists on occasion influence the appointment of administrative personnel. Farm organizations, for example, are likely to find a sympathetic ear at the Department of Agriculture and the veterans' groups have

## Top Lobby Spenders for 1955

| Organization | Total Amount Spent in 1955 |
|---|---|
| Natl. Assoc. of Electric Companies | $114,835.55 |
| American Federation of Labor | 114,079.74 |
| American Farm Bureau Federation | 113,610.00 |
| Congress of Industrial Organizations | 111,787.50 |
| Assoc. of American Railroads | 104,806.26 |
| Southern States Industrial Council | 100,244.64 |
| U. S. Cuban Sugar Council | 99,275.70 |
| Natl. Assoc. of Real Estate Boards | 93,801.89 |
| American Legion | 91,794.18 |
| Natl. Fed. of Post Office Clerks | 90,551.68 |
| General Gas Committee | 87,709.99 |
| Friends Committee on Natl. Legislation | 86,220.68 |
| Natl. Farmers Union | 82,648.34 |
| U. S. Savings & Loan League | 74,107.24 |
| Natl. Assoc. of Letter Carriers | 73,952.53 |
| Natl. Rural Electric Cooperative Assoc. | 73,234.52 |
| Council of State Chambers of Commerce | 71,367.33 |
| Colorado River Assoc. | 64,403.31 |
| Committee for Pipe Line Companies | 63,483.16 |
| Natl. Housing Conference | 62,711.48 |
| Public Information Committee of the Cotton Industries | 61,571.04 |
| American Medical Assoc. | 61,488.33 |
| Committee for Study of Revenue Bond Financing | 61,179.67 |
| Intl. Assoc. of Machinists | 59,748.61 |
| American Petroleum Institute | 54,564.00 |
| American Trucking Assocs., Inc. | 52,221.45 |
| Total | $2,125,398.82 |

Source: *Congressional Quarterly*, No. 6 (week ending Feb. 10, 1956), p. 137.

considerable influence in the Veterans' Administration. Close relationships are to be expected, but some regulatory agencies have been accused of having been captured by the very groups they are supposed to control—labor and the National Labor Relations Board during the New Deal, or the railroads and the Interstate Commerce Commission under various Republican as well as Democratic administrations.

*Lobbying and Public Opinion.* Lobbying, as we have seen, is no longer carried on only in committee rooms and legislative halls. Today the big money is spent on public opinion, in the hope that this most powerful force of all can be directed toward legislators and political executives. The National Association of Manufacturers spends more than $2 million a year in publishing separate periodicals for the nation's educators, for leaders of women's clubs, for farm leaders, and for clergymen. Motion pictures and a speakers' training program supplement the literature. In the halcyon 1920's, the National Electric Light Association (succeeded by the Edison Electric Institute) spent $20 million a year. Two other utility groups, in the early days of the New Deal, laid out more than a million dollars in a vain effort to defeat one bill. In more recent times, the American Medical Association spent a similar amount in its battle against national health insurance.

### Is Lobbying Bad?

At some point in its history, virtually every private interest group finds itself involved in the lobbying process. Some groups have existed for little else. Lobbying is an inevitable result of the First Amendment's protection of the right to petition. It is not only inevitable, however; it is useful. It is an instrument for apprising representative officials of the wants and fears of the citizen. We have already noted that public opinion is difficult for the politician to assess. We shall see in the next chapter that the political party tends to represent too many groups to be able to represent any one group adequately—at least from its point of view. (This inability is of course the national party's most impressive asset.) Between elections, at the operating level of government, lobbying in its broadest and best sense is simply the citizen approaching his government through a private group of his own choosing.

In the legislature, in addition, lobbyists provide much information to the harried representative submerged under thousands of bills and hundreds of issues; for the sympathetic legislator the lobbyists can serve as a good right arm in obtaining passage of a measure.

On the other hand, in both theory and practice, lobbying can and often does represent a genuine threat to effective democratic government. In the first place, the pressures of private interest groups tend to limit still further the average legislator's parochial viewpoint. Instead of keeping his eye on the national interest, the typical Congressman is apt to concentrate much of his energy on furthering the private interests of his own constituents, a practice which is eagerly cultivated by the interest groups which stand to benefit.

*Lobbying and Small Groups.* Furthermore, not all Americans are equally represented by lobbyists in what has been termed the "third house" of the legislature. Most people do not belong to influential organizations, and do not benefit except indirectly from their membership in an organization that participates in the lobbying process. Certain segments of society such as Indians, itinerant farm workers, and unorganized labor have been notoriously underrepresented and have suffered the consequences. As one recent report phrased it, "Each state has a medical society, often very potent, but try to find a patients' association." [4] Furthermore, the citizen's interests as a consumer are rarely protected by interest groups; as a matter of fact, the citizen as consumer is the target for and the victim of much of the lobbying work done by private interest groups. There has never been an effective consumer group, for the simple reason that citizens play so many other roles in life of more immediate interest than their role as consumer that no consumer group could remain intact on any single important issue. If the consumer is to have an effective voice as consumer he must turn to the ballot rather than the pressure group.

Another charge which can be levied against lobbies is that effective policy-making power in many organizations is concentrated in the hands of an inner circle composed of a few leaders buttressed by a professional staff and virtually immune to the crosscurrents of opinion of the membership at large. Safely ensconced behind bylaws and customs which make it difficult for dissenters to force any change, the top leadership of giant organizations can exert substantial influence at the highest levels of government with a minimum of responsibility to their own membership and even less to the welfare of the nation.

## Theory of Countervailing Power

In an effort to minimize the potential threat to our democratic institutions posed by private interest groups, some observers have framed a theory of "countervailing" power which holds that since most group struggles are competitive, interests tend to cancel out each other's influence. In certain fields this is undoubtedly true: labor competes with business on more or less equal terms over labor-management relations issues, for example, and on occasion the two groups fight to a draw. But in many cases this is not true. On many important issues great lobbies seek to combine with other great lobbies to form an irresistible force. Labor and management may cooperate in opposing tariff reductions—at the expense of the unorganized consumer. In its campaign to oppose national health insurance, the skilled legislative practitioners of the American Medical Association built up substantial support from such other potent organizations as the American Legion, the American Farm Bureau Federation, the United States Chamber of Commerce, and the American Bar Association. By the time the operation was finished, little countervailing power was left and the health insurance measure was dead. Lobbyists lobbying other lobbyists is a common practice which has become an art second only to that of lobbying in legislative halls and agency anterooms.

There is no reason to suppose that the big private organizations and groups in our society—moral as they may profess to be—would operate for long in the public interest without the regulatory powers and restraining influences of government. Dangers occur when the government itself finds it politically expedient not to "countervail"—especially since government in some cases is the only defender of the interests of the inarticulate and the unorganized in society.

## Control of Lobbying

It was only a little over a decade ago that Congress first took official recognition of lobbying and passed a law on the subject. Under Title III of the Legislative Reorganization Act of 1946, organizations and individuals seeking to influence Congress are required to register their names, sources of income, and how the money is spent. Since lobbying is protected under the Constitution, however, the law makes no effort to regulate lobbying activities. Even the limited provisions of the law cannot be enforced, for no

The map above shows the principal economic interests of various areas of the nation. It also serves as a pictorial guide to the homegrounds of some of the nation's most influential pressure groups, which have formed around the various producing groups scattered across the land. (Freely adapted from *The Reporter*, Vol. I, No. 11, Sept. 13, 1949, pp. 26–27.)

enforcement agency is provided. As a result many organizations do not file and others submit only partial information.

Weakening the law still further, the Supreme Court has held that it applies only to direct legislative lobbying, not to activities designed to influence the public.

## Lobbying and the Legislator

No study of private interest groups and lobbying would be complete without a discussion of the role played by the major object of all this effort and expense: the legislator. Although the average legislator represents a mixed district containing constituents with many interests the average Congressman or Senator or state legislator frequently leans toward only a few key interest groups. It should occasion no surprise that a Senator from Kansas is especially friendly to the representative of a farm organization, or that a Congressman from Gary works closely with officers of the United Steelworkers of America. The question remains, however, How friendly, and how closely?

In many cases, the acquaintanceship and the cooperation is so close as to put the legislator among the ranks of lobbyists himself. There are few lobbyists on Capitol Hill who cannot count on the support of at least one legislator. On some issues, it is hard to tell the legislator from the lobbyist. On certain controversial issues, such as public housing, the struggle appears to be between opposing private interest groups, marshalling their legislators and throwing them into battle.

It is no surprise, therefore, to find that former Congressmen have a habit of staying in Washington, after their service is over, and becoming lobbyists themselves. In 1955, fifty-three former members of the House and thirteen former United State Senators had registered as lobbyists. Under congressional rules, former members have one great advantage over their fellow lobbyists: they are entitled to enter the House or Senate chamber itself.

### Lobbying and the Administration

Dwarfing the lobbying efforts of private interest groups and of Congressmen are the legislative activities of the administration. When the President of the United States picks up his telephone to call a recalcitrant senatorial member of his party, or when a division head in a government agency trudges to Capitol Hill to testify against a pending bill, they are indulging in lobbying. This, of course, is not the work of private interest groups, but it is of concern here largely because government agencies will often work with such groups to advance or oppose a bill. During the great annual debates over the extension of federal rent control after the end of World War II, for example, housing groups could depend on substantial assistance—usually given unofficially—from certain government housing agencies.

### Interest Groups and Political Parties

Almost all private interest groups claim to be non-political. Actually, most of them are political; what they really mean is that they are non-partisan. Even organized labor, which is openly political and usually has Democratic leanings, has advanced under the banner of Samuel Gompers' famous dictum of non-partisanship, "reward our friends, punish our enemies."

It is probably inevitable that organizations which have spent eleven months of the year in seeking to influence elected representatives will approach the twelfth month, the one before election day, with both bitter and happy memories of legislative records and some desire to do something about them. Most of this election activity occurs at the local level with little national direction. Members of a city chamber of commerce may pass the hat in behalf of a friendly incumbent Congressman, while members of the local AFL-CIO central council will ring doorbells for his opponent. Interest groups are represented behind the scenes, too. The candidate himself probably belongs to several interest groups, as does his campaign manager and his principal supporters. Occasionally they all belong to the same organization, and then he may become known as a labor candidate, or a candidate of big business. Usually the relationship is subtler, but after election day the particular pressure group will be able to count on a reliable friend in Congress.

Some pressure groups support both candidates in an election, in hope that they will be remembered with fondness by the winner, whoever he may be. This is particularly common in one-party states, where the primary result determines the election and all candidates are members of the same party.

One of the most effective methods of lobbying is face-to-face contact between a Congressman and his constituents, brought together, usually, by a private-interest group. Below, a small delegation of union members discuss pending labor legislation with their Congressman in his office.

### Lobbying through Election Activities

The most politically active of private interest organizations at election time is the AFL-CIO, which through its Committee on Political Education seeks to encourage labor participation in the political life of the nation. Full-time field representatives stimulate registration and get-out-the-vote campaigns and organize political action institutes, while the national headquarters produces research reports and copious quantities of literature. Labor leaders are frequently divided in their support, however, and some eschew political activity entirely. As a result, labor's effectiveness at the polls, except in a few areas, is questionable.

Organized business groups make up in money what they lack in numbers, but again their success is spotty.

In the past, an occasional private interest group has given up in despair on both major parties and has attempted to form a third party. The American Labor party and the Liberal party in New York were originally founded by labor unions and their supporters. The Prohibition and the Vegetarian parties are still in existence, although rarely on any ballot. Such parties are usually a passing phenomenon, short-lived and unimportant.

## ARE INTEREST GROUPS GOOD FOR THE COUNTRY?

It would be hard to find an official of a private interest group who did not sincerely believe that the objectives of his organization were consonant with the public welfare. The textile manufacturer calls for higher tariffs against Japanese imports in the belief that his industry is necessary to the economic health of the nation, and the textile workers' union may join hands with the manufacturer on a journey to Washington to take their case to the House Ways and Means Committee. Home builders complain that federally sponsored housing is an unwarranted governmental interference in our private economy, while doctors oppose government health insurance as a threat to our nation's pattern of private medicine.

Opposing these groups are others who are confident that they, too, are fighting on behalf of the general welfare. The Committee for a National Trade Policy battles the textile industry in order, it says, to combat a general rise in tariff barriers which would cripple free trade and the world's economy. Urban housing authorities testify against the home builders to the effect that only federally-financed housing will overcome a critical shortage of dwellings, while organized labor fights the AMA in the belief that middle-income workers will never receive adequate health care without a national system of insurance.

Far below the surface are the thousands of individuals and groups who are looking for much less out of government. The typical lobbyist represents not the fourteen-million-member AFL-CIO or the thousands of retailers affiliated with the NRDGA, but a single construction company looking for an appropriation for a federal highway on which it can place a bid, or a Polish fraternal organization in Detroit pressing for changes in the immigration laws, or a milk-marketing agency in New Jersey interested in a three-sentence section of a farm bill.

Few of these organizations are consciously engaging in activity which would militate against the general welfare; rather they are each protecting and furthering their own interests in an intensely competitive society which takes pride in the accessibility of its government.

What is needed is not fewer private interest groups; any law limiting them would be unconstitutional, anyhow. What is needed is more public officials—legislators and administrators at all levels of government—who have the courage and the ability to exercise intelligent moral judgments in the public interest over the conflicting claims of private groups.

Such moral judgments constitute the real answer to any evils implicit in lobbying—although a strengthened lobby registration law and a more diffused method of financing political campaigns would undoubtedly work toward the same goal.

In the future, as the population increases and government continues to grow more complex, private interest organizations are bound to grow in size and influence. More and more they will direct their major efforts at the general public, in the knowledge that this is a *representative* democracy. This probability places an ultimate obligation on all citizens to search for the public interest and to resist the importunities of those who would use our instruments of government for selfish or limited purposes only.

The difficulty, of course, is that private and public interests are not easy to separate. Man is often more a rationalizing than a rational animal, and he has capacities both for highly selfish and highly altruistic actions. Furthermore, who is sufficiently skilled in the ethics and logic of events to deny definitively that the satisfaction of the desires of a particular private interest may not actually be in the public interest?

Yet with all these doubts, Americans hang on to the belief that a real distinction can, and often does, exist between the public interest and private interests—and that, in fact, the concept of a separate public interest is one of the great distillations of our heritage.

# CONCLUSION

### Synopsis

In our representative democracy, private interest groups are among the most important instruments available to the people to articulate their expectations of government. Most people who believe they have a claim on government seek to realize it through an organization. Interest groups span every occupation and industry as well as most nationalities and religions. They perform a variety of valuable functions in keeping each other in check and in keeping public officials informed of the impact, or possible impact, of public policies.

### Significance

The gentle art of lobbying is a legitimate and a necessary activity in a democracy. But it sometimes places an almost intolerable burden upon honest government officials seeking to develop policies in the national interest. This becomes increasingly true as interest groups grow in size, and as they consciously direct their major efforts at the general public. Fortunately, as James Madison pointed out many years ago, there is safety in the very plethora of interests in our big society. More important, the moral courage and intellectual acumen of our elected and appointed officials, and the homogenizing effect of our political parties, are our major guarantees that what Burke once called the "permanent forces" in the community will not be ignored.

## Prospectus

The greatest problem posed by interest-group activity is that it tends to confuse unduly what is necessarily confused anyway in a democratic society: public and private interests. In our democracy, as the next chapter attempts to demonstrate, some of the sting is taken out of what could become a poisonous confusion by our political parties—the most formalized of our political instruments.

## CHAPTER 12

# Political Parties

PARTIES are the supreme political instruments of American democracy.

They are also instruments of power and privilege for ambitious self-seekers. They are heart-warming devices for giving even the lowliest citizen a sense of identification with great men and great events. They are also purveyors of services for the scheming and the greedy. They are the great selectors of our leadership. They are also vehicles of corruption. They are our most effective channels for the formulation and presentation of great alternatives. They are also artful devices for the hiding of alternatives.

It is difficult under these circumstances to fashion an image of political parties which has any coherence. It is perhaps the supreme contribution of the man to whom this book is dedicated, Professor E. E. Schattschneider, that he more than any other political scientist in America has searched out the heart of American political parties and has seen with the eye of faith their remarkable promise—as fashioners of responsible majorities, as homogenizing agents of diverse group interests, as something more than sullen spiders of intrigue, spinning thousands of tiny and unrelated webs for the sole purpose of catching tawdry transient prizes.

American parties are in transition. The two chapters which follow attempt to paint an honest portrait of what they are presently like, how they operate, and what changes seem to be occurring which lend credence to Professor Schattschneider's optimism.

## Parties and the Constitution

No word can be found in the Constitution about political parties. Historians agree that this was no oversight but a deliberate omission, for many of the Founding Fathers, unhappily conscious of the history of factional disputes abroad, were hopeful of avoiding, in the words of the nation's first President, the "baneful effects of the spirit of party." Washington and many others feared that parties would be a divisive influence in our young and tender democracy, but some of his compatriots, such as James Madison, recognized that their rise would probably be inevitable. In actual fact, parties, in a rudimentary form at least, began to take shape before the end of Washington's second term.

Although they are not provided for in the Constitution, our major political parties function within the framework of our constitutional democracy. In other nations this is not necessarily true; there are parties in France, for example, that have promised if elected to power to change the form of government forthwith. In Germany in 1933 and in Italy earlier, such promises turned out to be no idle boasts, for the Italian Fascist party and the National Socialists in Germany, although elevated to power under approximately democratic conditions, promptly destroyed democratic government.

In the United States only the outlawed Communist party has taken issue with our constitutional regime; other political parties, no matter who their candidates or what their platforms, have accepted our framework of democratic government.

## How Many Parties

Since the Constitution makes no mention of parties, there is obviously no constitutional provision establishing two parties instead of three or four. Nevertheless, we have only two major parties, and we have always had but two.

Many factors have combined to produce a two-party system in America. In an important sense, our two-faction system is a product of our British heritage—particularly of the Restoration struggles between Tories and Whigs in the last half of the seventeenth century. In part, the Colonial struggle in many sections of eighteenth-century America between the seaboard, British-oriented, commercial and landed upper-class, and the frontier, small-farmer, debtor class produced a two-party faction mind-set. This evolved into the Federalist and the anti-Federalist split of the early days of our republic. Actually, the Jeffersonian cells—the "Democratic society" which developed in the 1790's to challenge the monopoly of the Federalist party —were probably the first party organizations worthy of the name in our history.

Our two-party system is due also to the quadrennial competition of winning the majority of electoral votes for the Presidency; and, at the local level, to the existence of constituencies from which only a single member can be chosen for certain important offices.

*Stability of Two-Party System.* The two-party system has played an important part in making this nation one of the most stable constitutional democracies in the world. Because there are only two parties, each one must necessarily embrace a wide variety of groups and ideas, and, within this embrace, the sharp edges and disrupting conflicts of different groups or sections tend to be worn down in the common quest for electoral victory. Interest groups which in another nation might charge boldly into the political arena, nominating and electing candidates, writing platforms and seeking to capture government for special purposes, in the United States seek to have their private interests adopted by a political party—or by both political parties. Since the political party is mainly dedicated to the task of capturing as many votes as possible, it normally will not embrace such a private interest until it is convinced that a majority of voters will not be outraged in the process.

Thus the two-party system is a force both for moderation and for unity. In addition, since parties tend to have a long life in the United States, they also provide a vital connecting link with the past. Finally, since only one party can control the administration at any one time, the nation has benefited—notwithstanding serious shortcomings—from considerably more party responsibility than could ever be provided by the coalition-type government found in nations with multi-party systems.

*Minor Parties.* Despite the evident permanence of our two-party system, American history is littered with the debris of minor parties. In some states they may be found on the ballot today. Minor parties, to a greater extent than their big brethren, combine the functions of pressure group and political party. They normally have grown around a controversial issue which the major parties have been unwilling to resolve. Some are little more than pressure groups designed primarily to promote one issue, such as the Prohibition, Greenback, or Free Soil parties. Some are real parties, interested in replacing existing parties, usually on a regional basis, such as the recently defunct American Labor party and the Liberal party in New York, or the Farmer-Labor party in Minnesota. A few have considered themselves as class parties, such as the Communist, which until its demise, took its orders from another country.

None of these parties has risen above the minor leagues, largely because of their single-mindedness and failure to appeal to a suf-

ficiently wide cross-section of the nation. A few have won temporary success, such as the Populists, who in the 1880's were electing
governors and congressmen by the score, at which time the major
parties, performing a traditional function, adopted most of the
populist program.

Today, because of the legal barriers erected in most states designed to hinder third party candidates from getting on the ballot,
it would be a virtual impossibility for a third party to achieve success on a nation-wide scale. And in their decline, private interest
groups are taking over their functions to an increasing extent.

Despite the proliferation of minor parties, minor-party candidates
have had a chance of victory in only two presidential elections since
1800: in 1824, when only one party survived as an effective force;
and in 1912, when Theodore Roosevelt ran on the Bull Moose ticket.
Robert LaFollette, on the Progressive ticket in 1924, garnered the
highest number of votes of any third-party candidate, but won the
electoral votes of only one state.

Even though they have never produced a President, minor parties
have had a sizable influence on American political life in promoting
issues that the major parties felt were too hot to handle. Some of our
proudest governmental achievements can be traced to the heroic and
at the time seemingly futile efforts of minor and now largely forgotten third-party movements.

Considering the changes that have occurred during the 175 years of our nation's
existence, our political parties have remained surprisingly stable, as the chart
below demonstrates. (Adapted from "Here We Go Again," Time, Inc. Copy-
right, 1956.)

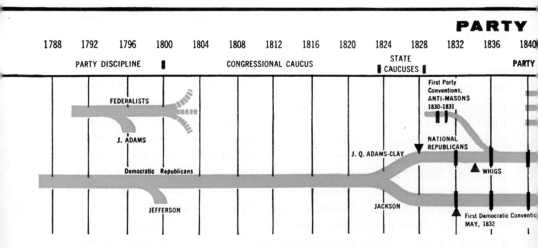

**PARTY**

| 1788 | 1792 | 1796 | 1800 | 1804 | 1808 | 1812 | 1816 | 1820 | 1824 | 1828 | 1832 | 1836 | 1840 |

PARTY DISCIPLINE     CONGRESSIONAL CAUCUS     STATE CAUCUSES     PARTY

FEDERALISTS

First Party Conventions, ANTI-MASONS 1830-1831

J. ADAMS

NATIONAL REPUBLICANS

J. Q. ADAMS-CLAY

Democratic Republicans

WHIGS

JEFFERSON

JACKSON

First Democratic Convention MAY, 1832

## One-Party States

What happens in areas or at levels of government where there is only one effective party, or none at all? In a number of states—in the South, in New England, and elsewhere—one of the two parties has established such a stranglehold on political life that the other party often does not take the trouble to nominate candidates for many offices. In some states the result has been a disintegration of the party in power; candidates for office compete with each other within the framework of the party. In a state such as Mississippi, where the Democratic party has no opposition to serve as a binder for its different factions, effective party control is vested in popular individuals and in local organizations, known as courthouse "rings." Here one-party politics in theory has led to multi-party politics in practice. In other states, such as Virginia, the party leadership at the state level is more firmly entrenched and party discipline more accepted at the local level. Here one-party politics has led to a monolithic pattern of power in state elections—although not in national elections.

## Nonpartisanship

At the other extreme, in some 16 states and in the majority of cities of over 5,000 population, in contests for judicial office, nonpartisan elections have driven the traditional political parties off the ballot. Nonpartisanship on the local level is the result of a wave

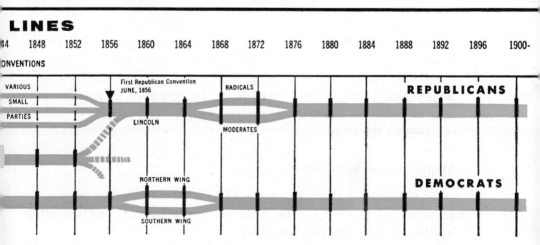

**LINES**

| 44 | 1848 | 1852 | 1856 | 1860 | 1864 | 1868 | 1872 | 1876 | 1880 | 1884 | 1888 | 1892 | 1896 | 1900- |

ONVENTIONS

VARIOUS
SMALL
PARTIES

First Republican Convention
JUNE, 1856

RADICALS

**REPUBLICANS**

LINCOLN

MODERATES

NORTHERN WING

**DEMOCRATS**

SOUTHERN WING

of revulsion against bossism and corruption in municipal party organizations around the turn of the century. Its proponents argue that since there is little relationship between city and state issues on the one hand, and national issues on the other, nonpartisanship helps to prevent municipal issues from being submerged under wider issues of greater importance. Other advantages are supposed to be a diminution of patronage and spoils, greater opportunity for civic reform, and a chance for voter competition in one-party areas. In some areas, where one party domination has led to corruption, nonpartisanship has been useful in breaking the stranglehold and encouraging decent government.

On the other hand, opponents of nonpartisanship point out that many city issues are in fact entwined with state and national issues, and the official ban on parties merely camouflages the usual party jockeying. On the whole, while not a panacea for the ills of local government, in some areas nonpartisan elections have served a useful purpose.

# WHAT POLITICAL PARTIES DO

### General Functions

The principal function of political parties—and the one to which all its other activities are keyed—is the nomination and election of candidates. In the process of attempting this goal, parties help in the popularization and sometimes the polarization of issues of vast consequence to our future. The political parties perform other services: they serve as humanizing intermediaries between levels of government (local and state, and state and national); and between branches of government (legislative and executive); they provide a rallying point and mediating service for pressure groups; they help educate and interest citizens in the processes of government; and, when out of office, they provide an alternative of men and often of issues to the in-party.

### Mediators and Stabilizers

That many of these functions or by-products are not always evident in practice should not blind us to the realities and the possibilities of dedicated party activity.

Certainly one of the happiest functions of party activity, and one which is observable in every major campaign, is that of mediating and moderating among men of strong will and intense belief. Both parties have shunned extremism on most issues (largely because most voters are not extremists), and in the process the parties have done much to prevent the polarization of opposing groups. Deadly battles may be fought out within the ranks of the party, but at election time it is usual for all sides to bury the hatchet inside the party and turn smiling faces toward the electorate. Although extremists exist in both parties, they are generally absorbed as they find it expedient to modify their positions.

This contribution to the stability of our democracy cannot be overemphasized; for when opposite sides take extreme positions there is always the danger, as one British statesman put it, that the "nation may not be so fundamentally at one that it can safely afford to bicker." Such a situation has developed only once in our national history—in 1860. The Civil War cost us a half million dead.

For all that is said ruefully about the integrity, intelligence, and courage of the men who make our parties run, the politician deserves a mighty salute for his ability to mediate among opposing forces. Without such mediation, violence would often be inevitable.

## Parties and Upward Mobility

One of the most significant but little recognized contributions of our political parties has been their service as ladders of upward mobility for ethnic, racial, and religious minorities. For many individuals from minority groups, political party activity has offered a way to advancement and influence in the community long before private industry or social organizations have opened their doors. In most areas, furthermore, the principal source of relief to a minority group suffering from economic or social oppression, is the political party, which recognizes the value of a vote despite the complexion or accent of the person casting it.

## The Party Hierarchy

Political parties do not rest upon a substantial base of active membership. Political party members pay no dues, fulfill no responsibilities, and assume no specific functions. Furthermore, party members may switch membership frequently (in most areas, an opportunity is available every time the citizen registers to vote in a primary election); and he may vote with impunity for candidates of the opposite party in a general election.

In sum, most Americans who vote belong to a political party, but most party members do not participate in the work of the party.

*Precinct Leaders.* The lowest level of party activity, therefore, is not the membership but the bottom rung of the official hierarchy. The occupant of this humble station may be known as a district leader (New York), a division worker (Philadelphia), a block leader (Alabama) or by several other names, according to the name of the smallest electoral district in the state. The most common name is the precinct worker and most precinct workers are members of a village, town, city and/or county committee, which makes them committeemen and women as well.

In past eras, the precinct worker was the principal link between the party and the people, a man who did favors, found jobs, interceded with judges and handed out financial favors at election time —in return for votes.

Today the old time type of precinct worker is becoming extinct. Merit systems of appointment have cut deeply into the patronage that maintained his loyalty; radio, television, movies and a nonpartisan press are replacing his function as a propagandist; scientific polls have replaced him as a source of information; tighter election laws and voting machines in many areas have restricted election day activities; and the political job which once supported the precinct worker is no longer attractive in a time of high factory wages. Precinct operations involving close acquaintanceship with the voters are particularly difficult in areas of rapid population change, which would include vast sections of the United States, such as the growing suburbs surrounding large cities.

But precinct leaders there still are, and they perform valuable functions—not so much in expounding the issues, which is usually done better by the press, but in stimulating registration and voting. In many areas, however, even this very important job has been taken over by such organizations as the League of Women Voters, Chambers of Commerce, labor unions, and other private groups acting in cooperation with the press, television, and radio stations. A careful study in Elmira, New York, during the 1948 campaign, showed that precinct or other party workers contacted only a quarter of the voters, largely by mail. The study also showed that personal contact had little effect on opinion, but that it did help stimulate registration and voting.[1]

*Ward and County Leaders.* The pattern of local political organization varies in different states, but the average precinct worker, where he exists, serves in an area containing 250 to 1000 voters. The next level of leadership in urban areas may be the ward from which city council members are chosen, or the state legislative district, from which members of the State House of Representatives are elected. Above this level is the county (in rural areas the county is directly above the precinct), and in most areas it is at the county level that the greatest power of political parties lies. The average county leader has considerable independence from the leaders at higher levels—state and national—and considerable control in the selection of leaders at the lower level. Although the county leader himself is formally elected by the ward leaders underneath (or the precinct workers in their alternate role of county committeemen), the election usually merely ratifies the choice of a few powerful sub-chieftains.

One measure of the strength of a political party is the depth and extent of its county organizations. Both parties boast strong county groups in the Northeastern states, whereas county organizations are few and far between in the West. The Democrats can claim some degree of organization in 2500 of the nation's 3050 counties, ranging from close-knit groups in such urban areas as Cook County (Chicago) and Hudson County (Jersey City) to mere skeleton groups, such as in Maine and Vermont. Because of the absence of strong Republican organizations in more than a dozen southern states, the Republican party can only claim power in 2000 counties. Its greatest influence tends to be in suburban areas.

# NATIONAL POLITICAL PARTIES

If the county leaders, collectively, retain most of the power to choose state-wide candidates and to select the principal election issues, nevertheless they must depend to some extent on patronage and favors emanating from the statehouse or the state party chairman. Traditionally, the real leadership break has lain between the state party organization and national headquarters. Until recently the latter has had little power and virtually no independence. In effect, the national political party has for most of our history been little more than a federation of state parties, and only when the party's leader has been President of the United States has the national party headquarters retained its place in the chain of authority.

There is substantial evidence to show, however, that in recent years the national headquarters of the two major parties have grown enormously in power and prestige. As Paul David has written,

Both parties now maintain strong and increasingly professional headquarters staffs at the nation's capitol, whether in power or out; this is a change that has come within the last generation. The national committee chairmanship has been taking on a new kind of importance in American political life; and this again is a sign of increasing emphasis upon the organizational aspects of political activity at the top of the party structure.[2]

Whereas once a political party could claim to have a semblance of permanent unity only at the state level, we are increasingly justified in referring to our *national* political parties.

### National Committee

Organizationally speaking, the national political party is run by a national committee which consists of a male and female representative from each state. The national committee, in turn, chooses the party chairman.

The committee itself seldom meets, but it is a symbol of internal party democracy, and many of its individual members are political powers in their respective states. The chairman of the national committee is in effect the chairman of the party as a whole.

Although the position of party chairman has increased in prestige and power in recent years, there is still truth to the description offered by Cabell Phillips:

His authority is limited and he must make common cause with a great variety of individual satraps and satrapies. . . . Lacking effective disciplinary powers, he must rely upon diplomacy and the subtle arts of leadership to weld his confederacy into a unified striking force.[3]

The power of the national chairman is of course enormously strengthened if his party controls the administration. Under these circumstances, the party chairman's function at election time is to publicize and defend the President's record, and encourage state and local leaders to do the same, at least insofar as their sectional preferences and prejudices will allow.

For the party defeated at the polls, a tug of war is apt to follow between the last presidential candidate, called the titular leader, and the party leaders in Congress. They seldom agree on all issues and some of these disagreements are not settled until four years later at the succeeding party convention.

*Special Campaign Committees.* At election time, much official party machinery is supplanted by *ad hoc* organizations established by the candidate, in part at least, to sidestep the legal limitations on the financing of campaigns. The presidential candidate will organize his own campaign cabinet; the gubernatorial or congressional candidate will create some kind of campaign committee and in extreme cases may ignore completely the regular party organization. Meanwhile special committees, to promote relations with farmers or unions or the foreign born, are hastily put together, and each party seeks to gather a committee of dissident members of the opposite party to support their candidate. In the intensity of its activity, organized labor is especially potent in election campaigns in a few areas, and some party candidates in heavily unionized communities may depend more on union campaign machinery than on their own party organization.

## Behind the Scenes

After having studied the official hierarchy of a national political party, the realistic student would do well to forget much of what he has learned. For notwithstanding an apparently foolproof organizational chart, the real locus of power in a political party will center around those whose resources and ability have made it possible for them to capture control. In some areas real political power may be exercised by a giant corporation or a large labor union or a farm organization. In other areas a governor or mayor or county executive may have built up a personal following which is impervious to the attempted inroads of formally elected party leaders. In one state, a county leader whose name rarely makes the front page may in reality call the tune to which the state party dances, while in another an industrialist with large financial resources may pay the fiddler.

It is difficult for the observer to locate the locus of power because it is constantly shifting, and there are always subterranean movements of unnamed forces seeking to capture it. Although some state parties have a high degree of political unity, many state organizations are heavily divided—between upstate and downstate, city and country, lowlands and plateau, or river valley and mountain. Even many

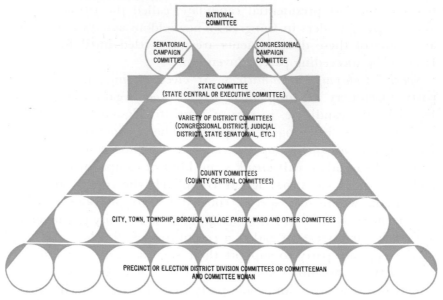

The organization charts of our two major parties are similar, but they give a misleading picture of the true source of authority, which may often lie somewhere near the middle of the hierarchy, rather than at the top (or bottom).

counties are split in this fashion, and in each division there are different party goals and conflicting party issues and entrenched leadership battling for dominance.

*Parties, Politics, and Money.* The only permanent factor in politics is the need for money. Merely to maintain the national headquarters staff during off years costs each party about one million dollars annually, while the cost of political campaigns is many times that figure. One estimate fixed the total cost to both parties of national, state and local election campaigns in 1952 at about 150 million dollars. On this basis, 1956 cost the parties about 200 million dollars. A senatorial campaign in a major state will cost not less than $150,000 and often will run as high as $500,000. The average congressman in a closely contested district will have to raise $25,000 for his campaign.

Where does the money come from? Both parties receive the bulk of their resources in the form of large gifts from a few major sources. Republicans get much of their money from bankers, brokers, manufacturers, utilities, insurance companies, mining and oil interests. Democrats receive contributions from brewers and distillers, contractors, builders, the professions, merchants, the entertainment industries and organized labor. These are rough categories only; some manufacturers, bankers, and brokers are Democrats and many professional men contribute to the G.O.P. A few wealthy families enrich political coffers by huge amounts: in 1956 the Du Ponts gave more than $85,000, the Mellons, $99,000, and the Rockefellers, $100,000, to the Republican party or to campaign committees. Labor unions in 1954 spent more than $2 million in the midterm elections, mostly in behalf of Democratic candidates.

The candidates themselves in many cases spend a considerable amount for their own election campaigns—it is not unknown for a wealthy would-be officeholder to obtain the nomination on the promise to invest a substantial sum in party activities, including his own campaign. Another source of political income is government workers, who, although under federal law and similar laws in most states cannot be solicited, are permitted to donate voluntarily. The line between soliciting contributions, and receiving voluntary contributions, is a difficult one to follow, however, and in many states and cities the law does little to hinder fund-raising among civil employees.

The last and least important source of funds is the average citizen. Only a small percentage of party members feel the impulse to contribute to the organization of their choice, and their small donations are cherished by party leaders mostly as symbols of party loyalty and activity.

*Limitations on Contributions.* Under the Federal Corrupt Practices Act of 1925, amended by the Hatch Act of 1939, the individual is barred from giving more than $5,000 to any single candidate or committee. This is easily bypassed by wealthy contributors, who can send in their gifts under the names of other members of their family, and by candidates, who can set up several different committees. Political campaign costs themselves are limited by law: presidential candidates are not supposed to spend more than three million dollars, senatorial candidates more than $10,000, and congressional candidates more than $2,500. But the limits are so unrealistic in the light of today's costs that candidates have perforce found numerous ways to evade the strictures of the law. Neither corporations nor labor unions are supposed to give directly to campaigns for federal office; both do by employing a number of devices to avoid detection or direct violation.

*The Effect of Money.* Ineffective laws and unwilling party members have led to the dependence of parties on a relatively few wealthy individuals or politically conscious groups. This in itself is not necessarily corrupting. One observer has pointed out, however, that "a man has to be a very humble person indeed to fork over tens of thousands of dollars to a political group and not acquire at least a little feeling of possessiveness." [4] Whether an individual signs a large check directly over to a political party, or whether a private interest group spends large sums independently in behalf of a candidate, the effect is to give the donor a vested interest in the officeholder which in some form or other is usually repaid. Direct corruption, at least at the federal level, is comparatively rare. The greater problem of party financing is akin to the problem presented by interest groups: the candidate's dependence on a few large contributors narrows his freedom of thought and action, and increases his insularity. It would be normally difficult for the Senator from a farm state to vote against a bill favorable to farm interests, if only because he might offend powerful interest groups back home and thus endanger his chances of re-election. The difficulty is compounded if his vote will also cut him off from his principal campaign contributors. The average legislator is, to some extent, faced by such a decision on every vote, and so is the elected administrative official every time he lets a contract or issues an administrative ruling.

Since the turn of the century there have been proposals, which are echoing again today, to appropriate government funds to pay for election expenses. The obvious danger of injecting the government into so sensitive an activity has so far deterred any legislation in this direction. Other voices have been raised to tighten laws surrounding political contributions, to lift spending limits to more realistic levels, to eliminate loopholes and provide enforcement. Some of these proposals may become law, but so long as the average member absents himself when his party passes the hat, legislation will not alter the present pattern of fund-raising.

Without question, the most fruitful proposal for raising the level of political morality in America has been made by Philip Graham, publisher of the *Washington Post and Times-Herald:* an annual, nation-wide campaign to secure widespread popular contributions for our political parties—thereby relieving the parties themselves and individual candidates from dependence upon a few "fat cats."

## BOSSES AND PATRONAGE IN TRANSITION

Edwin O'Connor's novel, *The Last Hurrah,* is an epitaph not only to a famous New England political boss, but in a sense to all party bosses everywhere. For this noted American landmark, so long typified in story and cartoon, is slowly changing or passing from the scene altogether. Many bosses built their political power on the services they performed for the hordes of immigrants landing on American shores before the 1920's; today legislation has reduced immigration to a trickle, and the immigrants' children are doctors or rising young businessmen. The growth of labor unions has also contributed to the demise of the boss, for with unionization came greater job security and an outlet for political ambitions for once downtrodden workers. The expansion of federal services, such as unemployment and workmen's compensation and old-age pensions, has deprived the political boss of further services which he could offer his clientele—although a few modern bosses have exploited these services to help cement their machines. One of the functions of the boss was to provide an easy entrance to government for the voter who wanted a favor or a job. Today many political jobs are covered by civil service regulations, and municipal government has been generally simplified and centralized, making it easier for the citizen to find his way around himself. Finally, our higher standard of living and broader educational opportunities have changed the average voter, especially in the city, from a docile and unknowing unit in the machine to an independent and reasonably well-informed citizen. The reformer of yesteryear, usually a temporarily outraged member of the upper classes who seldom could stick on the political firing line for more than a year or two, has been replaced by the ambitious young lawyer or community-conscious housewife who, once in politics, cannot be fazed or forced out by political bosses.

One of the most dramatic examples is the change that has overtaken Tammany Hall, the New York County (Manhattan) Democratic organization. Under such luminaries of the past as Tweed and Croker, Tammany Hall became the prototype of political machines, dedicated largely to the enrichment of its leaders and the perpetuation of power by fair means or foul. Today the Tammany Tiger is a changed animal. It still retains much of the atmosphere of the machine, but under the artful leadership of men like Carmine De Sapio room has been found for the independent-minded intellectual; a professor of law has even been elected a ward leader.

## The Contemporary Boss

The modern political boss has a different job to do than his ancestor. Instead of finding jobs for voters' relatives and easing the processes of naturalization for immigrants, he must produce effective candidates and publicize winning issues. The boss of today is a man like the late Edward Flynn of the Bronx Democratic organization, a sophisticated individual who built his machine like a corporation and even found places for Republicans in its ranks; or like J. Russell Sprague in Nassau County, Long Island, who has welded a wealthy suburban county into a Republican stronghold. Perhaps the best-known machine in the nation is managed by Senator Harry Byrd in Virginia. The Democratic organization he has established has been labeled "the most urbane and genteel dictatorship in America." [5]

In most states, however, few voters know the name of the boss, and generally his control is incomplete. The true boss, who years ago ruled only through his control of the party machinery, beyond the powers of any public office, is a rarity. Perhaps the strongest machines today can be found in rural areas, where their power is rendered less noticeable because there are fewer people and less money at stake. They may be centered on a rural courthouse or a country store, and their influence is inflated by the over-representation of rural areas in the state legislature. As a result, the state funds dispensed by rural machines usually come from the under-represented city taxpayer (see Chapter 25).

## Patronage

One of the foundations on which the old-time boss and the modern leader build their strength is patronage. The knowledge that a government job is available will often serve to harden, beyond any other factor, the political loyalty of an active partisan. As the Irishman is supposed to have said in New York, "For me soul, I go to church. To take care of me body, I join the Athletic Association. But to keep body n' soul together, I join Tammany Hall." [6]

Patronage is the parcelling out of government positions to those who have given their support to the party in power. Such support

The old-time machines did steal blatantly and openly. They had the Robin Hood attitude that it was O.K. to take things from the rich to give to the poor, with a percentage of the take for operating expenses and a good time for the boys. These days are gone, possibly forever.

—Warren Moscow

may have consisted of many years of substantial contributions, which may be worth an ambassadorship, or it may have been loyal service as a precinct leader, which may be worth an appointment to the police department for a relative. Patronage is one of the coins of the realm of politics, for party officials receive as much patronage from the level above as they have weight in party circles, and their power over their inferiors may be in proportion to the amount of patronage they can dispense.

Patronage does not necessarily mean the appointment of inferior officials, either as ambassadors or as policemen, for the average party organization is enhanced by good appointments and seeks to avoid scandal. Today, in fact, many party leaders regard patronage as a troublesome and overrated factor in building political organizations. With each appointment, so goes the saying, the party leader makes 99 enemies and one ingrate.

## Spoils

The other side of the coin of patronage is spoils, which is the dispensing of political favors to active partisans. Spoils may be found at the local level when a building code violation by a favored contractor is overlooked by an inspector or when fire and health inspectors ignore the deficiencies of a real estate development. On the national level spoils may be reflected in a negotiated contract or in the influence of a "five-percenter," a political fixer who sells his services to companies wishing to do business with the government for five percent of the worth of the contract. Spoils are present to a certain extent in every unit of government; excessive spoils may lead to inefficient government, scandal and defeat at the polls. An alert opposition party and a conscientious press are the best antidotes.

# CAN POLITICAL PARTIES BE IMPROVED?

Some critics of our parties attack their inability to take a stand on controversial issues and to carry through their promises after their candidates have won office. The goal of most recent proposals is summed up in two words—party responsibility—which would shift party power from the county or state level to the national level and make it possible for each party to follow a rationalized and identified path without turning to extremes. Among the tools suggested to accomplish this end are: (1) a party platform prepared in advance of the quadrennial nominating convention by a representative group of party leaders—binding on all candidates; (2) the selection of National Committees by the convention to insure better representation; (3) the elimination of the seniority rule and the filibuster in Congress (see below, pages 276, 383) ; and (4) greater use of caucuses, binding on legislators of each party.[7]

Defenders of the present party system fear that centralized parties might lead to bossism on a national level and government by direct majority rule, whereas much of our constitutional edifice is founded on a belief in rule by consensus in which majority rule is strained through a series of baffles. Furthermore, it is feared that centralized parties would destroy—or be destroyed by—the sectional prejudices of state and local organizations. For example, it is difficult to imagine the Democratic parties of the Southern states accepting as binding a civil rights platform written solely by the majority Democrats of the North.

But most important issues confronting the nation in the middle of the twentieth century are not regional or local in nature—they are nation-wide and world-wide. Their solution calls increasingly for the mobilization of responsible majorities that can make themselves felt —particularly in the behavior of our parties in the Congress.

The institutions of government in our society have been built by men and they can be changed and adapted by men. Responsible parties need not be monolithic; in fact, they cannot be in a pluralistic-federal society such as ours. But surely there is reason to believe that the nationalization of American politics—going on before our eyes— will, with the help of imaginative leadership, produce a national party system that will allow for intraparty diversity and compromise, but in the end will enforce an increased measure of party discipline based upon majority rule. To deny this chance or this hope is to select for deification every force and institution in our history which has found itself in a strategic position to promote an irresponsible system of "minority rule and majority rights," rather than the fundamental (even if paradoxical) expectation of democracy, "majority rule and minority rights." Parties need not disagree on everything in order to be responsible; but when party majorities *do* disagree, the voting public should have a more meaningful chance than at present to vote for one or the other. Otherwise, political accountability has little meaning, and the public develops a dangerously cynical belief that politics is nothing but a razzle-dazzle shell game of banter, barter, and booty.

# CONCLUSION

## Synopsis

Parties are evolving as responsible instruments of national power —even though the evolution is slower than many of us wish. But even while lacking formal means of insuring political accountability, our two-party system and the people who man it have been key instruments of our democracy. They have helped modify institutions that might have grown rigid; they have brought compromise when issues might otherwise have been solved only through force; they have afforded an outlet for those whose energies and ambitions had been otherwise frustrated; they have released new visions and defined new programs in the interest of larger rather than smaller segments of the population. They have provided alternative candidates and issues—keeping the political options of a free society alive.

## Significance

In the atomic era, when America's responsibilities are to the world, our need is not for fewer politicians but for more: for men and women who have skills of leadership and conciliation, and who can see through the superficial and sometimes tawdry scrim to the promise of American politics. Political parties are vastly significant and, in general, highly moral enterprises without which democracy as we know it could not survive. The need now is to make them more responsible instruments of national policy.

## Prospectus

The climax of political activity in a free society is election day. The ultimate political instrument of the American people is the ballot. Elections, consequently, are the subject of the next and final chapter in this Section.

## CHAPTER 13

# Elections

IF MOST MEANINGFUL party activity takes place behind closed doors, the ultimate goal of all party activity—elections—is carried on in full view. Not entirely, of course, for behind the written platforms, the election leaflets, television speeches, and motorcades lie planning, conferences, and hard work. But compared to off-year political party activities, elections, in the words of two veteran observers, have "all the glitter of a Hollywood first night, all the suspense of a Conan Doyle detective story, and the drama . . . of a major military battle. . . ." [1] Since approximately one million officials are elected annually, election campaigns are not a rare experience for the average American, at least in his role as a voter. And since it is the voter who is the arbiter of these military battles, he is the one who must be examined first.

## WHO VOTES—OR DOESN'T VOTE

Under the original constitutional document, all voting qualifications were left to the states. Four amendments have since modified this extension of power: the Seventeenth provided for direct election of Senators; the Fifteenth and Nineteenth made it unlawful to deny the franchise to any person because of race, color, previous condition of servitude, or sex; the Fourteenth gave Congress the power to reduce representation in the House to any states denying the vote to its citizens. The latter clause has never been invoked.

At the present time, in virtually all the states, would-be voters must be citizens, must have resided in the state for one year, in the county for from sixty to ninety days, and in the precinct for thirty days; and must be twenty-one years of age (eighteen in Georgia and Kentucky).

### Registration

In every state, voters must first register in order to vote. Two systems are in effect, permanent registration and periodic registration. Under the former system, which is employed in some forty states, a citizen need register in his community only once, and thereafter he remains on the election rolls. Under the latter system, voters must register before each election, or at least at periodic intervals, to maintain their status as voters. Permanent registration requires considerable administrative effort to maintain accurate rolls; periodic registration adds a stumbling block in the path of the voter. Neither system is perfect, but current practice favors some form of permanent registration.

### Literacy Test and Poll Tax

One of the most inexcusable defects of our democratic process is the denial of the right to vote to those who deserve the right. The two most common methods are the literacy test (in eighteen states) and the poll tax (in five states). In itself there is nothing undemocratic about a literacy test. In certain regions, however, the administration of the test has been perverted to disenfranchise those against whom the local boards of elections wished to discriminate, which has meant Negroes and in some cases low-income whites as well.

Neither the literacy test (where its administration is discriminatory) nor the poll tax, however, are principally responsible for the low percentage of American citizens who participate in the election process. In recent presidential elections, somewhere between a third and a half of all eligible voters in the United States have not voted. The national percentage is misleading, however, because it varies sharply from state to state and region to region. In eleven Southern states in 1952 the percentage added up to 39.1; in the rest of the nation it averaged about 70. The differential was caused by the low proportion of voters among Negroes, who are widely disenfranchised in the South through coercion or discriminatory voting requirements.

Different groups of people appear to vote in different proportions: men vote more than women (only very slightly more in 1956) ; urban more than suburban or rural; Westerners more than inhabitants of other areas; Northerners more than Southerners; Catholics more than Protestants; higher income families more than lower income; better educated more than the less educated; and more people vote in presidential elections than in the mid-term congressional elections or in off-year local elections.

Surveys show that most nonvoting is caused not by ignorance or by events beyond the voter's control (such as illness or sudden travel), but by apathy. A few students of the problem have proposed a system of compulsory voting, enforced by fines for unexcused nonvoting, but it is questionable whether an unwilling voter is an enlightened voter, and it is probable that certain other reforms, such as a shorter ballot, easier registration requirements, and strengthened political parties might be more useful than fines.

# NOMINATING THE CANDIDATES

The first step in the election process is the nomination of candidates whose names will appear on the ballot. Nominating methods have changed drastically during the nation's brief history. For twenty-five years following 1800, most candidates were nominated by legislators meeting in secret caucus. Following growing criticism of the lack of democracy, the caucus method began to yield to the political convention. Toward the end of the nineteenth century, conventions came under attack for a number of abuses, particularly for the control exercised by political machines, and by 1917 all but four states had adopted the primary system. Today the last major use of the convention is in nominating the candidates for President and Vice President.

## Primary Elections

Under the primary system, the candidate's name is placed on the primary ballot following the filing of a petition (bearing a certain number of names of enrolled party members) with county election officials. In a closed primary, which is common to most states, voters may cast their ballots only in the election of the party in which they have previously enrolled. In open primaries, the voter can decide which party primary contest he wishes to vote in at the time he casts his ballot. In many states, the primary is combined with a convention, held either before the primary election (to determine the official designees) or afterward (to write a platform). In some states, candidates must receive a majority of the votes, which often requires a runoff primary election between the two leading vote getters.

Nom. of
Pres.
Cand.

②

The nomination of a candidate for the Presidency is accomplished by a combination of primaries and conventions. There is no word in the Constitution about nominating Presidents, and today the process is almost entirely in the hands of political parties, with a minimum of state law touching on the details. The final choice is made by the major parties in the quadrennial conventions, but the convention is only the culminating movement in a vast panorama of activity throughout the nation. As one observer has pointed out, "The Presidential nominating process provides a quadrennial test of party organization from precinct to national committee" [2]

## The National Convention

③

In most states the delegates to the national convention are chosen in state conventions or by the state committee. In practice, however, the struggle among party leaders for a delegate's post is usually settled at the county level. At the turn of the century, abuses in this selection process led to a movement to institute the selection of delegates by primary election. Within fifteen years it became evident that strong party machines could control primaries as readily as conventions, and today only sixteen states still employ the primary method of selecting some or all of their convention delegates. These remaining primaries have uncertain influence; victorious convention delegates are not committed or announced for a particular candidate (at least after the first convention ballot) and because most presidential hopefuls do not enter them. Although primary victories helped President Eisenhower obtain the Republican nomination in 1952 (without this prestige he might never have overcome Senator Taft's lead), presidential primaries usually serve principally to kill off hopeful candidates. Wendell Willkie was the victim in 1944;

---

The free-for-all of an American election . . . has many times seemed only to put clowns, and worse than clowns, in high places. . . . But on the great occasions, on the supreme issues, it has the habit of doing the right thing; and if it does the right thing only at the eleventh hour, after many prophecies of disaster, it does the right thing handsomely. . . .

—*The* (London) *Economist* (Aug. 2, 1952

Harold Stassen in 1948; Estes Kefauver in 1956—although in this case his showing in the primaries undoubtedly contributed to his success in the vice-presidential contest at the Chicago convention.

*Presidential Qualifications.* Every four years the two major parties meet in convention to write their platforms and choose candidates for President and Vice-President. One of America's fondest myths is that every mother's son has a chance to become President. History demonstrates that the myth has very little basis in fact; the qualifications are so rigid that the party may have only a handful of persons available for the office. The record indicates that the potential candidate normally has had some experience in public office (only Wendell Willkie in recent years has broken through this rule); that his chief previous post has been in state government rather than in Congress—although there are several exceptions to this rule; that he comes from a large state with a doubtful vote, such as New York, California, Illinois, Ohio, or Pennsylvania (from 1868 to 1948, twenty-five of the forty two major party candidates came from New York or Ohio); that he is a Protestant (Alfred E. Smith has been the only exception); and that he cannot be identified with a particular nationality group. Working within this framework of political requirements, the convention's job may thus be limited to choosing from among only a few major possibilities.

The television camera has helped to make this quadrennial shindig one of the greatest shows on earth, not the least of its virtues being that the television viewer is probably getting a more complete picture of the convention panorama than are most of the participants. Certain accepted patterns and rules regulate the surface flow of the convention, but from the time the site is chosen months before there are likely to be deep political undercurrents behind

As a device for nominating Presidential and Vice-Presidential candidates, it is generally agreed that the national convention has served the parties well. As a platform-making organization, however, the convention receives a lower mark. The differing relative abilities of national conventions to perform these two types of functions is but another indication of the principal purpose of the major party. . . .

—Ivan Hinderaker

every move. The convention city, for example, must offer ample hotel rooms, a large hall, and a sizable purse. The Democrats picked Chicago because it was the home state of the leading candidate, Adlai Stevenson. The Republicans chose San Francisco at least partly to afford President Eisenhower an opportunity to mediate on the spot in case California's warring leaders were to have taken up political arms during the convention period.

*Keynote Address.* The first major address of each convention, known as the keynote address, is "an intensely partisan oratorical bender," but the keynoter is chosen for more reasons than his speaking ability. In 1948, old-timer Alben Barkley was picked to mitigate intraparty feuds in the Democratic party, and accomplished his task so well that he won the vice-presidential nomination. This was an exception, however, for the keynoter is normally a neutral who is not a serious candidate for anything.

*Convention Committees.* Each party convention selects its standing committees, none of which normally have much importance but any one of which may at one time or another be plunged into the middle of a battle. The first committee to report, the Credentials Committee, merely certifies the lists of qualified delegates, but in 1912 William Howard Taft won renomination over Theodore Roosevelt by controlling the Credentials Committee and disqualifying several pro-TR delegations. In 1952, the Eisenhower-Taft struggle was largely settled by the results of a fight over the seating of delegates from three states.

Normally the work of the Platform Committee, which starts public hearings a week before the convention opens, is little noted and not long remembered. But in 1948 a battle over the civil rights plank split the Democratic party.

Much of the ceremony and routine are well known to the television viewer: candidates are nominated to the accompaniment of cowbells and parades (an aspect of conventions which TV coverage is rendering obsolete); the states are polled in alphabetical order, with occasional exceptions when one state yields to another, or interruptions when a state delegation is polled individually. Voting continues until one candidates wins a majority, which may require only one ballot, like President Eisenhower's and Adlai Stevenson's nominations in 1956, or 103 ballots, like John W. Davis's victory in the Democratic convention of 1924.

*Behind the Scenes.* Events taking place behind the scenes, invisible to the television viewer, usually play a much larger role than the maelstrom on the floor. In the hotel-room meetings and

## "I Have The Same Trouble"

HERBLOCK

corridor conversations, weaker candidates may be trying to combine their strength against the leader, while uncommitted delegation heads are attempting to judge the best possible moment for jumping on the leader's bandwagon before his victory is clinched by a similar leap by another delegation. Kingmakers are doing their best to manipulate the convention course to their own particular advantage. Virtually every convention develops its own pattern and behind-the-scenes struggles. Several months before the 1920 Republican convention, an Ohio political leader named Harry M. Daugherty predicted that in the early morning hours of a certain day a small group of political leaders would meet in a hotel room and accept a dark horse, Senator Warren G. Harding of Ohio, as the candidate. His prediction came true, and out of that meeting came the twenty-ninth President of the United States as well as a new political term, "smoke-filled room." The next day, however, the rank and file of delegates, having accepted Harding, bolted their leadership and for Vice-President named Calvin Coolidge from the floor by acclamation.

Convention deals make strange bedfellows. Abraham Lincoln's managers promised a cabinet post to a notorious leader from Pennsylvania in order to win the nomination for Honest Abe, while in 1948 the liberal Governor Dewey clinched his nomination through a deal with conservative Pennsylvania boss Joseph Grundy—over the objections of liberal Governor James Duff of the same state!

*The Vice-President.* Until recently, the candidate for Vice-President was almost forgotten in the chaos of the presidential struggle. Often the post was given as a consolation prize to the forces who supported one of the defeated presidential hopefuls; often the vice-presidential candidate represented a different section of the country or different political leanings than did the head of the ticket. The conventions of 1956 perhaps marked a turning point in the role of the Vice-President. In order to help relieve the Chief Executive of some of his impossible burdens, the Vice-President has been given an increasingly important role in government. The importance of the vice-presidential candidate has been reinforced by our growing awareness of the mortality record of Presidents while in office. As a result, the selection of the vice-presidential candidates in 1956 assumed a new importance, and one which probably will not be diminished in future years.

*Convention System Criticized.* The smoke-filled rooms, the deals, the tremendous influence wielded by a few political leaders over the rank-and-file delegates, have all made the national convention a natural target of criticism. In support of the convention system, defenders claim that the successful and experienced politicians who control conventions have the clearest eye for the strongest candidate, and the behind-the-scenes compromises help modify divisive floor struggles and avoid eventual deadlock.

Anyone who watched the Republican convention in 1952 or the Democratic convention in 1956 must certainly be aware of the dramatic resolution of intra-party struggles that party conventions make possible in our national political life.

# THE ELECTION

Much of what the nation today accepts as normal in the voting process took many years to develop. In the nineteenth century, for example, it was usual for each party to print its own ballots and for

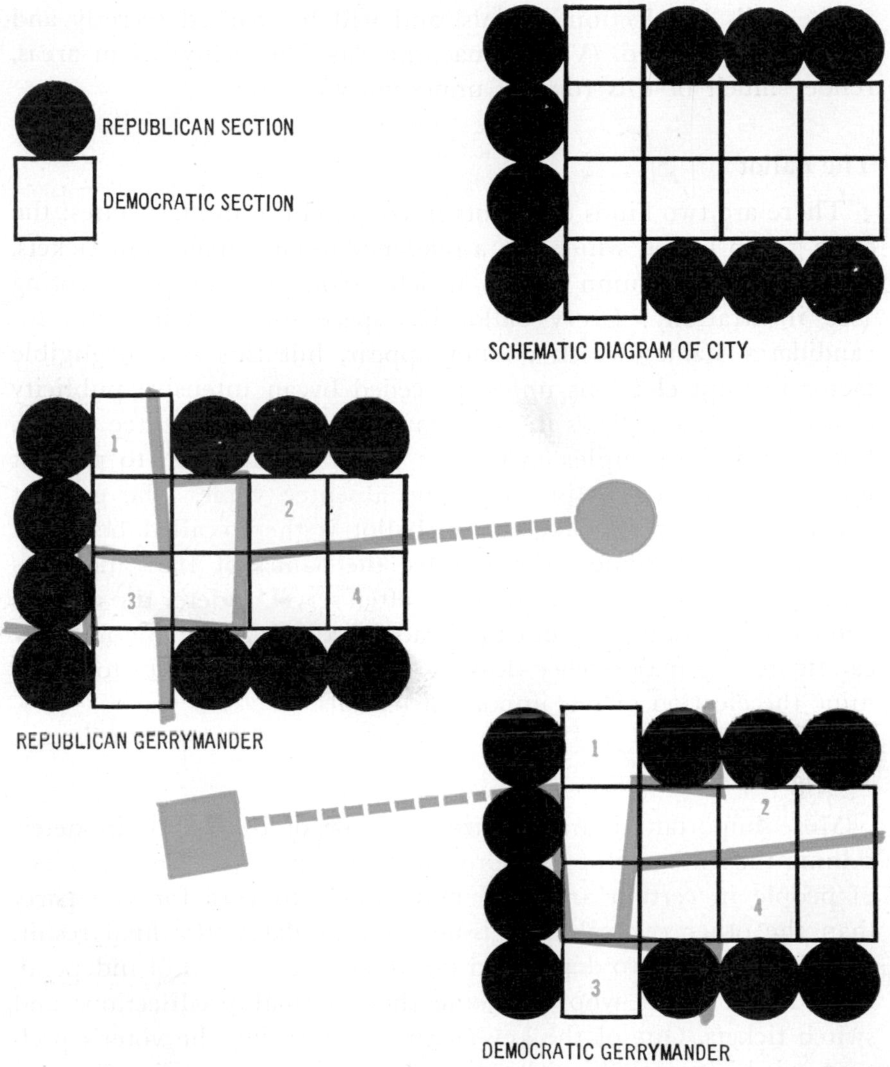

REPUBLICAN SECTION

DEMOCRATIC SECTION

SCHEMATIC DIAGRAM OF CITY

REPUBLICAN GERRYMANDER

DEMOCRATIC GERRYMANDER

The diagram above gives an example of the art of gerrymandering. In the imaginary city above, Republican and Democratic voting strength is equal, but is centered in different wards or areas. If the Republicans control the state legislature, district lines can be drawn to produce four "safe" Republican representatives and one Democratic. The reverse would be true if Democrats held a majority in the state legislature. (See page 262.)

the voter to obtain the ballot of his choice from his precinct leader before entering the polls. The opportunities for bribery, intimidation, and corruption were endless. Since the universal adoption of the Australian ballot, the electorate takes it for granted that the ballot will be printed by the government, will be given to voters at the polls by election officials, and will be marked secretly and deposited unopened. (Voting machines, used in many urban areas, render much of this routine unnecessary.)

## The Ballot

There are two kinds of ballots in common use in most states: the office group ballot, which has a tendency to encourage split tickets, and the party column ballot, which favors straight party voting (see illustration). Every ballot has space for write-in votes for candidates' names which do not appear, but this is a negligible factor in most elections unless preceded by an intensive publicity campaign. Election laws in most states provide for absentee voting, but usually the complex provisions which are designed to prevent misuse also serve to discourage the absentee voter. The greatest single problem pertaining to the ballot is the so-called bed-sheet ballot, which in some areas may list the names of 100 candidates for dozens of offices. The long ballot often serves to deter the average voter from marking any but the heads of the ticket, or the first few candidates for major office, leaving only a small minority to determine the election of less important officials.

## Voting Patterns

More important than the size or shape of the ballot in determining the outcome of elections are voting patterns. Certain kinds of people in certain areas are more likely to vote for one party than the other regardless of issues or candidates; the final result, therefore, is likely to depend on the votes of a handful of independents and of a few who overcome their normal predilections and switch tickets. One of the key factors determining the voter's preference is his geographical location. In certain areas entire states or clusters of states have been dominated by one party—the Democratic South, the Republican Dakotas, Maine, Vermont, New Hampshire, Oregon. Within the two-party states (and to a certain extent in one-party states as well), Democrats have been strongest in urban and low-income rural areas, while Republicans dominate small towns, suburbs, and the more prosperous rural areas. The House of Representatives gives graphic testimony to this division: of 172 "safe" Democratic seats (won by more than 60 percent of the vote in 1954), 45 were Southern rural and 50 were Northern urban districts. Of 79 Republican "safe" seats, 32 were small town districts.[3] Environment

# Official Presidential Ballot

Make a cross (X) or other mark in the square opposite the names of the candidates for whose electors you desire to vote. Vote in ONE square only.

DWIGHT D. EISENHOWER ---------------- President ⎫ Republican ☐
RICHARD M. NIXON ---------------- Vice President ⎭

ADLAI E. STEVENSON ---------------- President ⎫ Democrat ☐
ESTES KEFAUVER ---------------- Vice President ⎭

T. COLEMAN ANDREWS ---------------- President
(Better Government Under the Constitution) ⎫ Independent ☐
THOMAS HAROLD WERDEL -------- Vice President ⎭
(Better Government Under the Constitution)

FARRELL DOBBS ---------------- President
(Socialist Workers Party) ⎫ Independent ☐
MYRA TANNER WEISS ------------ Vice President ⎭
(Socialist Workers Party)

ERIC HASS ---------------- President
(Socialist Labor Party) ⎫ Independent ☐
GEORGIA COZZINI ---------------- Vice President ⎭
(Socialist Labor Party)

DARLINGTON HOOPES ---------------- President
(Socialist Party) ⎫ Independent ☐
SAMUEL H. FRIEDMAN ------------ Vice President ⎭
(Socialist Party)

# OFFICIAL BALLOT

If you desire to vote for an entire party ticket for state, congressional, legislative and county offices make a cross (X) or other mark in the circle (O) under the party designation at the head of the ballot. If you desire to vote for particular persons without regard to party, mark in the square at the right of the name of the candidate for whom you desire to vote, if it be there, or write any name that you wish to vote for in the proper place.

| REPUBLICAN | DEMOCRATIC | INDEPENDENT |
|---|---|---|
| O | O | |
| For Governor— VERNON W. THOMSON ☑ | For Governor— WILLIAM PROXMIRE ☐ | For Governor— BUTTERFIELD |
| Lieutenant Governor— WARREN P. KNOWLES ☑ | Lieutenant Governor— WILLIAM A. SCHMIDT ☐ | Lieutenant Governor— NASH |
| Secretary of State— ROBERT C. ZIMMERMAN ☐ | Secretary of State— MARGUERITE R. BENSON ☑ | Secretary of State— JOHN CLEESE |
| State Treasurer— WARREN R. SMITH ☐ | State Treasurer— WILLIAM S. CLARK ☑ | State Treasurer— VAL SINGLETON |

The Wisconsin ballot above combines the features of the office type ballot in its listing of presidential candidates and of the party type ballot in the listing of candidates for state office.

is a potent influence, strong enough to cause the voter to change a long-held preference, such as demonstrated by thousands of one-time New York City Democrats who, in moving to the suburbs, become Westchester Republicans.

Nationality, race, and religion also play a part in determining votes. The average white, native-born Protestant is a Republican; minority ethnic groups and Catholics are more likely to be Democratic. These racial and religious patterns are normally weakest among younger voters—except among Jews and Negroes, whose youth tend to be more Democratic than their elders. It is important to note that these party preferences exist regardless of economic level or basic political attitudes.

Whether class-consciousness influences voting is the subject of strenuous debate. In general, the blue collar or manual worker leans Democratic and the white collar worker and business man leans Republican—but do they follow these tendencies conscious of their class? No one is sure. Some students of the subject believe class-consciousness is a minor factor in voting; others see it becoming more important than geographical or sectional influences.[4]

About 80 percent of the voters, along the various lines described above, are party regulars; the other 20 percent are independent and may split their ticket. This percentage bears little relation to party enrollment: in California, for example, more people enroll Democratic than Republican but more people vote Republican than Democratic. In each area, however, it is the swing vote group which is the most cherished object of the election campaigning.

*Recent Trends.* Many of these patterns, which political scientists have been exploring for two decades, were rudely upset by the results of the 1956 presidential vote. Several states long dominated by single-party machines appear to have broken out of their strait jackets: Virginia, Florida and Texas, which have re-elected Republican Congressmen and twice supported a Republican presidential candidate; Oregon, which now has two Democratic Senators, three Democratic and one Republican Congressmen, and a Democratic governor; Pennsylvania, which has thrown out a long dominant GOP machine in Philadelphia and has elected a Democratic governor and Senator as well.

An equally unusual trend was the return of large blocs of Negro voters to the Republican fold. In the North, this was generally limited to a small percentage; in several Southern areas, however, the swing was more dramatic, in one case as high as 70 percent. It is the

Negro vote, plus increasing industrialization and urbanization and the rise of a larger middle class, which is behind the imminent break-up of the Democratic Solid South. In the West, long under Republican control, Professor V. O. Key questions whether the decline of Republican liberalism, especially in the public resources field, may not have thrown several states into Democratic hands for some time to come.

Over-riding the importance of President Eisenhower's personal victory, which might not be repeated by any other candidate, were these signs of change in our fundamental political tendencies. The new patterns have not yet solidified—it may take years before they do, but certainly something is happening to the balance of political influence which may mark the beginning of a new era in our national politics.

## The Campaign

No two election campaigns are the same. The pattern of a campaign is determined by many factors, including the size and location of the district involved, the relative strength of the two parties and of the candidates, dominant characteristics of the electorate, the absence or presence of important issues, even the state of the economy and whether there is war or peace abroad. Two candidates for the mayoralty of a small town may spend much of their time talking to friends and neighbors. They may each spend $50 for a campaign leaflet and for telephone calls, and unless an important issue is at stake the campaign may be chiefly characterized by the lack of electioneering. The broader the area and the higher the office, the more elaborate (and expensive) are the campaign techniques. In a statewide election, hundreds of thousands of dollars are spent for advertising and publicity materials, for paid speakers, for a headquarters staff, for radio and television talks.

In every American election there are two acts of choice, two periods of contest. The first is the selection of the candidate from within the party by the party; the other is the struggle between the parties for the place. Frequently the former of these is the more important, more keenly fought over, than the latter. . . .

—James Bryce

*Campaign Methods.* Each area of the country has its own customary campaign methods, dictated in part by the nature of the electorate. A congressional candidate in Mississippi buys radio time at 6 A.M. to catch the ears of voters before they go out into the fields, and he may spend days out in the fields with them. In close-packed Chicago, the sound truck and street-corner meetings, supplemented by as much door-to-door canvassing as the candidate can stimulate, are the effective methods to reach the electorate.

In the wide-open spaces of the West, a statewide candidate may visit his constituency by airplane, and hire a corps of stump speakers —campaign veterans or politically minded college students—to tour the small towns by car. In heavily populated Massachusetts, where it is impossible for the candidate to shake hands with more than a tiny fraction of the electorate, newspaper advertising, television talks, spot radio commercials, and billboards are a necessity.

The dominant groups in the community also help determine the nature of the campaign. A congressional candidate in a Chicago district which is more than 90 percent Negro, most of them voters, will pitch his campaign on quite a different level than will a congressional candidate in a Mississippi district 70 percent Negro, only a handful of whom vote.

*Intensity of Campaign.* The intensity of campaigns is often determined by the issues. Where there are none, electioneering may degenerate into invective and smears. Although John Foster Dulles and Herbert H. Lehman were among the most revered and irreproachable senior statesmen in the nation, when they opposed each other in a special senatorial election in New York in 1949 the campaign was marked by bitterness and harsh words. This is a likely development in any close-fought election; only where one party is dominant is the campaign apt to be relatively mild, for the favored candidate has little fear of defeat and the underdog seeks to avoid offending majority-party partisans.

*Coattail Influences.* The course of campaigns is also affected by the relative stature of other candidates on the ballot. In Ohio in 1950, virtually every congressional race was keyed to some degree to the re-election efforts of Senator Robert A. Taft; in 1956, every Republican candidate dogged the footsteps of President Eisenhower, just as Democratic candidates hung onto President Roosevelt's coattails in 1936. A strong candidate at the head of the ticket will normally help bring votes to local candidates of his party, except in areas where voters have become accustomed to ticket-splitting.

Ticket-splitting appears to be on the rise: in 1950 New York voters elected a Republican governor, a Democratic Senator, and an independent for mayor of New York City. In 1956, voters in a score of states split their tickets when they gave Republican President Eisenhower a thumping majority but elected Democratic Senators and Congressmen at the same time. The final result—a landslide victory for a Republican President, but a Democratic victory in both houses of Congress—was a body blow to a simple coattail theory.

*Campaign Effectiveness.* How effective are campaigns? Do they persuade voters to change their minds or are they merely a useless appendage to our political system, serving mostly to glorify the candidates in their own and their followers' eyes?

A number of skilled students of politics have suggested that most voters have made up their minds before the campaign begins, and those who have not are normally swayed by family, relatives, or friends rather than by electioneering efforts. In the light of the presidential election of 1948, this appears to be an overstatement, for it is almost universally agreed that President Truman's tactics played a part in the switch of a sizable number of votes in many states. One recent study of campaign timing indicated that about 80 percent of the electorate had made up its mind by the time the 1952 conventions had chosen Eisenhower and Stevenson as the candidates. The next most critical period for the voter was the last week before the election, when undecided voters finally made their decisions, and presumably a few voters changed their minds. But during the greatest period of the campaign, the span of three months between the convention and Election Day, relatively few voters were influenced by the sound and the fury.[5] The decision of both parties to abbreviate the campaigns in 1956, therefore, appears to have conformed to voter psychology as well as to campaign economy.

*Election Returns.* Regardless of the techniques or the pattern of the campaign, on election night every candidate retires to his headquarters, surrounded by his followers, to await the counting of the returns. It is one of the psychological quirks of the campaign that virtually every candidate, irrespective of adverse polls or heavy odds, by the end of the campaign has succeeded in selling himself on the possibility of victory. Finally the results come in, slowly at first, in a rush later, bringing rejoicing to one headquarters, gloom to the other (usually accompanied by satisfaction at leading the losing ticket, or at least in having run a good campaign). Once again the American people have made their choice.

# PRESIDENTIAL ELECTORAL VOTE 1900 TO 1956

| ELECTORAL VOTE BY STATES FOR 1956 | | 1900 | 1904 | 1908 | 1912 | 1916 | 1920 | 1924 | 1928 | 1932 | 1936 | 1940 | 1944 | 1948 | 1952 | 1956 |
|---|---|---|---|---|---|---|---|---|---|---|---|---|---|---|---|---|
| 11 | Ala. | 11 | 11 | 11 | 12 | 12 | 12 | 12 | 12 | 11 | 11 | 11 | 11 | 11 | 11 | 11 | * |
| 4 | Ariz. | Adm. 1912 | | 3 | 3 | 3 | 3 | 3 | 3 | 3 | 3 | 3 | 3 | 4 | 4 | 4 |
| 8 | Ark. | 8 | 9 | 9 | 9 | 9 | 9 | 9 | 9 | 9 | 9 | 9 | 9 | 9 | 8 | 8 |
| 32 | Calif. | 9 | 10 | 10 | 2 11 | 13 | 13 | 13 | 13 | 22 | 22 | 22 | 25 | 25 | 32 | 32 |
| 6 | Colo. | 4 | 5 | 5 | 5 | 6 | 6 | 6 | 6 | 6 | 6 | 6 | 6 | 6 | 6 | 6 |
| 8 | Conn. | 6 | 7 | 7 | 7 | 7 | 7 | 7 | 7 | 8 | 8 | 8 | 8 | 8 | 8 | 8 |
| 3 | Del. | 3 | 3 | 3 | 3 | 3 | 3 | 3 | 3 | 3 | 3 | 3 | 3 | 3 | 3 | 3 |
| 10 | Fla. | 4 | 5 | 5 | 6 | 6 | 6 | 6 | 6 | 7 | 7 | 7 | 8 | 8 | 10 | 10 |
| 12 | Ga. | 13 | 13 | 13 | 14 | 14 | 14 | 14 | 14 | 12 | 12 | 12 | 12 | 12 | 12 | 12 |
| 4 | Idaho | 3 | 3 | 3 | 4 | 4 | 4 | 4 | 4 | 4 | 4 | 4 | 4 | 4 | 4 | 4 |
| 27 | Ill. | 24 | 27 | 27 | 29 | 29 | 29 | 29 | 29 | 29 | 29 | 29 | 28 | 28 | 27 | 27 |
| 13 | Ind. | 15 | 15 | 15 | 15 | 15 | 15 | 15 | 15 | 14 | 14 | 14 | 13 | 13 | 13 | 13 |
| 10 | Iowa | 13 | 13 | 13 | 13 | 13 | 13 | 13 | 13 | 11 | 11 | 11 | 10 | 10 | 10 | 10 |
| 8 | Kan. | 10 | 10 | 10 | 10 | 10 | 10 | 10 | 10 | 9 | 9 | 9 | 8 | 8 | 8 | 8 |
| 10 | Ky. | 13 | 13 | 13 | 13 | 13 | 13 | 13 | 13 | 11 | 11 | 11 | 11 | 11 | 10 | 10 |
| 10 | La. | 8 | 9 | 9 | 10 | 10 | 10 | 10 | 10 | 10 | 10 | 10 | 10 | 10 | 10 | 10 |
| 5 | Me. | 6 | 6 | 6 | 6 | 6 | 6 | 6 | 6 | 5 | 5 | 5 | 5 | 5 | 5 | 5 |
| 9 | Md. | 8 | 1  7 | 2  6 | 8 | 8 | 8 | 8 | 8 | 8 | 8 | 8 | 8 | 8 | 9 | 9 |
| 16 | Mass. | 15 | 16 | 16 | 18 | 18 | 18 | 18 | 18 | 17 | 17 | 17 | 16 | 16 | 16 | 16 |
| 20 | Mich. | 14 | 14 | 14 | 15 | 15 | 15 | 15 | 15 | 19 | 19 | 19 | 19 | 19 | 20 | 20 |
| 11 | Minn. | 9 | 11 | 11 | 12 | 12 | 12 | 12 | 12 | 11 | 11 | 11 | 11 | 11 | 11 | 11 |
| 8 | Miss. | 9 | 10 | 10 | 10 | 10 | 10 | 10 | 10 | 9 | 9 | 9 | 9 | 9 | 8 | 8 |
| 13 | Mo. | 17 | 18 | 18 | 18 | 18 | 18 | 18 | 18 | 15 | 15 | 15 | 15 | 15 | 13 | 13 |
| 4 | Mont. | 3 | 3 | 3 | 4 | 4 | 4 | 4 | 4 | 4 | 4 | 4 | 4 | 4 | 4 | 4 |
| 6 | Nebr. | 8 | 8 | 8 | 8 | 8 | 8 | 8 | 8 | 7 | 7 | 7 | 6 | 6 | 6 | 6 |
| 3 | Nev. | 3 | 3 | 3 | 3 | 3 | 3 | 3 | 3 | 3 | 3 | 3 | 3 | 3 | 3 | 3 |
| 4 | N.H. | 4 | 4 | 4 | 4 | 4 | 4 | 4 | 4 | 4 | 4 | 4 | 4 | 4 | 4 | 4 |
| 16 | N.J. | 10 | 12 | 12 | 14 | 14 | 14 | 14 | 14 | 16 | 16 | 16 | 16 | 16 | 16 | 16 |
| 4 | N.M. | Adm. 1912 | | 3 | 3 | 3 | 3 | 3 | 3 | 3 | 3 | 4 | 4 | 4 | 4 |
| 45 | N.Y. | 36 | 39 | 39 | 45 | 45 | 45 | 45 | 45 | 47 | 47 | 47 | 47 | 47 | 45 | 45 |
| 14 | N.C. | 11 | 12 | 12 | 12 | 12 | 12 | 12 | 12 | 13 | 13 | 13 | 14 | 14 | 14 | 14 |
| 4 | N.D. | 3 | 5 | 5 | 5 | 5 | 5 | 5 | 5 | 4 | 4 | 4 | 4 | 4 | 4 | 4 |
| 25 | Ohio | 23 | 23 | 23 | 24 | 24 | 24 | 24 | 24 | 26 | 26 | 26 | 25 | 25 | 25 | 25 |
| 8 | Okla. | Adm. 1907 | | 7 | 10 | 10 | 10 | 10 | 10 | 11 | 11 | 11 | 10 | 10 | 8 | 8 |
| 6 | Ore. | 4 | 4 | 4 | 5 | 5 | 5 | 5 | 5 | 5 | 5 | 5 | 6 | 6 | 6 | 6 |
| 32 | Pa. | 32 | 34 | 34 | 38 | 38 | 38 | 38 | 38 | 36 | 36 | 36 | 35 | 35 | 32 | 32 |
| 4 | R.I. | 4 | 4 | 4 | 5 | 5 | 5 | 5 | 5 | 4 | 4 | 4 | 4 | 4 | 4 | 4 |
| 8 | S.C. | 9 | 9 | 9 | 9 | 9 | 9 | 9 | 9 | 8 | 8 | 8 | 8 | 8 | 8 | 8 |
| 4 | S.D. | 4 | 4 | 4 | 5 | 5 | 5 | 5 | 5 | 4 | 4 | 4 | 4 | 4 | 4 | 4 |
| 11 | Tenn. | 12 | 12 | 12 | 12 | 12 | 12 | 12 | 12 | 11 | 11 | 11 | 12 | 11 | 11 | 11 |
| 24 | Texas | 15 | 18 | 18 | 20 | 20 | 20 | 20 | 20 | 23 | 23 | 23 | 23 | 23 | 24 | 24 |
| 4 | Utah | 3 | 3 | 3 | 4 | 4 | 4 | 4 | 4 | 4 | 4 | 4 | 4 | 4 | 4 | 4 |
| 3 | Vt. | 4 | 4 | 4 | 4 | 4 | 4 | 4 | 4 | 3 | 3 | 3 | 3 | 3 | 3 | 3 |
| 12 | Va. | 12 | 12 | 12 | 12 | 12 | 12 | 12 | 12 | 11 | 11 | 11 | 11 | 11 | 12 | 12 |
| 9 | Wash. | 4 | 5 | 5 | 7 | 7 | 7 | 7 | 7 | 8 | 8 | 8 | 8 | 8 | 9 | 9 |
| 8 | W.Va. | 6 | 7 | 7 | 8 | 1  7 | 8 | 8 | 8 | 8 | 8 | 8 | 8 | 8 | 8 | 8 |
| 12 | Wis. | 12 | 13 | 13 | 13 | 13 | 13 | 13 | 13 | 12 | 12 | 12 | 12 | 12 | 12 | 12 |
| 3 | Wyo. | 3 | 3 | 3 | 3 | 3 | 3 | 3 | 3 | 3 | 3 | 3 | 3 | 3 | 3 | 3 |
| 531 | Total | McKinley 292 | Roosv. 336 | Taft 321 | Wilson 435 | Wilson 277 | Harding 404 | Cool'ge 382 | Hoover 444 | Roosv. 472 | Roosv. 523 | Roosv. 449 | Roosv. 432 | Truman 303 | Eisenh'r 442 | Eisenh'r 457 |
| | | Bryan 155 | Parker 140 | Bryan 162 | Roosv. 88 | Hughes 254 | Cox 127 | Davis 136 | Smith 87 | Hoover 59 | Landon 8 | Willkie 82 | Dewey 99 | Dewey 189 | Stev's'n 89 | Stev's'n 74 |
| | | | | | Taft 8 | | | LaFoll. 13 | | | | | | Thurm 39 | | |

[000] Republican    [000] Democratic    Progressive Roosevelt    Progressive LaFollette    States Rights Democrats Thurmond    [0][0] Vote divided

* See footnote 6.

# THE ELECTORAL COLLEGE

But will the choice of the majority become President? This is probable but not sure. For one peculiar aspect of our constitutional system is the Electoral College which makes it at least possible for a majority of voters to prefer one presidential candidate only to see his opponent elected to office. This has not happened frequently in recent history (twice since the Civil War), but there is no guarantee that it will not happen again.

Why is this so? What is the electoral-college system? How does it work? What problems does it present? Why is it attacked? Why is it defended?

### Presidential Electors

Under the Constitution, the President and Vice-President are not elected directly by the people. Instead, citizens vote on the first Tuesday of every leap-year November for a slate of electors. Sometimes these electors are not even mentioned on the ballot by name;

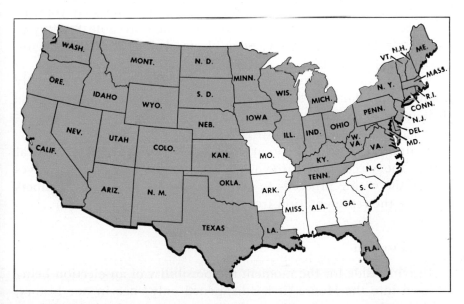

National elections are decided by majorities in each state, not by total popular vote. In 1956, President Eisenhower won about 84 percent of the electoral vote but only about 58 percent of the popular vote. Many of the states above which gave the President their electoral votes also elected Democratic governors or Senators.

but in fact the people who pulled either the Eisenhower or the Stevenson lever on November 6, 1956, were not voting directly for Eisenhower or Stevenson, but for a group of electors who, if elected, would in turn cast their electoral-college ballots for the people's choice in that state.

Each state has a right to the same number of electors as it has members in the national legislature. For example, New York has forty-three United States Congressmen and two United States Senators. It is therefore entitled to forty-five votes in the Electoral College. On a similar basis California is entitled to thirty-two electoral votes. The total number of electors in the Electoral College is 531, equivalent to 435 Congressmen and 96 Senators.

Before the November election, each party in each state chooses a full slate of electors. When the election is over, a state-unit system goes into effect. In other words, the popular winner in each state, no matter how slim his victory, receives *all* the electoral votes of that state. In 1956, for example, Eisenhower won a popular majority in California and thereby received all thirty-two electoral votes.

Although there is nothing but custom and party pressure which makes an elector cast his ballot for the presidential and vice-presidential candidates who have won the majority of popular votes in his state, (the few state laws in this area are unenforceable. See Ray V. Blair, 343 U. S. 214: 1952). State electoral delegations almost invariably vote as a unit.[6]

The outcome of the electoral-college balloting is not officially known until January 3 when Congress in joint session counts the ballots cast by the members of the Electoral College in their respective state capitols on a day in December fixed by federal law.

If, in the official count, no man has received a majority of electoral votes, the election is thrown into the House of Representatives where the voting proceeds to take place by states, not by members (that is, the representation from each state has only one vote).

### The Distortion

Leaving aside for the moment the possibility of an election being thrown into the House (it has happened only once in our history, in 1824), how does the electoral-college system make it possible to skew the popular vote to the point where the "losing" candidate might actually become President?

The following imaginary sample should make the process clear. Suppose that there were only 10 states in the Union, and that 112 (out of a total of 223) electoral votes were needed to elect a President.

| | Candidate A | | | Candidate B | |
|---|---|---|---|---|---|
| *State* | *Popular Vote* | *Electoral Vote* | | *Popular Vote* | *Electoral Vote* |
| Alabama | 25,000 | 0 | | 200,000 | 11 |
| California | 2,100,000 | 32 | | 2,000,000 | 0 |
| Mass. | 1,100,000 | 16 | | 1,000,000 | 0 |
| Montana | 90,000 | 0 | | 100,000 | 4 |
| New York | 3,100,000 | 45 | | 3,000,000 | 0 |
| Ohio | 1,000,000 | 0 | | 2,000,000 | 25 |
| Penn. | 1,000,000 | 0 | | 2,000,000 | 32 |
| N. Carolina | 80,000 | 0 | | 700,000 | 14 |
| Texas | 600,000 | 32 | | 400,000 | 0 |
| Wisconsin | 401,000 | 12 | | 400,000 | 0 |
| TOTALS | 9,496,000 | 137 | | 11,800,000 | 86 |

|  |  |
|---|---|
| **Candidate A wins electoral-college majority and becomes President** | **Candidate B wins popular majority but does not become President** |

## Reform: Pro and Con

Suggestions for reform of the electoral-college system have been many. In general, reform proposals have been aimed at one or more of three alleged evils in the present system:

1. A minority of popular votes may elect a President.

2. An election may be thrown into the House of Representatives with unpredictable consequences (including the possibility that *no one* might become President, since under the Constitution a winning candidate must receive the support of a majority of all the states).

3. An elector may "jump ship" and vote for someone other than the man winning the popular majority in the elector's state.

The most vigorous attempts in recent years to change the electoral-college system have centered around the so-called Lodge-Gossett Amendment. This proposed amendment, first introduced in the Congress in 1949 and since accompanied by a number of variations on its theme, would

1. Abolish the office of elector.

2. In each state, divide the electoral vote proportionally to the popular vote.

3. Make a 40 percent plurality sufficient for election (thus prac-

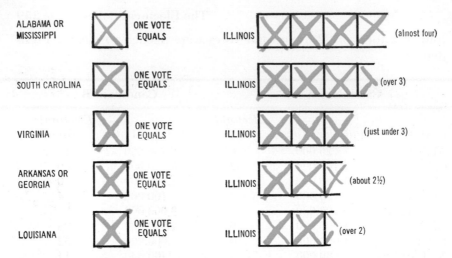

| | | |
|---|---|---|
| ALABAMA OR MISSISSIPPI | ☒ ONE VOTE EQUALS | ILLINOIS ☒☒☒☒ (almost four) |
| SOUTH CAROLINA | ☒ ONE VOTE EQUALS | ILLINOIS ☒☒☒ (over 3) |
| VIRGINIA | ☒ ONE VOTE EQUALS | ILLINOIS ☒☒ (just under 3) |
| ARKANSAS OR GEORGIA | ☒ ONE VOTE EQUALS | ILLINOIS ☒☒ (about 2½) |
| LOUISIANA | ☒ ONE VOTE EQUALS | ILLINOIS ☒☒ (over 2) |

Each member of the House is supposed to represent approximately the same number of people. In terms of population this is roughly true, but because of the barriers placed before Negro voters in some states, it is not true in terms of *voters,* as the chart above indicates.

EIGHT LARGEST STATES

NEW YORK
CALIFORNIA
PENNSYLVANIA
ILLINOIS
OHIO
TEXAS
MICHIGAN
NEW JERSEY

EIGHT SMALLEST STATES

NEVADA
WYOMING
DELAWARE
VERMONT
NEW HAMPSHIRE
IDAHO
MONTANA
NORTH DAKOTA

 SENATOR

■ 1,000,000 POPULATION

THE SIXTEEN SENATORS FROM THE EIGHT LARGEST STATES IN 1950 REPRESENTED 71.3 MILLION PEOPLE OR 47.3 PERCENT OF THE TOTAL POPULATION. THE SIXTEEN SENATORS FROM THE EIGHT SMALLEST STATES REPRESENTED 3.5 MILLION PEOPLE OR 2.3 PERCENT OF THE TOTAL POPULATION

As the diagram shows, the Senate grossly misrepresents the nation's population to an extent probably never envisioned by the men who wrote the Constitution 175 years ago.

Congress . . . is heavily weighted with members so distributed in more sparsely settled districts as to over-represent agrarian, suburban, middle-class interests with property-conscious and entrepreneurial biases. Considerably more than a majority of representatives in Congress represent districts with no city of as many as 50,000 inhabitants.

—Wilfred Binkley

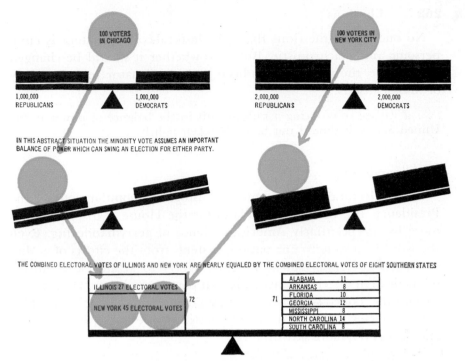

IN THIS ABSTRACT SITUATION THE MINORITY VOTE ASSUMES AN IMPORTANT BALANCE OF POWER WHICH CAN SWING AN ELECTION FOR EITHER PARTY.

100 VOTERS IN CHICAGO

100 VOTERS IN NEW YORK CITY

1,000,000 REPUBLICANS    1,000,000 DEMOCRATS

2,000,000 REPUBLICANS    2,000,000 DEMOCRATS

THE COMBINED ELECTORAL VOTES OF ILLINOIS AND NEW YORK ARE NEARLY EQUALED BY THE COMBINED ELECTORAL VOTES OF EIGHT SOUTHERN STATES

ILLINOIS 27 ELECTORAL VOTES

NEW YORK 45 ELECTORAL VOTES

72          71

| ALABAMA | 11 |
| ARKANSAS | 8 |
| FLORIDA | 10 |
| GEORGIA | 12 |
| MISSISSIPPI | 8 |
| NORTH CAROLINA | 14 |
| SOUTH CAROLINA | 8 |

Under the electoral college system, relatively small minority groups can have a crucial influence on national elections. As the diagram above shows, a shift of 100 votes each in Chicago and New York could throw a total of 72 electoral votes into one column or another, offsetting the combined vote of eight Southern States.

tically obviating the chance of an election's being thrown into the House).

The supporters of this amendment claim that it would get rid of the three major evils of the present electoral-college system and would develop a healthy two-party system throughout the country. This last is predicted because, under the change, any increase in minority strength in a state would be reflected in an increase in electoral votes nationally.

The opponents of the *Lodge-Gossett* and similar proposals take the position that both state and national legislatures in the United States presently overrepresent rural interests (or interests which dominate rural representatives); that the present electoral-college system is the only institutional mechanism for assuring that presidential candidates will listen to the demands of urban majorities (and minorities) in America; and that the chief interest of Southern sponsors of electoral reform is to diminish the alleged power of urban minorities, particularly the Northern Negro, in national politics. (Study the above charts carefully.)

No one really questions that the electoral-college system is cumbersome and anachronistic. But as to whether it should be changed at this time, the real issue has been posed by Senator John Kennedy of Massachusetts:

. . . if we are considering a radical shift in the balance of power in the United States, it should not be undertaken lightly. . . .

## Gerrymandering

If the Electoral College tends to distort the popular vote on the Presidency, the vote on candidates for the House is distorted even more by the peculiarly American science of gerrymandering. Even the word is unique to our nation; it stems from the efforts of a Massachusetts governor named Elbridge Gerry to arrange the outline of an election district to favor his own party's candidate. On the map the outline looked surprisingly like a salamander. The science which Governor Gerry invented in 1812 is still in use today, in his name, and on an even more skillful level.

The graph on page 249 shows what gerrymandering can accomplish in theory. In practice, since most state legislatures are themselves dominated by rural interests, and since state legislatures are responsible for redrawing congressional districts following the decennial census, gerrymandering has made the United States House of Representatives more representative of rural and small-town than of urban interests.

There is no automatic way of ending gerrymandering. So firmly is the practice imbedded in our political culture that if over the years urban forces were to capture control of state legislatures, they would undoubtedly rearrange congressional districts to favor their own interests.

The worst abuses of the system are generally contained by the fear of political reprisal; but short of some national supervision by a judicial or quasi-judicial body, gerrymandering will continue to skew our representative system.

# CONCLUSION

## Synopsis

Our electoral process is complex. Few would pretend that it produces an exact reflection of majority opinion in every election in all sections of the country. The long ballot, the opportunity for machine control of the nominating process at certain levels, the failure or inability of many voters to exercise their franchise, the electoral college, and the gerrymander—all on occasion produce skewed images of majority will. But some of these factors tend to cancel out; and, in general, the results of elections are sufficiently in conformity with public expectations to produce a sober and sportsmanlike willingness on the part of losing candidates and their supporters to accept defeat with equanimity. This last is the great hallmark of a successful democracy.

## Significance

Pressure groups and political parties in the long run are subject to the final endorsement or rejection of public opinion, which in turn expresses itself with some degree of finality only at election time. Free and honest elections have been rare in human history. They are rare today. Americans have reason to be grateful for a heritage which has increasingly extended the privilege of meaningful voting to all people. The privilege will become even more meaningful as our parties become more responsible policy instruments.

## Prospectus

This book began with a brief description of our value heritage, and then proceeded to show how our expectations of government have helped to translate a heritage of ideas into a living reality. We have now completed a section on the political instruments at our disposal for communicating with, and giving ultimate direction to, the activities of government. We turn in the following Sections to the formal instruments of government which exist to effect our political will. We look first at our national instruments: legislative, executive, and judicial.

# SECTION IV

## Our National Instruments

*I*t is not a new observation that the people of any country (if, like the Americans, intelligent and well-informed) seldom adopt, and steadily persevere for many years in, an erroneous opinion respecting their interests. That consideration naturally tends to create great respect for the high opinion which the people of America have so long and uniformly entertained of the importance of their continuing firmly united under one federal government, vested with sufficient powers for all general and national purposes.

The more attentively I consider and investigate the reasons which appear to have given birth to this opinion, the more I become convinced that they are cogent and conclusive.

—John Jay

## CHAPTER 14

# Congress

PUBLIC OPINION, interest groups, parties, elections—these are the major instruments of political communication and influence which exist in our society to link the American people to their chosen representatives.

We now turn to the representatives themselves and to the formal institutions of government which our political instruments are designed to affect and to work through. Like our political instruments, these formal and official instruments exist at every level of government in America. Actually it is through them that our expectations of constitutional government and our value goals as a people are ultimately realized.

In this section we examine our national instruments; in subsequent sections our state and local instruments and the vital interrelationships of all three levels of government.

In surveying our national instruments, we begin where the Constitution begins—with the United States Congress.

## WHAT CONGRESS DOES

### Legislative Powers in the Constitution

The outlines of congressional authority are drawn in Article I and include the power to set and collect taxes, borrow money, regulate commerce with foreign nations and among the states, coin money, declare war, provide for the armed forces, create a postal system, and establish federal courts under the Supreme Court. Many of these powers belong to Congress exclusively; they are forbidden to the states.

### Electoral Powers

Besides acting as a legislative body Congress has a number of other functions. The House of Representatives plays its part in the electoral process by serving as a selector of last resort if the Electoral College is unable to supply a majority for a presidential candidate. Since the passage of the Twelfth Amendment in 1804, the House, as we have seen, has performed this task only once. Within constitutional limits, each house also has the right to set the qualifications of its own members and to decide election disputes between candidates for membership.

## Impeachment

Congress serves as an agency for the *removal* for cause of top executive and judicial officers. To impeach a federal official (members of the armed forces and members of Congress are exempt), the House first passes a resolution, which is roughly equivalent to an indictment, and the Senate, sitting as a court, conducts the trial. Impeachment can only be voted for "treason, bribery or other high crimes and misdemeanors," and the Senate must provide a two-thirds majority to convict. The Senate has sat as a court but twelve times in history, and produced a guilty verdict only four times.

## Other Powers

Congress has broad investigatory powers. It can look into anything in connection with carrying out its other powers, and it has the right to subpoena witnesses and documents.

Congress has the right, within certain constitutional limits, to set its own rules and elect its own presiding officers. It also has extensive disciplinary powers, not only over its own members, who can be unseated by a two-thirds vote, but also over private citizens who interfere with its operations. This latter power has been used extensively by investigating committees against refractory or un-

We are of opinion that the power of inquiry—with process to enforce it—is an essential and appropriate auxiliary to the legislative function. It was so regarded and employed in American legislatures before the Constitution was framed and ratified. Both Houses of Congress took this view of it early in their history . . . and both Houses have employed the power accordingly up to the present time.
—U. S. Supreme Court, *McGrain v. Daugherty* (1927)

truthful witnesses. The former can be charged with contempt and the latter with perjury. Under normal procedure, the accusation is made in the form of a joint resolution, the case is turned over to the United States Attorney General and trial is held in federal court.

Congress has the power to admit new states and can set the qualifications which new states must fulfill before being considered eligible for admission.

Congress is the agency of government which initiates the amending of our Constitution. In every case to date, Congress has taken the first step by passing, by a two-thirds majority, proposed constitutional amendments for ratification in turn by three fourths of the states. Under an alternate method, Congress could instead call a constitutional convention to propose amendments for ratification by the states. (See page 48.)

Finally, the Senate has the power to ratify treaties with foreign nations, which it must do by a two-thirds majority, and to confirm all top executive appointments.

## GENERAL STRUCTURE OF CONGRESS

### Membership

The fact that Congress consists of two houses, the Senate, containing two members from each state, and the House of Representatives, with members elected from districts apportioned among the states according to population, is the result of a compromise in the Constitutional Convention between delegates from the large states and the small states. Originally, the Senate, which gives every state, regardless of size or population, an equal voice, was intended to be the more conservative body with a national outlook. Senators were originally elected not by the people, but by the legislatures of their respective states. Removing them from the reach of the mass of voters was intended also to remove them from popular prejudices and passions and enable them to maintain a more imperial viewpoint. The House, on the other hand, whose members were chosen directly at the polls, was supposed to be directly representative of the more radical and democratic-minded mass of people—small farmers, tradesmen, and workers. In the House, too, the larger states would have a larger voice in affairs of government.

In the century and a half that have elapsed since the Constitutional Convention, the situation has been in large part reversed.

The august and conservative members of the Senate, who by constitutional amendment (in 1913) are now elected directly by the voters, have tended to become a more liberal and representative body.

In most states, particularly those with a dynamic two-party rivalry, the rich and the poor, the urban and the rural, the farmer and the workers, all live in large numbers. Senators who are elected by statewide vote must pay the urban worker his due, the more so since in recent decades the weight of the population has shifted from the country to the city and from the farm to the factory. In the House, decades of gerrymandering by state legislatures, which are themselves not representative of their states (see page 396), have kept more than half the seats under rural or semirural control. Although city-dwellers and workers make up more than half the population, they have considerably less than half the Representatives in the House. (For further discussion of this point, see Chapter 15.)

The Senate has 96 members. The House has 435 members, a number which, within limits, the House can modify. A Senator, who is elected for a term of six years, must be thirty years old, a resident of the state which he represents, and a United States citizen for nine years. A member of the House, who is elected for a term of two years, must be twenty-five years old, a resident of the state from which he is elected, and a citizen for seven years. (A Representative need not be a resident of the district from which he is elected, but in every case he is.) Members of Congress receive a salary of $22,500, which includes a tax-free expense allowance of $3,000.

## Congressional Privileges

Members of Congress are exempt from arrest except for treason, felony, or breach of the peace, which in practice is reduced to meaning that a Congressman need not serve on a jury, testify in court, or respond to a civil action. Congressmen have no exemption from criminal law, and a few of them over the years have been convicted and sent to jail, usually for misuse of government funds.

More important, congressmen are immune from legal action resulting from words spoken in Congress and in congressional committees or written in official congressional publications.

Congressmen have one other privilege: their official mail can be sent postage-free, under congressional frank.

## Congressional Sessions

Each Congress has a life of two years and is numbered accordingly. This life is in turn divided into a first session, which convenes in the year following the elections, and a second session, which meets during the year of the subsequent elections. The organization of Congress, such as its committee line-ups and presiding officers, and all bills introduced, last through both sessions. Each session is supposed to open on January 3 (unless Congress changes it to avoid a Sunday opening) and, under the Legislative Reorganization Act of 1946, is supposed to adjourn as close to July 31 as possible. Congress usually finds itself with enough to do, however, to delay adjournment beyond July, except in presidential election years.

*Procedure.* The parlimentary and other rules of the House are readopted, with opportunity for changes, at the beginning of each new Congress; those of the Senate are considered to be permanent, although they may be changed by senatorial vote at the beginning of any Congress and possibly at other times as well. The difference is that the House must stand for re-election every two years, and thus in theory a new body is sworn in at the beginning of each Congress. In the Senate only a third of the members (plus candidates running for seats left vacant by death or resignation) are up for election between Congresses, and the Upper House therefore considers itself in uninterrupted session.

In any discussion of rules, which play an important part in the operation of Congress, care must be taken to differentiate between the formal and the informal varieties. In the words of one veteran, the Senate "has operated so long as a gentlemen's club that two sets of rules have developed, one written and the other based on custom. Only after specific warning is it considered fair to enforce the written rules." [1] Even in the House, although to a lesser extent (see below), informal agreement between congressional leaders is a more important factor in the daily congressional routine than the elaborate system of regulation and precedents. Without such agreement, any disgruntled member could tie up either house in knots. It can still be done, but custom also provides for powerful deterrents to any Congressmen rash enough deliberately to violate the unwritten rules.

*Staff.* Congress does not consist only of Congressmen. There are approximately 3,700 people on the congressional payroll. Each member of the House receives an allowance sufficient to hire two clerks and a secretary, while the individual Senator receives enough to hire a staff of twelve or more, plus a specific sum for an administrative assistant. The average administrative assistant is an influential member of the Washington scene in his own right, since he acts in the Senator's behalf in caring for constitutents' problems, and helping on matters of legislative and campaign strategy. In addition, each congressional committee is entitled to hire at government expense four staff experts and six clerks. The legislation establishing this allowance was intended to help build up permanent, nonpartisan committee staffs, but the exigencies of politics and personalities have in part vitiated this intention. At present, some committee staff members last only as long as the chairman of their committee; but others simply shift to a minority role on the staff and hopefully await the next election.

## Services

Finally, there are two services provided to all Congressmen. The Legislative Reference Service in the Library of Congress consists of about 160 experts in every conceivable field who are available to prepare materials and conduct original research for any member on any subject. The Office of Legislative Counsel, consisting of parliamentarians and legal specialists equipped to draft a bill in proper form to cover any issue on request, drafts or helps polish most of the bills introduced in Congress.

# CONGRESS AT WORK

The tourist who ventures into one of the galleries overlooking the House or Senate Chamber is likely to be disappointed by the scene below. In the House, on an average afternoon, thirty or forty members will be scattered around the long, curving banks of seats or clustered at the side doors of the chamber. A Congressman will be speaking into a microphone at one of the tables on the floor but no one seems to be listening, least of all the presiding officer. In the Senate, the scene is even more alarming. Perhaps five Senators are sitting at their desks, most of them poring over their morning mail or the previous day's *Congressional Record*, while one of their number is declaiming industriously into vacant air. Not even the press galleries are occupied.

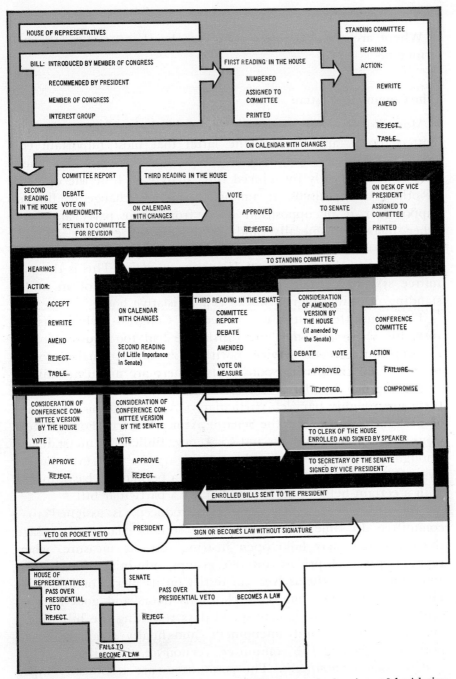

The illustration above diagrams the manifold steps a single piece of legislation must take before it becomes a law. But this is only half the story. There are many other less formalized steps, involving what Pendelton Herring has called the four I's of policy-making: Ideas, Interest, Institutions, and Individuals. (*Current Readings on the Congress,* Maxwell Graduate School of Citizenship and Public Affairs, Department of Political Science, Syracuse University, n. d., pp. 3–4.)

Where are the Congressmen? What has happened to the government?

## The Committee System

Most Congressmen could be found in their offices or in committee rooms, and it is in the latter that most important congressional business is transacted. It is in committees that members receive a newly introduced bill, analyze it, hear the opinions of others on it, discuss it among themselves, change it, line up support for it or opposition to it from their party and from other members generally, and finally, after the issues and the lines have been carefully drawn, vote it out for ultimate decision on the floor of the chamber itself or pigeonhole it. This is the committee system, virtually the beginning and the end of an understanding of how Congress works as a legislative body.

The committee system was forced on Congress early in its history, for the reason that the legislature had too many members and too much business to deal with to be able to make progress except by dividing the responsibility. There are nineteen standing committees in the House and fifteen in the Senate, and most of them are roughly parallel, particularly: Appropriations, Ways and Means (called Finance in the Senate), Armed Services, Foreign Relations, Agriculture, Banking and Currency, Judiciary, Interstate and Foreign Commerce. Many of these divide up the work even further by establishing subcommittees, either on a permanent basis, to deal with a certain field, or *ad hoc,* to handle a particular bill.

Every bill, once it is formally introduced, is assigned to a committee. In time, if the bill has a serious chance of passage, the committee may hold open hearings on the measure, where representatives of private interest groups, administration leaders, and Congressmen themselves can testify on its merits or iniquities. Hearings over, the committee closes its doors and goes into executive session, where it may spend days rewriting the bill, voting on each provision and amendment, and finally producing a report encompassing the committee version of the bill.

*Bipartisan Committees.* The committees are technically bipartisan; each party is represented in approximately the same proportion as its strength in the chamber. If the Senate, for example, has sixty-four Republicans and thirty-two Democrats, then each fifteen-member committee will have ten Republicans and five Democrats. In the Senate, every member serves on at least two major committees, and each committee has from thirteen to twenty-one members. In the House, the average member serves on but one committee, each committee having about thirty members.

*Special Committees.* Occasionally the House or Senate will create a special committee to deal with a special issue or pursue an investigation which for some reason cannot be entrusted to a regular committee. This practice, which tends to upset congressional routine, has declined since the Legislative Reorganization Act of 1946.

*Joint Committees.* To deal with a few important and particularly complex subjects, Congress has established joint committees, consisting of members from each house. A temporary joint committee is occasionally appointed to make an investigation; permanent joint committees are concerned with research into taxation, into the national economy, and with atomic energy.

## Committees at Work

The average bill, if it can be considered animate, owes its life or death to its committee. In the first place, the average bill deals with a subject of some complexity, and by the time committee members have finished living with it through hearings and committee voting, they are likely to know far more about its provisions than anyone else in the chamber. As a result, except in cases of bills of great importance and wide application, the average member will follow the lead of the committeeman who is of his party and perhaps from a similar district on almost any bill emanating from the committee. When an urban Democratic Congressman who is a Labor Committee member, for example, decides to vote for a bill on a labor-management subject, all the urban Democrats in the House serving on other committees are apt to take the cue. They are aware that he has been in closest touch with the private interest groups involved; they know that he must face the same kind of electorate they do; they know that he is aware of the tiny pitfalls and loopholes in each provision of the bill; they consider it reasonably safe to follow his lead in voting for it.

Furthermore, the committee collectively usually determines

whether the bill will ever reach the floor for a general vote. In this regard the average committee has more power in the negative; once a bill has been pigeonholed, it is extremely difficult for a Congressman, or even a group of Congressmen, who are not members of that committee to get it out. Only one practical avenue is open: if a majority of the chamber signs a discharge petition, then the bill is automatically brought out for a vote. But because of the sanctity with which Congress regards the committee system, including the right of a committee to pigeonhole a bill, discharge petitions are seldom successful.

Finally, the committee version of the bill usually carries considerable weight on the floor. The average measure is considered not in the round, but in parts. The main battles will be staged over certain key amendments, not on the subject of the bill as a whole. The committee version of a bill has been determined by a group of men who have been subjected to hundreds of opinions, on every aspect of the subject, from private interest groups, from party leaders, from the administration and from other interested Congressmen. Having passed through this crucible of fire, the committee version is likely to prove acceptable to a majority of the chamber as well.

### The Committee Chairman

Everything that has been said about the power of committees can be pinpointed, to a certain extent, in the single person of the committee chairman. The committee chairman, through custom and rules, has immense influence in determining the nature and the amount of the committee's work. Through his power to call meetings (and to adjourn them), to prepare agenda, and to choose the committee staff, the chairman, except in the rare event that he is deserted by most of the other members, has the first and last word on every bill before his committee. The chairman's influence is reinforced by his own special status before the public, in the executive departments and even within Congress itself. Finally, since the chairman often guides a bill once it reaches the floor, he represents the committee in leadership conferences which decide when a bill is to be brought up for consideration and he even chooses the members who shall speak for the bill.

*Choice by Seniority.* The concentration of responsibility in com-

mittee chairmen is in many ways useful to the Congress. The fly
in the ointment is the method used to select them. In a sense there
is no method; committee chairmen win their posts through seniority
—the length of uninterrupted time they have served on the committee—and retain their positions until they retire, die, or are defeated in election. A committee member may oppose his own party's
program, abominate his party's leadership, get along badly with
other committee members, and be generally incompetent; but if
he remains on his committee long enough, and his party has a majority, he will eventually become its chairman.

Committee chairmen are in fact chosen not by their peers or
superiors in Congress, but by the voters who return them to office
for term after term. A district which returns the same Congressman to office consistently is apt to be a one-party district, where
the political tides flow slowly and where elections are dominated
by a political machine or private interest group. In hard-fought
districts, where political cross-currents are swift, where party leadership is in flux and interest groups compete for favor, Congressmen
have short or erratic legislative careers and do not become committee chairmen. To a significant extent, therefore, the seniority
system detracts from democratic leadership, for it is the close-
fought, evenly matched district which more accurately reflects the
political emotions of the nation as a whole, while the one-party
district usually is representative of a single interest.

*Dual Leadership.* Because committee chairmen are not chosen
for their party loyalty, the seniority system also promotes a dual
leadership in each chamber. Ranged on one side are the official
party leaders; opposing them in many cases are the committee
chairmen. This is accentuated by the divisions which occur in each
party on various issues. The Democratic party had been committed to amending or repealing the Taft-Hartley law; helping to
block the way was a Democratic committee chairman from North
Carolina who favored retaining the law unchanged. A Republican
President found that part of his international program was being
undermined by a Republican committee chairman from Wisconsin
who represented the isolationist wing of the party.

A few defenders of the seniority system regard it as the only
method available to avoid bitter disputes and division over the
choice of committee chairmen, and give it added credit for recognizing experience. In effect, however, the argument revolves not

around political science but around politics: rural and conservative groups, from one-party districts (of both parties) which benefit from seniority, favor it; labor, liberal, and civil rights groups, who suffer from seniority, oppose it.

The seniority system of selecting chairmen is only one of the factors tending to promote the unrepresentative character of congressional committees. Another factor is the understandable tendency of Congressmen to seek posts on committees dealing with their special interests. Thus the Congressman from Iowa will try to obtain a seat on the Agriculture committee, and the Senator from Oregon will battle for a place on the Public Works committee. In time, some committees may cease to represent Congress as a whole, for they become dominated by the special interest groups in their particular field of legislation. The perfect theoretical picture of the nation as a whole delegating legislative responsibility to Congress, which in turn delegates it to a committee, may be badly distorted in practice.

## The Conference Committee

A different kind of committee, the conference committee, exercises a different kind of power in the structure of Congress. When the two houses pass different bills on the same subject, which is normal procedure, a conference committee of from three to five members from each house is appointed to prepare a compromise version. The result of their labors, which are often extensive and bitter, cannot be amended when it is returned to each house, but only passed or rejected as is. The conferees are supposed to confine themselves to the subject matter of the House and Senate versions of the bill, but it is not rare that the only suitable compromise appears to be the writing of a new provision, or the introduction of a new approach. The conferees may be criticized for "exceeding their instructions," but the conference report is usually passed by both houses. The power of conference committees has led to their being called "the little Congress."

## Congressional Investigations

One of the most controversial aspects of the committee system is the congressional investigation. There are two kinds of congressional hearings, which in practice are often intermingled: the investigatory hearing, in which the primary aim is to obtain information, and the regulatory hearing, in which the primary aim is to exercise control over the workings of executive agencies. Legislative hearings, which are held in connection with virtually every major piece of legislation, are mainly held to elicit the opinions and narrow the conflicts of various interest groups. Some hearings, especially in connection with appropriation bills, are partly regulatory in character, and bureaucrats frequently squirm under hostile questioning. (After the hearings, the bureaucrat condemns the Congressman for his parochial viewpoint and the Congressman attacks the bureaucrat for his unresponsiveness to public opinion. Often both parties are correct.)

Many hearings are held not in connection with a particular piece of legislation but as part of a general investigation, either into an aspect of the administration or into a field of public interest. Congress has every right and need to conduct such investigations, and some notable probes have uncovered corruption in government, infringements of civil liberties, racketeering, and unethical business practices. It is not the subject of an investigation which determines its merit, but the way it is conducted. Congressmen more interested in making newspaper headlines than in developing information, and more concerned with hanging an accusation on an opposing party or interest group than in regulating malpractice, have sometimes abused the congressional right to investigate. Despite its power to investigate, Congress does not have the power to determine the guilt or innocence of an individual or a group. This power is reserved to the courts. Defending investigations, some legislators have claimed that Congressmen need not be confined by judicial safeguards because no fine or imprisonment result from an investigation. On the other hand, sensational exposure, leading to loss of a job and ostracism, can be just as effective punishment to the victim as a jail sentence.

## Political Party Influence

The influence of politics and the political party extends deep into both houses of Congress, and is felt at the committee level as well as on a broader basis. The members of both houses are seated on the floor according to party, Republicans on the left (looking out from the platform), Democrats on the right. The leaders of Congress, including a majority party leader and minority party leader, with their assistants, sometimes called party whips, plan over-all party strategy, try to keep their respective membership in line and working together, and Congress functioning.

Strict party organization is achieved usually only in the first few days of a session, when each party, meeting in caucus, designates its committee line-ups and votes for its respective leaders. Each party in each house has a committee to determine committee assignments; since reelected members usually remain on their former committees, this is largely a task of assigning freshmen to vacancies and accommodating a few veterans who wish to shift.

Thereafter, party blocs are broken up into smaller groups, shifting with each major bill, revolving around sectional needs and political differences. The party *caucus* (called the *conference* in the Senate) seldom meets again and its members are usually not bound to follow caucus decisions when it does. In the Senate, an intermediate group, consisting of a smaller group of party leaders and called the Policy Committee, is endowed with a budget and staff and depending on its leadership may help preserve party unity on some issues. But throughout most of the session it is up to a handful of party leaders to establish party positions and to erect party lines. They meet with more or less success, depending on the issue and on their power relationship with committee chairmen, the President of the United States, and with individual Congressmen. A freshman member looking for a better committee assignment, a patronage-hungry member seeking some jobs for his supporters back home, a committee chairman who has a pet bill, an ambitious member who wants to head a special investigating committee, these are grist for the party leader's mill. He swaps favors; he negotiates; he cajoles. A dynamic and energetic leader may maintain considerable party solidarity (if outside forces, such as a party-splitting issue, do not interfere), while a weak or unlucky leader may be swept aside by the rush of events. It is this intermittency and fortuity that make many people wish to see more responsible instruments of party leadership developed in our national government.

# THE HOUSE OF REPRESENTATIVES

By the nature of their membership and the role they play in the legislative process, each house of Congress has certain peculiarities and differences which have developed over the years. In the potentially unwieldy House of Representatives, certain institutions and rules maintain a degree of efficiency in procedure—and also limit the freedom of movement of the individual member.

## The Rules Committee

The House Rules Committee, for example, has an entirely different function from that of its counterpart in the Senate. After a bill has gone through the mill of hearings, consideration and rewriting in a regular House committee, it then must go to the Rules Committee, which serves as a kind of traffic officer for almost all legislation reaching the floor. The Rules Committee may also delay a bill to death, or amend it or even substitute a different version more to its liking. Eventually it also provides a rule regulating the length of debate and the number and kinds of amendments which may be offered when the bill reaches the floor. As an extra source of influence, the Rules Committee receives firsthand all proposals to change House rules—including measures to change the power of the Rules Committee.

No Congressman will deny that the Rules Committee has an important function in preserving some kind of order in the schedule of House business. More than this, it also stands between the average beleaguered member and an unworthy bill which he might find it embarrassing to oppose on a record vote. Some bills, which the nation cannot afford to have passed, are accompanied by such high-pressure lobbying that the average Representative would hesitate to vote against them when they come to the floor. Occasionally the Rules Committee performs a signal service to the nation by quietly pigeonholing such a bill until too late in the session for floor action. To be able to perform this service, the members of the Rules Committee must come from politically secure districts, which are usually Democratic one-party districts in the South or Republican one-party districts in the Middle West. In both cases, the Congressman is likely to be a conservative; in any case, he is not representative of the House as a whole.

If Rules Committee members disregarded their own political tendencies in the exercise of their important powers, there might be little objection to their work. However, it is only natural that a conservative Southerner might sincerely believe that a civil rights measure poses the same kind of threat to the nation as a veterans' pension grab, and that a conservative Middle Westerner might have equal misgivings about a public housing bill. As a result, the Rules Committee stands accused of exploiting its exalted position to impose on the House its own brand of political leadership, rather than of serving as an impartial traffic controller. Following the sweeping electoral victory of President Roosevelt in 1936, for example, a handful of men composing a majority on the House Rules Committee became a two-year roadblock against the President's program.

### Speaker of the House

At the summit of the small group which directs the activities of the House is the Speaker, the most important single individual in the chamber. Elected by the majority party members meeting in caucus, the Speaker's official powers are reinforced by his informal powers. The former include the recognition of speakers (largely at his own discretion), the settlement of parliamentary disputes, the appointing of members of special and conference committees, and the assigning of bills to relevant standing committees. The latter, which stem in part from his recognized leadership of the majority party in the House, depend partly on his own personality, on the strength of his party, and the relations between Congress and the President and may, if all the factors coincide, make the Speaker second only to the President of the United States in influence.

House rules and customs themselves exert a quieting influence on the individual member. There is no such thing as a filibuster—excessive speechmaking to prevent action—because there is a ban on any debate which is not strictly to the point and because no member can talk more than one hour on one subject. The Rules Committee usually limits debate even more by the rule it gives to individual measures; the Committee of the Whole House, a parliamentary sleight of hand by which the chamber transforms itself into a working body during most debate in order to lower quorum requirements on the floor, imposes even stricter limits on discussion. Since all these rules and limits are adopted by majority vote and enforced by the Speaker, it is extremely difficult, if not impossible, for a small group of Congressmen to impose their will on the House once a measure reaches the floor.

# THE SENATE

The Senate, on the other hand, glorifies the individual Senator to such an extent that although there is complete freedom for every member, the chamber's operations occasionally are brought to a dead halt. This, too, is dictated by the nature and functions of the body. The individual Senator is likely to be an important leader in the state and perhaps a recognized national authority in a certain field. Not even the President can cross swords with an influential Senator without risk to his program. This is bolstered by the Senate's own high regard for itself as the most exclusive club in the world, whose members, elected for a term of six years and often re-elected for several terms, watch Presidents come and go.

## Filibusters

There are virtually no limits on the right of a Senator to speak on the floor on any subject that enters his head for as long as he can remain on his feet. Southerners have used this right to indulge in frequent filibusters—or threats of filibusters—to delay action on civil rights bills, but the record for one man was made by a Westerner, Wayne Morse of Oregon, when he occupied the floor for 22 hours and 26 minutes. Besides exhaustion, the only weapon to curtail the filibuster is cloture, under which sixty-four Senators can limit each member to one hour on the floor. In the opening days of the 85th Congress in 1957, a bold attempt was made in the Senate —and with some success—to ease the rigid rules protecting the filibuster. But limitation of debate by simple majority vote is still a long way off.

Senator Wayne Morse of Oregon naps on a cot in the Senate lobby during a filibuster. Morse himself holds the filibuster longevity record of over 22 hours.

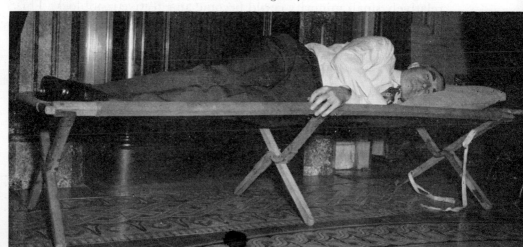

The Rules Committee has no special powers in the Senate and there is no powerful presiding officer to regulate senatorial affairs. Bills are taken up in the order they are reported by committee, or are taken up out of order by unanimous consent. Although the presiding officer is technically the Vice-President of the United States, his place is usually filled by a junior member who happens to be on the floor. Presiding officers must recognize speakers in the order of their request and they have little else to do.

## Treaty Ratification

In addition, the Senate has two special functions which give its members, individually and collectively, great influence in the nation. One is the power to ratify treaties—which in practice means to be consulted on every step of the way, from the time a treaty is first broached, until it is signed, sealed, and delivered. To insure good relations with this powerful body, the Secretary of State usually consults on all matters of foreign policy with the chairman and members of the Foreign Relations Committee. (In our history, the Senate has approved 900 out of 1,100 treaties, but the 200 it turned down included some of the most significant.)

In recent years the Senate has been obliged to share some of its exclusive jurisdiction over foreign policy with the House of Representatives. This development has come partly because an increasing number of foreign policy bills involve money (foreign aid, technical assistance, etc.); partly because the Senate leadership has wished on occasion to avoid the unwieldy two-thirds vote of approval which is required on every treaty. To pass the average non-controversial treaty, involving, say, international control over narcotics or safety measures for international air travel, the two-thirds requirement poses no particular obstacle. Against other treaties, which the Senate leadership and the administration would like to see approved, a relatively small minority could become an effective roadblock. This, and the fact that House approval would be necessary for their effective implementation, has led to the adoption of certain foreign policy measures, including the European Recovery Act (Marshall Plan), and the Point-Four Program (technical assistance to other nations), through *joint resolution* which requires a majority vote of both houses.

## Confirmation of Nominations

It has already been demonstrated that the individual Senator is a more influential factor in the political field than the average individual Representative. Senators not only represent entire states: they sometimes dominate them. No Representative has ever equaled the power of Senators like Huey Long in Louisiana, or Robert A. Taft in Ohio, or Harry Byrd in Virginia. Some of this senatorial power comes from the upper chamber's constitutional right to confirm nominations. This brings the subject back to patronage (see p. 236). The Senate has a constitutional right to approve or reject nominations for judicial office and for executive agencies after they are submitted to it by the President. In practice, the administration clears nominations before they are announced, which means that individual Senators belonging to the administration party often have the right to choose the nominees in the first place. Furthermore, through a custom known as senatorial courtesy, the Senator from whose state the nominee hails can exert an absolute veto power by labeling the nominee "personally obnoxious," a feeling which the Senate as a whole always respects.

The power of individual Senators over executive appointments enhances the strength of the upper chamber at the expense of the administration. In day-to-day life in the nation's capital, however, the power of the administration to propose and of the Senate to dispose is in somewhat equal balance, weighted on one side or the other by the momentary influence of the Senator in question, by the determination of the administration, and even by the reputation of the nominee.

# THE CONGRESSMAN—UNDER THE MICROSCOPE

Who is the average congressman? If he is in the Senate, he is likely to be fifty-eight years old, a lawyer who has previously served in public office, with an income by his own estimate, if he had not been in the Senate, of $47,000 a year. In the House he is also a lawyer, fifty-three years old, with the possibility of previous political experience, and with an income, if he were in private practice, of $22,000 a year. (The income figures were tabulated in a survey made several years ago, before congressional salaries were raised.) Not all congressmen are lawyers, of course, but more than half of them are. About a third are from business or the banking fields, and the rest are journalists, teachers, farmers or other professional men. Only a handful are likely to come from the ranks of organized labor. At the beginning of the 85th Congress, only three were Negroes and sixteen were women. Almost three quarters were Protestant; about 20 percent were Catholics; a handful were Jews.

If Congress represented the nation precisely, there would be more younger people, more women, more Negroes. The educational level would be lower and the occupational spread would be much wider.

Despite the preponderance of lawyers, however, Congress on the whole does mirror the average American's nonprofessional and nonlegalistic approach to governmental problems. The average congressman may embrace many of the voter's weaknesses, but he also reflects the voter's strengths; and the fact remains that he has earned the respect of at least part of his community and that, in general, he is endowed with enough integrity, ability, and experience to do his job. No doubt a Congress composed exclusively of engineers, scientists, philosophers, and poets would perform on a higher plane, but there is also no doubt that such "eggheads" would soon outdistance the voters. This would result either in their removal at the next election or the end of government by consent.

William Allen White, the Kansas editor who spent much of his life in national politics, once described a certain successful congressman in these terms:

> In Congress he rose rapidly, because of his facility of speech, but also because he had a logical mind, a sound, healthy body and could work in committee, talk on the floor, and hurry through the [Executive] departments getting jobs for his friends.

The description was of William McKinley, who later was twice elected President, and it may still serve as an accurate picture of the average congressman today.[2]

## Influences

To whom is the congressman responsible? What are the influences which impel him to vote as he does? How do the various influences described in Section III, such as public opinion, private interest groups, and political parties, compare with each other in their effect on one man?

*From Home District.* Certainly the strongest influences on any Congressman, especially on a member of the House, comes from his home district. Of these home pressures the least effective come from vague, ill-defined public opinion, as expressed in the scattering of letters and post cards received every day in the congressman's office. More important is the pressure exerted by the local branches of major interest groups, especially from one with which the congressman himself is or has been allied.

Of equal importance may be the attitudes of the party leaders in the congressman's district or state.

*The National Party.* In the absence of strong pressure from home, a number of other influences enter the picture. Pressure from party headquarters (from the national committee or from the administration, depending on whether the congressman's party is in power) is important for members from two-party states, and may be buttressed by a promise of patronage or other favors (or a threat to withdraw them). Party leaders in Congress itself often try to maintain a semblance of party discipline and unity on certain votes, exerting a pressure which may also be reinforced by promises of favors or threats to withdraw them. There is also a certain amount of trading among members: you vote for my bill and I'll vote for yours—a practice known as "log-rolling." A Congressman who is intensely interested in a certain bill for his district may trade away his freedom of action on dozens of other bills in return for votes for his measure. In the House, there may be pressure exerted on a member by his fellow partisans from the same state; this is especially common among delegations from one-party states. It might be awkward, for example, for a Democratic Representative from Alabama to explain why his vote was different from the votes cast by the other eight Democratic members from the same state.

*From Congressional Leaders.* Certain congressional leaders and committee chairmen in either chamber exert influence far beyond their titular powers and sometimes even beyond the ranks of their own party. Conservatives of both parties, for example, would often follow the lead of former Republican Senator Eugene Milliken on tax matters, or Democratic Senator Harry Byrd on appropriations and the budget, or the late Senator Pat McCarran on immigration. In the House, Representative Francis E. Walter has similar influence in immigration matters, while Representative William L. Dawson has considerable influence on Northern members on civil rights issues. Finally, the average congressman is also influenced by his own ideals, his conscience, his background, and his experience. There is more honest searching for the public interest in the Congress than is generally credited. The Congressman inevitably draws upon his background and his world-view in making a decision. These resources have helped put him in Congress in the first place because they mirror to a certain extent the ideals and background of his constituents. No political figure is impervious to external influence or to the dictates of conscience. Fortunately, there are few Congressmen who have eliminated all self-respect and, like a weather vane, move only as the winds of influence play from the various points of the political compass.

# WHAT'S WRONG WITH CONGRESS?

One of the favorite occupations of critics inside and outside government is to attack Congress. Many attacks are ill-considered and unfair to the victim, for much of what Congress does it is compelled to do. Its squabbles and conflicts are on the surface because Congress is a public institution to a much greater extent than the judiciary or the administration, where warring factions retreat behind closed doors. By its nature Congress is argumentative and controversial: a Congress speaking with unanimity could not exist in a democratic society and would not be representative if it did. Congress throws its weight around in various places because it is endowed by the Constitution with a number of broad powers which have been granted to no other branch of government.

But still and all, there is considerable validity in the central indictment of Congress: that it fails to devote sufficient of its energies to establishing clear-cut, responsible national policies and programs.

## Inefficiency

In part this failure is due to inefficiency. Congress is swamped with minutiae, particularly with constituent errands. The energy spent on these petty matters prompted Professor Schattschneider to comment that it was a little like "using a cyclotron to warm a cup of coffee." By cutting red tape and helping bewildered constituents find their way down the right governmental corridor, the congressman often performs a humanizing function in big government. Unfortunately, however, many constituents turn to their congressman only after the proper governmental agencies have

# "There Must Be Some Better Way We Can Run This"

rightly resisted their requests. Such constituents are out to get more than they are entitled to get, and in the process make their congressmen accessories to the whine, if not the crime.

Inefficiency also results from the exaggerated prerogatives of Senators to talk without restraint as to time or topic. Self-discipline is in order here, even if the ultimate right to "talk until the Senate sobers up" is retained.

In the area of congressional behavior, diagnosis is easier than cure. The Legislative Reorganization Act of 1946 identified many of the most difficult problems of Congress, but the basic troubles still remain. The 1946 reform cut the number of committees; congressmen are now harried by the competing demands of *sub-* committees. The reform act added staff to committees and to individuals in order to lighten the legislator's burden; now, with the assurance of staff help, the member may take on new duties and spread his energies even thinner.

## Minority Interests

But inefficient or superfluous machinery is not the key issue. The fundamental problem is the seeming inability or unwillingness of Congress to adopt a more consistently national viewpoint. Often what appears to be managerial inefficiency, such as the Rules Committee's predilection for delaying legislation in the House, actually reflects an inherent fear of majority rule and an inherent determination to protect not the rights, but the importunities, of minority interests.

As long as an individual member feels that his primary loyalty should be to his district's interest, he would be derelict in his duty if he did not use every means at his command to enforce his own views on the body as a whole, even against the wishes of a majority of other members. And if, by the adroit use of parliamentary stratagems, the single member is victorious, his district may rejoice in having elected a "superior" representative.

But the national interest—what Edmund Burke called the "permanent forces" in the community—may suffer seriously if not disastrously in the process.

Proposals to change some of the trappings of this parochialism, such as the power of committee chairmen and the seniority system of electing them, inevitably come up against one of the original pillars of our constitutional philosophy. Just as a fear of majority rule produced the checks and balances among various divisions of government, so the Congress has established roadblocks against attempts to dilute the power of organized minorities in determining or vetoing national policies.

In the long run, basic reforms in the operation of the United States Congress will come as the reflection of deep changes in our social, economic, and political life; from the necessities and leadership of the future. Actually, in times of widely recognized crisis, Congress has almost without exception demonstrated sufficient unity to take decisive action—usually, however, under what Professor

Rossiter has called the "constitutional dictatorship" of the Presidency.

The difficulty is that life today is a perpetual crisis. We have been living on top of a volcano for so long that we have, almost inevitably, become relaxed and inattentive. The fact is that the charming irresponsibilities of the nineteenth century are no longer permissible. We need an educated, responsible, and nationally oriented Congress *all* the time, not just part of the time.

How to approximate this goal is a task for Presidents, for political parties, for the electorate generally, and for the best minds in America in the years ahead.

# CONCLUSION

**Synopsis**

Congress is one of the most complex and fascinating instruments of government ever devised. Within its formal structure, a kaleidoscope of committees, political leaders, blocs, and ordinary members in varying states of confusion and parliamentary sophistication, maneuver for mastery. Set upon by every pressure and influence of a democratic society, it is perhaps little wonder that its members have a tendency to duck unequivocal decisions and evade clear-cut expressions of policy.

**Significance**

The question may well be raised: If Congress were more responsible in a political sense, would this not destroy its usefulness as a regional and economic conciliator in this vast and sprawling nation? The only answer is a counter-question: If Congress does not become more responsible—more conscious of its role as a critical evaluator, modifier, and endorser of integrated policy proposals—will there be any vast and sprawling democratic nation left to conciliate?

**Prospectus**

Congress is not walls or halls, but people. There is no "Representative Swanson," and never was; and there is no Welfare Committee. The Food and Drug Administration *does* exist, in the Department of Health, Education, and Welfare, but to the best of our knowledge it has never been called upon to act in a case like the fictional one described in the next chapter. But description does not have to be real in order to be true. What follows is neither the high road nor the low road of congressional activity; but neither is it an exceptional road.

## CHAPTER 15

# "Representative Swanson"

### A Call from the President

REPRESENTATIVE THOMAS SWANSON was not likely to forget this day for some time. Although he had been in Congress five years, and had on four occasions spoken to the President of the United States in person, this was the first time the President had called him on the telephone to ask him for his vote on a pending measure. Swanson had planned to vote for the bill anyway; evidently the party whip assigned to his state delegation in Congress had reported him as uncertain. The fact that the President had called him personally was a sign not only of the importance the White House gave to the measure but also that the vote the following afternoon would be close.

Swanson sat at his desk in his office for a few moments, musing over his memory of the call. The President had opened the conversation by asking about Swanson's wife, who had been going through a seige of influenza. A sign of careful staff work. The President had used careful phrasing in asking for Swanson's vote: "Congressman, I am calling to tell you how important the Secretary of State and I feel that foreign aid is to our efforts to maintain our defenses abroad. As you know, the bill is scheduled for floor action tomorrow and I certainly hope that we can count on you to support our efforts to obtain an authorization of at least four and a half billion dollars. You've probably read the hearings and noted that most of the money is destined for military aid, but the fund for economic assistance is equally important."

Swanson had assured the President that he would vote for the full amount in the administration's bill, including economic assistance, and after a few amenities the call had ended.

## Job Recommendations

Now Swanson wondered if he should have used the opportunity to ask about the opening in his district for a job with the Bureau of Internal Revenue. He had submitted a name, and cleared it in advance with the National Committee, but a month had passed without word from the White House. Meanwhile he had heard rumors that the Treasury Department had favored another candidate for the job, a man who had played no active role in his party back home for several years but who was close to one of the United States Senators from the state.

Despite the temptation, Swanson knew that he could not bring up the Internal Revenue job in connection with a vote on the foreign-aid bill. The latter was too remote from party politics, and although some Congressmen might have demanded a pound of flesh for their vote, Swanson had a higher sense of the proprieties. He would bring up the patronage matter instead next week, when the White House congressional liaison staff member came around to talk to him about a pending tariff bill.

## A Bill Is Introduced

The day he received the call from the White House was also the day that Representative Swanson had introduced—by handing it to a page on the House floor, who had deposited it in the hopper by the Speaker's desk—a bill which was close to his heart. On the face of it, an amendment to the Federal Food and Drug Act was not likely to stir up a great national debate, but the mere act of introduction had already involved Swanson in a series of battles with several parties and cost him two months of time-consuming effort.

It had all begun a week after his election to a third term. One of his supporters, a man who could be counted on for a $500 contribution for every election campaign, was the comptroller of a drug and patent medicine manufacturing company in his district. (The comptroller, who had the improbable name of Hubert La Salle, was undoubtedly reimbursed by the company for the $500, which was probably listed as entertainment or some other business expense.) One of the company's most profitable products included among its ingredients a newly discovered chemical which the Food and Drug Administration, after extensive tests, had decided

This air view of part of Capitol Hill in Washington, D. C., shows the Capitol in the middle, with the two House Office Buildings below it and the Senate Office Building at top right. A second Senate Office Building is being completed to the right of the present structure.

came under the category of narcotics. As a result, the buyer of the product would require a doctor's prescription. The company had intended its new product for the patent medicine market, and the decision had been a heavy blow to its plans.

La Salle came to Swanson with the company's request: Could the Congressman introduce an amendment to the Federal Food and Drug Act removing this particular chemical, and others of the same nature, from the provisions of the narcotics act?

In describing the problem, La Salle assured Swanson that when the narcotics section of the law had been written, many years earlier, chemists had little knowledge of the chemical in question or of its various components. It was entirely safe—La Salle had the results of extensive tests to prove it—and without a change in the law, millions of Americans would be denied an inexpensive medicine which could provide substantial relief from pain.

To clinch his argument, La Salle showed Swanson correspondence with the agency, and an official report written by an agency examiner, which showed that the agency itself might support such a change in the law. At Swanson's request, he also arranged an appointment with an official of the agency when Swanson returned to Washington.

## A Bill Faces Opposition

And so the merry-go-round began. Perhaps La Salle was not aware of it, but it developed that the Food and Drug Administration was not fully sold on the change in the law. It agreed that the chemical in question perhaps should not be covered by the narcotics provisions, but it feared any legislation which might result in a substantial emasculation of the narcotics section. At Swanson's request, La Salle spent two weeks in Washington working with agency scientists and legal representatives, seeking to write a satisfactory bill which would cover the subject but not weaken existing law more than necessary. The bill was taking shape when a scandal blew up involving an agency action against a manufacturer of a highly doubtful insecticide. The scandal involved political influence reaching as high as a member of the President's cabinet, and the Food and Drug administrator, evidently deciding that the agency's interests would be best served if it drew in its horns for a while, called off all work on Swanson's bill.

La Salle was understandably annoyed. At Swanson's suggestion, he enlisted the support of a well-known doctor who wrote a letter of support to the administrator. The latter remained obdurate. Swanson called the Secretary of Health, Education, and Welfare, who had jurisdiction over the Food and Drug Administration, but the Secretary, fearing the opposition of organized medicine, was not enthusiastic about the bill. Swanson then played his master card. Although he was not a member of the Appropriations Committee, one of its ranking members had recently asked Swanson for support for a certain bill. Swanson now called the member and asked for a reciprocal favor. The member agreed, and put in a telephone call to the Secretary, suggesting that the Secretary could help his department's pending appropriation bill by removing the roadblock on the narcotics amendment bill. The Secretary thought it over for a few days, and then gave in.

Within the following week, La Salle had received agency approval of a final draft of the bill and Swanson had obtained the agreement of a friend in the Senate to introduce it in the upper chamber at the same time that he introduced it in the House.

After the bill was introduced the Speaker of the House, as a matter of routine, assigned the bill a number (HR 846) and referred it to the Welfare Committee. Swanson had a lunch date with the committee chairman the next day but despite his most persuasive efforts, he left the table feeling that the chairman was not going to extend himself in behalf of the bill. Two weeks later he called up one of the committee staff members to find out if hearings had been scheduled. The staff member said they had not, and suggested that prospects were not auspicious. It appeared that another staff member, who was highly regarded by the committee chairman, was fervently opposed to the bill and had sold his point of view to the chairman. As it was related to Swanson, a major medical association, opposing the bill for reasons of its own, had sent its legislative representative to discuss the matter with the staff member and persuaded him that any amendment weakening the narcotics section of the Federal Food and Drug Act would be ill-advised. Once again Swanson found himself in an impasse.

## Lobbying for and against the Bill

Foreseeing the possibility of full-scale opposition by the medical organization, Representative Swanson advised La Salle that the complexion of the battle had changed. It was time to seek the support of the pharmaceutical trade association, to hire a lawyer in Washington who could do some direct lobbying on Capitol Hill, and to arouse some support in the home districts of the committee chairman and ranking committee members. And so the campaign began.

In the course of the next two months, the pharmaceutical association, which boasted an office and an executive secretary in Washington, devised an attractive brochure and a lengthy brief in support of the amendment and sent them to every member of Congress. Efforts on the part of the executive secretary to persuade the committee staff member that his fears about the bill were needless were not particularly productive. Meanwhile, however, another drug company located in the home state of the committee chairman took up the cudgels and approached the governor, state party leaders, and several other Congressmen for their support.

The medical association, busy with other matters, at first paid little attention to the matter. An article attacking the amendment appeared in its monthly magazine and another in its weekly news sheet mailed to association leaders in each state. As the pharmaceutical association's efforts became more apparent, however, the opposing organization stepped up its efforts. The next issue of the news sheet urged medical leaders to write their Congressmen in opposition to the bill. The executive vice-president had lunch with three influential congressmen, one of them a doctor in private life, and discussed lobbying strategy. It was agreed to try to persuade the agency to reverse its support of the bill and to seek administration assistance.

On the other side of the battle, the drug companies had succeeded in obtaining the cooperation of a union which represented most of the workers in the industry, and Congressmen began to receive letters and post cards, all suspiciously alike, urging support of the bill. The number of communications, which was large, influenced the average Congressman less than the fact that the union itself had taken an interest in the subject.

### Political Action on the Bill

With the entrance of the union into the battle, there began to be a faint stirring of political interest in the bill. The union legislative representative dropped in to see the minority leader, who promised his support. The Speaker had already been approached by the medical association and had made no commitments. In fact, he had been under pressure by the medical association in regard to a number of other bills that session, and, slightly peeved at their excessive interest in what appeared to him to be a permissible measure, he checked with the Food and Drug Administration and with the White House and found that neither agency was eager to fight the bill. Privately he told Representative Swanson that if he could persuade the committee chairman to schedule hearings and report out the bill, he would help him obtain speedy floor consideration. With the outright support of the minority party and the guarded assistance of the Speaker, Swanson stepped up his telephone calls and visits to other congressmen asking for their support. Meanwhile the drug companies expanded their publicity efforts, and soon there appeared a number of articles in women's magazines and another over the signature of a well-known columnist who was widely syndicated in the press, announcing that a new miracle painkiller would be available to everyone without a prescription as soon as Congress bestirred itself to amend an obsolete law.

The committee chairman, who was the eventual target of much of this effort, finally gave in. No one knew what convinced him, but it may have been when one of the articles was picked up and reproduced in one of the leading general-circulation magazines, which also named the committee chairman as the culprit, or when the governor from his home state called him and asked him to schedule some hearings. It was just eight weeks after HR 846 had been introduced that the committee chairman called Swanson and told him that hearings were scheduled to begin ten days later. Swanson thanked him kindly and gave a private sigh of relief.

### Favors to Constituents

The sigh encompassed more than the good news, which came to him at 7:30 in the evening. It was also in gratitude at the end of one of the most difficult days he had ever experienced as a congressman. It had started off badly when his wife had confessed she was homesick and wanted to return to her home town for a week. Swanson could not afford the expense, but he told his wife to go anyway. When he arrived in his office, he found two political associates from his district making themselves comfortable on the leather couch. One of them had a son in the Army who wanted to transfer to the Air Corps, and he asked Swanson to intercede

ibers of Congress
id much of their
serving the needs
their constituents,
ite the press of ur-
national problems.
ve, Senator William
ell of Connecticut
es as guide and
to a group of Girl
its.

for him at the Department of Defense. The other visitor was a minor party official who had decided to press his request for a job with the local civil defense organization. Swanson knew that regular channels existed for such matters, but he also had no desire to alienate his supporters, so he spent an hour on the telephone arranging appointments in an effort to assist them.

Adding to his worry was a letter from the head of one of the local fraternal groups, attacking the congressman's party—as if Swanson were solely responsible—for its failure to support a certain bill. Swanson knew that the fraternal organization did nothing for him at election time, but he did not want to risk goading it to outright opposition, so he replied in placating terms.

## A Day's Activity

Although he had meant to spend an hour reading a few committee reports on forthcoming bills, he found the rest of the morning taken up with other constituent requests. While eating a sandwich in his office, he made a few telephone calls to congressional friends and to one of the party whips and so determined how he should vote.

He had barely survived the afternoon. Two hours had been spent meeting with drug company executives and several other interested congressmen, working out strategy on HR 846. Three times during the meeting the bell indicating a record vote had sounded and with the other congressmen he had to hurry the half mile of corridors to the House chamber to cast his vote. At 4 P.M. his own committee had held an executive session, marking up a major bill which had already gone through the hearing stage, and Swanson found himself the spokesman for a minority of committee members who wanted to change the bill. Swanson had fought hard to be assigned to this committee, but in view of his frequent differences of opinion with the chairman, he now entertained some thoughts about asking the Speaker for a new assignment when a vacancy elsewhere next occurred.

The news at 7:30, that hearings were scheduled on HR 846, was perhaps the only pleasant event of the day.

## Hearings

The hearings were not noteworthy. Swanson himself testified, his written statement having been prepared by the drug associa-

Statues of former members of Congress, which are located in various public halls of the Capitol, serve as a constant reminder to present members of some of their noted predecessors and of the great traditions of this remarkable legislative body. Above is Henry Clay, known as the Great Compromiser, who served in the House and Senate a total of more than 40 years.

KENTUCKY

HENRY CLAY
1777 — 1852
LEADER AND STATESMAN

tion secretary with the assistance of a lawyer from the agency. He had suggested a few questions to a friend on the committee, and he answered them creditably. The committee staff member, who still nursed his opposition to the bill, asked several questions with an unpleasant twist, but Swanson maintained his composure. For two days various drug and chemical company executives and a union official succeeded each other on the stand in rapid succession in support of the bill; not more than two committee members were ever in the room at any one time and the staff member asked most of the questions. The committee chairman never appeared. On the third day, three spokesmen for the medical association opposed the bill. The final witness was the general counsel of the agency, who gave an excellent demonstration of a man who could not make up his mind. Under the probing of one of the committee members friendly to Swanson's cause, the unhappy counsel finally agreed that the bill, if passed as written, would cause no harm.

## Renewed Opposition to the Bill

A week after the close of hearings, Swanson began to hear disquieting rumors. It began to appear that the medical association leaders, now somewhat alarmed, had decided on a new strategy: amend the bill to make it broader in application, and thus bring down the opposition of the agency. Swanson's behind-the-scene efforts were redoubled. Six of the committee members favorable to HR 846 spent most of one day with pharmaceutical association leaders learning as much as they could digest about the chemical industry. Another tactic produced even better results. Several leading doctors were uncovered in different states who refused to follow the lead of the medical association and they were encouraged by the drug companies to write to the committee in support of the bill as written. This tactic gave to the committee members the firm impression that the medical association was split on the issue, and the best arguments of the association's chairman could not repair the damage.

Nevertheless, despite growing support for his bill, Representative Swanson became increasingly concerned as the committee chairman still refused to hold executive sessions to mark up the bill. Three weeks after the hearings ended, Swanson, with a measure of malice aforethought, called a meeting in his office of more than forty congressmen with the widely publicized purpose of planning action to force the committee to discharge the bill. At the meeting, a petition was produced and all those attending signed it. Swanson did not expect to be required to obtain the 218 signatures necessary before the discharge petition took effect; the threat was usually enough. And this proved to be the case. Three days later the recalcitrant committee chairman called a hasty meeting of his group and in three hours the bill was voted out without significant changes.

## Floor Debate on the Bill

The next stop was the Rules Committee. Here no difficulty was expected. True to expectation, the Rules Committee chairman had little interest in HR 846, and his committee gave it a rule without benefit of hearing. Under the rule, proponents and opponents of the bill would each be allowed one hour on the floor. Five amendments and a motion to recommit the bill would be entertained, to be followed by a vote on the bill itself. The committee chairman, refusing his privilege of managing the floor debate on the bill, turned the job over to a ranking committee member. Another committee member, opposed to the bill, assumed the reins of the opposition.

The scene on the floor when the bill came up for consideration belied the bitter struggles that preceded it. The House, as is customary during consideration of a bill, had converted itself into the Committee of the Whole, which required a quorum of only 100 members instead of 218. During the debate on the bill, however, average attendance on the floor was closer to 40 until the actual voting began.

Representative Swanson himself spoke for twenty minutes on the bill, devoting most of his talk to opposing the pending amendments. Several other members interested in HR 846 shared the remaining twenty minutes of time allotted for the proponents. The opponents failed to fill their hour.

### The Bill Is Voted

The key to the bill's success was the vote on the first amendment. On a quorum call, more than 200 members came into the chamber from committee rooms and offices. On a call for a teller vote, the members filed down the center aisle, those favoring the amendment first, then those opposing it. A few moments later the presiding officer announced the vote: 85 for the amendment, 92 against. Swanson quickly conferred with his associates and, fearful that the small margin might hurt his cause in the Senate, demanded a record vote, in which each member's vote would be recorded by name. A fifth of the congressmen present supported his motion, so the bells rang and the rest of the membership streamed slowly into the chamber. Slowly the clerk read each name in alphabetical order. The yeas and nays echoed through the chamber. Five minutes after the roll call was completed, the presiding officer announced that the amendment was defeated, 202 to 119. It was evident that a smaller proportion of the membership wished to be recorded by name against the bill.

The members streamed out of the chamber following this vote, and the other four amendments and the motion to recommit to committee, which would have killed the bill, were turned down quickly by voice vote. A final voice vote passed the bill itself. At this point the House moved out of the Committee of the Whole, and another vote, also by voice, with the Speaker in the chair, confirmed the previous decisions.

As Swanson left the chamber, he looked up at the galleries, saw Hubert La Salle, and smiled broadly.

## The Senate Concurs on the Bill

Action in the Senate followed a swifter course. By the time the House had passed the bill, the appropriate Senate committee had already reported the bill. The only fly in the ointment was the determined opposition of several Senators, who had pointedly informed the committee chairman that they would have a great deal to say about the bill when it came to the floor. Unable to dissuade them, the committee chairman was forced to agree to several changes in the bill. When the bill came to the Senate floor, under a unanimous consent agreement engineered by the majority and minority leaders, it took only ten minutes to vote on the two amendments and then to pass the bill. A Senator who had been delivering a three-hour address on foreign policy yielded the floor for the ten minutes required for consideration of the bill, stepped into the lobby for a cup of coffee, and then returned to conclude his address.

## Conference Committee Acts on the Bill

Three of the members of the House committee—the chairman again took no part—were appointed to the conference committee by the Speaker. A few days later they met with three members of the Senate committee which considered the measure—members appointed to the Conference Committee by the Vice-President. In a session of four hours, the senatorial delegation succeeded in persuading the House delegation that if they did not accept the two amendments passed by the Senate, a filibuster would certainly ensue in the upper chamber, which might result in the bill's defeat. Returning to the House with their conference report, the House managers claimed that the Senate had really bowed to the House rather than vice versa, and urged the House to approve the report. The House did so by voice vote.

## The President Signs the Bill

Following Senate passage, the bill, now an Act of Congress, was sent to the White House for presidential action. Two weeks before, an Executive Office staff member, assigned to keep track of the bill, had asked the Secretary of Health, Education and Welfare for a written statement on the bill as soon as it was passed. The Secretary's report to the President indicated that there was nothing objectionable in the bill. A few days later the President signed the measure, and it was published in the Federal Register as Public Law 246 of that session of Congress.

# CHAPTER 16

# The President and Congress

It is roughly a mile from the White House to Capitol Hill. For most of our history that mile has been a long one. President Truman, when congratulated on the length of his honeymoon with Congress, is reputed to have said, "If this is a honeymoon, God help marriage!" For most American Presidents the Congress has seemed an almost chronic irritant. To many Representatives and Senators, Presidents have been objects of fear, suspicion, or envy.

## CONFLICT

This mutual hostility, except on rare occasions, has not been a personal matter. It has been constitutional and political. Most Americans understand this. Like parents who become upset when their children are squabbling, but who become quietly terrified if there is no noise at all, mature Americans accept the struggle between President and Congress as necessary and, in part, as desirable. As a recent Secretary of State has put it, "The relations between the executive and legislative branches of our government were not designed to be restful. We must not be disturbed and think that things have gone amiss when power striking against power, and being restrained, produces sparks." [1]

### Constitutional Causes of Conflict

We have observed earlier some of the constitutional sources of friction between the President and the Congress (see pp. 44–45). It is perhaps well to make three summary comments at this point:

307

1. The three branches of our national government (executive, legislative, and judicial) are established by the Constitution as co-equal centers of power.

2. Each branch has certain clear checks upon the other two.

3. The exact differences between "legislative" functions, "executive" functions, and "judicial" functions are not spelled out in the Constitution with the consequence that mutual encroachments have been inevitable.

It is remarkable under these circumstances that the equilibrium among the three branches throughout our constitutional history has been so dynamic that numerous scholars still argue without agreement as to which branch of the national government is the most powerful.

## Political Causes of Conflict

Important as these constitutional abrasives are in creating sparks, political abrasives are equally effective. Take appointments, for example.

*Appointments.* It is a matter of political custom that when presidential appointments are submitted to the Senate for confirmation, the rule of "senatorial courtesy" is followed. This rule, as we have seen, means that if the President has not "cleared" the nomination with at least one of the Senators (of the President's own party) from the nominee's home state, the Senator can block the appointment by stating on the floor of the Senate that the appointment is "personally obnoxious" to him. The power of confirmation is a continuing source of possible friction between the legislative and executive branches of government.

*Two-Party System.* Another political abrasive is the extra-constitutional two-party system which has been superimposed upon our constitutional system of staggered elections. A President is elected for four years; Senators for six years; and Representatives for two years. A combination of circumstances over which the President may have little or no control may combine to give the opposition party control of one or both of the houses of Congress. The loggerheads which develop may be serious, as in 1930-1932 during the depression; or almost negligible, as during the last two years of Eisenhower's first administration.

*Two Points of View.* The most significant political abrasive is the fact that the President and the Congress represent different con-

| | PRESIDENCY | SENATE | HOUSE OF REPRESENTATIVES |
|---|---|---|---|
| Legend | DEMOCRATIC / REPUBLICAN | DEMOCRATIC MAJORITY / REPUBLICAN MAJORITY | DEMOCRATIC MAJORITY / REPUBLICAN MAJORITY |
| 1928 | REPUBLICAN (HOOVER) | 56 REP., 39 DEM., 1 OTHER | 270 REP., 164 DEM., 1 OTHER |
| 1930 | REPUBLICAN (HOOVER) | 48 REP., 47 DEM., 1 OTHER | 220 REP., 214 DEM., 1 OTHER |
| 1932 | DEMOCRATIC (ROOSEVELT) | 59 DEM., 36 REP., 1 OTHER | 313 DEM., 117 REP., 5 OTHER |
| 1934 | DEMOCRATIC (ROOSEVELT) | 69 DEM., 25 REP., 2 OTHERS | 322 DEM., 103 REP., 10 OTHERS |
| 1936 | DEMOCRATIC (ROOSEVELT) | 75 DEM., 18 REP., 3 OTHERS | 333 DEM., 89 REP., 13 OTHERS |
| 1938 | DEMOCRATIC (ROOSEVELT) | 69 DEM., 23 REP., 4 OTHERS | 262 DEM., 169 REP., 4 OTHERS |
| 1940 | DEMOCRATIC (ROOSEVELT) | 66 DEM., 27 REP., 3 OTHERS | 267 DEM., 162 REP., 6 OTHERS |
| 1942 | DEMOCRATIC (ROOSEVELT) | 57 DEM., 38 REP., 1 OTHER | 222 DEM., 209 REP., 4 OTHERS |
| 1944 | DEMOCRATIC (ROOSEVELT – TRUMAN) | 57 DEM., 38 REP., 1 OTHER | 243 DEM., 190 REP., 2 OTHERS |
| 1946 | DEMOCRATIC (ROOSEVELT – TRUMAN) | 50 REP., 46 DEM. | 246 REP., 188 DEM., 1 OTHER |
| 1948 | DEMOCRATIC (TRUMAN) | 54 DEM., 42 REP. | 263 DEM., 171 REP., 1 OTHER |
| 1950 | DEMOCRATIC (TRUMAN) | 48 REP., 47 DEM., 1 OTHER | 235 DEM., 199 REP., 1 OTHER |
| 1952 | REPUBLICAN (EISENHOWER) | 49 DEM., 47 REP. | 221 REP., 213 DEM., 1 OTHER |
| 1964 | REPUBLICAN (EISENHOWER) | 49 DEM., 47 REP. | 232 DEM., 203 REP. |
| 1956 | REPUBLICAN (EISENHOWER) | 49 DEM., 47 REP. | 235 DEM., 200 REP. |

Executive-Legislative Party Divisions, 1928–1956. (Adapted from the *New York Times,* Nov. 11, 1956.)

stituencies. It is commonplace to say that the President represents the whole nation while members of Congress represent localities. But the implications of this banality are important. The rival institutions of President and Congress give the nation an unusual, valuable, and somewhat dizzying pair of bifocals. One lens, the President's, tends to focus upon the inclusive and the general. The other lens, of Congress, tends to focus upon the exclusive and the specific. The world does not look the same through the two lenses. Take, for example, the knotty question of whether the United States government should lower tariffs on Japanese textiles. Low tariffs may be endorsed by the President as the best way to strengthen our national security by strengthening the economy of a strategically located ally. But a congressman coming from a textile area has another kind of image. Textile manufacturers and workers may have deluged him with telegrams and letters; or he may simply visualize in his own mind what could happen to his friends and neighbors if the local textile mill should fail as a result of Japanese imports. World peace is a complicated issue, and surely a 10 percent tariff rise on *one* commodity affecting *one* foreign country will not tip the scale. The President replies that if textiles have their way, a thousand other commodities with as serious a claim should also have *their* way, and then the economic stability of our allies and consequently our own national security would really be threatened.

This is but one example of the tensions which are created between the President and the Congress as a result of the differences in their points of view.

*Two National Interests.* Another way of putting this is to say that in reality there are at least two national interests: the total national interest, and the national sum of special interests. This formulation smacks of an attempt by the French political philosopher Jean Jacques Rousseau in the eighteenth century to distinguish between what he called the "general will" and the "will of all." Whatever the dangers, and they are real, of making the "general will" or the "total national interest" into a fuzzy, romantic, and ultimately despotic concept, it remains true that the President probably comes closer to seeing the whole picture of our polity and its needs than does any one congressman, or all of our congressmen put together. This is true not only because of the singular and exalted constitutional position of the President, but because of the development over the years of our party system, and of our strangely fashioned jigsaw puzzle of congressional districts. Without going into details, and at the risk of oversimplification, it is sufficient to say here that the outlines of our congressional districts have been so drawn by rurally dominated state legislatures that what Professor Binkley calls the "producer" interests in the country (particularly agriculture and business) tend to find their strength in the Congress, while the "consumer" interests (workers, family farmers, and low-income groups generally) tend to find their strength in the White House. Insofar as there are frictions between these various groups in our society, these frictions tend to be reflected in executive-legislative relations.

*Jealousy.* A final political abrasive is jealousy. Most Senators and a good many members of the House of Representatives have been, at one time or another, bitten by the presidential bug. Lost in the relative anonymity of the numbers 96 or 435, they look with understandable envy at the prestige and power of the single chief executive. It is small wonder that those members of the Senate and the House who have risen to positions of power in the committee system of the Congress, and consequently who can vie meaningfully with the President in attempting to control segments of the executive branch, hold tenaciously to their prerogatives.

# COOPERATION

It is perhaps a wonder that with all these abrasives the machinery of government does not grind to a halt. Except for one major breakdown—during and immediately after the Civil War—the machinery has operated with considerable success for over a century and a half. There have been periods of real strain when executive-legislative tensions have bound the gears dangerously. There have been periods of felicity when executive-legislative relations have been so lacking in friction that the machinery has raced—again, some would say dangerously.

### Pressures for Accommodation

On the whole, however, the system has not failed us. This is because there have been pressures and lubricants leading to accommodation. The fact is that the President and the Congress need each other—just as the nation needs their cooperation.

*Personal Standards.* First of all it should be remembered that most members of Congress are capable of decent, reasonable, and intelligent reactions to human need and to enlightened leadership. Because the press tends to play up conflict we frequently forget how much of the public's business is conducted in a spirit of mutual respect and honest compromise.

And we forget something else: the sobering and edifying effect of high public office on most public officials. Many men who start out in politics for reasons solely of personal ambition, professional prestige, or financial gain end up identifying themselves with what Edmund Burke once called the "permanent forces"—the most inclusive and long-range goals of the society. There is, among reasonable men, a will to accommodate and a will to grow.

*National Security.* In the second place, the contemporary demands of national security induce cooperation between the President and Congress. Differences in emphasis and direction there may be, but the kind of friction which developed between President Wilson and the Republican leaders in the Senate over the League of Nations in 1919 is almost unthinkable today. Congressional leaders, regardless of party, have come to understand the necessity of executive initiative in foreign affairs, and have usually responded with alacrity to presidential leadership in times of crisis. It is significant that some of our most crucial departures from traditional patterns of foreign policy (such as the Truman Doctrine and the Marshall Plan) were endorsed by the Congress immediately following World War II when the President was of one party and the two Houses of Congress were controlled by the other. President Eisenhower from 1952 to 1954 found as much or more support for his foreign policies from Democrats as he did from members of his own party.

Politics, in the sense of honest criticism and alternative suggestions, need not stop at the water's edge. But on some issues of national security a united front between parties and between branches of government is imperative. Rather elaborate machinery now exists to ensure the exchange of ideas and information between the leaders of the Congress and the leaders of the administration necessary for speedy cooperation on critical international issues.

*Presidential Influence.* In the third place, even when immediate issues are insufficiently dramatic to force the President and the Congress together, the President is not without leverage. Aware of the President's enormous potential influence with the public, most Congressmen prefer not to buck him on issues when they feel the public may be on his side. Presidents are newsworthy. What they say hits the front pages of every major newspaper in the country. Television and radio are at their beck and call. In a major campaign, presidential candidates have infinitely greater communications resources at their disposal than legislators do. In the 1948 campaign, for instance, President Truman's most effective phrase—whether justified or not—was "that do-nothing Republican Congress." Few Congressmen can win re-election on a record of obstruc-

---

It was Woodrow Wilson's great contribution to the Presidency to have made the provision of the Constitution for the Presidential message to Congress the basis of dynamic legislative leadership. The extraordinary significance of the State of the Union Message today owes much to the imagination and initiative of the only political scientist to have become chief magistrate of the United States.

—Wilfred E. Binkley

tionism—or even on a record which makes plausible a presidential charge of obstructionism. It should be remembered in this connection that the ultimate prize of partisan politics is the Presidency. If the opposition party controls the Congress and wants in the next election to control the Presidency as well, it must pay some attention to the President's constituents.

*Party Loyalty.* Finally, of course, the President has instruments of conformity at his disposal as party leader. When the President and the majorities in both houses of Congress are of the same political persuasion, the President has a number of devices for holding at least some of his legislators in line. Patronage is not so important today as it once was, but in some circumstances it is still an effective presidential weapon. More important, perhaps, is the granting or withholding of presidential recognition—political and social. It means much to a lowly congressman to be able to say to his friends and constituents, "As I told the President the other day. . . ." In the Republican campaigns of 1954 and 1956, congressmen stood in line waiting to have their pictures taken with President Eisenhower in the hopes that his coattails would help.

There are, then, lubricants to counteract in part the abrasives which exist between the President and the Congress. Whether one is interested in trying to reform executive-legislative relations depends in part on whether he considers the present lubricants adequate.

# THE PRESIDENT AS LEGISLATIVE LEADER

Most important legislation now originates in the executive branch of the government. Even when the Congress is in the hands

Yet he has ample means to make himself heard above all other voices. On his Inauguration Day, it is his word alone which fills the land, as he sets the tone for his administration. What he says on that day he can restate four times throughout his term when he delivers the State of the Union Address, informing the nation of what he has done or what he feels should be done.

—Sidney Hyman

of the opposition party, legislative initiative is normally allowed to come from the President.

The President has four formal means for suggesting to the Congress what he wants in the way of legislation: the State of the Union Message, the Budget Message, the President's Economic Report, and special messages.

### State of the Union Message

The Constitution provides that the President "shall from time to time give to the Congress Information of the state of the Union, and

"Big, Ain't It?"

recommend to their consideration such Measures as he shall judge necessary and expedient. . . ." (Art. II, Sec. 3). In spite of this clear statement, most Presidents until the twentieth century "operated on the assumption that leadership of the legislature was an extra-legal encroachment on the principle of Separation of Powers." [2] In recent years, however, the State of the Union Message has become a highly significant state document. A great deal of work goes into its preparation, and into dovetailing it with the Budget Message and the President's Economic Report. By the time it is ready for delivery early in January, the State of the Union Message is, in effect, the legislative program of the President.

The preparation of the State of the Union Message has become a highly skilled job for presidential assistants in the White House and in other parts of the Executive Office. Annually, every agency of government is asked to submit its proposals for new legislation and new programs. These proposals are then analyzed and organized for an eventual screening by the President himself. The President, with the advice of his cabinet members and other advisers, sets priorities, adds new items, and lops off what he considers to be unimportant.

Once the State of the Union Message has been delivered to the Congress, follow-up drafts of bills are prepared (usually by executive branch officials, but often with the advice of friendly Senators, Representatives, or members of congressional staffs). The various bills are then introduced by leading Congressmen of the President's party and referred to appropriate committees, at which point the legislative process begins.

### The Budget Message

The federal budget is often thought of primarily as an exercise in astronomy, or as an instrument of presidential control over departments and agencies. It is certainly the latter; but it is also an instrument of presidential leadership in the legislative field, and it is an important instrument of national economic stabilization.

Soon after the President has delivered his State of the Union Message, he sends his Budget Message to Congress. Essentially the Budget Message is a statement of how much the various programs of government will probably cost in the ensuing fiscal year (July 1 to June 30), and how much revenue may be anticipated to cover these costs. If the anticipated costs are higher than the anticipated revenues, the Budget Message will indicate the need for more taxes or more borrowing. If the anticipated revenues are higher than the anticipated costs, the President may recommend applying the balance to lowering taxes or to reducing the size of the national debt.

*Preparation of Budget.* The spending side of the budget is prepared initially by the Bureau of the Budget, an agency created in 1921 and now an important unit in the Executive Office of the President. Every summer the Budget Bureau sends out calls to the various departments and agencies of the executive branch setting forth general presidential targets and asking the agencies to submit their estimates of how much they think it will cost to carry out their responsibilities during the fiscal year beginning a year hence and ending two years hence. These agency estimates are sent back to the Budget Bureau in the late summer and early fall. At various stages during the autumn these figures are revised on the basis of budget hearings with the individual agencies, and as a result of conversations between the Director of the Budget and the President.

In December, the final corrections and changes are made. The huge manuscript, filled with figures, is sent to the Government Printing Office to be printed and bound. The President's Budget Message, which normally forms a preface to the budget itself, is of course only a general summary of a vast and complex document.

The detailed budget, once it reaches Capitol Hill, becomes the Bible of the House and Senate Appropriations Committees and their respective subcommittees which hold extensive hearings and finally report out appropriation bills for consideration by the respective chambers.

The revenue side of the Budget is prepared in large part by the Treasury Department, although constant liaison is maintained between Treasury, the Budget Bureau, and the Council of Economic Advisers on tax policies and programs. And, of course, the President has the final word in any executive branch recommendation to the Congress on tax measures.

Once the recommendations are received by the Congress they are sent to the powerful Ways and Means Committee of the House, the Finance Committee of the Senate, and to the well-staffed Joint Committee on Internal Revenue Taxation for study, modification, and action.

## The Estimated 1958 Federal Budget
### (In billions of dollars)

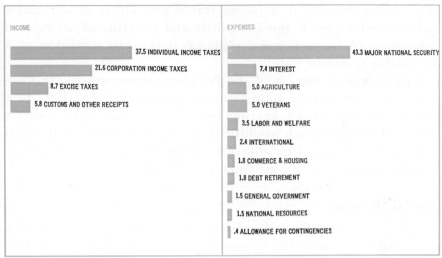

INCOME

| | |
|---|---|
| | 37.5 INDIVIDUAL INCOME TAXES |
| | 21.6 CORPORATION INCOME TAXES |
| | 8.7 EXCISE TAXES |
| | 5.8 CUSTOMS AND OTHER RECEIPTS |

EXPENSES

| | |
|---|---|
| | 43.3 MAJOR NATIONAL SECURITY |
| | 7.4 INTEREST |
| | 5.0 AGRICULTURE |
| | 5.0 VETERANS |
| | 3.5 LABOR AND WELFARE |
| | 2.4 INTERNATIONAL |
| | 1.8 COMMERCE & HOUSING |
| | 1.8 DEBT RETIREMENT |
| | 1.5 GENERAL GOVERNMENT |
| | 1.5 NATIONAL RESOURCES |
| | .4 ALLOWANCE FOR CONTINGENCIES |

This is the estimated budget of the federal government for the fiscal year ending June 30, 1958. Note the cost of defense expenditures relative to other budget aggregates.

## The Economic Report

The third formal message forwarded by the President to the Congress each January is the Economic Report, a document prepared in large part by the Council of Economic Advisers in the Executive Office of the President. The Council of Economic Advisers was established by the Employment Act of 1946—a law which provides that it is "the continuing policy and responsibility of the Federal Government to use all practicable means . . . to promote maximum employment, production, and purchasing power." In his Economic Report, the President gives a picture of the economic health of the union; points to any danger spots he sees; and recommends legislative action to achieve the purposes of the act.

This function is not assumed lightly. To those who have grown to adulthood since 1940, the availability of productive jobs and the enjoyment of a reasonably high standard of living seem normal attributes of life in America. Unfortunately, it has not always been so, and there is no automatic way of assuring continuing economic prosperity and stability in the future. Government, with its enormous impact upon the economy through its policies of spending, taxing, and borrowing, is a powerful force which the Employment Act dictates must be harnessed for the general economic welfare.

Although politically it is inconceivable that either of our major parties would permit the indignities and suffering of widespread joblessness to happen again, vigilance is the first condition of a reasonable economic stability.

The Economic Report of the President, when sent to the Congress, is referred to the Joint Economic Committee. The Joint Economic Committee holds hearings on the report, and finally issues a report of its own which has little direct legislative effect but which helps educate other legislators and the public to the possible economic consequences of legislation in the hopper.

## Special Messages

Some of a President's most important legislative recommendations may be made to the Congress in the form of special messages. Frequently, the State of the Union Message will alert Congress to the fact that the President intends to submit special messages on various issues in the near future. The advantage of special messages is that they give added weight to the President's legislative requests in particular areas of public policy. An item which may have been buried in a long State of the Union Message is suddenly given form, stature, and special recognition. The staggering of special messages to maximize the publicity given to each has become quite an executive art. Inaugural messages, of course, are frequently used to dramatize important policy goals of the President.

## Legislative Generalship

President Truman, with unwitting prophecy, once likened the President's desk to a general's. He outlined what he called the five "vital steps of strategy": "first, estimate your own resources; second, estimate your enemy's resources; third, form a judgment as to what is to be done; fourth, implement that judgment with a plan; fifth, persuade your leaders of the value of that plan and mass your forces for the attack."

This rather austere formula is rarely followed (at least in such careful sequence) by American Presidents in their dealings with the Congress; but it serves to suggest that strategy and tactics, rather than pious hopes, are necessary if a President is to be a successful legislative leader.

In recent years, Presidents and the heads of important departments have hired staff assistants whose major job it has been to maintain friendly relations with the Congress. In addition, recent Presidents have spent sizable blocs of time with various legislative leaders—particularly with the majority leader of the Senate and the Speaker of the House—in an attempt to win support for particular proposals. The Vice-President who is also, of course, the president of the Senate, has been used increasingly as an important bridge between the President and the Congress.

Even when the President does not intervene personally, various members of the cabinet may testify for or against particular bills, or may take on informal legislative campaigns for the President. In the Bureau of the Budget is a small "legislative reference" staff which has the responsibility of establishing, for the guidance of both the Congress and the executive agencies, the relevance of each major piece of legislation to "the program of the President."

*Presidential Pressure.* If, in spite of these various instruments and techniques of legislative generalship, the Congress sulks, balks, or wanders far afield, the President has more extreme and ultimate weapons. If the President has high public prestige, he may appeal over the heads of Congressmen to their constituencies—using the vast and powerful media of television, radio, and the press to arouse public interest. Or he may refuse patronage or political support to recalcitrant Congressmen. Or he may call Congress into special session as President Truman did in 1948 to put the legislative body on the political hot seat. Finally, he may use the veto—both as a threat and as an actual weapon.

## Veto

In our early history, the veto power of the President could hardly have been considered a major instrument of legislative generalship. Jackson was the first President to use the veto effectively as a strategic and tactical weapon; and not until the twentieth century has its power been made consistently operational. The veto is a powerful instrument. As Corwin and Koenig have pointed out, "The general effectiveness of the veto as a Presidential weapon is attested by the fact that from the first inauguration of George Washington to the second inauguration of Franklin D. Roosevelt only sixteen per cent of the vetoes of public bills were overridden." [3]

Being powerful, the veto has a deterrent value even when it is not actually used. If a "bad" amendment is about to be offered to a "good" bill, for example, oftentimes all the President has to do to have the amendment killed is to suggest that he would veto the entire bill if the amendment were included.

When a bill is passed by both houses of Congress and submitted to the President for signature, Executive Office machinery goes into operation. In the White House staff and in the Bureau of the Budget particularly, men are assigned the task of advising the President as to what course of action he should take. The bill may be submitted to half a dozen major departments or agencies for comment. If one agency feels that the bill should be vetoed, someone in that agency may be asked to prepare the draft of a veto message for consideration by the President. Or representatives of a number of agencies may be called together to develop a unified position on what the President should do. In the last analysis, of course, it is the President himself who must decide whether to sign or not to sign. If he does not veto within ten days, the bill automatically becomes law without his signature—with one exception. If the President receives the bill from the Congress within ten days of legislative adjournment, the President may simply do nothing and the bill automatically dies. This is known as a pocket veto.

## Item Veto

As matters now stand, the President must sign or veto a bill as a whole. He cannot accept 90 percent of a bill, for example, and reject 10 percent. Many reformers and many Presidents have overtly or secretly wished for the power of item veto which would enable the President to discriminate *within* bills as well as *between* them. Congress, however, jealously guards the privilege of sending any kind of package it wants to the President. It may, for example, tack onto an ordinary pay bill a "rider" which could never have gotten past the President as a separate bill. But if the President vetoes the pay bill in order to stop the rider thousands of federal employees might not be paid for weeks.

The item veto is an important executive weapon in many states and municipalities. It will probably be a long time, however, before it is allowed the President. As matters now stand all a President can do is to grit his teeth, issue a hot statement to the press, and sign—unless he wishes to risk the possible consequences of a veto, which in some circumstances must seem like burning down the barn in order to catch a rat.

# WHO CONTROLS THE EXECUTIVE BRANCH?

Inevitable frictions between the President and the Congress necessarily create tensions within and between the departments and agencies of the executive branch. Some agencies, like the Army Corps of Engineers or the Federal Bureau of Investigation, have extremely close contact with powerful sources of strength in the Congress. In terms of practical politics these agencies are virtually autonomous units in the executive branch, even though in theory they are responsible through department heads to the President. But these examples are relatively rare.

Most agencies feel themselves pulled by the polarized magnets of President and Congress. In terms of effective power, is an appropriations subcommittee any less important to the life of an agency than the President? In recent years, one or another of the military departments have found themselves caught in the following whiplash: the President has cut their budget; the House has sustained the President; the Senate has raised the appropriation; the raise has been sustained in conference committee; the extra appropriation has been voted by the Congress; the President has directed the Secretary of Defense not to spend the extra money.

Or an investigating committee of the Congress may request certain types of information from a federal agency. The agency may be perfectly willing to comply; but the President may order the agency not to comply. Congress may figure that the agency *asked* the President to issue the order of noncompliance and may therefore threaten to cut the agency's budget next time around.

We shall discuss other implications of executive-legislative relations in Chapter 17. Suffice it to say that every responsible bureau-

---

The President is controlled not only by the Congress acting as the legislature enacting the laws which the President is bound to execute, and appropriating the funds with which he executes them: the Senate also exercises a high degree of control over the President through its sharing with him of a large part of the executive power.

—Louis Brownlow

crat usually knows that he has to live with two kinds of authority —legislative and executive. He hopes that he will not be caught in the middle too often.

## REFORM

It would be strange indeed if the tensions produced by the peculiar nature of our executive-legislative relations had not, on occasion, caused frustration, buck-passing, and public outrage. Some students of government have looked longingly at the British parliamentary system in which real friction between the Cabinet and the Parliament is virtually impossible. Some have suggested the creation of a special executive-legislative council or a new kind of cabinet which would provide for a regular channel of communication (and presumably cooperation) between the President and Congress. Some people have suggested more highly disciplined parties which could act as a consistent bridge between the White House and Capitol Hill. Others have concluded that more felicitous and responsible relations between the two branches of government will occur only when incumbent Presidents learn the art of legislative as well as popular leadership.

Some students of the subject are satisfied with things as they now are—feeling that the pressures for accommodation during real emergencies are already sufficient, and that in nonemergency periods it is wise to have stiff competition between the two branches.

Perhaps we can conclude that in the perilous age in which we live, the wisdom of our Founding Fathers must be supplemented by our own wisdom in devising means of cooperation which transcend but do not traduce the separation of powers. Our political parties, working in conjunction with presidential leadership, seem the most plausible instruments of cooperation and responsibility.

## CONCLUSION

### Synopsis

The friction between President and Congress is a normal, if somewhat disquieting, aspect of government in America. The sparks fly from constitutional abrasives and from political abrasives—particularly from the fact that the President and the Congress are both representative instruments of the American people, but represent different constituencies and, frequently, different parties. The President's constituency is national in scope and heavily urban in character; congressional constituencies are local in scope and tend to be rural or small-town in character. The President through his various messages to Congress, through his threat or use of the veto power, and through less formal channels maintains considerable legislative initiative. He is not automatically the master of Congress, however; and he must compete with the Congress—or, more accurately, with segments thereof—for control of the departments and agencies of the executive branch.

### Significance

Sparks are fun to watch, but they can also be dangerous. The American people are less than logical when they return to office a President of one party and a Congress of another. It is becoming increasingly important, not only that the President and the Congress work together on fundamentals, but that the voting public be able to hold someone responsible for what happens. Even if today accommodation on important matters is the rule rather than the exception, the exception can be of critical importance to our safety and welfare. And responsibility to the voting public becomes all but impossible if the Presidency is controlled by one party, and the Congress by another—or, more realistically, by a series of cross-party factions. Perhaps the major institutional reforms needed in the American national government are (1) responsible centers of power in what is presently a highly splintered legislative branch, and (2) responsible political instruments which can act as a bridge between the President and the Congress on important issues.

### Prospectus

In the absence of such reforms, the American people must look to the President for an uncommon virtuosity in "handling" Congress while somehow managing his other vital functions. In the turbulent days of the mid-twentieth century, these other functions cannot be ignored. What these other functions are, why they are important, and how they are performed is the subject of the following chapter.

## CHAPTER 17

# The President as Chief Executive

THE NOUN OR adjective "executive" comes from the verb "to execute" which, in turn, derives from the Latin *ex* meaning "out" and "sequi" meaning follow. The Thorndike-Barnard dictionary claims that "execute" is synonymous with "perform, accomplish, fulfill, complete, kill, hang, and electrocute."

Presumably, then, an executive is one who "follows out" by performing, accomplishing, completing, killing, hanging, or electrocuting.

Since humans often like to have things performed, accomplished, or fulfilled, but dislike being killed, hanged, or electrocuted, executives have enjoyed a highly ambiguous reputation throughout history.

Herodotus in the third book of his *History* tells of seven Persians who once sat in a caravansary bemoaning the fact that chief executives such as monarchs tend to become tyrants. On the other hand, the Persians acknowledged that democracies tend to degenerate into mob rule; so that government really should be in the hands of the one best man—the monarch. But, after all, the one best man tended to degenerate into a tyrant.

These circular fears of Herodotus's Persians about sum up 2500 years of political theory on the subject of executives. Executives are necessary; but if left unchecked they can be dangerous to liberty.

It is obvious in retrospect that our Founding Fathers were caught in the same circular logic as the ancient Persians. Some of the most eloquent passages of the *Federalist Papers* are devoted to the justification of a strong, single executive who would really not be very strong or very single after all.

# THE NATURE OF THE AMERICAN PRESIDENCY

The American Presidency is what it is today by virtue of democracy's need for leadership and its fear of tyranny. The Constitution does not define the executive power, but simply says that it shall be vested in a President who shall be elected periodically and who shall be subject to certain constitutional restraints.

Although no two incumbents have looked at the Presidency through identical eyes, and some have seen more flexible "powers" in the office than others, the fact is that a presidential ethic has developed over the years which is clearly understood by most informed Americans. One may ask, for example, why the President as Commander-in-Chief of the Army, Navy, and Air Force does not call up the Pentagon and order troops to march on Capitol Hill and shoot all Representatives, Senators, and Supreme Court Justices who disagree with him. The answer of course is that if a President tried anything of the sort, the officer who answered in the Pentagon would probably respond by sending an ambulance to the White House to take the President to a mental hospital. Our expectations about our constitutional instruments make such a presidential order inconceivable. America has had strong Presidents and weak Presidents, but it has always enjoyed Presidents who respected the constitutional framework of the Republic. It is true that upon occasion Presidents have acted in ways destined to raise the cry of unconstitutional behavior; but if one accepts Professor Corwin's definition of the executive power as "that power most readily usable in an emergency" who is to be the judge of the limits of presidential authority? For who defines an emergency situation? The Congress and the courts may censure after the fact and may set guide lines for future presidential behavior, but they are hardly in a position to restrain a President who conscientiously believes that swift action is needed to preserve the nation. President Lincoln acted in the spirit of the Constitution, even though he defied the letter of the Constitution, when he ordered the Treasury to print money without prior congressional authority during the early weeks of the Civil War. Mr. Truman acted unconstitutionally when he seized the steel mills during the Korean crisis; but as soon as the Supreme Court had spoken, the President conformed without a murmur.

In short, America has been blessed with a series of constitutionally minded chief executives.

# THE FUNCTIONS OF THE CHIEF EXECUTIVE

In the previous chapter we have examined the President's role as legislative leader. We now turn to the other functions of the American Presidency which combine to make the job unique—and impossible.[1] No matter how the responsibilities are defined and catalogued, one thing is certain: the Presidency has emerged in the twentieth century as the most powerful office in the United States and in the free world.

## Chief of State

Unlike Great Britain which mercifully separates its ceremonial from its political leadership, the United States has pushed both responsibilities onto one man. The President must be more than the top political executive; he must be, in the words of President Taft, "the personal embodiment and representative of [the people's] dignity and majesty."

Professor Rossiter has eloquently sketched the dimensions of the President's role as Chief of State:

As figurehead rather than working head of our government, he greets distinguished visitors from all parts of the world, lays wreaths on the tomb of the Unknown Soldier and before the statue of Lincoln, makes proclamations of thanksgiving and commemoration, bestows the Medal of Honor on flustered pilots, holds state dinners for the diplomatic corps and the Supreme Court, lights the nation's Christmas tree, buys the first poppy from the Veterans of Foreign Wars, gives the first crisp banknote to the Red Cross, throws out the first ball for the Senators (the nine, not the ninety-six), rolls the first egg for the Easter Bunny, and in the course of any month greets a fantastic procession of firemen, athletes, veterans, Boy Scouts, Campfire Girls, boosters, hog callers, exchange students, and heroic school children.[2]

Some would contend that the ceremonial functions of the President are precisely what give him his unusual influence. It is unquestionably true that the role of Chief of State gives the President a majesty which enhances his executive status and political prestige. But if, under the burdens of office, the President must cut some

# SUPREME COURT DEFINES POWERS DELEGATED TO OR CLAIMED BY THE PRESIDENT

## (Six Representative Cases)

| Case | Situation | Majority Opinion | Decision | Minority Opinion |
|---|---|---|---|---|
| Prize Cases 2 Black 635 (1862) | Following opening of military hostilities but before Congress declared war, President Lincoln declared naval blockade of South. During period, four vessels, together with cargoes, were captured as prizes by Americans naval vessels. Owners challenged power of President, acting as Commander-in-Chief of naval forces, to seize vessels before formal declaration of war by Congress. | President constitutionally empowered to resist force with force in event of foreign attack, without Congressional declaration of war. Whether President, in supressing insurrection, justified in using force is for political departments of government to decide and not Court. President must decide what degree of force crisis demands. Proclamation of blockade itself is official evidence to Court that state of war existed. | Emergency actions of President constitutional. [ 6-4 ] | Evidence demonstrates no intention on part of one of ships to break blockade. Seizure under circumstances not warranted. Ship and cargo should have been restored to owners. War in material sense not same as war in legal sense. Civil war can exist, and legal consequences applied, only through formal declaration by Congress. War carried on by President against insurrectionary districts of South was personal war against those in rebellion until Congress acted. |
| Myers v. United States 272 U.S. 52 (1926) | Myers appointed by President, with advice and consent of Senate, as postmaster for four years. Before term expired, was ordered by President to resign. Refused and was removed from office. Myers sued for salary in court of claims, charging removal unconstitutional because not approved by Senate. Court of claims decided against Myers. Myers appealed. | Constitution empowered President to exercise removal power without restriction over certain officers he may appoint. Constitution vests executive power in hands of President and empowers him to select officers to assist him. Without removal power, President would be unable to exercise official duties as chief executive. Attempts by Congress to restrict removal power over appointed officers unconstitutional. | Decision of lower court affirmed. President can fire executive officers he appoints. [ 6-3 ] | Arguments drawn from executive and appointive powers of President not adequate to support facts of case. Myers' office created by Congress and details of that office depend on Congress alone. President's duty to see that laws faithfully executed does not require that he achieve more than Congress wills to leave within his power. |
| Humphrey's Executor (Rathbun) v. United States | President, believing that views of Humphrey, member of Federal Trade Commission (one of so-called independent regulatory | Congress distinguishes between purely executive officers, as in Myers' case, and member of an independent regulatory | President does not have powers concerned. | |

| Case | Facts | Reasoning | Judgment | Note |
|---|---|---|---|---|
| 295 U.S. 602 (1935) | commissions), incompatible with own, requested resignations. Humphrey refused, and President removed him despite congressional law limiting removal to cases involving "inefficiency, neglect of duty, or malfeasance in office." Humphrey died and executor took case to court of claims which certified it to the Supreme Court. | commission, acting in part as judge. Congress created FTC as agency independent of President. To permit President to remove members of agency would destroy its independence from presidential will and political whims. | [9-0] | |
| United States v. Curtis-Wright 299 U.S. 304 (1936) | Congress in an attempt to limit a war between Bolivia and Paraguay, passed joint resolution giving President power to prohibit sale of war materials to belligerents. Curtis-Wright, charged with conspiring to violate presidential order pursuant to joint resolution, claimed that such delegation of power to President was invalid. District court agreed with Curtis-Wright, and United States appealed. | Congressional legislation in regard to foreign affairs must often "accord to the President a degree of discretion and freedom from statutory restriction" not admissible if domestic affairs alone were involved. Steady stream of precedents as well as currently practical reasons why Congress should leave exercise of power in foreign field to President's unrestricted judgment. | Judgment of district court reversed.<br><br>[7-1] | President must not have infettered discretion even in foreign field. |
| Youngstown Co. v. Sawyer 343 U.S. 579 (1952) | Prolonged labor dispute in steel industry during Korean war led President to direct Secretary of Commerce, Sawyer, to seize and operate steel mills. President acted on basis, not of statutory authority, but of powers he felt inherent in office during emergency. Steel companies asked for and received injunction from federal district court restraining Secretary of Commerce. Federal *circuit* court stayed injunction and Supreme Court moved in – with dispatch. | Constitution gives no authority to the President to seize private property except as Congress shall by law direct. Neither the "Executive power" per se, nor presidential prerogatives as Commander-in-Chief justify or sanction presidential usurpation of law-making power. | Judgment of district court affirmed.<br><br>[6-3] | Under this view, the President is left powerless at the very moment when the need for action may be most pressing. This is not a "time for timorous executive action." |

functions from his daily agenda, his ceremonial duties can probably be minimized with the least possible damage to the public welfare or to his own effectiveness. Increasingly, the Vice-President and various presidential aides and subordinates are being used to share the ceremonial burdens of the Presidency. At no time, of course, would the President want to give up all ceremonial duties and opportunities; but means must be provided to enable the President to delegate some of his responsibilities as Chief of State to other high officials of the government if he is to meet his primary obligations.

## Chief Administrator

The President, fairly or unfairly, is held responsible by the American people for the way in which the national government is managed. Section 3 of Article II of the Constitution says in part, ". . . he shall take Care that the Laws be faithfully executed."

The managerial role of the President has never been an easy one to perform; the responsibilities are enormous and for most of our history have been quite beyond the grasp of our Presidents. In spite of a rather clear-cut constitutional mandate, it has only been in recent years that Presidents have "tooled up" to handle their managerial responsibilities—and even so, the managerial job is still uncommonly difficult.

What makes the job of effective management so frustrating for our Presidents? At least five factors can be isolated: size, turnover, Congress, preoccupation, and federalism.

*Size.* The executive branch of the national government presently consists of approximately seventy separate departments and agencies. These departments and agencies are manned by well over two million federal employees, and spend nearly $70 billion annually. The Post Office Department alone has a payroll of over 500,000 workers, and the civilian contingent of the Department of Defense is even larger. No human mind can possibly encompass the entire federal enterprise. Inefficiencies and cross-purposes are bound to arise. For these the President is ultimately held accountable even though he may have no effective opportunity to know of the problems or to do anything about them. In 1948 and again in 1953, former President Herbert Hoover served as chairman of commissions authorized by the Congress to study the organization and activities of the executive branch. The two Hoover Commission reports are replete with stories of duplication, waste, inefficiency, and jurisdictional confusion within and among the departments and agencies. Some of this managerial inefficiency is inexcusable; but much of it is the inevitable concomitant of big, sprawling, multipurpose government. The anomalies continue under Republicans and Democrats alike. Big business and big labor face similar problems; but the problems are magnified by the size and character of democratic government.

*Turnover.* No large enterprise can be smoothly managed if the rate of turnover of personnel is inordinately high. In the national government turnover is a constant threat to efficient operation. Without some turnover, of course, we should have a dictatorship, not a democracy. But the serious turnover is not that which occurs following elections. When it is recognized that in some of our most important departments the average tenure of assistant secretaries is less than a year and a half, and the annual turnover of clerical and blue-collar workers is upward of 25 percent, some indication of the seriousness of the problem may be grasped. Fortunately, an increasing number of steps are being taken by the President and by the Civil Service Commission (see Ch. 18) to recruit and hold able executives and subordinate personnel.

*Congress.* Attempts of the President to streamline the organization of the executive branch often run afoul of congressional interests—or of private interests favored by key Congressmen. A President, for example, may recommend that veterans' hospitals and military hospitals be combined. Powerful veterans' organizations like the American Legion or the Veterans of Foreign Wars may oppose such a move on the grounds that the interests of the hospitalized veteran would become subordinated to the interests of hospitalized military personnel. Since many congressmen are veterans, and since all congressmen have veterans in their home districts, any attempt by the President to change the existing pattern of hospitalization for veterans to achieve what he might believe to be over-all governmental efficiency may be doomed.

And, of course, Congress exerts powerful influence upon the management of the executive branch through its powers of appropriation, investigation, and confirmation.

This should not lead the reader to the conclusion that Congress is necessarily obstructive when it comes to matters of efficient administration. Actually, Congress ferrets out dozens of administrative inefficiencies and anomalies every year and thus keeps many departments and agencies on their toes. Furthermore, Congress has been at least a permissive partner to most of the important administrative reforms of the past two decades.

The point must be made, however, that it is a little unrealistic to hold the President personally responsible for the management of the executive branch when Congress is necessarily involved in actions and decisions which minutely affect the management of every department and agency. And, as we shall see in the following chapter, the General Accounting Office, which is responsible to Congress, and the Civil Service Commission, which is directly responsible to no one, have an immediate and intimate effect upon managerial discretion in the executive departments and agencies.

*Preoccupation.* For reasons which will become clear as this chapter unfolds, Presidents have precious little time to spend on their managerial duties. For over a hundred years, largely out of self-protection, Presidents have tried to unload most of the managerial headaches of running the government onto subordinates—department heads or, more recently, staff in the Executive Office of the President. As questions of foreign policy, national defense, and domestic economic stability come increasingly to dominate the attention of Presidents, they can scarcely be expected to spend many hours laboring over the most efficient administrative home for the Smithsonian Institute, or a new purchasing system for the Forest Service. Increasingly, therefore, the job of maintaining efficient day-to-day operations in the executive branch must be delegated; but it must be delegated in such a way that politically responsible officials can be held ultimately accountable for the conduct of the government's business. This is not a simple endeavor.

*Federalism.* Whatever the virtues of a federal form of government (and they are many), the existence of a series of layers of authority

---

The saving grace of our executive bureaucracy . . . is that nearly everybody in it works for the President. To be sure, each political executive is also responsible horizontally to four or five Congressional committees. . . . But when the chips are down on any one issue all political executives are accountable to the President—which is another way of saying that if they get into a tight spot, they can generally pass the buck to him.

—Harlan Cleveland

does not always make it easy for the citizen to know which layer of government to praise or to blame; and managerial symmetry is rarely achieved. In highway construction, in welfare, in education, in crime detection, in conservation, and in a host of other fields all three levels of government are involved—federal, state, and local (see Chapter 25). If the road in front of our house is disintegrating, we may write to the President of the United States if we care to, but the chances are that a more proximate authority is responsible—even if federal funds are involved in the form of grants-in-aid. Harmonious administrative arrangements among three levels of government are not always easy to achieve.

These, then, are some of the factors which make the President's role as chief executive difficult to perform. Difficult or not, fair or not, the American people will continue to hold their Presidents responsible for the efficient conduct of the public business.

## Chief Diplomat

The Constitution makes it quite clear that initiative in foreign affairs shall be in the hands of the President. The following excerpts from Article II warrant special attention:

He shall have Power, by and with the Advice and Consent of the Senate, to make Treaties, provided two thirds of the Senators present concur; and he shall nominate, and by and with the Advice and Consent of the Senate, shall appoint Ambassadors, other public Ministers and Consuls . . . he shall receive Ambassadors and other public Ministers. . . .

In addition, the Supreme Court has held that the President has implied constitutional powers to enter into executive agreements with other nations, and that these agreements, unless specifically disapproved by the Congress, have the force and validity of treaties. Some of the most dramatic relations with foreign powers in our

---

It is chiefly in its foreign relations that the executive power of the nation finds occasion to exert its skill and its strength. If the existence of the Union were perpetually threatened, and if its chief interests were in daily connection with those of other powerful nations, the Executive Department would assume an increased importance in proportion to the measures expected of it, and to those which it would execute.

—Alexis de Tocqueville, 1835

history have been marked by presidential actions without formal congressional clearance—at least until after the fact. The Louisiana Purchase, the Monroe Doctrine, the Boxer Protocol of 1901, and the destroyer-bases exchange worked out between President Franklin Roosevelt and Winston Churchill during the early months of World War II are but a few outstanding examples. And, of course, the President's prerogatives as Commander-in-Chief of the armed forces of the nation give him an instrument of influence which is of direct relevance to the conduct of diplomacy.

Since World War II, Presidents have taken particular pains to keep congressional leaders informed of new developments and unusual dangers in international affairs. Even though diplomacy in its preliminary phases must now—as always—be carried on in confidence, interbranch and interparty understanding is maximized by the conscious effort of the President and the Secretary of State to keep Congress and the public informed of major developments. Perhaps typical of the new understanding between the President and the Congress was the Concurrent Resolution passed by a Democratic Congress in the spring of 1955 allowing a Republican President discretion in the handling of a delicate situation off the China coast. In the atomic age, with national survival at stake, diplomacy must be conducted with precision and assurance—but with the moral weight of an entire people behind it.

It should also be remembered that more than American opinion is involved. America is today the most powerful nation on earth. But our power depends in large measure upon our relationships with the other free nations in the world. No nation on earth can today be diplomatically, economically, or militarily sovereign. Our long-range survival in the struggle against world Communism depends ultimately upon our ability to exercise restrained leadership in the cause of peace and freedom.

Because of the diplomatic and military prerogatives of the President, and because he is the Chief of State and chief executive of the most powerful nation on earth, other free nations tend to look with deference to his pronouncements and actions in the international field. This places an exalted—if terrifying—responsibility upon our Presidents to consider in all of their diplomatic activities— whether conducted through the UN, through our various alliances, or unilaterally—what our Declaration of Independence once called a "decent respect to the opinions of mankind."

## Commander-in-Chief

The presidential functions of chief diplomat and of Commander-in-Chief are so intimately related in the atomic age that they hardly deserve separate treatment. When President Truman authorized the dropping of the first atomic bomb on Hiroshima in 1945 he plunged the world into a new diplomatic as well as military era. Some of the dimensions of this era have been suggested in Chapter 7. Without question, the most open-ended of the President's powers are those which involve the security of the nation from external attack. As Justice Jackson wrote in the famous steel seizure case in 1952,

That comprehensive and undefined presidential powers hold both practical advantages and grave dangers for the country will impress anyone who has served as legal adviser to a President in time of transition and public anxiety. We should not use this occasion to circumscribe, much less to contract, the lawful role of the President as Commander-in-Chief. I should indulge the widest latitude of interpretation to sustain his exclusive function to command the instruments of national force, at least when turned against the outer world for the security of our society.

Whatever the limits on the President in the normal exercise of his peacetime functions, his powers are virtually limitless in providing for the common defense under emergency conditions.

## Chief of Party

In many of the President's roles he is effectively above the charge of partisanship. Certainly he does not open a cancer drive as a Republican or a Democrat. When he accepts the credentials of a foreign ambassador he is not looked upon as representing only one faction of the American people.

The fact remains, however, that all Presidents are creatures of partisan effort. Parties nominate Presidents, campaign for Presidents, and create the overwhelming bloc of votes in the majority that elects Presidents. Furthermore, the record of the President in office is accepted by most Americans as the record of the party in power. This is true even though both houses of the Congress may be in the hands of the opposition party.

Presidents are always the chief of their own party. This does not mean, however, that they are necessarily the boss of their own

**"It's a petition to the President containing fifteen hundred signatures, and she wants me to read it back!"**

party. As we have seen, American political parties are not monolithic and highly disciplined organizations. Party members in Congress may defer to the President during an election, but may buck many of his proposals during a congressional session. Many of the Congressmen who cheered President Eisenhower the loudest at the San Francisco Republican convention in 1956 were men who had voted against many of his most important bills in the preceding six months. Even as astute a politician as Franklin Roosevelt found himself slowed to a walk in his second and third terms by the leaders of his own party in Congress.

As Clinton Rossiter has put it, "The party that makes him also brakes him—this is the lot, not entirely happy, of the modern President."

### Voice of the People

Andrew Jackson is generally given credit for turning our constitutional pyramid upside down and making the President rather than the House of Representatives "the tribune of the people." Not until the twentieth century, however, did this reversal become the pattern. The concept of the Presidency as the proper vehicle for the reflection of the most widespread democratic forces in our society is certainly foreign to the intent of our Founding Fathers. In their scheme of things, the House of Representatives was to reflect the voice of the people; the Senate was to reflect the voice of property and education; and the Presidency was to be the final bastion of detached, almost introspective, conservatism. This initial ideal was transfigured by the relentless march of democratic forces during the nineteenth century. Through gerrymandering and the logic of producer influence in single-member constituencies, the House of Representatives has become, in the absence of widely recognized crisis, the most conservative representative organ in our national government; the Senate retains its place in the middle; and the President has become the recognized voice of the whole citizenry. But this is more than a matter of conservatism versus liberalism, constituency versus nation, property versus voter. Franklin D. Roosevelt once called the Presidency "the greatest pulpit in the world." True moral leadership is never vague or syrupy; it is a call to battle for precise causes worth sacrifice of time, money, and energy. It is a call to the big "oughtnesses" of our time. The people have many voices, and the President can echo whichever voice he chooses. If he uses his "pulpit" to pronounce "peace" when there is no peace, or if he refers to "spiritual principles" without recognition that in our heritage such principles have invariably involved toil and sacrifice as well as generosity and friendliness, he fails to tap the vast strength which is potentially at his disposal to meet the terrifying issues of our age.

## Protector of Domestic Tranquillity

The President is the grand protector of domestic tranquillity. Certainly no single person can command more resources to meet the exigencies of a natural disaster or a social explosion than the President. In recent years when vagrant hurricanes have lashed the populous shores of the northeastern United States, citizens have called mayors, mayors have telephoned governors, and governors have telegraphed the President. The only difference among these appellate layers is that at the level of the White House, as Mr. Truman's desk sign put it when he was President, "the buck stops here." If domestic violence in the form of race or industrial riots should break out, the ultimate instruments for restoring order would be those designated and ordered into action by the President. Certainly in the face of nuclear attack, the President would be expected to rule by executive decree. He is, in short, the ultimate protector of the people against physical violence and disorder.

## Manager of Prosperity

The Employment Act of 1946 made explicit what had increasingly been taken for granted during the previous fifteen years: the President has an obligation to be the chief watchdog of the economy. If financial panic or widespread unemployment or runaway inflation should threaten the country, all eyes would turn to the White House for recommendations and action. Even in periods of general prosperity it is commonplace for public officials in isolated depressed areas to ask the President for assistance. Traditionally, Republicans have been less inclined to accept government action to redress imbalances in the private economy than have Democrats. It is for this reason that the following words of a Republican President in 1953 are not without significance:

Government must be alert and sensitive to economic developments, including its own myriad activities. It must be prepared to take preventive as well as remedial action; and it must be ready to cope with new situations that may arise. This is not a start-and-stop responsibility, but a continuous one.[3]

## The President Is Many Men

The above list of presidential responsibilities serves to confirm the opinion of most qualified observers that the American Presidency is an impossible job. That as many of his functions are carried on as successfully as they are is a tribute to the dedication of the men who have accepted the responsibility of office; it is even more a reflection of the fact that today the Presidency is a gigantic enterprise carried on by hundreds of highly trained men and women.

*Presidential Assistance.* Presidents have always had some kind of help in the discharge of their duties. It is true that in terms of legally sanctioned staff assistance in the White House, it was not until 1857 that Congress appropriated money for a presidential "clerk." Prior to that time, however, some Presidents hired relatives or friends to do clerical work—paying them out of personal salary; and some Presidents like Andrew Jackson established what came to be called "kitchen cabinets"—small groups of personal friends and advisers who kept backstage, but nonetheless who helped Presidents perform some of their exacting roles.

These largely informal and desultory arrangements for assisting the President lasted well into the present century. As late as 1932, President Hoover had only forty-two assistants in the White House, and most of these were clerks.

# THE EXECUTIVE OFFICE

Today the Presidency is staffed with over 1200 employees. The explosive growth in the presidential institution is largely a product of the past quarter century. Although there are a number of historical landmarks delineating this development, the most significant are probably the following:

1. The Budget and Accounting Act of 1921. Among other things, this Act established a Budget Bureau (originally housed in the Treasury) responsible to the President, with the task of helping the President in his administrative and legislative roles by assisting in the preparation of an executive budget and by carrying out related functions.

2. Following the recommendations of the Brownlow Committee in 1938 ("the President needs help"), the creation of an Executive Office of the President containing various units such as the White House Office, the Bureau of the Budget, and various planning, personnel, and emergency units which set precedents for later developments.

3. The Employment Act of 1946 which created the Council of Economic Advisers in the Executive Office of the President.

4. The National Security Act of 1947 which established the National Security Council and the National Security Resources Board (now superseded by the Office of Defense Mobilization) in the Executive Office framework.

5. The creation during the first Eisenhower Administration of a Cabinet Secretariat.

Some of the constituent units of the Executive Office warrant further discussion at this point.

## The White House Office

Closest to the President in his daily routine is the staff of the White House office. Actually, many of those listed as working in the White House have their offices in the old State-War-Navy

Building on the corner of Pennsylvania Avenue and 17th Street. The White House office includes a variety of functions and, of necessity, a variety of skills. No two Presidents will ever organize the White House in an identical manner; for organization at this level of intimacy is a matter of temperament and administrative habit. But every President needs at least the following kinds of intimate assistants:

1. A *press secretary* to act both in an advisory capacity to the President on the handling of news emanating from the White House; and in the capacity of a buffer between hungry news reporters and the President.

2. An *appointments secretary* to bring some kind of order out of the chaos of requests that come from those who wish a piece of the President's limited time.

3. *Staff secretaries and clerks* to handle the hundreds and sometimes thousands of pieces of mail and official memoranda which swamp the White House every day.

4. *Personal secretaries*, both for the President and his wife.

5. A variety of *special assistants, administrative assistants, special counsels, advisers, and uniformed aides* to absorb as much of the shock of the daily presidential load as possible; to help keep the President informed in various key areas of public policy; to prepare drafts of presidential messages, speeches, letters, memoranda, and other official documents; and to assist the President in matters of protocol, personnel recruitment, legislative relations, and executive branch coordination.

6. A physician to the President.

7. A household staff (cooks, maids, grounds-keepers, etc.).

Without these kinds of assistance at his immediate beck and call, no President in the nuclear age could possibly handle the enormous responsibilities which have been thrust upon him by the Constitution and by democratic expectations.

### The Bureau of the Budget

Besides the White House office a number of other important units exist within the Executive Office of the President. The oldest and largest is the Bureau of the Budget which, as we have noted earlier, was established by the Budget and Accounting Act of 1921 and was moved into the Executive Office of the President when the latter was created by the Reorganization Act of 1939. The Budget

Bureau does more than help the President prepare the annual executive budget—although this is its major responsibility. Through its various staffs for statistical standards, legislative reference, and management and organization, it facilitates unified purpose and encourages administrative efficiency throughout the entire executive branch.

## Council of Economic Advisers

Created in 1946 and reorganized in 1953, the Council of Economic Advisers is made up of three members, one of whom is designated by the President as chairman. Operating with the assistance of a small staff of professional economists, "the Council analyzes the national economy and its various segments; advises the President on economic developments; appraises the economic programs and policies of the federal government; recommends to the President policies for economic growth and stability; and assists in the preparation of the economic reports of the President to the Congress." [4]

The chairman of the Council also acts as chairman of the government's Advisory Board on Economic Growth and Stability which consists of top level officials from the following departments and agencies: Agriculture, Commerce, Labor, State, Treasury, Federal Reserve, and the Bureau of the Budget. This Advisory Board attempts to relate departmental policies and programs to the over-all economic objectives of the Employment Act.

## National Security Council

No component of the Executive Office of the President better illustrates the impact of the nuclear age upon American government than the National Security Council. Created by the National Security Act of 1947 and formally located within the Executive Office of the President by Reorganization Plan No. 4 of 1949, the NSC is a top-level interdepartmental committee devoted to assessing and appraising "the objectives, commitments, and risks of the United States in relation to its actual and potential military power, in the interest of national security." [5]

The NSC is composed of the President, the Vice-President, the Secretary of State, the Secretary of Defense, the Director of the Office of Defense Mobilization, and the heads of such other departments and agencies as the President may direct.

Reporting to the NSC are the Central Intelligence Agency and the Operations Coordinating Board. The former is a sizable agency devoted, as we have seen, to collecting and collating intelligence related to the national security; the latter is a small unit designed to provide, in the jargon of government, for the "integrated implementation of national security policies by the several agencies."

A special assistant in the White House acts as a kind of chief of staff of the National Security Council. His is one of the most important responsibilities in the national government. In this nuclear age it is he that must keep the President informed and the NSC alert on those issues which involve the juxtaposition of our diplomatic objectives and our military capabilities.

### Office of Defense Mobilization

The functions of the Office of Defense Mobilization have been outlined earlier (see page 121). It is sufficient here simply to remind the reader that the Office of Defense Mobilization has the job of planning for the coordination of military, industrial, and civilian mobilization in the face of possible war. The ODM was made a part of the Executive Office of the President by Reorganization Plan No. 3 of 1953.

### Special Commissions

In addition to these formal and continuing units of the Executive Office, the President has other sources of help. He may, for example, appoint a special presidential commission to study some important area of public policy and make recommendations. In recent years such critical issues as civil rights, education, highways, and intergovernmental relations have been studied by presidential commissions, and many of the recommendations of these commissions have been incorporated in presidential messages to Congress, in legislation, and in administrative actions. Sometimes a commission may be a way of avoiding action on a particularly controversial subject; but, in general, presidential commissions have shed light without undue heat on some of the critical issues of our time.

### National Party Headquarters

In a real sense the national headquarters of the President's party is an adjunct of the Executive Office of the President. The national chairman and his key staff are in frequent communication with the President or with assistants in the White House on such matters as patronage, legislative relations, and campaign strategy. Before congressional elections, and especially before presidential elections, many roles in the White House and in the national headquarters of the President's party are interchangeable.

## THE CABINET

The President has, of course, the assistance of his political executives—the heads of the great departments and agencies of the national government. Collectively, along with top officials in the Executive Office, some of them sit as the President's cabinet. Individually, depending upon their personal relations with the President and the nature of their responsibility, they may serve as special advisers to the President. The Secretary of State, for example, is the President's key personal adviser in the field of foreign policy. Most cabinet members at one time or another assist the President in his ceremonial duties.

For most of American history, however, the cabinet has not been an effective instrument either for the formulation of policy or for the coordination of program. Even today with the existence in the White House of a Secretary to the Cabinet whose job it is to prepare agenda and background materials in advance of cabinet discussions and to check with departments and agencies on their implementations of cabinet decisions, it is highly doubtful whether the cabinet is a very important instrument of policy initiative or agreement. Its most useful present roles seem to be in fostering a "team" sense among the top executives of the government and in providing a forum for general discussions of national and international problems.

Historically, one reason the cabinet has not functioned smoothly and effectively as a policy-making and policy-coordinating body is because few of its members have been solely and continuously "the President's men." Although the nomination of cabinet officers is rarely blocked by the Senate, many department heads in our history have been selected by the President in order to appease a dissident faction of the President's own party. Only a few Presidents have heeded the wise advice that James Buchanan gave to Franklin Pierce:

A cabinet ought to be a unit. . . . He who attempts to conciliate opposing factions by placing ardent and embittered representatives of each in his cabinet, will discover that he has only infused into these factions new vigor and power for mischief.[6]

Another reason why fashioning the cabinet into a team has been difficult is because department heads almost inevitably become engrossed in the substantive problems of their own agencies and quickly lose track of the general concerns which occupy the mind of the President.

# UNOFFICIAL ASSISTANCE

Presidents turn, of course—as they always have—to friends and relatives outside the formal structure of government for advice and assistance. The Presidency always has been, and probably always will be, a lonely job. Disinterested advice may not be so hard to find today as it was before career positions were developed in the Executive Office; but it is still rare. Some presidential friends like Amos Kendall (to Andrew Jackson), Colonel House (to Woodrow Wilson), Harry Hopkins (to Franklin Roosevelt), and Milton Eisenhower (to Dwight Eisenhower) have had enormous influence upon events and have assuaged for their Presidents the loneliness of august power. Many wives of our chief executives have served as extensions of the eyes and ears and heart of the President. No matter how formalized the channels of communication to and from the President become, the chances are overwhelming that most of our Presidents will continue to search out the advice and assistance of a few people, personally close to them, who want nothing but to serve whom they love.

But of the President's work which might be increasingly shared by the Vice President without compounding the ground for strain, only one area holds some promise—the purely ceremonial functions. . . . The Vice President's share in the ceremonial burden might be enlarged and at the same time carried off with more grace if he was furnished with an official residence of his own.

—Sidney Hyman

# THE VICE-PRESIDENCY

The President, if he is fortunate, has a key aide in the person of the Vice-President. This statement is qualified because on occasion in our history the Vice-President has represented a faction in the President's party which has been basically unsympathetic with the President's program or hostile to the President as a person. The only constitutional responsibility of the Vice-President is to preside over the Senate. Unofficially, however, many Vice-Presidents in American history have been effective mediators between the President and Congress. More recently they have been used with increasing frequency to lighten the President's ceremonial burdens and to act as ambassadors of good will abroad.

Since the major constitutional purpose of having a Vice-President is to ensure a smooth succession to the Presidency in case the incumbent dies in office or is disabled, and since in this century two Presidents have died in office and two have been disabled for extended periods while in office, it is being increasingly recognized that a Vice-President must be given as thorough knowledge of the problems and duties of the Presidency as possible and must be initially chosen by his political party with presidential qualifications in mind.

## SUCCESSION AND DISABILITY

Although the question of presidential succession was settled by a new act in 1946 which provided that the Speaker of the House

In the case of Presidential disability, what is it that devolves upon the Vice President? Is it the "powers and duties" of the office, or is it the office of the Presidency itself? Furthermore, who is to determine whether the President is unable to discharge the responsibilities of his office? Who raises such a question? Who decides when a disabled President is capable of reclaiming his powers? . . .

—Peter Frelinghuysen, Jr.

and the President-Pro-Tem of the Senate were next in line after the Vice-President, the question of presidential disability is still hotly debated. As a result of President Eisenhower's heart attack in the fall of 1955, congressional and lay attention was focused on the question of who was to decide whether the President was too ill to carry out his constitutional responsibilities. There are many thoughtful students of the subject who feel that the problem is too important to be ignored. There are others, however, who think that the issue should be left hanging—precisely as our Constitution leaves it.

# CONCLUSION

## Synopsis

The Presidency has emerged in the twentieth century as the most powerful office in the United States and in the free world. In the preceding chapter we found that the President was Chief Legislator in the American system of government. In this chapter we have found that he is also Chief of State, Chief Administrator, Chief Diplomat, Commander-in-Chief, Chief of Party, Voice of the People, Chief Protector of Domestic Tranquillity, and Chief Manager of Prosperity. To meet these responsibilities, the Presidency has become highly institutionalized. A variety of staff units and staff assistants now exist in what is called the Executive Office, to help the President do his many jobs. In addition, Presidents turn to their cabinet officers, the Vice President, special *ad hoc* committees, and personal friends for aid and advice. But the awful responsibility of decision is still the lonely prerogative of the President himself.

## Significance

America has been blessed by the fact that, for most of its history, Presidents have conscientiously articulated what they believed to be in the public interest, have given unsparingly of their energies to the job at hand, and have cheerfully—sometimes gratefully—relinquished the reins of office when their elected term expired to return to a relative civilian anonymity. More important, in the big crises of our age, most of our Presidents have not been afraid to decide and to lead.

## Prospectus

Subordinate to the President, the Congress, and in some respects to the courts, are all but a few of the departments and agencies of government. Spread over the United States (some of them are spread over the world), the federal departments and agencies have a wide variety of functions and have assumed a wide variety of forms. Many of their functions were traced in Section II. We now turn to questions of organization and management.

## CHAPTER 18

# Departments and Agencies

THE DEPARTMENTS and agencies of the national government are the operating instruments of the President and the Congress in representing the public will. The day-to-day business of government as it affects the lives of people around the globe is carried out through a multitude of dissimilar and highly complex organizations. These organizations exist to carry out policies which have developed over time in response to a variety of public and private needs and demands—for assistance, for protection, for favors, for freedom.

## THE GROWTH OF THE EXECUTIVE BRANCH

The Constitution says very little about the executive departments and agencies of government. It is quite clear, however, from the language in Article II, Section 2 that executive offices and officers were envisioned.

The first departments were State, Treasury, and War, although other "offices" were created by the first Congress: notably that of the Attorney General and that of the Postmaster General. By present standards, these departments and offices were tiny affairs. Their heads were looked upon not as administrative managers, but as personal assistants and advisers to the President. When the United States Capitol was moved to the District of Columbia in 1800, the entire record of the executive branch was sent in seven packing cases.

In the next half century or so, however, the executive branch grew as the nation grew. From 1800 to 1860, nonmilitary federal employees jumped from 3,000 to 50,000. As the responsibilities of government developed, department heads were forced to construct or to accept increasingly complex patterns of organization. By 1849, the bureau system of subordinate units within the departmental structure had become sufficiently entrenched to lead one Senator to declare that the bureaus were already "substantially independent of the departments." In that same year, the Department of the Interior was created as a kind of holding company over such formerly independent offices as the General Land Office, the Office of Indian Affairs, the Pension Office, and the Patent Office.

Agriculture, which had been created as a noncabinet department under a commissioner in 1862, achieved cabinet status in 1889. In 1902, Congress created a Department of Commerce and Labor, but in 1913 split the department into two separate departments each of cabinet rank. The most recently established cabinet departments are Defense (1949), and Health, Education, and Welfare (1953). Both of these evolved, however, from other agencies or departments, some of which have roots deep in our past.

### Rate of Growth

This bare chronology of departmental development gives little sense of the rate of growth in the size and number of federal departments and agencies. As a generalization one can say only that prior to 1930, and excepting World War I, the rate of growth was steady but on the whole slower than the rate of growth of most other institutions in our society.

During the 1930's and 1940's, however, under the impact of convulsive economic and military eruptions, the federal establishment exploded. In the twenty-five years following 1930, federal expenditures jumped over 2000 percent. Federal employment tripled. New agencies sprang up, flourished, and died. Many were reincarnated. Many were fused. Although much of this activity was due to the insistent demands for economic and military security, new expectations about the general role of government in our society produced startling increases across the board.

Today there are approximately 70 departments and agencies in the federal establishment with over 2000 component units (bureaus, offices, branches, divisions, and the like)—some big, some small; some old, some new; some single-purposed, some multipurposed; some concentrated geographically, some widely scattered. Needed to run this gigantic, diffused enterprise are over 2,300,000 civilian employees (and more than an equal number of military personnel) spread across the land and around the globe.

In order to understand more fully the size and complexity of our national administrative system, a tenfold classification of agency types may be of value:

1. Cabinet departments
2. Departmentlike agencies
3. Independent regulatory commissions
4. Other multiheaded agencies
5. Government corporations
6. Multi- and bilateral international organizations
7. Quasi-official agencies
8. Interdepartmental agencies
9. Auxiliary agencies
10. Congressional agencies

The diversity suggested by these ten categories makes a simple and meaningful description of the national administration extremely difficult. To paraphrase D. N. Chester, the elephant and the squirrel are both animals, and the Department of Defense and the Arlington Memorial Ampitheater Commission are both agencies of the national government, but the differences are not without importance.

## CABINET DEPARTMENTS

Only ten major agencies of the national government are of cabinet rank. These are called departments and, except in two cases, are headed by officials called secretaries (the top official in the Department of Justice is called the Attorney General; the top official in the Post Office Department is called the Postmaster General). The ten cabinet departments (there are three noncabinet departments: Army, Navy, and Air Force) are as follows:

1. Department of State
2. Department of the Treasury
3. Department of Defense
4. Department of Justice
5. Post Office Department
6. Department of the Interior
7. Department of Agriculture
8. Department of Commerce
9. Department of Labor
10. Department of Health, Education, and Welfare

There is no particular logic as to why these ten departments should have the prestige of cabinet rank, and certain other agencies should not. All that can be said is that, historically, cabinet rank has symbolized the recognized importance of the functions of an agency, and that these ten agencies have had their functions so dignified.

## Size

The largest cabinet department is the Department of Defense, which as we noted earlier, includes three subordinate military departments: Army, Navy, and Air Force. The Department of Defense spends more money and has a larger number of civilian employees than any other agency in the federal government. The size of the enterprise defies comprehension. Seven percent of our national active labor force is employed directly by the Department of Defense. This amounts to more than twice the manpower of the ten largest corporations of the world combined.[1]

At the other extreme is a department like Labor with only a few thousand employees and with annual expenditures of less than one percent of those of the Department of Defense.

Regardless of size, however, all cabinet departments have certain things in common. They are each headed by a single political executive who is appointed by the President to serve at his pleasure (the advice and consent of the Senate in cabinet appointments is usually a formality). These top executives have the privilege of sitting weekly in the President's cabinet meetings, and they have directly subordinate to them a number of political executives, usually called under- or assistant secretaries, who have special policy responsibilities over a group of related activities. Below the assistant secretaries are, of course, the bureau chiefs, branch chiefs, field office supervisors, and other administrative officers (usually career) who are responsible for the conduct of the day-to-day operations of the national departments.

## Organization

Close to the top of each one of these departmental pyramids are staff and auxiliary officers—sometimes political appointees but usually career officials—who specialize in such matters as legal advice, personnel, budgeting and administrative housekeeping; in other words, the machinery and the legality of administration. Their

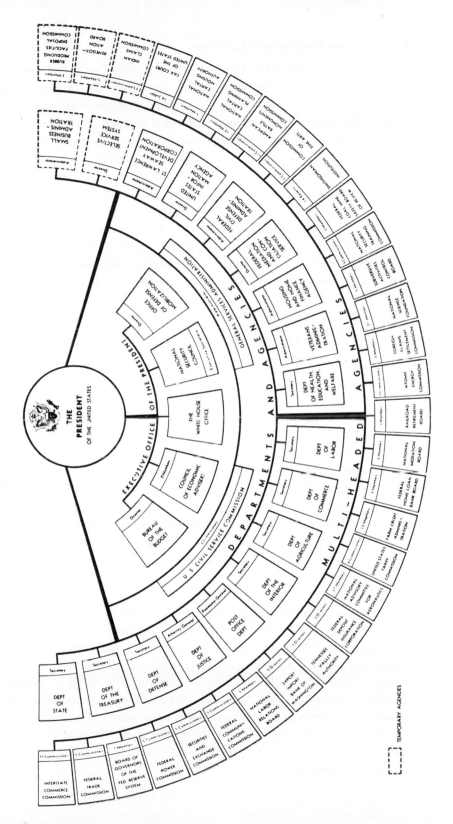

THE PRESIDENT OF THE UNITED STATES

EXECUTIVE OFFICE OF THE PRESIDENT

DEPARTMENTS AND AGENCIES

MULTI-HEADED AGENCIES

TEMPORARY AGENCIES

job is to help those who have the top responsibility to do their jobs more effectively, and to provide necessary continuity during political change. For just as a President must attempt to build a unified team out of his cabinet members, so each department head must attempt to build a unified team out of the various units and officials which make up his department. This is not always easy. There are centrifugal forces at work in each department and in the government as a whole which make a sense of common purpose difficult to attain. One of the most important achievements of the first Hoover Commission was inducing Congress to vest substantial legal power, which had formerly been lodged at the bureau level, in the secretaries of departments—thus enabling them to exercise the authority necessary for effective departmental coordination.

# DEPARTMENTLIKE AGENCIES

Next in rank and importance to the departments themselves are the departmentlike agencies. These, like the departments, vary greatly in size and are run by single administrative heads directly responsible to the President. Actually, in terms of budget and personnel, some of these single-headed independent agencies are far larger than some of the cabinet departments. The Veterans' Administration, for example, has a budget of nearly $5.0 billion annually and a permanent roster of over 175,000. Its centers, domiciliaries, district offices, and regional offices are spread all over the United States. In some large states like New York and California, a dozen to a score of separate VA "stations" are maintained.

## Organization

Nothing is better suited to confuse the student of American government than to be informed that the major functional subdivisions of the Veterans' Administration are called "departments." It is unfortunate that a governmentwide terminology cannot be adopted so that words like "office," "administration," "branch," "bureau," "division," "service," and "staff" can have a common meaning in all agencies and departments. As matters now stand, a bureau in one department is called an office, or department, or division in another. This unnecessarily confuses the public's picture of agency organization and responsibility.

Even the pyramidal organization charts of cabinet departments and departmentlike agencies are in some cases misleading. Some departments and agencies are little more than administrative holding companies for a variety of federal enterprises which have little relationship to each other. The Housing and Home Finance Agency, for example, has various subordinate "administrations" which have sharply contrasting functions. Its two largest subdivisions, the Federal Housing Administration and the Public Housing Administration were once powerful and warring independent agencies. They are no longer independent, but their respective philosophies and clientele interests still differ enormously; and it is a real question whether in terms of effective power with the Congress the heads of these two subordinate units are not so powerful as the top Administrator of the Housing and Home Finance Agency himself. Similar questions can of course be raised about cabinet departments like Health, Education, and Welfare; Justice; Interior; and Defense.

Besides the Veterans' Administration and the Housing and Home Finance Agency, some of the more important departmentlike agencies in the Federal government in recent years have been the United States Information Agency, the Federal Mediation and Conciliation Service, the Small Business Administration, the Selective Service System, and the Federal Civil Defense Administration. Until 1953 the functions of the Department of Health, Education, and Welfare were performed by what was called the Federal Security Agency—a departmentlike agency of considerable size and responsibility.

# INDEPENDENT REGULATORY COMMISSIONS

As we have noted in earlier chapters, the federal government exists not only to render direct and indirect services to the citizenry; it exists to regulate various privately managed enterprises. Some of the regulatory activities of the government are conducted through cabinet departments or departmentlike agencies: for example, the meat-inspection activities of the Department of Agriculture, or the building-inspection activities of the Federal Housing Administration.

But regulation is most particularly the job of a group of agencies called independent regulatory commissions.

## Attributes

Independent regulatory commissions have these attributes:

1. They are multiheaded, generally bipartisan agencies, governed by a board of five to seven members appointed on an overlapping basis for terms of five or more years.

2. The chairman of the board serves as chief administrative officer of the agency, but, in theory at least, his voice is no greater than that of any other board member in the rule-making and the adjudicative aspects of the agency's work.

3. The term "rule-making" implies that the agency has the power, within general limits set by the Congress, to issue rules and regulations which have the force of law. This is sometimes referred to as a "quasi-legislative" function.

4. The adjudicative aspects of the agency's work involve the commission's sitting as a kind of court to hear cases arising under the rules promulgated. This is frequently referred to as a "quasi-judicial" function.

5. Although commissioners are appointed by the President with the advice and consent of the Senate, the Supreme Court has ruled in the Humphrey Case that, except as Congress provides, the President may not remove them except for "cause" (malfeasance, misconduct, and so on). In the making of policy, the commissions are presumed to be independent of presidential influence.

## Component Groups

Today, in the order of their establishment, the independent regulatory commissions include the Interstate Commerce Commission (1887), Federal Reserve Board (1914), Federal Trade Commission (1915), Federal Power Commission (1930), Federal Communications Commission (1934), Securities and Exchange Commission (1934), National Labor Relations Board (1935), and the Civil Aeronautics Board (1940).*

## Criticism, Pro and Con

Almost from the beginning the independent regulatory commissions have been the subject of bitter controversy. The claims and

* In its present form.

This dramatic statue in front of the Federal Trade Commission building in Washington, D. C., symbolizes the restraining responsibilities of the regulatory commissions. The wild horse suggests a vigorous economy in the process of being tamed by government.

counterclaims have been many. Some students of the subject have contended that the commissions have too much leeway—that they are in effect little congresses and little supreme courts with life-and-death powers over important segments of the economy, and that they are effectively responsible to no one but themselves. Other students have echoed this complaint and have added that all too many regulatory commissions are in effect captive agencies—responsive, not to the public interest, but to the interests of those private groups which the commissions are supposed to regulate. The charge is that the railroads have captured the I.C.C.; the airlines, the C.A.B.; the networks, the F.C.C. Still other students have complained that the commissions have violated the Anglo-Saxon legal precept that the functions of prosecutor and judge must be separated —although much of the sting of this complaint was blunted by the Federal Administrative Procedure Act of 1946 which set up a series of procedural guarantees to minimize the dangers of purposefully or inadvertently violating the spirit of our legal heritage.

The defenders of the commissions claim that vast, complex, and highly technical aspects of our economy like transportation and communications cannot be regulated in the public interest by anything so ponderous and intellectually diffuse as the Congress; that delegated authority to make precise rules to meet new situations is a necessity in this age and that Congress so realized when it established the regulatory commissions; that presidential "politics" should be kept far removed from quasi-legislative and quasi-judicial policy-making; and that, although some of the commissions are rightfully sensitive to the problems of the people being regulated, the public interest has been in most cases the guiding light of the regulatory agencies.

### Problem of Policy Coordination

Perhaps the most serious accusation made against the regulatory commissions has been that their policies can operate out of phase with presidential policies. If, for example, the President is doing everything within his power to control inflationary pressures, the actions of the Federal Reserve Board and the Interstate Commerce Commission might negate much of what the President is trying to do. That this in fact rarely happens, that commissioners are reasonably responsive to the programmatic aims of the President, does not destroy the argument that dangers of cross-purpose exist, and that when cross-purpose occurs one of the contending parties is in effect responsible to nobody.

The most dramatic suggestion for dealing with this problem of policy coordination was made twenty years ago by the President's Committee on Administrative Management which suggested the following reorganization:

1. Abolish the independent regulatory commissions as now organized.

2. Transfer the rule-making function of each commission to the regular department of the government most logically concerned (for example, I.C.C. to the Commerce Department, N.L.R.B. to the Labor Department, and so on), and subject rule-making to policy guide lines set by the President and his department heads—always, of course, within the general legal framework set by the Congress.

3. Keep the quasi-judicial functions separate from departmental and presidential control, but place the instruments of administrative adjudication in the regular departments of the government for "housekeeping" purposes (space, files, desks, and so on).

The first Hoover Commission Report in 1949 recommended minor administrative changes in the regulatory agencies (such as vesting in the chairman of each commission the administrative responsibilities of the agency), but in general it gave its blessing to the idea of maintaining in our governmental system a number of independent regulatory commissions. Short of some national crisis which can be traced to the independent action of some regulatory agency, it is probable that they will continue to live and to function, in Professor Cushman's phrase, as a "headless fourth branch of government."

# OTHER MULTIHEADED AGENCIES

Many agencies of our national government do not focus in a single administrative head. We have already noted that the independent regulatory commissions are multiheaded agencies; but there are many agencies whose major functions are not regulatory which are run by a board or commission.

Some of these will be discussed below under other categories for reasons which will be apparent when we come to them. Some multiheaded agencies are too tiny to warrant much attention in a book of this kind: the American Battle Monuments Commission or the Commission on Fine Arts, for example.

Some, like the United States Tariff Commission, Foreign Claims Settlement Commission, Indian Claims Commission, the Tax Court, and the Railroad Retirement Board, have a variety of judicial functions which in some ways make them far more like courts than like administrative agencies. Their job, in other words, is to sift and weigh evidence and to make settlements or recommendations for settlement which seem equitable under the law. Actually, it is a fair generalization that when judicial questions must be handled by an administrative agency, the Congress with a few notable exceptions has seen fit to make such an agency multiheaded.

### Atomic Energy Commission

No one would pretend, however, that the major task of the Atomic Energy Commission is either regulatory or judicial (although its functions are sufficiently vast to involve the commissioners in both kinds of responsibilities, especially since the passage of the Atomic Energy Act of 1954). The big job of the AEC is research and production within general but crucial guidelines of policy. For example, the AEC had to decide whether resources should be diverted from the production and improvement of atomic fission weapons to develop nuclear fusion weapons. Because of the fantastic and almost totally unpredictable nature of the problems created by the development of atomic energy, Congress provided in the Atomic Energy Act of 1946 for a multiheaded civilian agency to take over atomic development activities from the military. As Morgan Thomas has put it in his book, *Atomic Energy and Congress:*

In placing this unique program in the hands of a five-man commission, rather than a single administrator, Congress indicated its realization that many tough policy problems would arise after this formal transfer of authority.[2]

It should be noted, however, that under the five commissioners of the AEC, and responsible to them, is a general manager. As the Special Senate Committee on Atomic Energy reported:

This form of organization is based on administrative experience developed in both government and industry. Such experience points to the need for a high level policy group which can discharge its functions without the additional burden of passing on current operations. Day to day administration is best directed by a single manager.[3]

It will be interesting to watch over the years to see how the form of organization changes as atomic energy problems change. Already, the chairman of the AEC, rather than the commission itself or the general manager, has become the focal point of AEC policy and administration. Scholars and practitioners of government are struggling to develop a more systematic conception of the various forms of organization needed at various stages in the life of an institution. Within the federal government, the Administrative Management Staff of the Bureau of the Budget (assisted occasionally by the reports of special commissions like the two Hoover Commissions) attempts to do what it can to recommend administrative reorganizations which will fit the needs of a rapidly changing government of vast and complex proportions. Many distinguished social scientists are addressing themselves to the same kinds of questions. But no one pretends at this stage that he has all the answers. "When should a multiheaded organization be changed into a single-headed organization?" This may seem to the reader like a dull and unimportant question. Actually, it is the kind of question that may be at the heart of successful, efficient, imaginative, and economical government.

# GOVERNMENT CORPORATIONS

Government corporations are business-like enterprises which have been endowed by Congress with functions and prerogatives not generally permitted other agencies of government.

Although most government workers are employed outside of Washington, citizens tend to think of the nation's capital as the administrative center of the national government. This is in part because of the magnificence of the public buildings in the District of Columbia. The dignity and spaciousness of these buildings is suggested here by the Department of the Interior located at 19th Street and Virginia Avenue.

Prompted first by the demands of World War I for goods and services which a free market economy could not provide within the nation's timetable of urgency, government corporations as a flexible instrument of administration received their greatest boost during the depression years of the 1930's.

At present, some government corporations provide banking or underwriting functions in areas where risks are too long or too high to attract private lenders (for example, Federal Crop Insurance Corporation, the Federal Deposit Insurance Corporation, the now defunct Reconstruction Finance Corporation). Some government corporations are developmental in a broad sense: the Tennessee Valley Authority, the Virgin Islands Corporation, or the St. Lawrence Seaway Development Corporation, for example. A few have been directed toward answering in direct operational terms a particular social or economic need, such as low-cost housing for low-income families (Public Housing Administration).

## Privileges

What ties these various enterprises together is the fact that most of them enjoy privileges not generally extended to other agencies of government:

1. They may sue and be sued.

2. They may present to the President and Congress a "businesslike" budget which allows an operating flexibility in expenditures for program not permitted other types of agencies.

3. They may receive a commercial rather than a government audit.

In addition, some government corporations are not bound by civil service regulations. The Tennessee Valley Authority, for example, has its own personnel system.

Only a few of the government corporations are directly responsible to the President and the Congress. Most of them are tucked away in side pockets of other departments and agencies, but within those side pockets they exercise considerable autonomy.

Over the years, and particularly since the Government Corporation Control Act of 1945, these businesslike enterprises have gradually discarded some of the features which they once had and which linked them in theory and practice to their business counterparts. Today, without such trappings as capital stock, and in many cases without boards of directors, government corporations still retain many of the advantages and flexibilities inherent in having a separate legal personality.

But it would be a mistake to think of them as autonomous in any fundamental sense. As Harold Seidman, one of the world's leading authorities on public enterprises, has put it, "The United States government corporation is today nothing more nor less than a government institution tailored to the requirements of certain types of operating programs." Through controls established in the 1945 Act, the President and the Congress—either directly or through other agencies—have the responsibility of coordinating the programs of the government corporations with the other major programs of government. But this does not mean that the operating flexibility, which has made the government corporation such a vital and useful instrument of democracy, has in any serious way been limited.

# MULTI- AND BILATERAL INTER-NATIONAL ORGANIZATIONS

With the growth of America's international obligations, and with the increasing impact of technology upon world affairs generally, the United States government has found it imperative to participate in a variety of multi- and bilateral international organizations. These represent half-blind feelers of twentieth-century man probing for ways in which to make increasingly secure and felicitous his necessary relationships with his fellow men the world around.

Some of the more important of these organizations have been listed above (see p. 70). It is only necessary to note here that participation in such organizations creates a variety of administrative problems for the national governments concerned, including our own. The machinery of decision-making is ponderous in any modern nation. When two or five or fifteen or sixty or seventy-six nations attempt to reach a firm agreement on any important policy issue, the problems of clearance and communications become at times almost insurmountable. Furthermore, the sensibilities of sovereignty are easily injured, and any powerful nation must walk and talk with care in the presence of weaker partners. Even if the overpowering issue of war and peace were not pressing, the perfection of administrative forms and diplomatic skills for the efficient managing of international affairs unquestionably would be among the priority items on the agenda of twentieth-century man.

# CAREER OPPORTUNITIES IN

Selected introductory statements from *FEDERAL CAREERS, A*
ing Office, 1956. This is the most comprehensive, attractive and
purchased from the Superintendent of Documents, U. S. Govern-

Careers in public service offer satisfactions and rewards found in no other calling. Many people choose careers in Government for the sheer satisfaction of participating in challenging, far-reaching activities of Federal agencies. They draw a feeling of pride from the privilege of serving all of the American people. They enjoy the excitement of being in the midst of vital work, of helping—if only in a small way—to further the progress of a great nation. . . .

Federal employees work in thousands of offices, laboratories, and installations throughout the United States, in the Territories and possessions, and in most foreign countries. They perform almost every kind of work found in private employment as well as some jobs peculiar to Government. . . .

You can get an idea of the Government's manpower needs when you consider that more than 20,000 Federal employees are at work in the physical sciences, nearly 50,000 in engineering, 10,000 in the social sciences, 17,000 in personnel administration and industrial relations, 15,000 in the biological sciences, 66,000 in medicine and allied fields, 8,000 in education, 77,000 in accounting and fiscal work, and 18,000 in mathematics and statistics. . . .

If you desire additional information about these programs or the kinds of opportunities offered, write to the agency in which you are interested. As a further source, the Civil Service Commission and the agencies publish pamphlets and other employment literature which can be obtained on request or which may be available at your college placement office or library. Representatives of the Commission and many agencies make annual recruiting visits to colleges and universities. Your placement officer or department head can tell you about visits scheduled for your school and can arrange interviews for you.

# THE FEDERAL GOVERNMENT

*Directory for College Students,* United States Government Print-
useful brochure available on Government careers. Copies may be
ment Printing Office, Washington 25, D. C. for 60 cents.

More specific information concerning *current* employment opportunities and
open examinations can be obtained at your college placement office, your local
post office, the personnel offices of the agencies and installations, and offices of
the Civil Service Commission as listed below:

CENTRAL OFFICE.—The United States Civil Service Commission, Washington 25, D. C.

FIRST REGION.—Post Office and Courthouse Building, Boston 9, Mass.
(Area of Maine, New Hampshire, Vermont, Massachusetts, Rhode Island, and Connecticut.)

SECOND REGION.—Federal Building, Christopher Street, New York 14,
N. Y. (Area of New York and New Jersey.)

THIRD REGION.—United States Customhouse, Second and Chestnut
Streets, Philadelphia 6, Pa. (Area of Pennsylvania, Delaware, Maryland,
and Virginia.)

FIFTH REGION.—Peachtree-Baker Building, 275 Peachtree Street, NE,
Atlanta 3, Ga. (Area of North Carolina, South Carolina, Georgia, Florida,.Tennessee, Alabama, Mississippi, Puerto Rico, and Virgin Islands.)

SIXTH REGION.—Post Office and Courthouse Building, Cincinnati 2,
Ohio. (Area of Ohio, Indiana, Kentucky, and West Virginia.)

SEVENTH REGION.—New Post Office Building, Chicago 7, Ill. (Area of
Michigan, Wisconsin, and Illinois.)

EIGHTH REGION.—1114 Commerce Street, Dallas 2, Texas. (Area of
Arkansas, Oklahoma, Louisiana, and Texas.)

NINTH REGION.—New Federal Building, Twelfth and Market Streets,
St. Louis 1, Mo. (Area of Missouri, Kansas, Iowa, Nebraska, Minnesota,
North Dakota, and South Dakota.)

TENTH REGION.—Building 41, Denver Federal Center, Denver, Colo.
(Area of Colorado, New Mexico, Utah, Wyoming, and Arizona.)

ELEVENTH REGION.—302 Federal Office Building, First Avenue and
Madison Street, Seattle 4, Wash. (Area of Montana, Oregon, Idaho,
Washington, and Alaska.)

TWELFTH REGION.—128 Appraisers Building, 630 Sansone Street, San
Francisco 11, Calif. (Area of California, Nevada, and Hawaii.)

# QUASI-OFFICIAL AGENCIES

The United States government enjoys the services of two quasi-official organizations which operate under congressional charter, cooperate with other departments and agencies on many matters, but receive no direct appropriation from the Congress and have no continuing administrative relationship to the President. The first is the National Academy of Sciences. The second is the American Red Cross. Both organizations are presently struggling to find their exact and proper role in relation to a government which has increasingly moved directly into the very problems of science, welfare, and disaster relief with which these quasi-official agencies have traditionally been concerned.

# INTERDEPARTMENTAL AGENCIES

As the business of government has expanded so have the necessities of coordination. It makes little sense, for example, for the Civil Aeronautics Board to prescribe safety rules for *civilian* aircraft if all *military* aircraft are to be allowed to fly when and where they please.

Washington is cluttered with interdepartmental committees. Most of these were initially established on an *ad hoc* basis by administrative order to take care of some particularly ramifying issue. They remain either because of inertia or because the issue refuses to go away. No one really knows how many formal and informal interdepartmental committees of this kind exist. The number is surely in the hundreds, if not thousands.

Some interdepartmental committees have received either Executive-Order or statutory recognition. In a number of areas, in other words, the President or Congress has created permanent administrative mechanisms to deal with policy problems where the need for interagency coordination is vital and continuing. The National Security Council, discussed in the previous chapter, is such a mechanism.

Some of the more important interdepartmental agencies outside the Executive Office framework are the Air Coordinating Committee, the Interdepartmental Committee on Scientific Research and Development, the National Advisory Committee for Aeronautics, and the National Advisory Council on International Monetary and Financial Problems. Each has a staff which, like the cabinet secretariat established by President Eisenhower, attempts to keep the separate departmental members informed of issues to be settled and policies agreed upon. Some interdepartmental agencies like the NACA are virtually operating departments in their own right.

### Need for Coordination

The ultimate question about interdepartmental committees and agencies is, of course, Who will coordinate the coordinators? This is not a new question, but its importance has not diminished since it was first officially flagged by the first Hoover Commission in 1948. Not only did the first Hoover Commission recommend that there should be an inventory of interdepartmental committees by the President's office at least once a year and that those whose work was completed should be terminated; it recommended also the creation of a new staff secretary in the White House, one of whose principal functions it would be to keep the President currently informed of the work and of the decisions of interdepartmental committees. Neither of these recommendations has been specifically carried out, although there is evidence that the various staffs in the Executive Office of the President are increasingly concerned with the problem.

## AUXILIARY AGENCIES

There are two major executive-branch agencies below the level of the President's office which have what is called by professional administrators an auxiliary function. Auxiliary agencies do not serve the public directly, but serve the other agencies of government which in turn serve the public.

One of these agencies, the General Services Administration, assists other parts of the government in matters of housekeeping: supplies, office space, transportation, record-keeping, property procurement, maintenance, disposal, nonpersonal services, and so on.

The other major auxiliary agency is the United States Civil Service Commission which helps secure and retain personnel for the government by administering a merit system covering 85 percent of all civilian federal employees.

Of the two agencies, the Civil Service Commission is much the older; although the functions of the GSA have been carried on in one form or another since 1789. The Federal Property and Administrative Services Act of 1949, which established the GSA, simply followed some of the recommendations of the first Hoover Commission in consolidating a number of related service functions in one giant agency especially designed for the purpose.

### Civil Service Commission

The United States Civil Service Commission was created by the Civil Service Act of 1883. In some ways independent of both the President and the Congress, the commission is composed of three members, one of whom serves as chairman and chief administrative officer.

At the core of any merit system (the Civil Service Commission administers only one, albeit the largest one, of a number of merit systems in the national government), is the concept that positions covered by the system should not be filled on the basis of politics or religion or personal favoritism, but on the basis of merit as determined by open competitive examinations, or by other appropriate procedures established by the rules of a disinterested body.

Since 90 percent of all federal employees work outside of Washington, D. C., the Civil Service Commission operates twelve regional offices in addition to its central office in the District of Columbia.

*Reorganization.* Under substantial attack from many quarters, including both Hoover Commissions, the Civil Service Commission is in the process of rapid reorganization and massive decentralization. Instead of viewing its job simply as that of "keeping rascals out," it is increasingly turning its attention in a positive sense to the needs of federal departments and agencies for skilled and dedicated personnel. The problems are enormous: federal employee turnover is high; skilled personnel are scarce—especially during periods of extended full employment; tens of thousands of different skills and aptitudes are needed to meet the many demands of modern government; and the many regulations laid down by the Congress governing hiring, promotion, pay, grades, pensions, awards, and veterans' preference are complex and often difficult to administer equitably and efficiently.

But observable progress is being made by the Commission in attracting trained people into government service. In 1955, a new

Federal Service Entrance Examination was established to make it simpler for college students, regardless of their major field, to secure a place on a civil service register. The FSEE is given frequently at convenient locations all over the nation. Passing it opens up a wide variety of fascinating and well-paying careers in the public service for college-trained men and women.

Government at all levels needs trained and resourceful people, both in the career service and in the political executive positions above the career service. The Task Force Report on Personnel and Civil Service of the Second Hoover Commission gave special attention to the question of how the supply and quality of government personnel could be increased—especially at the levels of top management. Most of its recommendations deserve careful study and implementation.

# CONGRESSIONAL AGENCIES

Three giant agencies of the federal government are not part of the executive branch at all. Responsible directly to the Congress are the Government Printing Office, the Library of Congress, and the General Accounting Office.

The Government Printing Office fills orders for printing and binding submitted by Congress and the various executive agencies; furnishes, on order, blank paper, inks, and similar supplies; and distributes government publications to interested officials and the general public as required by law.

The Library of Congress, the largest library in the world, exists primarily for service to the Congress—as its name implies; but it also provides a range of library services to the executive agencies of government and to the public at large. It is truly a national library service for the entire country.

The General Accounting Office is the administrative arm of the Congress to see that appropriated funds are disbursed honestly and in conformity with the law by the various agencies of government. The Controller General, who is appointed for a fifteen-year term, is the agency's chief officer. He has the power to disallow any agency's expenditures if in his judgment such expenditure would violate legislative intent (this is known as the function of preaudit). The GAO also, of course, has the responsibility of checking vouchers and receipts after a financial transaction has been completed (postaudit). In addition, the General Accounting Office is called upon to make special and annual reports to the Congress on matters of financial management in the various agencies of government.

Many political scientists feel that the Controller General has too much power; that his pre-audit responsibilities, particularly, interfere with the necessary discretion of agency heads, and add unnecessary red tape to the complex processes of government. No one questions, however, the desirability of an independent postaudit of government expenditures, although the GAO needs considerable streamlining in the handling of this function.

# BUREAUCRACY AND DEMOCRACY

Even ten categories are insufficient to contain all the agencies of the national government; but perhaps enough has been said to suggest that our government is vast and complex. We have learned in this century that big organization is necessary to accomplish the various goals of our society. This is as true in business and labor and agriculture as it is in government.

But we have also learned that big organization has problems of its own. When many people are harnessed to a single, huge, highly variegated enterprise, a series of difficulties and dangers arise: problems of communication among people, among agencies, and between headquarters and field offices within a single agency; problems of impersonality and inertia; problems of morale; problems of red tape; problems of overlapping and duplication of effort.

### Investigations

The four major public investigations into big government in this century: President Taft's Commission on Economy and Efficiency (1910–1913), the President's Committee on Administrative Management (1936–1938), the first Hoover Commission (1947–1949), and the second Hoover Commission (1953–1955) have all wrestled with these problems of bigness and have made many valuable suggestions for increasing efficiency and responsibility in big government.

Terrifying as the image of big government can be, we do the cause of responsible self-government little good by conjuring up a parade of imaginary horribles every time we hear the word "bureaucracy." We might as well rail against the size of General Motors, the United Steel Workers, or the A & P. Big institutions are a necessary part of our life. Our job is to make them and keep them our efficient servants rather than our masters.

And it is wise to remember that just as the "bureaucrat" of the American Telephone and Telegraph Company is, among others, the friendly man who installs the new dial on our phone, so the "bureaucrat" of the federal government is, among others, the postman who delivers our mail or the meat inspector who protects us.

# CONCLUSION

## Synopsis

Under the impact of depression and war, the federal government has expanded enormously in this century. This growth has often been experimental; it has rarely been orderly. As a result, at least ten different kinds of administrative patterns are now observable among the vast congeries of agencies which make up the operating part of our national government.

## Significance

Big government is not easily managed or directed efficiently. Coordination of effort is particularly difficult when both the Congress and the President have constitutional and political prerogatives which directly affect matters of agency organization and management, and when clientele interests from the outside sometimes resist having "their" agency "coordinated." There is no easy solution to this problem. In spite of Hoover Commissions and internal management studies, some splintering is bound to remain.

## Prospectus

The King of England in the seventeenth century was deemed to be under "God and the Law." But ultimate law in England is determined by act of Parliament. In the United States, law receives its ultimate sanction from decisions of the Supreme Court of the United States. The decisions of the Supreme Court, and the federal courts under it, set the general framework within which the President, the Congress, the federal departments and agencies, and, where federal law is applicable, state and local officials, make and enforce public policy. To the work and organization of the federal court system we now turn.

## CHAPTER 19

# Federal Courts

Although the Judiciary is the least dramatic of the three broad divisions of our Federal government, this fact should not hide the importance of the Federal court system as a branch of government and as an influence on the life of every citizen.

Considering the volume of business handled by modern federal courts, and the importance of their role in the democratic process, they are given surprisingly scant treatment in the Constitution. Article III established a few categories of original jurisdiction for the Supreme Court—and that is all that is specified. Extension of the Supreme Court's jurisdiction, and the creation of other Federal courts inferior to the highest tribunal, were left entirely to Congress.

## JURISDICTION OF COURTS

### Supreme Court

Clearly within the purview of the Supreme Court, according to Article III, are cases arising out of disputes about the Constitution or under federal laws and treaties; admiralty and maritime cases; cases between citizens of different states, or between a citizen of one state and the government of another state, or between two states; cases involving ambassadors and other diplomatic personnel; cases to which the United States government is a party. The Eleventh Amendment modified this to the extent of permitting a citizen to sue a state only with the state's consent, and then in the courts of that state.

### Federal versus State Courts

A volume would be necessary to describe the complex and interlocking relationships between Federal and state courts. Federal courts are not necessarily superior to all state courts. Only the Supreme Court has appellate jurisdiction over state courts, and this privilege is limited. Furthermore, each time Congress has extended the jurisdiction of Federal courts, it has usually not restricted state courts from sharing the jurisdiction. Many violations of federal laws are left to the jurisdiction of state courts, and the only broad category which is restricted to Federal courts are cases involving governments or citizens of different states.

In a nutshell, state courts have jurisdiction over certain types of cases; Federal courts have jurisdiction over a few; only the United States Supreme Court has superior jurisdiction over all other courts.

### High Repute of Federal Courts.

These complex relationships have led to a certain amount of confusion over jurisdiction; some cases revolve entirely around the issue of whether trial should be held in state or Federal courts. The confusion could have been avoided by awarding state courts original jurisdiction in all cases (except those mentioned in the Constitution) and reserving Federal courts for appeals. But by and large the two systems have worked out remarkably well, and the retention of original jurisdiction in Federal courts has been an important factor in preserving justice. Federal courts have acquired a reputation unmatched by the average state court, and in certain areas where regional passion tend to corrupt justice, only a Federal court could be trusted to remain unprejudiced.

# THE HIERARCHY OF FEDERAL COURTS

### District Courts.

At the bottom of the hierarchy of the Federal court system are the eighty-four district courts. (The District of Columbia court and territorial courts are also considered as sharing the same station.) From one to sixteen judges—the number depends on the volume of business—sit in each district court and their principle function is in the field of original jurisdiction. All violations of federal crimes are tried in district courts, usually before one judge and a jury.

Assisting the district court are United States commissioners, who are empowered to issue warrants of arrest and to hold preliminary hearings in criminal cases. United States marshalls, who have limited police functions, and court clerks and court reporters assist in the dispensing of justice.

## Courts of Appeals.

Sitting as an appellate court for the district courts are the United States Courts of Appeals, of which there are ten circuits, or regions, plus the District of Columbia Court of Appeals. Created by Congress in 1891, the Courts of Appeals help take the appellate load off the back of the United States Supreme Court. All cases tried in a district court may be appealed to a court of appeals; few may be appealed beyond them to the Supreme Court. Circuit courts also hear appeals from decisions of legislative courts (see below) and from independent boards and commissioners.

Each circuit court has three to six judges, although only two judges are necessary for each case. (Cases on appeal, of course, do not use a jury.) Judges of the Supreme Court are each assigned a circuit and may sit in on cases—but they never do.

## Legislative Courts.

Other Federal courts, established by acts of Congress, do not come under constitutional provisions regulating the judiciary. They are called legislative courts; their judges are not necessarily appointed for life and they are restricted to a specific jurisdiction.

*The Court of Claims* is largely limited to cases arising out of contractual disputes with the United States government. Under the Constitution, the government must give its consent to be sued by a citizen. The Court of Claims was created to replace Congress as the agency empowered to accommodate citizens who had a case against the government. In accepting a case it automatically gives the government's consent to be sued. Five judges of the Court of Claims sit in Washington, D. C., for all cases.

*The United States Customs Court* hears cases arising under the tariff regulations passed by Congress. Nine judges usually sit in New York City.

*The United States Court of Customs and Patent Appeals* is the appellate court for the United States Customs Court and for cases decided in the United States Patent Office. Its five judges usually sit in Washington, D. C.

*The United States Court of Military Appeals,* the most recently

Ranking under the United States Supreme Court are the Courts of Appeals. The nation is divided into 10 circuits, shown above, in each of which is located an Appeals Court. There is also an Appeals Court in the District of Columbia.

established legislative court, was created in 1951 to sit as a final court of appeals over cases arising under the Uniform Code of Military Justice. It is the GI's Supreme Court, consisting of three judges.

*The United States Territorial Courts,* mentioned above, are actually legislative courts, but in their widespread functioning they resemble the district courts. They are located in Hawaii, Alaska, Puerto Rico, the Virgin Islands, and the Panama Canal Zone.

# THE UNITED STATES SUPREME COURT

Sitting above and apart from every other court in the land are the nine justices of the United States Supreme Court. The guardian and symbol of justice in a land where justice is one of our highest goals, the United States Supreme Court has awesome responsibilities. Under the Constitution, it must take original jursdiction only in cases involving high foreign diplomatic personnel and cases to which a state is a party. Most of its work is of an appellate character, subject to the decisions of Congress and of the Court itself, and over the years has increasingly exercised its discretionary power *not* to hear cases.

Cases which originate in state courts can be appealed only if a question of federal law is involved, and in most such cases the Court will only choose to hear an appeal if it considers the subject of sufficient applicability and importance to warrant special attention. The Court also has considerable discretion in accepting appeals from Federal courts; with certain exceptions, it can refrain from taking any but the most important cases.

Most cases are brought to the Supreme Court not through the formal appeal process but through a writ of certiorari. If the Court accepts a request to issue a writ, in effect it orders up the case from a lower court, either state or federal.

The Court can refuse to hear a case for four reasons:

1. Because the plaintiff is not sufficiently affected by the law under dispute.

2. Because it is not a true "case of controversy."

3. Because it involves a political question, which must be settled by the executive department or by the legislature, but not by the courts.

4. Because it refuses to issue a writ of certiorari; this may be accomplished without additional comment.

As the chart shows, there are three layers in the Federal court system: District Courts, Courts of Appeals, and the Supreme Court.

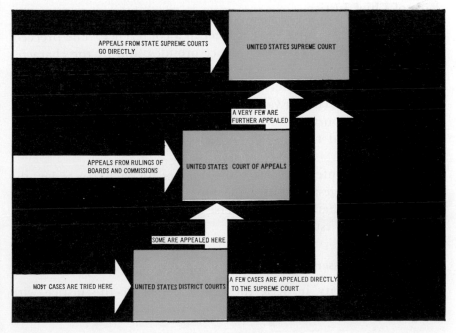

## The Supreme Court at Work

The Supreme Court hears about a hundred cases a year. It sits in session from the first Monday in October through the month of June. It divides its session into four-week periods: two weeks to hear arguments, followed by two weeks to consider the cases and write opinions. A minimum of six justices must participate in every case, and a majority of those participating must agree to a decision. If there is a tie, the most recent lower court decision in the case is automatically sustained.

The sessions of the Supreme Court blend a modicum of ceremony with the pressing search for justice. At high noon on public hearing days, the eight associate justices and the Chief Justice, dressed in black judicial robes, file into court and take their places in the huge chamber of the massive Supreme Court Building. Attorneys for each side are allowed a maximum of one hour to plead their case, but the smoothly practiced phrases of the lawyer may be frequently interrupted by judicial questioning or ignored altogether as the justices discuss the case among themselves. Rhetoric is apt to fall flat; the justices get most of the facts in the case by reading the elaborate briefs prepared by each side.

## Role of Chief Justice.

On Saturday the nine justices meet in a conference. The proceedings are top secret. The Chief Justice presides, and by the character of his leadership may exert considerable influence on the Court as a whole. Some of our Chief Justices, such as John Marshall, Roger B. Taney, and Charles Evans Hughes, impressed their own personalities on the Court. Others, such as Harlan F. Stone and Fred M. Vinson, preferred to share the reins of leadership with the Court as a whole.

During the conference, each justice gives his views in order, the justice with longest seniority speaking first. Following discussion, the justices cast their votes, in reverse order, the justice with the least seniority voting first.

## Majority and Dissenting Opinion

For the majority justices, the Chief Justice or the justice with greatest seniority assigns one of the number to prepare the written opinion. If, after the opinion is written, a majority justice does not agree with the reasoning employed, he is privileged to write a separate, concurring opinion. Minority judges follow the same pattern in preparing the dissenting opinion. Dissenting opinions are important and sometimes, if the Court over a period of years decides to reverse a precedent, the former dissenting opinion may bcome law.

The development of justice in America has been given special impetus by a few great and gifted innovators, such as John Marshall, Roger Taney, Oliver Wendell Holmes, Louis D. Brandeis, and Benjamin Cardozo. These were the trail blazers, who made or overturned precedent and wrote brilliant opinions which sometimes were not fully accepted until a generation later. But the average jurist is more traditional in outlook, more conservative in imagination, and more dependent on the opinions of his predecessors.

# THE SELECTION OF JUDGES

In a democratic society, how do the people set about finding able judges?

All federal judges are nominated by the President of the United States with the advice and consent of the Senate, and their terms are for life (assuming what the Constitution calls "good Behaviour"). Before 1913, when Senators were not directly elected by the people, the candidates they proposed for presidential nomination were apt to reflect the views of the conservative classes of the community. Today, with the membership of the Senate elected by popular majori-

| Name of Court | Number | Number of Judges | Salary | |
|---|---|---|---|---|
| Supreme Court | 1 | 9 | Chief Justice | $35,500 |
| | | | Associate Justices | 35,000 |
| Court of Appeals | 11 | 63 | $25,500 | |
| District Court | 91 | 295 | 22,500 | |
| Court of Customs and Patent Appeals | 1 | 5 | 25,500 | |
| Court of Claims | 1 | 5 | 25,500 | |
| Customs Court | 1 | 9 | 22,500 | |
| Court of Military Appeals | 1 | 3 | 25,500 | |

**Judges of the Federal Courts**

ties in each state, federal judges are more truly representative of the people as a whole.

# THE JUDICIAL BRANCH VS THE EXECUTIVE AND LEGISLATIVE BRANCHES

The relationship of the judiciary to the executive and the legislative branches of the government is established in broad outline in the Constitution. The basic functioning of the courts is well insulated against harassment or tampering by the other branches of government, but nevertheless each branch has been endowed with certain powers over the others.

The legislature, for example, can decide, within the broad limits set by the Constitution, what kind of cases should come before the federal judiciary; it can create or abolish courts below the level of the Supreme Court; it can fix the number of judges on all Federal courts. The size of the Supreme Court has been changed six times in our history, and in every case the change was intended to influence the decisions of the Court. Finally, through its right of confirmation of judicial appointments, the United States Senate can exercise some control over the shape of justice.

On the executive side, the President's power to appoint judges has been utilized by most chief executives to nominate men who have been sympathetic to their views and who have usually been members of the same political party.

Against these potentially dangerous sources of interference, the federal judiciary has strong defenses and some powers of its own. Chief among the defenses is the fact that federal judges, under constitutional mandate, hold office for life and can be removed, through the impeachment process, only for treason, bribery, or other high crimes. In addition, the salaries of federal judges cannot be reduced during their term of office.

## Power of Judicial Review

The chief influence of the courts over the other branches of government is exercised through the power of judicial review. Taken in its broadest meaning, judicial review is the right of the courts to scrutinize all executive decisions and activities, and to enjoin or compel such activities in the light of constitutional or legislative mandate. The same power of judicial review extends over the legislative branch, which under the eyes of the courts must function within the boundaries of the Constitution.

The courts are a party, therefore, to every legislative and executive act. Has Congress passed a law which violates the spirit of the Constitution? The courts can declare the law void. Is the administration applying a congressional law too harshly? The courts can rule that it must be stopped. Is the administration failing to enforce a legislative measure? The courts can enjoin the administration to begin enforcing it.

This broad power of judicial review has been a vital influence in the development of American democratic government. In effect the courts stand as a supreme traffic officer, patrolling the activities of the other two branches of government, regulating to a certain extent their relationships with each other and with the citizenry.

If the courts possessed such power without limitation, they could well become the dominant branch of government. Such has not been the case.

### Limitations on Judicial Review

The Supreme Court has limited its own right of judicial review. It will not issue advisory opinions on proposed legislation or on executive decisions; it will only give an opinion based on an actual case. Furthermore, the plaintiff in a case involving constitutionality must have a substantial interest. Since this has been interpreted to mean more than the interest of a mere taxpayer or citizen, in some types of broad legislation it may be virtually impossible to find a plaintiff with the required degree of interest in the law. Finally, the Court has given itself the responsibility of vetoing legislation only when a "clear" violation of the Constitution is involved. (This restriction, however, has been frequently ignored.)

All courts, of course, are limited by their inability to enforce their own decisions. Without an armed force or a treasury or the power of public opinion as expressed in votes, the courts must depend on our respect for the law and for the courts' role in interpreting it. Seldom in our history, however, has a major court opinion been ignored by another branch of government—even if this possibility acts to deter judges from abusing their power and majesty in a democratic society.

## Life Appointments for Judges

When conflicts have arisen, however, they have been intense. Federal judges are of course appointed for life. A tide of political change sweeping over the nation will bring with it a new administration and new congressional majorities, but may then crash against the barrier of a bench appointed by previous administrations and confirmed by previous Congresses. No force except death or retirement can alter the complexion of the bench, or compel it to accept new political ideals which have won the accptance of a majority of the nation. Eventually, of course, death will win out. New judges who share the new ideals will be appointed in place of the old and the conflict between the branches of government will ease—until changing conditions and conceptions inspire a new set of political attitudes.

## Attempt at "Court Packing"

Judicial review came to a climax in the years 1935–1938. In 1932 the nation had elected a President and Congress which were resolved to make sweeping changes in our economic relationships. But when new laws were passed, they were met with the veto of the Supreme Court. In 1935 and 1936, the Court invalidated eight out of ten measures coming before it. In 1936, President Franklin D. Roosevelt was re-elected by an overwhelming majority, and the stage was set for a showdown between a popularly elected government and a Court whose members had been appointed years and even decades before. Roosevelt's answer was a bill which gave the President power to appoint a new justice to the Court for every incumbent justice who did not retire at the age of seventy. (Most of the justices at the time were elderly.) The maximum size of the Court was to be limited to fifteen justices.

Opponents of the proposal called it "court-packing" in recognition of Roosevelt's intention to add more liberal-minded members to the Court. Others agreed with the President that the Court, flying in the face of popular opinion, was weakening the power of government to cope with the crisis of depression. But most people feared the placing of the Court under the domination of the executive branch.

Roosevelt's bill was in effect defeated by the Court itself when it began to reverse its own decisions. The President lost his battle for the Court bill, but he won the war against the roadblock imposed by the Court. The principle of judicial review remained undisturbed, although future Supreme Courts may be more reluctant than in the past to stand in the path of social and economic tornadoes caused by the confluence of crisis and popular leadership.

### Courts and Election Returns

Might not this pattern of conflict be avoided if judges were more studious in following the election returns? Do courts have the privilege of blocking progress which has been clearly called for by the majority of the people? There can be no unequivocal or doctrinaire answer to questions such as these. At times in our history the courts have wisely resisted popular passions, particularly in preserving minority privileges; at other times they have prevented government from taking obvious and necessary steps to accommodate changing conditions, particularly in the economic area. The courts have undoubtedly been influenced to a certain extent by the election returns. If they had not grown with the country their power would have been long since destroyed. Courts, like all instruments of democratic government, must retain a measure of public support. "The Constitution is what the judges say it is. True, but ultimately the Constitution is what the people want it to be." [1]

# REFORMING THE COURTS

The chief weakness of the Federal court system lies in its lack of direction. Congress has established a clear-cut hierarchical system of courts, but the judges are largely independent of each other and possibly the only cement binding a judge to the larger requirements of the bench is his desire to have his opinions sustained in higher courts.

To help bring together the various elements in the court system, Congress established the annual Judicial Conference. Once a year the Chief Justice of the Supreme Court and the senior justices of the Courts of Appeals meet with the Attorney General, with officers of the Administrative Office of the Courts and occasionally with members of the House and Senate Judiciary committees to devise new methods of bringing harmony to the courts and to avoid delays in

# THE CITIZEN IN THE FEDERAL COURTS: A CASE STUDY

On the night of July 31, 1940, Federal revenue agents moved to arrest the McNabb family, Tennessee mountaineers, suspected of selling "moonshine" (untaxed whiskey). In process of arresting, one Federal agent was shot and killed from ambush. McNabbs escaped, but four of them were soon apprehended, and the fifth voluntarily surrendered. The five were put in jail, and for two days were periodically questioned, by local arresting officers. McNabbs did not request counsel, nor were they told they were entitled to it. They were told, however, that anything they said might be used against them. Benjamin McNabb admitted having fired the first shot, but denied firing the second. Freeman and Raymond McNabb admitted being present when shooting occurred. Barney and Emuil made no incriminating admissions. McNabbs indicted, and case taken to Federal district court.

During trial in district court, judge accepted confessions as admissible, but his decision was challenged by defense. Judge advised jury that defendants' admissions should be disregarded if found involuntarily made. Admissions by McNabbs constituted crux of case. Standing on constitutional freedom from self-incrimination, McNabbs refused to take witness stand before jury. Barney and Emuil, who made no incriminating confessions, were acquitted. Freeman, Raymond, and Benjamin *convicted of murder in second degree and sentenced to 45 years in prison.* Convicted McNabbs appealed.

Circuit court of appeals heard case in December, 1941. McNabbs charged that admissions or confessions were not free and voluntary, but were obtained by coercion. Circuit court declared that voluntary confession made without compulsion is admissible in evidence, and found no evidence in case of any duress or coercion in McNabbs' admissions. Circuit court also argued that Benjamin's admission together with other evidence constituted ample basis of guilt, and that admissions of Freeman and Raymond, together with other evidence, constituted basis of their guilt as aiders and abettors to second-degree murder committed by Benjamin. *Circuit court upheld judgment of district court* (123 Fed 848). McNabbs petitioned Supreme Court for writ of *certiorari,* that is, they requested that the Supreme Court review their conviction. Supreme Court granted *certiorari* and ordered circuit court to send case up for review.

Supreme Court heard case in October, 1942, and on March 1, 1943, rendered decision. Court admitted that incriminating statements by McNabbs constituted crux of government's case, and that convictions could not stand if such evidence were excluded. Court refused to consider constitutional question of whether use of confessions in trial violated constitutional protection against self-incrimination. Court argued that main question was whether incriminating statements by McNabbs were made under legal circumstances. Under its power to review rules of evidence in Federal trial courts, Supreme Court, by 7 to 1 decision (one justice not participating), found that arresting officers, in interrogating McNabbs without first taking them before nearest United States commissioner or judicial officer, violated laws of Congress. Court argued that treatment of McNabbs was misuse of law-enforcement process. Interrogation without benefit of counsel was violation of law. Confessions thus not admissible in evidence. *Judgments of lower courts and conviction of McNabbs reversed.* In June, 1943, Supreme Court denied petition to rehear case and said that any new evidence or issues could be heard in retrial of case (318 U.S. 332).

Case retried in district court. Government introduced new evidence showing that Freeman, Raymond, and two other McNabbs acquitted in first trial, had actually been brought before U. S. commissioner in Chattanooga on morning after arrest; that they pleaded "not guilty" and, unable to produce bail, were committed to jail. On following morning Freeman, Raymond, and Benjamin were brought before U. S. commissioner on warrant charging them with murder of Federal officer. They pleaded "guilty" and were committed to jail without bail. On basis of this new evidence, they were *convicted of voluntary manslaughter instead of second-degree murder and sentenced to imprisonment for 9 years and 3 months.* They appealed judgment.

Circuit court of appeals heard case again in June, 1944, and concluded that questioning of McNabbs involved no evidence of coercion, violence, or any other denial of due process. *Judgment of district court and conviction of McNabbs affirmed* (142 Fed 904).

On November 6, 1944, Supreme Court denied petition of McNabbs for *certiorari*, that is, it refused to bring case up from circuit court for review.

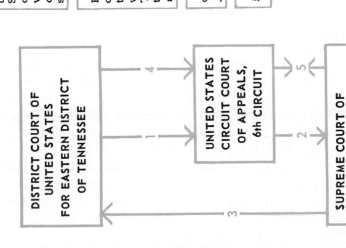

justice. In recent times Congress has also given the Chief Justice and senior appeals justices the power to shift district judges to ease congestion in court calendars.

The Administrative Office of the United States Courts functions under the direction of the Judicial Conference. Its duties are mainly concerned with housekeeping and with administrative functions of the courts, which include issuing warrants, appointing juries, admitting attorneys to practice, supervising receivers in bankruptcy cases, naturalizing aliens, performing marriages, and issuing writs.

Despite occasional delays and confusion, the Federal court system has established and maintained a unique reputation in its solemn work of dispensing justice.

# CONCLUSION

## Synopsis

Endowed with only a skeleton of form and function in the Constitution, the Federal court system over the years has acquired power and prestige. Despite occasional delays and blind resistances to inevitable forces, it has established and maintained a unique reputation in America in its solemn work of dispensing justice. Standing at the apex of the Federal court system is the United States Supreme Court, with its self-appointed role as guardian of the Constitution. Sometimes lagging behind, sometimes leading, the conscience of the nation, the Supreme Court stands at the center of our governmental process, tempering the passions of men and factions with an equal passion for order and justice.

## Significance

The pursuit of justice, as Chapter 5 attempted to show, takes many paths, but the principle one is through laws and the courts that interpret them. Although, in terms of manpower and money, the Federal court system is the smallest of the three branches of government, its resources have nevertheless proved ample to the performing of its function of dispensing justice under the Constitution. The fact that its work brings it into occasional conflict with the legislature and the executive has frequently been of benefit to the nation—for the usual outcome has been the tightening of reins upon loose or runaway executive or legislative power, or the speeding up of the reflexes of the courts.

## Prospectus

In a democracy, and especially in a federal system such as ours, government is nothing if not complex. We have to this point examined the instruments of government at only one of three major levels of activity in our Constitutional system. We now turn to a second level—the state—and to the various instruments which exist for the making and executing of public policy in what is, in many parts of the country, a scarcely visible limbo of American government.

# SECTION V

## Our State Instruments

*T*he governments of the states deserve to be objects of their citizens' concern. They seldom are. And when they are, the concern is about their powers—that they are being robbed of powers by the national government or that they are robbing cities and towns of powers appropriately local. Few worry constructively about how well the states use the powers they have. Yet if the states fail the test of competence, of capacity for use of power, they weaken their claims to repossess powers lost to the national government, to retain powers now in hand, and to expand powers over complex urban-area problems.

—James W. Fesler

## CHAPTER 20

# State Legislatures

Up to this point we have concentrated our attention largely upon policies and instruments of the national government. This is not surprising in view of the gargantuan responsibilities we have asked our national government to undertake in recent years.

But we should not forget that we still have a federal system. The difficulty is that when we turn from a study of national government to a study of state governments we are confronted with an uncomfortable analytical and descriptive problem. There is only one national government to be analyzed and understood; but there are forty-eight state governments, forty-eight governors, forty-eight state legislatures, and forty-eight separate systems of state courts and state administrations. In a nation in which Texas, the largest state, embraces a quarter of a million square miles, and Rhode Island, the smallest state, encompasses only a thousand; in which New York contains over 15 million people and Nevada only a little more than 200,000; in which California's government spends $2 billion annually and Delaware's less than $70 million; what meaningful generalizations can be made about state government in America?

Specifically, since we are starting with legislatures, what meaningful generalizations can be made about the law-making bodies of our forty-eight states? In short, what do the other forty-seven state legislatures have to do with us?

## Mutual Influence

In the first place, what happens in those forty-seven state legislatures may affect the citizens of the forty-eighth state as well. Whether the innovation is procedural, such as the establishment of a new committee system, or substantive, such as a new law regulating public schools, it is apt to have some influence on other states. Some of the nation's most important reforms have come through the initiative of states: workmen's compensation; relief; legislation limiting child labor; the establishment of public schools and state universi-

## STATE PROFILE: THE LEGISLATURE AND THE EXECUTIVE

| State | Total No. of Legislators | Salary of Legislators per Session | Frequency of Regular Legislative Sessions | Limitations on Length of Regular Sessions | Power of Item Veto by Governor | Length of Governor's Term in Years | Annual Salary of Governor | Number of Top Executives Appointed by Governor Alone |
|---|---|---|---|---|---|---|---|---|
| Alabama | 141 | $ 3,780 | Odd Years | 36 L | Yes | 4* | $12,000 | 6 |
| Arizona | 108 | 480 E | Annually | 60 C | Yes | 2 | 15,000 | 3 |
| Arkansas | 135 | 1,200 T | Odd Years | 60 C | Yes | 2 | 10,000 | 2 |
| California | 120 | 12,000 E | Annually | 120 C | Yes | 4 | 40,000 | 6 |
| Colorado | 100 | 3,600 T | Annually | 30 C | Yes | 2 | 17,500 | None |
| Connecticut | 316 | 600 T | Odd Years | 120 C | Yes | 4 | 15,000 | None |
| Delaware | 52 | 2,000 T | Odd Years | 150 C | Yes | 4 | 12,000 | None |
| Florida | 133 | 2,400 E | Odd Years | None | Yes | 4* | 20,000 | 5 |
| Georgia | 259 | 400 E | Annually | 40 C | Yes | 4* | 12,000 | None |
| Idaho | 103 | 600 E | Odd Years | 60 C | No | 4* | 10,000 | 6 |
| Illinois | 235 | 10,000 E | Odd Years | None | Yes | 4 | 25,000 | 1 |
| Indiana | 150 | 3,600 E | Odd Years | 61 C | No | 4* | 15,000 | 8 |
| Iowa | 158 | 2,000 T | Odd Years | None | No | 2 | 12,000 | 1 |
| Kansas | 165 | 450 E | Annually | 60 L | Yes | 2 | 15,000 | 2 |
| Kentucky | 138 | 1,500 E | Even Years | 60 L | Yes | 4* | 15,000 | 7 |
| Louisiana | 140 | 2,700 E | Annually | 60 C | Yes | 4* | 18,000 | 1 |
| Maine | 184 | 1,250 E | Odd Years | None | No | 2 | 10,000 | None |
| Maryland | 152 | 3,600 E | Annually | 90 C | No | 4 | 15,000 | 7 |
| Massachusetts | 280 | 9,000 E | Annually | None | Yes | 2 | 20,000 | None |
| Michigan | 144 | 8,000 E | Annually | None | Yes | 2 | 22,500 | 2 |
| Minnesota | 198 | 4,800 E | Odd Years | 90 L | Yes | 2 | 15,000 | None |
| Mississippi | 189 | 2,000 T | Even Years | None | Yes | 4* | 15,000 | 1 |
| Missouri | 191 | 3,000 E | Odd Years | 150 C | Yes | 4* | 25,000 | None |
| Montana | 150 | 1,200 T | Odd Years | 60 C | Yes | 4 | 12,500 | 6 |
| Nebraska | 43 | 1,744 E | Odd Years | None | No | 2 | 11,000 | None |
| Nevada | 64 | 900 E | Odd Years | 60 C | No | 4 | 15,000 | 8 |
| New Hampshire | 423 | 200 T | Odd Years | None | No | 2 | 12,000 | None |
| New Jersey | 81 | 10,000 T | Annually | None | Yes | 4 | 30,000 | None |
| New Mexico | 96 | 1,200 E | Odd Years | 60 C | Yes | 2 | 15,000 | 4 |

| State | | | | | | | | |
|---|---|---|---|---|---|---|---|---|
| North Carolina | 170 | 1,350 | Odd Years | 90 C | No | 4* | 15,000 | 3 |
| North Dakota | 165 | 300 E | Odd Years | 50 L | Yes | 2 | 9,000 | 2 |
| Ohio | 169 | 10,000 E | Odd Years | None | Yes | 2 | 25,000 | None |
| Oklahoma | 165 | 3,950 E | Odd Years | None | Yes [1] | 4* | 15,000 | 1 |
| Oregon | 90 | 1,200 E | Odd Years | None | Yes | 4 | 15,000 | 6 |
| Pennsylvania | 260 | 3,000 E | Odd Years | None | Yes | 4* | 25,000 | 1 |
| Rhode Island | 144 | 300 T | Annually | 60 L | No | 2 | 15,000 | None |
| South Carolina | 170 | 2,000 T | Annually | None | Yes [2] | 4* | 15,000 | 1 |
| South Dakota | 110 | 1,050 T | Odd Years | 60 C | Yes | 2 | 12,000 | 3 |
| Tennessee | 132 | 750 E | Odd Years | 75 C | Yes | 4 | 12,000 | 10 |
| Texas | 181 | 3,000 E | Odd Years | 120 C | Yes | 2 | 25,000 | 1 |
| Utah | 89 | 1,000 E | Odd Years | 60 C | Yes | 4 | 10,000 | None |
| Vermont | 276 | 1,600 E | Odd Years | None | No | 2 | 11,500 | 1 |
| Virginia | 140 | 1,080 T | Even Years | 60 C | Yes | 4* | 17,500 | 2 |
| Washington | 145 | 2,400 E | Odd Years | 60 C | Yes | 4 | 15,000 | None |
| West Virginia | 132 | 3,000 T | Annually | 60 C | No | 4* | 12,500 | None |
| Wisconsin | 133 | 4,800 E | Odd Years | None | Yes | 2 | 18,000 | None |
| Wyoming | 83 | 480 E | Odd Years | 40 C | Yes | 4 | 12,000 | 2 |

E – Plus Expenses Including Travel.

T – Plus Travel Allowance Only.

C – Calendar Days.

L – Legislative Days.

[1] In General Appropriation Act Only.

[2] In Appropriation Bill.

*Governor cannot be re-elected for two consecutive terms.

SOURCE: *The Book of the States, 1956-1957.* Chicago: Council of State Governments, 1956.

ties; government research into disease. It is readily apparent that the ability of one state legislature to meet the problem posed, for example, by the need for workmen's compensation, is of considerable importance to other states wrestling with the same problem.

## A Training Ground

In the second place, state legislatures have served as training grounds for many of the nation's leaders, past and present. A President named Lincoln and two Presidents named Roosevelt took their apprenticeship in government in state legislatures. Many governors, senators, and representatives have also started their climb up the political ladder in the state legislature. In what sort of institution are these future national leaders receiving their first impressions of democratic government? How are state governments equipped today to handle their responsibilities? Generalizations here are not only possible; they are required if we would understand government in America.

# THE POWERS OF THE LEGISLATURE

Despite the average citizen's ignorance about state legislatures, these bodies in many respects have broader powers than the United States Congress. Most of the powers of Congress are carefully delineated in one article of the Constitution; state legislatures have all other powers of government except certain ones specifically denied them by the federal or state constitutions.

## Administrative Powers

The average state legislature has considerable authority in the administration of the state. It appropriates money; confirms nominations; impeaches state officials who are derelict; investigates government operations; and takes the initial step in amending the state constitution.

## Social and Economic Powers

The state legislature also has considerable influence in the social and economic affairs of its citizens through its power to raise taxes;

provide for education; establish institutions for the needy, the aged the disabled, and the delinquent; regulate industry, labor, and agriculture; provide for the protection or disposal of natural resources; and establish criminal and civil law.

Buying a house or renting an apartment? The state legislature provides for the licensing of real-estate operators, regulates rents, and maintains minimum health and fire standards. Getting married or divorced? Both activities are circumscribed by state law. Own a business? It is regulated and taxed under state law. Signing a contract? Both parties are protected by state legislation. In trouble with the police? The limits of legal behavior and of the power of police are largely set by state legislatures. In sum, state legislatures touch human activities profoundly and extensively.

### Limitations on Power

But there are some limits, set both by the federal and by state constitutions. Under the federal document, as we have seen, state legislatures cannot coin money; pass laws impairing the obligations of a contract; deal with foreign governments; abridge the privileges and immunities of a citizen; deprive a citizen of life, liberty, or property without due process; or deny equal protection of the laws to citizens.

In most state constitutions there are five general kinds of limitations on the power of state legislatures. (1) A bill of rights protects the basic freedoms and privileges of the citizen. (2) Other provisions prevent the state legislature from favoring one corporation over another. (3) State legislatures are curbed in their power to incur debts. (4) All state constitutions set the broad framework of state government, including the powers of executive officers and the qualifications of voters, and the state legislature must function within this framework. (5) And finally, most state constitutions set forth certain general principles in regard to local government, public institutions, and education which the legislature may not disturb.

### Too Much Business

One guide to the powers of the individual state legislature is the number of words in the state constitution. Generally the longer the constitution, the more restrictions on the power of the legislature. Vermont, Connecticut, Indiana, Iowa, and New Jersey have fairly short constitutions. Those of Alabama and California are relatively long. Louisiana's constitution is gargantuan.

It is not surprising that with a foundation of such broad powers, the average state legislature is overwhelmed with business. Where local governments have not been given sufficient power to run their own affairs, state legislators spend much of their time dealing with particular problems of particular cities and towns. Many constitutions forbid special legislation affecting only one city, but state legislatures can get around the restriction without too much difficulty. The result is apt to be extensive logrolling among legislators from different cities.

A wider adoption of home rule would eliminate much of this, but on the other hand it would also limit the state's power to meet major problems posed by intercity relationships, such as the conflicts between a city and suburban towns. (See Chapter 25)

# ORGANIZATION OF STATE LEGISLATURES

### Two Houses vs One House

Not so many years ago one of the leading topics for college debating teams was bicameralism versus unicameralism: two houses versus one house in the state legislature. Since early in our history, the nation has shown a decided preference for the two-house system. In the formative years, each of the two houses in the states represented different classes, just as the United States Senate, which was originally elected by indirect vote, was intended to represent the wealthy propertied classes, while the United States House of Representatives was intended to represent the urban and rural masses. Today distinction according to class between the two houses of American legislatures no longer holds true at any level of government.

All states except Nebraska retain the two-house legislature. Nebraska has boasted a one-house legislature for two decades. Despite the early success of this experiment, there are powerful voices in that state presently clamoring for a return to bicameralism. And certainly no other state has taken much interest in the possibility of combining two houses into one. Today college debating teams turn to livelier subjects. Why?

The major weaknesses of state legislatures, which will be discussed below, cannot be solved by the adoption of unicameralism. Furthermore, the greatest weakness of all, the lack of equitable representation, could be made even worse if one house were dispensed with.

## State Legislatures: Facts and Figures

The chart on pages 392–93 provides the basic facts about the state legislature in each state. Summarizing quickly:

1. In most states the lower house is called the House of Representatives, and the size ranges from 35 members (Delaware) to 399 (New Hampshire). The average membership is 100.

2. In all states the upper house is called the Senate, and the average membership is 40.

3. Altogether there are about 7,500 state legislators. Businessmen, lawyers, and farmers, in that order, comprise two thirds of the state legislators. In every state the job is part time, and the salary ranges from $6,000 a year to a per diem of a few dollars. One bad effect of low pay is that salaried workers seldom serve; only those of independent means, or those who can readily take time away from their jobs, can afford to be state legislators. Low salaries also tend to reinforce the general lack of prestige of state legislators, which has led to a remarkably high turnover. High turnover means a low level of experience, and this in turn leads to less effective state government.

4. In most states the legislature meets in alternate years, usually beginning in January. In half the states the session is limited by the constitution to two or three months. In recent years, however, a trend has started to return to annual sessions, or at least to resort

The diagram above dramatizes the extent of rural over-representation, and urban under-representation, in state legislatures. This serious distortion of democracy in state government will inevitably be countered by direct federal-local relationships which will simply by-pass the states entirely.

to annual special sessions, because the volume of business has been too heavy to be dealt with satisfactorily in one biennial session. This has been especially true in regard to state budgets, which are difficult to blueprint for a two-year period without a knowledge of future tax income.

# UNEQUAL REPRESENTATION—THE PROBLEM

We shall see that state legislatures are criticized for many weaknesses, but none is so widespread or so vital as the failure of most state legislatures to represent fairly the people they are supposed to govern.

People living in urban areas are seriously underrepresented in all but a handful of states, and even in the best arranged state legislatures, city dwellers have less influence than their country cousins. In 1947, it was estimated that urban centers with 60 percent of the population of the nation elected only 25 percent of the state legislators.

## Estimating Representation

One way to measure the failure of state legislatures to represent the people is by estimating the minimum percentage of the population which can elect a majority of the legislators. Although American political concepts contain sufficient conservatism to make representation based upon a simple popular majority unlikely in most of our legislatures—national, state, or local—any substantial deviation from the principle of majority rule can fairly be challenged as contrary to our democratic faith. State legislatures almost without exception are sufficiently violative of majority representation, to warrant continuing attack by those who believe in the principle of majority rule. Under strict democratic theory, of course, not less than 51 percent of the people should be able to elect a majority of the legislators. As the percentage declines—the smaller the minority exercising control—the larger the underrepresentation of the majority. In state senates, the figures indicate that the proportion of the population exercising majority control in:

14 states is above 40 percent

# "It's A Crime How Those Big City Machines Operate"

15 states is between 30 and 40 percent

10 states is between 20 and 30 percent

 9 states is below 20 percent.

In state houses of representatives, the proportion of the population exercising majority control in:

11 states is above 40 percent

22 states is between 30 and 40 percent

 9 states is between 20 and 30 percent

 4 states is below 20 percent.

Now let us examine a few individual states in detail. In Connecticut, less than 10 percent of the people elect a majority of the state representatives; Hartford, with a population of 170,000, has two representatives in the State House, but so does Union, which has a population of 290. In the same state, the 10 representatives from the 5 largest cities, representing more than half a million people, are often outvoted by 12 representatives from the 6 smallest towns, representing fewer than 3,000 people. In California, the 40 percent of the population who reside in Los Angeles elect only one member of the state senate, which has 40 members altogether. In Illinois, Cook County has more than half the population and pays more than half the taxes, but elects only 37 percent of the legislature.

The situation is getting worse, not better. Since 1937, representation in thirty-eight states has been further warped; in only ten has it improved. How has this distortion of democracy happened and what are its results?

## Causes of Inequitable Representation

Inequitable representation has grown through three failures of government. First, in those legislatures where one or both houses are elected on a basis roughly of one member per county, such as in California, a distortion of representation is bound to occur. More people live in urban counties than rural, and as a result the city dweller's vote counts for less.

Second, many states have failed to redistrict as their population has shifted, leaving rotten boroughs scattered through the state. For example, Mississippi has not changed its districts since 1890, Delaware since 1897, Tennessee since 1900, and Illinois since 1901.

Third, in many states the redistricting process has been corrupted by gerrymandering.

In most states, the failure to redistrict or the resort to gerrymandering has been the responsibility of the state legislatures themselves. In these states, rural legislators, who years ago actually did represent the majority of the population, have been understandably reluctant to change the apportionment of the legislature in recognition of growing urban population, if only because they did not relish the prospect of voting themselves out of their jobs. Not only the individual but the political party is involved; rural legislators (in two-party states) are frequently Republican, urban voters are frequently Democratic; and it has been too much to expect one party to vote itself into a minority.

In some areas, rural Republicans have been supported by conservative business interests in the cities, who prefer a Republican legislature, regardless of origin, over a Democratic legislature more responsive to labor and liberal groups. As a result, in almost all two-party states, the Republican Party has established a stranglehold on one or both houses of the legislature.

## Results of Unequal Representation

One result of skewed representation is increasing resentment by urban interests which have been neglected or even discriminated against by state legislatures, in everything from education grants to taxing powers. This does not mean that urban voices are never listened to. If this had been the case in Connecticut, for example, Republican governors would never have been elected to office; obviously without a part of the big city votes, most gubernatorial candidates cannot be elected. This leads to concessions to urban interests by the rural legislative majorities who want their party to control the governorship. But many people would claim that what is needed is not occasional concessions, but equitable representation. Many people decry the "march to Washington" in the past twenty years. The fact is that, in part, this march has been made inevitable by the unwillingness of state legislatures to take care adequately of the deep social and economic problems in their own urban constituencies.

Another result of distorted representation shows itself at the level of the national legislature: since state legislatures are charged with the responsibility for establishing congressional districts (changes are supposed to be made after each decennial census), rural interests have benefited from gerrymandering in the United States House of Representatives (see pp. 249).

Finally, in many states, particularly those with large urban populations, there has been an increasing tendency for the legislative and executive government to be split between the two major parties: rural overrepresentation guarantees Republican control of the legislature while urban votes tend to elect a Democrat to the governorship. In state after state, divided responsibility has led to heated and unending conflict between executive and legislature. Responsible government has been the chief victim.

Unfortunately, there is no automatic remedy for the failure of our state legislatures to represent the people more equitably. The most representative states have turned over the responsibility for fixing legislative apportionment to nonlegislative commissions, or to the governor, or have provided that the results of a reapportionment can be challenged in the courts. Hopefully such methods will eventually be adopted by most states.

# STATE LEGISLATIVE PROCEDURES

For the student who has an understanding of the procedures and rules of the United States Congress, there will be few surprises in an examination of how state legislatures operate.

In most states, the lieutenant governor presides over the senate, while the house elects its own speaker from the majority party. Unlike the Speaker of the United States House of Representatives, house speakers in the several states are usually empowered to appoint committees in addition to such other powers as assigning bills to committees, refereeing parliamentary battles, and scheduling legislation on the floor. Thus in the states the speaker has more power than the speaker in Congress, and it is often wielded to gain additional power. For example, a speaker may use his power to assign members to committees to reward those who supported him in the election for the speakership. Friends may receive choice committee assignments; opponents may not. Seniority plays a lesser role than in the United States Congress.

### The Committee System

Like its counterpart in Congress, the committee system plays an important role in the legislative process in the states. In most state legislatures, however, there are too many committees, and these are too large. The result is that the average legislator serves on too many committees and can give serious attention to none of them. As an extreme example, in Georgia the legislator may belong to as many as thirty-five committees and subcommittees.

Three states, all in New England, have taken an important step in improving the efficiency of the committee system by establishing joint house-senate committees. Joint hearings save time, and disagreements between the houses are often settled before the particular legislation reaches the floor, thus obviating the need for conference committees.

## Party Organization

No generalization will suffice in describing party organization in state legislatures. In Nebraska's one-house legislature, nonpartisanship has been in force (not without strain) for many years. In the western and southern states, especially where one party dominates, conflicts arise not between parties but among factions. In most of the eastern and north-central states, partisan lines are rigidly maintained, and the party caucus plays a role it has not played in the national legislature for many years.

## Passing a Bill

The formal procedure for getting a bill through a state legislature is roughly similar to the procedure in the United States Congress. Bills are assigned to committees; public hearings are held; committees report bills to the floor; floor debates culminate in final votes. As in the Congress, much of the decision-making is done behind the scenes, under pressure from party and various private interest groups.

There are, however, certain significant differences among states, and between the states and the national legislature:

1. In some states a record vote is required on all legislation. In many states, the voting process is speeded up by electric voting devices, reducing the time required from a half hour or more to a few minutes.

2. In most states, amendments to a bill must be germane, and there is considerably less opportunity for delaying action than there is in the United States Senate.

3. Although all but one state (North Carolina) provide for a gubernatorial veto, less than a third allow a pocket veto (see page 320). Most states, however, permit the governor to veto certain items in appropriation bills without forcing him to veto the entire bill. (This item veto is unknown in the Federal government.) The gubernatorial veto is used more frequently in most states than the presidential veto is at the federal level. Because of the time limits on sessions, legislatures frequently spew out hundreds of bills in the closing days, many without adequate prior thought or debate. After the legislature adjourns and goes home, the governor can veto as many bills as he wishes without fear of being overriden. In New

York, a governor has vetoed as many as one quarter of all the bills passed in a session.

4. The last-minute chaos in state legislatures dwarfs the closing rush in Congress. In Pennsylvania one year, the legislature passed almost a hundred appropriation bills in thirty-six minutes. A bill was killed in the closing days of a Connecticut session when a legislator pocketed it for a few hours and prevented one house from taking it up for consideration. Occasionally the official clock may be stopped by a vote as it approaches midnight of the last day—and remain stopped for several days.

## Legislative Councils

To cope with short and infrequent sessions and inexperienced legislators, about half the states, starting with Kansas more than twenty years ago, have established "legislative councils." Composed of legislators from both houses appointed by the presiding officers, and endowed with a professional staff and a budget ranging from $10,000 to $100,000, legislative councils are in session all year 'round, investigating, holding hearings, establishing policy, developing new legislation, and helping coordinate various legislative and executive branch activities. These small groups have afforded invaluable assistance to the cause of efficient government, and as their effectiveness has grown so has their power. In some states, a bill which reaches the floor without the endorsement of the legislative council is doomed to defeat.

Certain states have established interim committees, which are, in effect, regular committees functioning between sessions, with fact-finding and policy powers. Usually their efforts are keyed to one important issue. Occasionally they have abused their powers.

Regardless of the possible abuses, however, both legislative councils and interim committees have helped state legislatures fulfill more responsibly their vital role in state government. Both devices need an adequate staff if they are to perform at a high level.

## Lobbying in the States

The low salaries of legislators, the unequal representation, the gargantuan size of some legislatures, and lack of party organization in most legislatures make them peculiarly susceptible to lobbying —to a degree not witnessed in the United States Congress, for example. Decades ago, lobbying reached such heights of influence and depths of impropriety that Lincoln Steffens commented, "The legislators came from the country, and they came bought. They had no power; [received] low salaries; they took orders absolutely." [1]

*Individual Influence.* The Congress has never been so dominated by industrial or political leaders, or by interest groups as have state legislatures. Penrose and Grundy in Pennsylvania, Huey Long in Lousiana, Mark Hanna in Ohio, and Frank Hague in New Jersey could boast a degree of power unequaled by any figure in the nation's capitol. Only a few years ago a somewhat unbelievable character named Arthur H. Samish, representing an association of California brewers, spent at least $500,000 in six years of lobbying and boasted, with few to contradict him, "I am the legislature."

*Corporation Influence.* In the smaller states, especially where party lines are not maintained, certain corporations may be larger and richer than the state itself. The Anaconda Copper Company has long had a powerful influence in Montana, similar to the influence of the DuPont family in Delaware; this is a phenomenon which is not found in the United States Congress.

*Interest Groups.* The average lobbyist at the state level, however, represents the same kind of group as his counterpart in Washington. In northern cities, studies have shown that there is an organized group for every seven people. Many of these groups exercise great influence in their states, including the Catholic Church in New York, the Mormon Church in Utah, and pension groups in California and Colorado. The American Legion and the Chamber of Commerce are active in every state of the union; labor unions are strong in industrialized states, weak in the South and in predominantly agricultural states. Approximately two hundred professions come under state licensing provisions, a fact which prompts considerable

---

Some two hundred professions, from architects to undertakers, are licensed in some or all states, commonly by separate licensing boards for each profession, and more professions seek licensing laws every year. The politics involved in getting the bills passed, obtaining satisfactory appointments on the boards, issuing rules, policing the professions, opposing other professions (lawyers versus realtors, M.D.'s versus osteopaths and chiropractors) is infinitely complex and never ending.

—Dayton D. McKean

lobbying by professional groups. Public employees and teachers engage in legislative work, as do many cities seeking their proper share of state funds. Much lobbying is sponsored by public interest groups, such as the League of Women Voters and Parent-Teachers' Associations, who are anxious to improve their communities.

The strength or weakness of parties in the various states has a strong effect on the influence of private interest groups. Where parties are strong, interest groups tend to work through them; where parties are weak, interest groups tend to dominate the legislative process and agenda.

Thirty-eight of the states have lobbying laws, usually requiring disclosure of information, but higher standards of public education, public morality, and public participation in government have been far more effective than laws in elevating lobbying practices.

## Direct Legislation

During the early part of the century, largely because of the domination of one-party state legislatures by party bosses and interest groups, about a third of the states adopted various measures for direct legislation. The *referendum* is a method of putting a measure on the ballot for direct vote of the people. Almost all states require a referendum vote on amendments to their constitutions. *Initiative* provides a method of obtaining a popular vote on a bill regardless of the action of the state legislature. *Recall* provides the electorate with a method of displacing state or city officials between elections. The *protest referendum* in twenty-one states gives the electorate an opportunity, through the use of petitions, to delay bills passed by the legislature until a popular vote decides the issue.

Although these measures of direct democracy were passed in the full flush of a reform movement, over the years they have proved to have little effect in improving democratic government. Under certain conditions, in fact, the referendum has been employed to the advantage of forces which have little interest in anything but their own narrow goals. Initiative, for example, requires such great resources in manpower and money to obtain the necessary signatures on petitions and to publicize the issue among the electorate, that it has become less a tool of democracy than a weapon of interest groups. The referendum has provided state legislatures with a loophole through which they can avoid the responsibility of determining potentially embarrassing issues and throw the responsibility to the voters at large. Often the issue may be too complex for ready comprehension by the mass of voters, and as a result political machines or private interest groups capture control of the process.

# THE REFORM OF STATE LEGISLATURES

The weaknesses of state legislatures—their unrepresentative character, their inefficiency, their lack of a sufficient number of experienced legislators—has caused citizens to turn to other institutions to achieve their goals. It was partly the inability and unwillingness of state legislatures to perform their proper functions that led to the larger role and greater power of the executive branch within the states and at the national level.

State legislatures still have a major role in the day-to-day life of the nation, especially in helping to preserve a useful measure of local autonomy and decentralization. To make it possible for state legislatures to perform their functions more adequately, students of the subject have suggested a number of changes in their composition, their operations, and their privileges.

## Improve Representation

1. As has been suggested above, the greatest weakness of state legislatures has been their unrepresentative character. Gerrymandering and the failure to redistrict; the one-party control of state legislatures in two-party states; the unbreakable rule of rural interests in industrial and urban states, have led to a deep-seated distortion of the will of popular majorities at the state level. The state legislature should be made more representative.

## Expand Legislative Sessions

2. Many years ago, during the same wave of reform that produced referendum and recall, legislative sessions were foreshortened to discourage corruption and special interest legislation and to force legislatures to stick to more important business. Today, with several state budgets totaling more than $1 billion annually and legislative business growing by leaps and bounds, a two- or three-month session every other year is insufficient to accomplish the job.

In several states, the so-called split session has proved of some help to harried legislators. The opening session, of thirty days, is reserved for the introduction of new bills. A thirty day recess then permits legislators to return to their homes, study the pending measures, and consult with their constituents. A concluding thirty-day session is reserved for consideration and disposition of the bills. Although the purpose of the split session procedure has often been evaded, it has generally been a useful improvement in procedure.

If split sessions are not adopted, state legislatures should institute a deadline for the introduction of new bills.

### Raise Legislative Salaries

3. Legislative salaries should be raised to attract better legislators with more staying power. In addition, more staff assistance should be provided to individual legislators and to legislative committees to take off their shoulders the minor burdens which now steal time from more important matters.

### Overhaul Archaic Procedures

4. Legislative procedures need considerable overhauling. Committees should be combined and legislators should be assigned to a smaller number of committee posts. Greater use should be made of joint committees, interim committees, and legislative councils. Committee practices can be streamlined and greater coordination developed between the two houses of the legislatures.

### Hold State Elections in Odd Years

5. To help clarify state issues, which are frequently submerged under the weight of national issues, elections for state officials should be held in odd years.

Charles Beard once wrote:

. . . our legislatures are not organized to bring public opinion to a focus, to secure the definition of questions, to concentrate debate on issues, to formulate laws on clear principles of public policy. They are miscellaneous assemblies of citizens, chosen independently, subject to local influences, often with little experience in public affairs, busily engaged in making a living, eager 'to get things done and get home.' Though generally zealous for the public good, members of the rank and file are often without the knowledge or power necessary to effect their purpose.[2]

With a greater potential role than ever before, state legislators have their work cut out for them. If they fail, they have only themselves to blame if government centralization continues.

# CONCLUSION

### Synopsis

No two state legislatures are alike, but all share a large part of the responsibility of governing the people of the United States. Unfortunately, state legislatures have not generally succeeded in meeting their responsibilities efficiently and intelligently. Their rules are often cumbersome, their members underpaid, and their actions subject in many cases to the destructive influences of those pressure groups which crawl and feed only when apathy and public ignorance are prevalent. Most important, because of gerrymandering and an unwillingness to bring up to date archaic patterns of representation, most state legislatures fail to come close to being truly representative of popular majorities.

### Significance

In a working democracy, the people will ultimately find ways of fulfilling their expectations of government. In recent decades, the shift of governing power from the state to the federal level has been caused not only by the national nature of the problems but also by the inability or unwillingness of state legislatures to meet the expressed needs of the people—particularly of urban majorities. This shift will continue until the states and their legislatures take the necessary steps to put their own houses in order.

### Prospectus

The failures of state legislatures have driven an increasing number of people to look, not only to the national government, but to the state *executive* for a source of responsive government. The result has been a great increase in the power and prestige of the governor in many of the states. To the state executive and his problems we now turn.

## CHAPTER 21

# The State Executive

THE OFFICE OF governor as sketched in the first state constitutions in 1776 reflected the deep-seated belief that a strong executive is an instrument of tyranny. With the memory of arbitrary prerevolutionary royal governors strong, the new state constitutions provided for an executive carefully restricted in power. The governor's term of office, in most states, was limited to one year. He had no veto power, and no power to convene or dissolve the state legislature. Even the appointment of other state officials was denied him, as the movement grew for popular election (or legislative appointment) of top administrative officers. And several states required that the governor's few remaining powers be exercised only with the consent of an executive council. It is no wonder that in 1788 James Madison wrote:

The legislative department is everywhere extending the sphere of its activity, and drawing all power into its impetuous vortex.

The founders of our republics . . . seem never to have recollected the danger from legislative usurpations, which, by assembling all power in the same hands, must lead to the same tyranny as is threatened by executive usurpations.

## Expansion of Office

But as the United States changed, so did the state constitutions and the earlier concept of the state executive. During the first half of the nineteenth century, state governments felt the influence of vast political, economic, and social forces which could not be dealt with adequately by part-time state legislators or hog-tied governors. Inevitably, the role of the executive was expanded; and governors, under the impact of Jeffersonian and Jacksonian ideas, became increasingly the symbol of popular democracy—especially as they came to be popularly elected. The governor was granted new powers; constitutional prohibitions against re-election were relaxed; and impeachment became more difficult.

Meantime, the new Federal Constitution had not been without influence. Following this national model, most of the states granted the veto power to their governors (limited, however, by a two-thirds or majority vote in each house of the legislature). Many states extended the governor's term of office from two to four years.

But with all these changes, the governor's power was still limited. In most states he had no power to appoint the officials with whom he had to share the management of the state. These officials were either chosen by the state legislatures or elected by the people. In either case, political loyalty rather than competence seemed to be the major qualification for office—for the first half of the nineteenth century was the heyday of the spoils system. In states where the officials were popularly elected, voters were often called upon to select more than twelve state administrative officers (the so-called bed-sheet ballot)—an impossible task for the voter. Furthermore it often happened, then as now, that heads of the state departments and the governor were of different political parties and hence different philosophies, making it difficult, if not impossible, for the governor to carry out a consistent program.

This system of diffused and circumscribed state executive power was perhaps tolerable as long as the business of the state remained meager and simple, but states became increasingly impotent during the second half of the nineteenth century and the first half of the twentieth, as matters requiring their attention became more numerous and complex. Unfortunately, in many parts of the nation, the anachronism of a constitutionally weak and splintered state executive is still with us.

## The State Executive Today

A modern governor—elected by and responsible to millions of people, head of a complicated bureaucracy, responsible for executing programs that touch most directly many important aspects of people's lives, and spender of millions or billions of dollars in state funds—bears little resemblance to a governor in the days of Jefferson or Jackson. Nevertheless, the state executive today is a creature in part of the inertias, habits, fears, and expectations of a bygone era. The kinds of men who become governors, the ways in which they are nominated and elected, the powers they wield, the duties they perform, the techniques they use, how they manage their relations with state legislatures and state administrative agencies, reveal much about America's past, as well as its restless present.

# OFFICE OF GOVERNOR

## Qualifications

Who may serve as a state governor? The qualifications of office are specifically outlined in most state constitutions. A candidate must be a citizen of the United States, must have attained a minimum age—usually thirty—and must have been a citizen of the state for a specified period. In the early years, of course, eligibility for office included a property qualification.

## Nomination

For many years, candidates for governor, along with other state officers, were nominated by state party conventions. During the first quarter of the twentieth century, however, this pattern of selection gave way in most states to the direct primary. Contrary to the expectations of those who led in the movement, there is little evidence that the primary has had any considerable beneficial effect upon the health of party politics or upon the caliber of the men selected for governor and other state offices. Actually, in recent years there has been a countermovement against the primary, and two states —New York and Indiana—have already returned to the convention system.

## Election

Election of the governor is by popular vote in all states except Mississippi, where the governor is selected through an intricate popular and electoral vote system. In most states election is by plurality, while in Georgia, Mississippi, and Vermont a majority is required. If no candidate secures the required majority, the election is thrown into the state legislature. Election of the governor and other executives in most states is held in even-numbered years, corresponding to election of congressmen and state legislators. In four states they are elected in odd-numbered years.

### Term of Office

In almost two thirds of the states the governor's term of office is fixed at four years, while in the remainder it is two years. The shorter term is more prevalent in the North and Northeast, while four-year terms are more common in the South and West. In one third of the states, however, where there seems to be a strong fear that governors may perpetuate themselves in office by manipulating their own re-elections, state constitutions prohibit a consecutive second term. This feature, of course, is an inherited characteristic of the traditional fear of executives and it tends to weaken the hand of the governor as his term nears its end. His relationships with state agencies and with the state legislature are colored by their knowledge of his impending descent from power.

### Salary

The salary of the governor, a useful indication of the importance of the office, varies from the modest $9,000 paid annually to the governor of North Dakota to the more liberal $50,000 received by the governor of New York. Most governors receive between $10,000 and $15,000. In some states an executive mansion is provided for the governor and his family, and sometimes he is reimbursed for expenses related to the execution of his duties. A primary characteristic of the modern state governor, however, is his low salary, a residual feature of the historic suspicion of executives and the conception of the governorship as an honorary office rather than one of power and importance. Low salaries for governors did not seem consequential in a laissez-faire society. Actually, most state salaries are abysmally inadequate. One state treasurer, for example, who is responsible for the expenditure of millions of dollars, has a salary of $2,500 per year. Most lieutenant governors, attorney generals, secretaries of state, and treasurers receive far less than men in comparable positions in business. In a real sense, we have bargain-basement government in the several states. With few exceptions, salaries paid our top state executives seem to indicate that state government in this country is not only neglected, but actually held in contempt.

### Removal

Removal of the governor is through impeachment or recall. In all states he may be impeached: charges are leveled against him by the lower house of the legislature and he is tried by the state senate. In about one fourth of the states the governor may be removed by popular recall, upon petition of a specified number of voters. Impeachment and recall, however, have been infrequently used by the states. So far, only ten governors in the history of the nation have been impeached. Five of these were removed during the unsettled years of Reconstruction following the Civil War. Only one governor has been recalled: Lynn J. Frazier of North Dakota, accused of seeking to "socialize" his state. Removed by recall in 1921, he was elected to the United States Senate the following year.

### Succession

The question of succession to the governorship has not been subjected to as much attention as that of the Presidency. In most states the lieutenant governor is the heir-apparent, while in those states which do not provide for the office of lieutenant governor, the president of the senate or the speaker of the house is second in line. An important criticism of this practice has been that it too easily permits the opposing party (as a result of one-party legislature domination) to secure control of the office and thus frustrates the popular will as expressed in the preceding election. Those who recognize the steady expansion in the importance of the state executive foresee a growing concern with questions of succession and continuity.

## THE EXECUTIVE "TEAM"

In the popular mind, the state governor is a chief executive; he is like the President of the United States, but on a smaller scale. There is theoretical justification, of course, for the analogy, but in practice the positions are hardly comparable. Unlike the Presidency, the state executive power is not normally centered in the hands of a single elected executive. State constitutions frequently provide for a half dozen or more elected officials, and many of these, like the governor, have executive responsibilities.

### Lieutenant Governor

The lieutenant governor in most states has relatively few responsibilities. He presides over the state senate, and if the governor dies or is disabled, succeeds to that office. In practice, he frequently is a member of the opposition party, or leads a faction of the governor's party that is opposed to the governor. Thus he sometimes becomes an influential obstacle to the programs of the administration of which he is supposedly a part.

## Secretary of State

The office of secretary of state generally serves as an umbrella under which a variety of diverse and unrelated functions may be grouped. He is custodian of state records and keeper of the state seal; he supervises elections, issues certificates of incorporation, and publishes state laws. In some states he registers corporate securities and issues automobile licenses. The secretary of state generally inherits those functions and duties which are not easily classified, which do not seem fitted for existing agencies, and which are not considered sufficiently important to merit the establishment of new agencies.

## Attorney General

The office of attorney general, often considered an important political position and steppingstone to the governor's chair, is assigned the role of chief counsel to the governor. Duties include the provision of legal advice to state officials, representation of the state in the courts, supervision of prosecutions by local prosecutors, and related responsibilities. Opportunities for favorable publicity in his work give an attorney general a political advantage over other members of the executive team. Many young lawyers, ambitious for high state and national political prominence, look upon the office of attorney general as a choice plum.

## Treasurer, Auditor

The fiscal functions of state government are generally concentrated in two top elective offices: state treasurer and auditor. The treasurer is custodian of state funds and in some states he is responsible for the collection of taxes. The auditor, on the other hand, has two major tasks: he authorizes disbursements from the treasury and conducts periodic audits of other state officials who are responsible for spending state funds. The auditor is the financial watchdog of the state government. No money is supposed to be spent unless he conducts a preaudit—signs a warrant or statement certifying that the expenditure is authorized and that the funds are available in the treasury. After the money is spent he may conduct a postaudit to ascertain whether the funds have been appropriately spent. In view of the nature of his tasks, it is generally agreed that his postaudit role, as financial watchdog, should be independent of the governor, and it usually is.

Most state constitutions provide that "the supreme executive power shall be vested in the governor who shall take care that the laws be faithfully executed." In view of the number of separately elected executive officials, this constitutional mandate is easier said than done. In all too many cases the "executive" is a team of high-spirited and unruly horses. Separately elected state officials often behave not as teammates but as enemies of the governor. In 1950 Thomas E. Dewey, as Governor of New York, declared: "It's a serious handicap to a governor to have to pick daggers out of his back every morning tossed by other elected state officials."

### The Rise of the State Agencies

Like the office of the governor, state administrative agencies have grown in size, cost, and complexity. Actually, expansion of state administration has, in the twentieth century, been explosive.

In the state of New York, there were 10 administrative agencies in 1800, 20 in 1850, 81 in 1900, and over 170 in 1925. Today more than 1.25 million people are employed directly by state governments in the United States, representing about 17 percent of the more than 7,000,000 people on public payrolls at all levels of government in the United States. Not considering defense expenses, state and local governments combined spend more annually than the Federal government.

No citizen can escape the impact of this growth. The influence of state government has extended over public welfare, public health, highway transportation, public schools, business, industry, and the professions. Engineers, doctors, bankers, industrialists, labor leaders, farmers, teachers, and others either feel the hand of state government control or turn to state government for favors or support. Whether it serves as regulator, promoter, or manager, the state government requires administrative agencies, personnel, budgets, public buildings, office equipment, books of rules and procedures, and the rest of the paraphernalia of bureaucracy in a democracy to fulfill its functions. The result has been called the administrative-service state. Education, highways, public health, and hospitals alone in recent years have accounted for about 67 percent of all state employees and about 63 percent of state payrolls. As long as the people demand that these government services continue, large, complicated, and expensive state administrative organizations will remain with us. The job is to see that they function efficiently and responsibly.

But whose job is this?

# THE GOVERNOR AS ADMINISTRATIVE LEADER

If a governor is really to govern as an efficient administrative leader, he must have the power, the tools, and the will to act.

## Appointment and Removal

Two of the most important tools of efficient and responsible administration are the powers of appointment and removal. Understandably, these powers have been limited by the expansion of the civil service movement. About one half of the states today have merit systems. They are generally administered through state civil service commissions or single personnel directors, popularly elected or appointed by the governor. A popularly elected civil service commission, or a personnel director over whom the governor has little control, can become an opponent of the governor rather than a teammate. Thus, in some instances, the merit principle, conceived as a device for improving management, has become an obstruction. Many state capitols still ring with the echoes of frustration and despair of governors whose programs have been hamstrung by a stubborn and autonomous civil service board or commission.

## Patronage

To escape the prison of an overly restrictive civil service system, many governors have drawn on their political power as party leader and have assiduously exploited their remaining measure of patronage. In most states the question of where the career civil service should leave off and responsible political leadership begin is unanswered.

## Budget

Another preëminent instrument of leadership is control of the executive purse strings. In the past, the governor's fiscal powers have been strictly limited, reflecting the principle of separation of powers and the traditional colonial distrust of executives. The concept of the budget as a comprehensive plan of action for government, as a frame of reference within which policy decisions may be made rationally and coherently, or as an effective managerial tool was until recently unknown or ignored. The legislature acted on individual appropriation bills, without coordinating them and without full knowledge of the state's fiscal resources, needs, and plans. On the executive side, departments and agencies made budget requests to the legislature without consulting each other and without reference to a coherent and unified executive program of action. There was no place where an over-all view of the state executive's financial needs could be measured and evaluated.

There has been progress, however, in recent years. In more than forty states the governor has been empowered to prepare the state budget. The executive budget is then voted upon as a unified plan by the legislative body. In most of these states the governor is assisted by a budget officer or director in charge of a department of finance or administration, or by a commission. Where the governor is empowered to appoint and to remove the budget staff, his control is strengthened. In those states where the budget commissioners are popularly elected, as in Florida, the governor's budgetary power rests on his qualities of political or personal leadership. In most states, the governor, through his power to veto items in appropriation bills, has been able to rule on the *wisdom* of expenditures as well as their *legality*. The recent Commission on Intergovernmental Relations, appointed by President Eisenhower, revealed in 1954 that the governor's budget role is strong in about two thirds of the states, moderately powerful in about one sixth of the states, and weak in the remainder.

Improvements in the governor's administrative tools are only one aspect of a broader wave of reform that has recurrently swept over the nation and the states since World War I. The hallmark of the movement has been an underlying belief that most weaknesses of

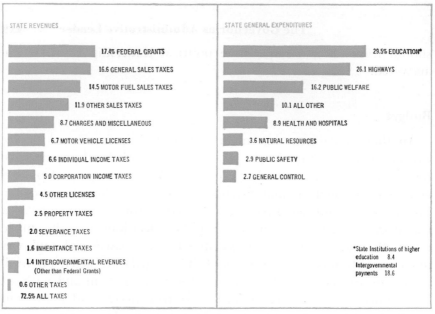

STATE REVENUES

17.4% FEDERAL GRANTS
16.6 GENERAL SALES TAXES
14.5 MOTOR FUEL SALES TAXES
11.9 OTHER SALES TAXES
8.7 CHARGES AND MISCELLANEOUS
6.7 MOTOR VEHICLE LICENSES
6.6 INDIVIDUAL INCOME TAXES
5.0 CORPORATION INCOME TAXES
4.5 OTHER LICENSES
2.5 PROPERTY TAXES
2.0 SEVERANCE TAXES
1.6 INHERITANCE TAXES
1.4 INTERGOVERNMENTAL REVENUES
(Other than Federal Grants)
0.6 OTHER TAXES
72.5% ALL TAXES

STATE GENERAL EXPENDITURES

29.5% EDUCATION*
26.1 HIGHWAYS
16.2 PUBLIC WELFARE
10.1 ALL OTHER
8.9 HEALTH AND HOSPITALS
3.6 NATURAL RESOURCES
2.9 PUBLIC SAFETY
2.7 GENERAL CONTROL

*State Institutions of higher
education   8.4
Intergovernmental
payments   18.6

Note, on the revenue side, that federal grants presently constitute the largest single source of state income, and, on the expenditure side, the dominant places of education, highways, and welfare.

government might best be eradicated by concentration of administrative authority and responsibility in the hands of a chief executive, through administrative reorganization and improvement of managerial techniques. The movement has been motivated not so much by a negative fear of the dangers of arbitrary government as by a concern with the *capacity* of governments to govern responsibly.

### The Problem of Power and Responsibility

Many years ago the Russian Czar Nicholas, shortly before his death, declared: "I do not rule Russia; 10,000 clerks do." The American governor might well declare with the Czar: "I do not rule the state executive branch of government; scores of independent heads, commissioners, board members, and state legislators do." The executive power for over a century has been diffused, fractionalized, and atomized. Leslie Lipson has described this as "Lilliputian administration." New agencies and offices, generally independent of the governor, were created to handle new functions and responsibilities. As law followed law, each new agency seemed to beget a new agency. The trend has gone on, despite the years of efforts to simplify and rationalize the jungle of state administrative organization. A recent state government study, for example, has revealed that in Alabama there are 117 separate administrative departments and agencies, in Colorado 140, in Connecticut 172, in Ohio 122, in Texas 124, and in Oregon 110. In one state alone the legislature has established such separate boards and commissions as the following—all of them effectively removed from responsible political control:

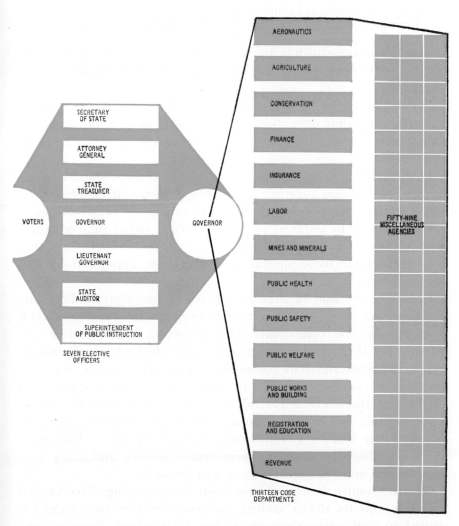

Seven elected officers, thirteen major departments, and fifty-nine miscellaneous agencies—hardly an organizational pattern conducive to political responsibility or administrative efficiency.

Athletic Commission
Board for Vocational Education
Commerce Commission
Harness Racing Commission
Highway and Traffic Problems Commission
Horticulture Society
Housing Commission
Inter-Racial Commission
Rural Electrification Administration
Spanish-American War Commission
Swedish Centennial Commission
Training School for Boys and Youthful Offenders Commission

The usual prescription for remedying this chaotic system embodies a set of principles which have become a dogma of administrative reform:

1. Administrative authority and responsibility should be concentrated in the hands of a chief executive who in turn may be held accountable for the performance of the executive department of government.

2. Related activities and functions of government should be integrated or brought together in a single department or agency.

3. Such functions as purchasing, budgeting, or personnel management should be assigned to single directors rather than to multi-member boards'and commissions.

4. A chief executive should have a cabinet, appointed by and responsible to him.

Following the lead of President Taft's Commission on Economy and Efficiency in 1911 at the national level, several states undertook to reorganize and consolidate their sprawling administrative machinery. By 1925, nearly fifteen states had engaged in administrative self-analysis and had reorganized their departments, agencies, boards, and commissions. The movement slowed down during the 1930's, but there was a revival following World War II. Again, following the lead of the national government, many states established "Little Hoover Commissions." Since 1947, about two thirds of the states have conducted administrative studies, and many have consolidated and reorganized their governments.

Over-all results, however, have been disappointing. Preoccupied with the hope for dollar savings, the reorganization movement has tended to deal with symptoms rather than causes. Despite some progress in devising and utilizing improved administrative techniques, the majority of American governors are still not chief executives in any meaningful sense of the word.

### Number of Agencies in a Sample of 23 States in 1950

| State | Total State Agencies | No. of Major Depts. | No. of Other Agencies |
|---|---|---|---|
| Alabama | 117 | 26 | 91 |
| Colorado | 140 | 9 | 131 |
| Connecticut | 172 | 32 | 140 |
| Delaware | 76 | NA | NA |
| Florida | 87 | 26 | 61 |
| Georgia | 29 | 12 | 17 |
| Illinois | 75 | 15 | 60 |
| Iowa | 87 | 35 | 52 |
| Kentucky | 93 | 22 | 71 |
| Louisiana | 102 | NA | NA |
| Massachusetts | 56 | 20 | 36 |
| Minnesota | 101 | 35 | 66 |
| Nevada | 104 | 39 | 65 |
| New Hampshire | 84 | 47 | 37 |
| North Dakota | 75 | 36 | 39 |
| Ohio | 122 | 12 | 110 |
| Oregon | 110 | 78 | 32 |
| Pennsylvania | 49 | 42 | 7 |
| South Dakota | 64 | 33 | 31 |
| Tennessee | 87 | 12 | 75 |
| Texas | 124 | 54 | 70 |
| Wisconsin | 71 | 25 | 46 |
| Wyoming | 76 | 33 | 43 |

NA—data not available.
Source: Council of State Governments, *Reorganizing State Government* (Chicago, 1950).

The record demonstrates that there is no magic in new administrative forms and methods. Streamlined organizations, paper merit systems, centralized purchasing agencies, IBM accounting machines, and the professionalization of public service are not enough. In themselves they guarantee nothing. The executive, whether he is a president, governor, or state highway commissioner, must have the power, the tools, the knowledge, the political skill, and the will to act in the general interest.

## THE GOVERNOR AS POLITICAL LEADER

About seventy years ago, Woodrow Wilson, a political scientist who was to become a state governor and a President of the United States, drew a distinction between "politics" and "administration," between the deciding of *what* governments will do and the actual carrying out of the tasks of government. This has been a useful distinction, but it tends to conceal the fact that politics and administration are often two sides of the same coin.

## A Party Politician

Like the President of the United States, the state governor is usually a party politician. He generally rises on the ladder of party advancement, and in seeking the highest state office he must win the support of his party organization. Once in the governor's chair, his success depends greatly on the measure of his control or influence over the state party organization. Frequently, the more powerful governors have personal party machines loyally behind them. The governor's use of patronage, his personal influence with members of his party in the legislature and with the voters of the state, his skill in exploiting radio, television, and the press, and his ability in furnishing policy leadership and direction generally—all these help to determine his effectiveness as governor.

## Legislative Powers

An important aspect of the governor's political leadership is his growing legislative role. As the governor's political role in state government has grown over the years, his legislative functions have almost inevitably expanded.

Today he may call and adjourn special sessions of the legislature, send them messages, and veto legislation. In addition to these legal legislative functions, he may exercise political influence which is generally not spelled out by constitution or statute. These various extralegal or informal powers, however, may be more effective than the formal legal ones if used with skill and courage. The governor may, for example, develop close friendships in the legislature. He may mobilize support for particular measures in the legislature by attaching his personal and official prestige to them and by personally promoting them through informal contacts with key members of the legislature. He may invoke his power as party chief, or appeal directly to the voters of the state above the heads of the legislators. The extent to which a governor exercises these legislative powers varies widely from state to state, according to the personal capacity of the incumbent governor, the traditional constitutional position of the governor in the state, and the immediate political situation within which he must operate.

### National Prominence

The governor is a politician in still another sense: he is commonly a contender for national prominence. The state governorship in particular has become a steppingstone to higher public office. From 1900 to 1956, with one exception, at least one major candidate for President of the United States in every election has been a governor. Woodrow Wilson of New Jersey, Calvin Coolidge of Massachusetts, Alfred E. Smith, Franklin D. Roosevelt, and Thomas E. Dewey of New York, and Adlai E. Stevenson of Illinois are some of the governors who have traveled this route. To an even greater extent, former governors have gone on to the United States Senate, where, in recent years, nearly a third of the membership has consisted of former state chief executives.

# THE GOVERNOR AS CHIEF OF STATE

Finally, as chief of state, the governor is the symbol of the power and authority of state government. In fulfilling his ceremonial role, in representing the state in its dealings with other states and with the national government, in serving as commander-in-chief of the state militia and leader of the state in time of war, riots, floods, or hurricanes, in commuting criminal sentences and granting pardons and reprieves, and in exercising his police functions, the governor has become more than an administrative and political leader.

It is in the exercise of emergency and police functions in particular that the power and prestige of the state executive have been enhanced. Regulation of persons and property has traditionally been the responsibility of locally elected officials, but in recent years many of these functions have been transferred to the state. The role of the governor in such areas as state police administration, public health, housing, fish and game preservation, and flood control has accordingly grown. Governor Abraham A. Ribicoff of Connecticut, in the great floods of 1955, has illustrated this point. Perhaps nothing he said or did in the previous year of his incumbency brought him and the office of governor the prestige which he won in a few critical days in his able leadership of a state which had been ravaged by wind and water.

## The Endless Quest for More Responsible State Government

Even if the governor should become an effective administrative and political leader, even if he were empowered to act as a chief executive and were armed with an arsenal of administrative tools of direction and control, even if he always carried his ceremonial functions with dignity, there is no guarantee that he would serve as a responsible servant of the people. There is always the possibility that he might use his power against the general good. If state government is to be responsible—and operate in such a way that the people get the kind of government they want and the electorate can hold political authorities unequivocally accountable for public policies—there must be more than a naive faith in strengthening the hand of the governor. Improvements must be made in the legislative process and the political party system as well, and newspapers must continue to help the public identify and control irresponsible legislators and executive officials.

# CONCLUSION

## Synopsis

The governor, as administrative leader, political leader, and chief of state, and armed with a variety of personal, political, and administrative tools of government, has shifted from figurehead to leader in most American states. Expansion of his role, however, has been accompanied by a growth in state executive departments and agencies frequently led or controlled, not by the governor, but by separately elected officials or independent boards who, in theory, are the governor's teammates or subordinates, but in practice are often his competitors for power and influence.

## Significance

The diffusion of state executive power and the unrepresentative character of most state legislatures combine to suggest that our state governments need more serious attention than they have received from concerned citizens interested in efficient and responsible government. The state is a vitally important instrument of government in America—both in terms of what it is presently charged with doing, and as a link between much federal and local activity. Certainly the state's role should increase rather than decrease as the metropolitan problems of our urban areas overwhelm less inclusive political jurisdictions. But if it is to perform its necessary functions, the state as an administrative and as a policy-making unit must become more visible, more disciplined, and more responsive to human need.

## Prospectus

State legislatures and state executives are important to the political health of America. But so are state courts. Long neglected as objects of concern by the general public (and by students of government), the importance of the work of these tribunals justifies attention to their organization, personnel, and procedures.

# State and Local Courts

FROM EARLY TIMES, courts of law have seemed remote and mysterious instruments of government. The imposing marble halls of the courthouse, the black robes of the judge, the austere drama of the trial, and the complex language of the lawyer all contribute to the difficulty of citizen understanding.

The majesty of the law is, of course, upheld to some extent by the austerity and mystery of legal rituals; but these rituals have tended to obscure the citizen's appreciation of the fact that courts of law are fundamental instruments of government in a constitutional democracy.

## The Public and the Courts

Actually, public attitudes toward the courts have been characterized by a striking ambivalence: like and dislike, trust and fear, respect and disdain. On the one hand, courts tend to be viewed as the source of all social wisdom and social justice. On the other hand, the personnel, paraphernalia, and maxims of the judicial process are frequently mocked—or worse, they are totally ignored by all except those who have direct business with the court system. In 1945, for example, the American Institute of Public Opinion found in an opinion poll that only 36 percent of their respondents knew how many justices normally sit on the United States Supreme Court. With respect to state and local courts, the confusion and ignorance are even more pronounced.

## THE COURT SYSTEM

In each state there is a single court system which embraces all state and local courts and tribunals. These state and local courts and tribunals handle the great bulk of judicial work in the United States—approximately 90 percent of it.

Basically, of course, courts are a substitute for more primitive forms of justice obtained through violence. Instead of an aggrieved person resorting to private vengeance through retaliation, he "litigates" in a courtroom. The role of the court as a substitute for violence is reflected in the term "litigation" which is derived from the Latin *litis* meaning "contention" or "strife."

## Double Role of the Court

A court has a double role: (1) as the instrumentality through which the force of law is applied (behind every policeman stands the judge); and (2) as the vehicle through which impartial judgment can be made in mediating the conflicts between members of society, and between individuals and the organized state.

This double role is reflected in judicial symbolism. Hundreds of cities and towns in America have a statue of Justice seated before their courthouse: one arm often raised with the sword of the force of law; the other arm bearing the scales of careful and impartial study– and her eyes closed to prevent favoritism in either role.

## Other Functions

In addition to these judicial functions, state and local courts have a number of quasi-administrative and quasi-executive duties:

1. They advise legislative and administrative bodies on the meaning of the law.

2. They serve as administrative or law-enforcement agencies in carrying out certain duties, such as the approval of business licenses or the removal of local officials.

3. They administer property, through regulation of executors of estates, guardians of children, trustees of funds, and receivers of bankrupt property.

4. They make rules of judicial procedure and administer the elaborate paraphernalia of justice—the court buildings, administrative personnel, and budgets.

## Jurisdiction of State and Local Courts

The "jurisdiction" of state and local courts—their power to hear and try cases and to interpret and apply the law—has not been clearly and simply written down in one place. State and local judges must consult many different sources in the process of determining, interpreting, and applying the law to a particular case. They must be guided by provisions of the United States Constitution and the laws of Congress, which set the broad limits within which state and local courts operate. Under congressional statutes, for example, cases involving charges of crime against the states are generally tried in state courts, while in certain instances (for example, if a United States government official is involved) the case may be removed to a Federal court. Judicial cases involving a "diversity of citizenship"— involving the citizens of two or more states and amounts not over $3,000—fall under the jurisdiction of the state and local court system. State and local judges must also be guided by state law, as embodied in state constitutions, state statutes, state administrative orders, in the charters, ordinances, and administrative orders of local governments, as well as in the body of inherited legal customs and traditions known as the "common law."

### Complexity Due to Derivation of Law

The complexity of the courts and their work is largely due to the fact that the body of law has been derived from different sources and may be expressed in different forms. Over the years, several categories of law have evolved, with important consequences for the courts. As new social problems have developed, the body of law has been enlarged and redefined by the courts in the process of administering justice. New courts have been organized to handle new kinds of offenses, and new judicial procedures have grown out of new ideas about justice. This we have already noted; but it is perhaps wise at this point to review a few items. (See Chapter 5.)

Criminal courts and procedures, for example, have developed from the statutory definition of such crimes as murder, robbery, and arson. Civil courts and procedures have evolved from the attempts by government to mediate disputes over property rights, business contracts, and marital relations. Equity courts and procedures developed centuries ago in England from the need for remedies which were unavailable under existing legal practice. Many equity procedures have been inherited by state and local courts in the United States which exercise them in practicing "preventive justice," that is, in issuing orders to prevent the breaking of the law or the violation of individual rights. Probate courts and procedures have developed to meet the need for special judicial machinery in dealing with disputes over wills and estates, over the commitment of mentally ill people to institutions, or over custody of children from broken homes. More recently, special family courts, marital courts, juvenile courts, and women's courts, employing different judicial techniques, have been established to deal with new and difficult social problems.

In each of the different categories of law there are important differences in the kind of offenses involved, in the procedures practiced by the courts, in the rights of the accused, and in the punishments inflicted upon the guilty. Civil law, criminal law, equity, probate, and common law, for example, involve somewhat different court machinery and procedures. The structure, jurisdiction, procedures, and even the names of many state and local courts reflect this enlargement and redefinition of the categories of the law.

# ORGANIZATIONAL STRUCTURE OF STATE COURT SYSTEMS

Legally, all state and local courts constitute a single court system within each state, organized in the form of a pyramid of three or more levels. Some courts have *original jurisdiction,* that is, they are trial courts where cases originate; others have *appellate jurisdiction,* that is, they review the decisions of the trial courts below them in the pyramid. Some cases may originate in trial courts and rise through the channels of appeal or review to the highest court of the state, a "court of last resort." All courts in the system, however, are subject to state law. Local courts, for example, have no independent existence. Their decisions may be overruled by higher state courts; they may even be reorganized or abolished by state law, and local officials may exercise no veto over such action.

## The Court System Pyramid

At the base of the judicial pyramid or hierarchy are a variety of *minor* or *inferior* courts which have an important role to play in the administration of justice. They include justice of the peace courts, magistrate courts, municipal courts, traffic courts, juvenile courts, family courts, and other specialized tribunals. It is these so-called inferior courts which carry most of the daily judicial chores in the state court systems. Most civil and criminal trial cases are handled by the *major trial courts* at the next level, and above them in many states are the *intermediate appellate courts*. At the apex of the judicial pyramid in each state is the *supreme court* or *court of last resort*.


# INFERIOR COURTS

### Justice of the Peace Courts

At the bottom of the judicial pyramid, located in most *rural* areas of the United States, is the justice of the peace court. It is a one-man tribunal, presided over by the so-called JP. He is usually elected for a two- or four-year term by the voters of his town or township, with jurisdiction generally extending throughout the county. Through him rural justice is administered at the "grass roots." For many rural residents, the justice of the peace is the only judicial officer with whom they ever have legal dealings.

*Powers.* His powers include the following:

1. He handles such minor infractions of the law as traffic violations, disturbing the peace, defacing public property, profane or blasphemous language, drunkenness in public, petty theft, violation of sabbath or "Sunday laws," and other misdemeanors.

Drawing by George Price,
© the New Yorker Magazine, Inc.

2. In more serious criminal cases, he may conduct preliminary hearings and may bind over an alleged offender to a grand jury for indictment and trial.

3. In civil suits his jurisdiction is limited to disputes involving no more than $100 or $200.

4. He may send offenders to the local jail or workhouse for 30 days.

5. He performs marriage ceremonies, notarizes documents, and administers oaths.

His decisions may, of course, be appealed to the higher courts.

The justice of the peace generally holds his court proceedings informally, without a jury, and without permanently recording the procedures. In many cases, JP's have been known to hold court wherever they happen to be: in a real-estate office, a grocery store, a barber shop, or at home.

*Weaknesses.* The weaknesses of the system are many. W. Brooke Graves has described justices of the peace as "usually local politicians of the smallest caliber." Generally not required to have legal education or experience, they are not considered competent to administer justice. A 1950 study of sixty-one typical Minnesota JP's, for example, revealed the following: almost half were engaged in the insurance or real-estate business or were retired, fewer than 8 percent had ever had any law training, fewer than 6 percent were college graduates, and only about 4 percent had ever previously held public office.

*Fee System.* The fee system, by which over half of all justices of the peace are compensated, is much criticized. Paid not by salary but by the fees he collects, a JP's income depends on his volume of business. Thus, there is a tendency to engage in such practices as splitting fees with arresting officers, advertising his services, or deciding disputes against the defendant. The record reveals that many justices of the peace have joined other local officials in operating "speed traps" in order to collect fines from speeding motorists passing through rural areas.

There is a lack of uniformity and administrative efficiency among JP courts. In Franklin County, Ohio, for example, in one recent year some courts handled less than six cases, while others conducted more than two thousand.

*Obsolescence.* The office of justice of the peace has been universally recognized as obsolete and former incumbents are being replaced by legally trained and salaried magistrates. In Ohio, for example, in 1955 JP's were replaced by formal municipal courts in eight Ohio counties, while throughout that state there are now over 400 townships in 65 counties without any justices of the peace.

An important obstacle, however, is the political intrenchment of the justice of the peace in his community. The office continues to serve many local party organizations as a source of patronage.

## City Magistrate Courts

The urban counterpart of the JP is the city magistrate who presides over a court of limited jurisdiction, variously called the magistrate's court, city court, justice court, police court, recorder's court, and a variety of other names.

In many cities magistrates generally exercise the same range of powers or jurisdiction as the JP courts, but are restricted to cases arising within the municipal boundaries. Much of their work involves violations of city ordinances or minor infractions of state laws.

The judges of these courts may be elected by popular vote or appointed by the governor, the city council, or a commission. The office is usually a reward to local lawyers for party service. The terms in most cities vary from two to four years. In California, Oregon, and Tennessee the terms are six years; in Pennsylvania and New Hampshire they are five.

Magistrates generally receive salaries ranging from a few hundred dollars a year to five or six thousand. In Texas they may receive up to $10,000 in the larger cities.

Even though trained in the law and paid by salary rather than fees, some city magistrates are still subject to many of the weaknesses of their rural counterparts. Ten years ago the following critique of magistrate courts was made. It is still relevant in all too many areas:

Most of the daily work of these courts is made up of handling minor offenses. Day in and day out these lesser judges dispose of hundreds of small-fry offenders. The magistrate's headquarters, if not in the precinct stationhouse, is usually special quarters in a drab neighborhood, and it is a dreary place indeed. An hour or so before the magistrate arrives, dozens of nondescript persons mill about, some sitting on the hard seats provided for witnesses and spectators. Police officers with their charges are waiting for 'His Honor.' There is no dignity. Rather it is bedlam. Most of the spectators are smoking. Many have their hats on. Spitting on the floor is not unusual. Newspaper reporters are on hand in the hope of getting a story or two.

The magistrate finally arrives, and all stand at halfhearted attention. He is almost always late. He disposes of his cases as rapidly as possible, meting out justice in what seems a careless and high-handed manner. He uses the slang of the street, injecting an occasional oath to demonstrate his authority. There is a great deal of whispering between him and lawyers for the various defendants. Many cases are fixed, especially if those charged with offenses have some political influence.[1]

## Special Courts

With the rapid rise of the modern city, many social problems have developed which place a heavy burden on local judicial machinery. From the simple, unspecialized magistrate court has come a proliferation of many special courts and tribunals of limited jurisdiction, organized for particular judicial purposes.

*Traffic Courts.* Following the lead of Chicago in 1912, most of the larger cities have established special traffic courts, either as independent tribunals or as divisions of municipal courts, to deal with offenses involving local traffic ordinances. Their load has been heavy. Automobiles and their drivers cause annually nearly 40,000 deaths, 350,000 personal injuries, and property damage amounting to over $1 billion. In 1947, the Traffic and Ordinance Court of Detroit, Michigan, disposed of 543,151 traffic cases. In 1956, New York City collected $12 million in traffic fines alone. Bumper-to-bumper traffic jams in the streets have created legal log jams in many of our courts.

The record of traffic courts is not much better than that of the magistrates and justices of the peace. Since more Americans come in contact with traffic courts than with any other judicial body in this country, there is considerable justification for the alarm expressed by Arthur T. Vanderbilt, Chief Justice of the New Jersey Supreme Court and a man whose name has become synonymous with efficient and enlightened court reform in the United States:

What they see and hear—and sometimes smell—in these courts do not tend to create respect for the law or for the judges and lawyers administering the law. And people are coming to these courts by millions each year as defendants or as witnesses in traffic matters—15,400,000 as defendants in 1951—in comparison with the relatively small number who experience justice from the courts of last resort in the state house. These local tribunals collectively can do more to undermine respect for law than the appellate courts can possibly overcome, try as they will. From the judicial point of view this aspect of the work of the traffic courts is quite as significant as the necessity of curbing the constantly growing

The number of traffic cases in American courts is staggering. Here is a typical day in a New York City traffic court. It might be any large city in America.

loss of life and property. Thoughtful judges and lawyers do not need to be told that our kind of government cannot exist long, once respect for law is destroyed.[2]

*Juvenile Courts.* Another special judicial body is the juvenile court. Shifting populations, congestion, cultural conflicts, social and economic extremes, and other unsettling conditions of urban life have contributed to a sharp rise in crime and antisocial behavior among children and youth. In New York City, for example, a recent report revealed that approximately 24 out of every 1,000 children and young persons aged five to twenty years in that city were registered with social agencies as people with problems. While not all of them commit offenses against the law, many of them are prone to antisocial behavior. Of all persons arrested for major crimes in the United States in 1955, over 42 percent were under the age of eighteen years. During the past few years the number of youthful offenders appearing before the courts has increased by about 60 percent.

At one time, youthful offenders were treated like hardened criminals, but as the problems of juvenile crime and maladjustment have grown in intensity and complexity in the large cities of the United States, many municipalities have followed the example of Chicago, a city which pioneered in 1899 by establishing under Illinois law a special juvenile court. Illinois was the first state to recognize that young people in trouble need understanding and rehabilitation, not repression and punishment. With the help of probation officers, child psychologists, psychiatrists, counselors, and social workers, the juvenile courts are fighting valiantly against one of America's most serious social problems.

*Family Courts.* In addition, the rising problem of divorce and broken homes has forced many American cities to establish family or domestic relations courts. They are found today in Boston, Chicago, Philadelphia, and many other cities. In New York City there has been a domestic relations court since 1933, consisting of a family court division and a children's court division.

The purpose of the family court is not to prosecute offenders but to seek reconciliation through informal conferences and other procedures. In a sense, these courts may be called courts of treatment rather than courts of law. Recognizing that the typical factors in most family disputes involve such problems as nonsupport, alcoholism, temperamental incompatibility, mothers-in-law, other relatives, religion, disagreements over children, or other difficulties, these courts seek to mobilize the assistance of experts outside of the legal profession. They work on the assumption that fines and jail sentences will be unnecessary if ailing marriages can be made healthy.

There are other special courts in the cities. In most urban communities women do not receive special treatment before the law, but in a few large cities there are special women's courts, presided over by judges who are presumably trained to deal with the woman offender.

*Small-Claims Courts.* In many cities there are special small-claims courts, designed to settle claims for amounts considered too small to warrant the use of the more cumbersome and costly judicial machinery of other courts. They generally employ informal procedures, without the necessity of a lawyer's services, with court charges reduced to as little as 75 cents. The small-claims court is another example of the unending attempts on the part of governments to extend justice to all citizens.

### Unified Municipal Courts

To avoid the decentralization, inexperience, and incompetence of the justices of the peace and many magistrates, and to escape the overlapping, complexity, and confusion involved in the multiplication of special local courts, some large cities have established unified municipal courts in which judicial labors have been divided into specialized categories and assigned to specially competent judges, operating under the administrative supervision of a chief justice.

In 1940, Chicago pioneered in establishing a fully unified municipal court system which has become a model for other cities throughout the United States. Based on a functional division of labor in which judges with special judicial skills can exercise their competence, the Chicago court has sought to avoid the widespread condition described by Dean Landis, when he referred to some judges as "jacks-of-all-justice."

*Chicago Municipal Court.* Taking the place of the justice of the peace and magistrate courts found elsewhere in Illinois, the Chicago Municipal Court handles a heavy load of civil cases, generally involving small amounts, in addition to a variety of violations of city ordinances and misdemeanors against Illinois state laws.

The Chicago court is administered by one chief justice, thirty-six associate justices, a clerk, and a bailiff elected for six years by the voters of the city. The judges are assisted by a staff of administrative personnel appointed largely on the basis of party loyalty. The court consists of the following specialized branches:

Auto Safety and Accident Court
Auto Theft Court
Boys' Court
Building, Housing, and Fire Safety Court
Business License Court
Criminal Branch (Reckless Homicide)
Domestic Relations Court
Emergency Building and Neighborhood Conservation Court
Felony Court
Narcotics Court
Ordinance Violations Bureau

This is not an unfamiliar sight to most Americans. Courtroom scenes have inherent drama. This fact has not been lost on the motion picture and television industries.

Speeders and Traffic Court
Traffic Violations Bureau
Women's Court

The Chicago model has been followed in Baltimore, Cleveland, Detroit, New York, and other cities. While the organizational and procedural details vary from city to city and state to state, unified municipal courts have greatly raised the standards of justice in the United States.

# MAJOR TRIAL COURTS

Above the level of minor courts in each state stands a tier of major trial courts, counterparts to the Federal district courts. They are known by a variety of names. In California, for example, they are called superior courts; in Oregon, circuit courts; in Texas, district courts; and in New York they are known as supreme courts.

## Organization

These major trial courts are organized on a geographic basis, that is, their jurisdiction generally conforms to county lines, with their headquarters located in the county courthouses. There is generally a trial court in each county, while in some states several counties are combined as judicial districts, with one or more district courts in each district. Where judicial districts embrace several counties, the judge "rides the circuit," that is, he travels from one county to another, according to a schedule established by the state legislature, holding "terms" of court at each county courthouse, where he is usually assisted by a resident clerk.

## Judges

The judges of these trial courts are, in most states, elected by the voters for terms varying from four years to life. The state of Washington, for example, elects its trial judges on a nonpartisan ballot for terms of four years. California elects its trial judges of the Superior Court on a nonpartisan ballot for six years. In Delaware, judges of the Superior Court are appointed by the governor, with the consent of the state senate, for terms of twelve years, while in

Massachusetts trial court judges are appointed by the governor of life, with the consent of the governor's council.

Judicial salaries generally rank high among those of state officials. California, for example, pays its Superior Court judges $15,000 to $18,000. In Connecticut the figure is $18,500, in Illinois $19,500, and in New York $24,000 to $30,000.

## Jurisdiction

These major trial courts have both original and appellate jurisdiction. In exercising original jurisdiction, that is, as courts of first instance, they handle all civil and criminal cases considered too serious to be tried in the minor courts. While there is some variation among the states, there are usually no limitations on the maximum amount of money involved or on the seriousness of the crimes committed.

In about half the states, the major trial courts also handle probate cases, that is, wills, estates, guardianships, and related matters. The remainder of the states have separate probate or surrogate courts, presided over by probate judges, most of whom are elected for terms ranging from two years in Idaho, Kansas, and Utah, to life in Massachusetts.

Most major trial courts also handle cases in equity—cases involving an aggrieved person who cannot find some available remedy under the traditional provisions of civil, criminal, or common law. Such a person may seek to obtain preventive action through an equity writ, to prevent irreparable damage to his freedom, his property, or his reputation. Equity and common law have been incorporated into the same general code of law in most of the states and are generally administered by the same courts. In Arkansas, Delaware, Missis-

---

Suppose that, after hearing witnesses, a trial judge finds that Shadrach and Abednego had a certain conversation on a certain day. While an upper court usually will not question that finding, it will not feel similarly obliged to acquiesce in the trial judge's further conclusion as to the meaning of the words of those two men or as to the intention manifested by those words. . . .

—Jerome Frank

sippi, and Tennessee, however, separate chancery courts, at the level of the major trial courts, have been established.

### Assistants

Attached to or working in most of the major trial courts are special officers and agencies who participate in the trial process. Generally, there is a *coroner,* who investigates deaths due to unknown causes, a *bailiff* who serves as official court attendant, and a *sheriff* who serves legal papers and performs other official duties. The central figure in the trial process is the *prosecutor,* sometimes also called the district attorney or the commonwealth's attorney. Generally, he investigates an alleged crime and participates in the decision on whether an alleged offender is to be held for trial. If a trial is to be held, he prepares the case for the state and conducts the prosecution.

*The Jury.* In most cases, the decision on whether a person is to be held for trial is technically made by a body of men called the *grand jury.* They may, if they believe the facts warrant, indict the alleged offender and order him to trial.

Another important group of participants in the drama of the trial are the members of the *petit* or *trial jury.* The United States Constitution, it will be remembered, contains three separate provisions (Article III, Section 2, and the Sixth and Seventh Amendments) which guarantee the right of jury trials in federal courts. Similarly, state constitutions preserve the right of trial by jury in state courts.

Usually composed of twelve men and women who supposedly represent a cross-section of the people, the jury decides questions of fact rather than law. That is, they listen to the opposing "facts" presented by the prosecution and the defense, and then decide which "facts" are the truth. Theoretically, the jury serves as the "conscience of the people," as a mirror of the popular common sense. The jury is thus conceived as a device through which the law might be softened. As G. K. Chesterton has said: "I would trust twelve ordinary men but I cannot trust one ordinary man."

In practice, however, the jury system is widely criticized as unrepresentative and incompetent in deciding complicated questions of fact. Furthermore, it is argued, facts cannot be divorced from law, and juries are particularly unqualified to interpret and apply the law. Carl Becker, for example, has summed up the critique of the jury system as follows:

Trial by jury, as a method of determining facts, is antiquated, unscientific, and inherently absurd—so much so that no lawyer, judge, scholar, subscription-clerk, cook, or mechanic in a garage would ever think for a moment of employing that method for determining the facts in any situation that concerned him.[3]

In reply it is pointed out that a jury contributes to more equitable justice by doing precisely what it is intended to do—decide questions of fact, not on the basis of legal theory or special competence, but on the basis of common sense.

There is a growing tendency among state courts, wherever possible, to dispense with juries. Jury trial may be waived by the parties to the dispute, particularly in civil cases.

Not all the work of these major trial courts is concerned with trials and original jurisdiction. They also have limited appellate jurisdiction to review cases from justice of the peace and magistrate courts. Most of the serious trial business is conducted in the major trial courts. Their decisions are considered final, so far as the *facts* of the case are concerned, but disputed questions of *law* involved may be appealed to higher state courts. In practice, the trial courts have the final word in approximately 90 percent of the cases they handle.

# INTERMEDIATE APPELLATE COURTS

In about one fourth of the states there are intermediate appellate courts which are counterparts of the Federal circuit courts of appeals. Like other state and local courts, they are known by a variety of names: district courts, courts of appeals, superior courts, or circuit courts.

In some states there may be only one intermediate appellate court, while in other states there may be several judicial districts each served by one such court. Each intermediate appellate tribunal has from three to nine judges who sit together and decide cases by majority vote. They are elected in most states, their terms ranging from three years in Illinois to twelve years in California.

Their jurisdiction varies considerably, but in general it is limited to the review of civil and criminal cases appealed from the major

# A CASE STUDY: THE CITIZEN IN THE STATE COURTS

On July 23, 1947, *Mr. Dayton Williams* executed a will in which he gave one half of his estate to *Mrs. Allen Lewis*, whom he married six weeks later; one fourth to his son, *Mr. Donald Williams;* and one fourth to his brother, *Mr. Charles Williams.* A few days after execution of the will, *Mrs. Lewis* left Illinois for Reno, Nevada, where she obtained a divorce from *Mr. Lewis* six weeks later. *Mr. Lewis* was represented there by his attorney. On the same day she obtained her divorce, she married *Mr. Dayton Williams,* and after a short honeymoon they returned to Illinois and lived there until *Mr. Williams'* death in September, 1953.

**County Court of Fayette County**

In settling the estate, the will came before the county court of Fayette County for validation, that is, for probate, in September, 1953. The county court invalidated the will because an Illinois statute provided that "marriage by the testator ⌐Dayton Williams⌐ shall be deemed a revocation of any existing will executed by the testator prior to the date of the marriage." Thus, if the will was held invalid under Illinois law, the estate would automatically be divided equally between the late Mr. Williams' wife and son, thereby eliminating the brother's one-fourth interest as designated in the will.

**Circuit Court of Fayette County**

Accordingly, the brother appealed the ruling of the county court, and the case was taken up by the circuit court of Fayette County. Here the will was declared valid, on the grounds that the Nevada divorce was invalid and therefore no legal marriage had taken place between Mrs. Lewis and Mr. Dayton Williams. At this point, Mr. Williams' brother, having apparently won the case took the unusual step of appealing to a still higher court, insisting that the marriage between his brother and Mrs. Lewis *was* valid, but even so it would not cause the revocation of the will. As the case involved the

**Intermediate Court of Appeals By-Passed**

constitutional question of whether Illinois courts must honor a legal procedure of the state of Nevada, it proceeded directly to the supreme court of Illinois, without review by the intermediate appellate court of Illinois.

The supreme court of Illinois proceeded to examine two major questions:

1. Was the circuit court correct in denying full faith and credit to the Nevada divorce decree on the grounds that Mrs. Lewis had failed to establish a legal home in Nevada?

The supreme court decided that the circuit court had erred. The Nevada decree stated that Mrs. Lewis had been a legal resident of Nevada at the time of the divorce and that her husband had had legal representation. Accordingly, the supreme court ruled that the requirement of the United States Constitution that "full faith and credit shall be given in each state to the public acts, records, and judicial proceedings of every other state" applied in this case, and thus Illinois courts must recognize legal divorce decrees by the courts of Nevada.

2. Since the will, even though executed six weeks before the marriage, was evidently made in view of the forthcoming marriage, could the Illinois statute be considered to apply here?

Previous decisions had held that where a will expressly indicated that its provisions were to apply to a future marriage, the marriage could not be supposed to revoke the will. But, in other previous cases, if the intention was not expressly stated, the will was ruled to have been revoked by marriage, no matter how clear the unexpressed intent was. In the present case, no such *expressed* mention was made in the will. The Illinois supreme court said, nevertheless, that, in the view of the judges of the court, the intention was clearly present at the time of making the will and that the will was therefore *not* invalidated by the marriage. The Illinois supreme court in this case then specifically overruled previous decisions to the contrary as "unsound." Thus, the decision of the circuit court was upheld, even though the reasoning behind it was condemned.

Ordinarily, probate cases are easily disposed of by the lower courts. In this case, however, there were several significant issues:

1. The rule reaffirming the necessity to give full faith and credit to the court actions of another state, even though its finding appears questionable;

2. The process of judicial review, whereby a high court effectively amends an apparently forthright statute, by relying on the concept of "intent";

3. The process of reviewing previous judicial decisions, whereby a higher court declares its previous decisions are "unsound" and establishes a new rule;

4. The process whereby the intermediate appellate court can be by-passed and a case taken directly to the state supreme court when a constitutional issue is involved;

5. The necessity imposed by the Federal Constitution upon state courts to consider federal questions.

**Supreme Court of Illinois**

trial courts. In some states they exercise original jurisdiction in certain kinds of cases. Despite the diversity, they all serve primarily to help the highest state appellate court carry the increasing burdens of appeals work. Cases which involve the constitutionality of state laws, legality of state offices, felonies, and other serious matters must be reviewed in some states first by the intermediate courts of appeals before going to the court of last resort. In other states, such as in Arizona, Connecticut, Michigan, and Oregon, cases of this type go directly to the top of the judicial hierarchy.

# APPELLATE COURTS OF LAST RESORT

At the top of the pyramid in several states are courts of last resort. These courts are known by a variety of names in the United States. In thirty-eight states appellate courts are called supreme courts. It is the Supreme Court of Errors in Connecticut, the Supreme Court of Appeals in Virginia and West Virginia, and Supreme Judicial Court in Maine and Massachusetts, and the Court of Appeals in Kentucky, Maryland, and New York.

The court generally sits at the state capital, but in several of the states it may also convene in other important sections of the state. In approximately one third of the states the court consists of divisions that sit and decide cases separately.

### Justices: Numbers, Terms, and Salaries

Most of these courts consist of from three to nine justices. Arizona, for example, has five, California seven, Delaware three, Iowa nine, Michigan eight, New York seven, and Texas nine. One justice in each court is the chief justice—highest ranking judicial officer of the state. Selection of the chief justice varies widely. For example, Alabama selects him directly by popular election, California through appointment by the governor, Colorado by court rotation, Kansas by seniority of service, Rhode Island through election by the legislature, and Oregon through majority vote of members of the highest court.

Terms of justices vary in most states from six years to life. In Arizona it is six years, in California twelve years, in Louisiana fourteen years, in Missouri twelve years, in Pennsylvania twenty-one years, and in Massachusetts and Rhode Island it is for life.

Salaries are generally high. They range from $8,500 in Idaho to $23,000 in California, $24,000 in New Jersey, $25,000 in Pennsylvania, and $35,500 in New York. In Connecticut, Delaware, Georgia, Maine, Maryland, Massachusetts, and other states the salaries of justices exceed those of the governors.

## Jurisdiction

These appellate courts of last resort, or supreme courts, are far removed from the minor court world of disputes over unpaid bills, divorce decrees, alimony, troubled children, parking fines, and bent automobile fenders. Their jurisdiction extends rather to issues of basic legal and constitutional philosophy. Through their power of judicial review, approximately 99 percent of their work is devoted to the final legal interpretation of state constitutions, state statutes, municipal ordinances, principles of common law, their own previous decisions, and, since Federal courts are bound by state supreme court decisions on questions of state law, to some of the intricacies of federalism.

The supreme courts in several states are also required to render advisory opinions on request of the governor or legislature. Such opinions are normally restricted to grave matters of government and do not have the binding effect of a regular judicial precedent.

# AN APPRAISAL OF STATE COURT SYSTEMS

In 1818 the Illinois Constitution declared:

Every person ought to find a certain remedy in the law for all injuries and wrongs which he may receive in his person, property or reputation; he ought to obtain by law right and justice freely, and without being obliged to purchase it, completely and without denial, promptly and without delay.

Over one hundred years later, state court systems in the United States today still do not fully satisfy this prescription for justice.

Sometimes described as "statutory omelets," most state court systems are a confusion of organization, procedure, and jurisdictions. There are so many courts of so many kinds that it is often hard to tell where a case should be heard—and at what level. Moreover, a court system built for a bygone age is badly hampered by delayed and expensive justice. In 1955, for example, approximately 34,000 personal injury cases were awaiting trial in the Circuit and Superior Courts of Chicago. And justice is a costly prize, not only for the states in operating forty-eight different systems, but for the individuals who contest within them.

Should everyone be provided with a defense lawyer? The Sixth Amendment to the United States Constitution says "Yes" as far as Federal courts go; but the states have not guaranteed this. In most states, an alleged offender can secure highly competent legal advice only if he can pay for it.

### Selection or Election?

A further problem arises in the method of selecting judges, for justice can be no better than those who administer it. In three quarters of the states, judges are elected by the voters. In other states, judges are appointed by the governor or by the legislature.

Whether judges should be appointed or popularly elected has been a subject of debate for many years. Both methods have produced outstanding jurists; both methods involve the risk of introducing undue partisanship into our judicial life.

It is easily understood why some political organizations and leaders take great interest in candidates for the bench. Judgeships are valuable forms of patronage and once in office judges have considerable patronage powers of their own. Judges can appoint referees, guardians, receivers in bankruptcy cases, and trustees and administrators of estates—all grist for the patronage mill.

The fact is that there is no easy way of eliminating partisan politics from the processes of judicial selection. Most students feel that selection by executive appointment and for extended terms is preferable to selection by election—this, even though governors almost inevitably defer to local political leaders for judgeship nominations, particularly at the municipal level.

The remarkable thing is that "bad" politics has had so little effect upon the integrity of our court system. There are a number of reasons for this. It is in part because most political leaders know that "good appointments are good politics"; it is in part because most politics is not bad, and is in fact an almost ideal training ground for judges who are constantly faced with subtle issues of adjustment and public acceptance. Most important of all, the donning of a judicial robe by itself has a remarkable effect upon erstwhile attorneys. The most opportunistic and expediential lawyers are frequently transformed into models of judicial incorruptibility and decorum when they identify themselves officially and symbolically with the stream of justice which has upheld the dignity of Western man since the days of Solon. All this is fortunate, but it is not enough. The Jacksonian spoils system does not mix well with our expectations of judicial incorruptibility.

Tempering the political selection of judges is the influence exerted by the American Bar Association and its state and local affiliates. Basically a trade union of lawyers, the bar association supervises bar examinations, keeps an eye on judges, recommends legislation to improve the administration of justice, and often endorses candidates for election or appointment to the bench. Although generally a conservative influence politically, the bar association helps mitigate irresponsible partisanship in the choice of judges.

# COURT REFORM—PROPOSALS AND PROGRESS

The reform of courts has been slow and difficult compared with improvements in other state and local agencies. At the same time, a recent awareness and improved understanding of the problems of administering justice has been encouraging. Four general tendencies characterize reform efforts:

1. *Over-all court reorganization and unification.* New Jersey and California, for example, have been very active in reducing the number of courts and justices while streamlining the administration of the judicial branch considerably.

2. *Procedural changes aimed at reducing delays in the law.* Oregon has been experimenting with the use of temporary judges and with lawyers serving as judges. The Supreme Court of Los Angeles has refused to postpone trials except for adequate reasons, thus helping to break the case log-jam. Other states are finding that increased informal negotiation between counsel and judge has ended many cases promptly, inexpensively, and fairly.

3. *The provision of legal assistance to those who cannot afford it.* "Public defender" organizations such as Legal Aid Societies and law school clinics, are growing rapidly in numbers and importance. Without them, poorer people have often been at the mercy of

"shyster" lawyers, or young and inexperienced lawyers assigned to defend them. Often the poor have had no help at all.

4. *Improvements in the selection of judges, in their length of term, and in their salaries.* At least two states have contributed significantly to improved methods of selecting judges. Appeals judges in California are appointed by the governor subject to approval of a commission, while in Missouri, the governor selects judges from a slate submitted by a nominating panel of lawyers and laymen. In both states, these judges run for election on their records at a later date.

The tenure of judges varies from two years (Vermont) to life (Massachusetts). The average tenure ranges from four to six years. Many states are actively striving for longer and more secure terms for judges.

In the matter of salaries, more than half of the state legislatures meeting during the last few years have increased judicial salaries.

# CONCLUSION

## Synopsis

Despite the ignorance, confusion, and ambivalent attitudes of the American people about courts of law, state and local judicial bodies play an important role in helping us achieve key expectations of government. In each of the states there is a single court system—a pyramid embracing all state and local courts and tribunals: inferior courts which handle a variety of minor and special cases; major trial courts which handle more serious cases; intermediate courts of appeal; and, at the top in each state, an appellate court of last resort. In recent years there has been progress in overcoming the complexity, confusion, delay, and expense of the state court systems; but court reform is still in its infancy.

## Significance

Most Americans never come into direct contact with the Federal courts of the United States. Our faith, or lack of faith, in the justice and efficiency of our courts derives almost entirely from our experience with state and local courts. If the cause of justice is not promptly, intelligently, and humanely served at the local level, our respect for law at all levels will inevitably be eroded. Widespread doubt about the integrity and efficiency of our judicial instruments is an attitude which we as a democratic nation based upon the rule of law cannot afford.

## Prospectus

In this Section we have examined the instruments of government which operate at the level of the states. We turn finally to our myriad instruments of local governmnt. Legal creatures of the states, local governments in America have a significance of their own. Their importance to the success of the entire democratic enterprise is frequently overlooked. So is the fact of their interdependence—with each other, and with other levels of government.

# SECTION VI

## Our Local Instruments

*E*ducation takes place not only in schools, but in family and community as well, and it seems safe to venture the suggestion that the process of coming to our senses will involve a new faith in community life and family life as well as a new concern for education in the things of spirit and mind. We cannot turn the job over to the society as a whole, for Americans live their lives in communities; nowhere else can men come to know themselves and their fellows more intimately and completely than in communities. It is here, first of all, that faith in man can be re-created for Americans, and it is here that loyalty and freedom can once more be put in their proper relation. If Americans fail to maintain and to build democratic communities, they will fail to maintain a democratic nation."

—Blaine E. Mercer

## CHAPTER 23

# Towns, Townships, and Counties

HOWEVER MOMENTOUS the decisions reached in state capitols, in the federal buildings along the Potomac, or in the steel and glass sky-scraper of the United Nations along New York's East River, it is in our local communities that instruments of government come most directly into daily contact with the American people.

To those who have never experienced the excitement and fasci-nation of local government, the work of mayors, city managers, selectmen, town councils, village councils, sheriffs, health officers, planning consultants, or directors of sanitation may seem undramatic. But what these officials do, and the way in which they do it, has a vital bearing upon our ability to realize our expectations of con-stitutional government.

No incumbent mayor or city councilman will ever sign a treaty of peace ending all war; no city engineer will ever build a hydrogen bomb; no police chief will ever command a victorious United Na-tions army; but these local officials are the men and women who will determine whether the several communities in which we live will remain relatively civilized and decent. If this job could be uniformly well done throughout the world, a meaningful treaty of peace among nations would be but a ceremonial flourish—a ratifi-cation of a pre-existing state of felicity and order.

## ROLE AND TASKS OF LOCAL GOVERNMENTS

The importance of local governments in our lives can be expressed in a number of ways. Local governments permit diversity and flexi-bility within our national and state constitutional system. Local gov-ernments help reconcile conflicting national and local goals and needs. They also tend to maintain a balance between national uniformity and local diversity. They increase the sense of popular participation in public affairs among the citizenry—a sense so vital to the continuation of democracy. Local governments give phrases like "domestic tranquillity," "general welfare," and "blessings of liberty," their most immediate and poignant meaning. Finally, local governments are our primary resource for the training of future leaders in our democracy and in the world. A selectman who has to take his next-door neighbor's property for a new road will never forget the twin propositions which haunt all humane governments: that all forward movement is at somebody's expense—and that no forward movement is at somebody's expense.

In short, in Professor Schattschneider's words, "The best thing about local government is that it is local."

# REGULATORY AND PROMOTIONAL FUNCTIONS

As America passed from a continental wilderness to a nation of tremendous metropolitan areas and vast cultivated plains, local governments were inevitably loaded with an increasing burden of work.

Local activities may be divided initially into two categories: *regulatory* and *promotional*.

## Regulatory Functions

The regulatory function exists for the protection of persons and property, and includes the following:

    Abatement of air and water pollution
    Building inspection
    Custody of law violators
    Fire protection
    Police protection
    Public health regulation
    Traffic safety and control
    Regulation of business, trades, and other activities
    Zoning of land for industry, commerce, residences, and other uses

These regulatory activities have traditionally accounted for the great bulk of local government work in the United States. In a sense, they may be viewed as the things which local governments do to ensure domestic tranquillity.

## Promotional Functions

The second major category of local government activities may be described as *promotional*—activities dedicated to releasing the energies of people. The promotional tasks of local government, like similar activities at the state and national level, have been growing rapidly in the past few decades. Many of these were noted in Section II, particularly in the chapter on the general welfare. Random examples include the following:

> Airport construction and maintenance
> Charities
> Correctional institutions, such as industrial schools for boys
> Hospital and medical services
> Libraries
> Parks, playgrounds, and recreation
> Public markets, wharves, and warehouses
> Public schools
> Public utilities, such as electric, gas, water, street railway services
> Sewerage disposal
> Street maintenance

A note of caution is in order at this point. While these two broad categories serve a useful purpose in describing the work of local government, the distinction is not clear cut. Promotion and regulation are increasingly two sides of the same coin. The promotion of one person's interests restrains another's. Building inspection, once exclusively a regulatory function, is now an integral part of general welfare programs such as urban renewal. The decision by the city of Los Angeles to promote the interests of autoists and truckers by improving the system of freeways effectively restrained the interests of many whose lands were taken through *eminent domain*. Antinoise ordinances promote the interests of those who retire early in the evening, while these same ordinances restrain the exuberance of the young. Fire regulations restrain the interest of people who clutter their attics, but promote the safety of the larger community.

In sum, there is no clear-cut distinction between "ensuring domestic tranquillity" and "promoting the general welfare," but together they help to "secure the blessings of liberty."

## Legal Basis of Local Government

Legally, all local governments are creatures of the states. They are, in the eyes of the law, public corporations, established for purposes of providing local service and regulation. From the practical point of view, all these public corporations may be regarded as alike. Legally, however, there is a distinction between two categories:

1. *Municipal corporations:* cities, villages, boroughs, and incorporated towns which have presumably been called into existence in response to the initiative and the desires of the local population who prefer local self-government under a charter—a form of local constitution.

2. *Quasi-corporations* (units of local government which act as if they were municipal corporations): counties, towns, townships, school districts, and a variety of other special units, which have been created not on local initiative but at the instigation of the state, for administration of state laws, regulations, and programs.

Municipal corporations generally operate under the terms of charters which spell out a city government's structure, powers, functions, and procedures. Some municipal charters, called home-rule charters, allow considerable local independence from state regulation.

Quasi-corporations, on the other hand, are not based on charters but operate under many different provisions contained in state constitutions and legislative statutes.

None of these local governments is considered "sovereign" in the sense that powers are reserved to it as to state governments. Local governments generally have only the powers permitted them by state law.

# ORGANIZATION OF LOCAL GOVERNMENT

One of the most striking characteristics of local government in the United States is the great variety of organizations through which the tasks of local government are carried out. In this country today there is a crosshatch of over 116,000 separate—but often overlapping —organized units of local government. The list includes more than:

```
 3,000 counties
17,000 towns and townships
16,000 incorporated villages and cities
67,000 school districts
12,000 park, water, sewer and other special districts
```

There are basically five different types of local government in the United States:

1. *New England town government:* the first form of local government established in America and found today in the six New England states.

2. *Midwestern township government:* a variation of the town, centered in a belt running from the state of New York westward to the Great Plains.

3. *County government:* the largest unit of local government, found throughout the United States but particularly active in the South and West. In about eight midwestern states, the township and the county share local government responsibilities in rural areas.

4. *Municipal government:* the major form of government in urban communities including thousands of incorporated villages and cities throughout the nation.

5. *Special districts:* units established for special purposes such as education or water, rather than for general government.

# THE NEW ENGLAND TOWN

The way local governments are organized in the United States—even their names—bears witness to their deep historical roots. Less than twenty-five years after the landing of the Pilgrims at Plymouth Rock, for example, the early settlers of Massachusetts divided the colony into four "shires" or counties, not only resembling their English models, but actually named after them: Essex, Middlesex, Norfolk, and Suffolk. The county was found too large for effective local self-government in New England, however. Thus, the "town," derived from the early Anglo-Saxon "tun" (a small enclosed place), was adopted and became the primary unit of local government in New England. The county remained as a legal subdivision of the state in New England, but it never became a full-fledged unit of general government there.

### Evolution of Towns

The town evolved naturally from New England life. It embraced a smaller area of land than the county and was based on the grouping of people in relatively tight communities. The so-called proprietors of the early town government were the heads of local families,

This rather drab town hall hardly suggests the number or the importance of the tasks that local governments are called upon to perform in the middle of the twentieth century.

and all other citizens were free to participate in deciding public questions through a romanticized instrument of direct democracy—the town meeting. It was in this assembly that the town discussed and decided such questions as the need for a new town well, or a road, or a bridge, or perhaps a town hall. As the burdens of town government grew, there was a division of labor. The town meeting appointed a committee, called a board of selectmen, which supervised the activities of the town government and sought to coordinate them. Several administrative officers—a constable, treasurer, overseer of the poor, mender of fences, and others—were also appointed to help carry out particular tasks. The town meeting, however, retained its position as the basic policy-making and financial body.

## Towns and Municipalities Compared

With some modification, the New England town prevails today in more than 1,400 rural communities. Towns are generally not municipal corporations. That is, they were created by state initiative rather than local option, and they operate under broad constitutional and statutory provisions rather than municipal charters. In effect, however, towns enjoy as much self-government as municipal corporations, and they can do practically anything that an incorporated city can do—levy taxes, borrow money, own property, sue and be sued, enact local ordinances, make contracts, enforce police, fire, and health regulations, and provide a variety of community services. As some towns have grown and lost their rural character they have requested incorporation and a municipal charter in order to secure the benefits of municipal organization and administration.

## The Town Meeting

The chief instrument of town government remains the annual or special assembly of qualified voters of the town, organized as the town meeting, and presided over by the moderator. As many towns have grown, they have found the mass meeting cumbersome and ill-suited to handling complex community problems. Consequently, many growing towns have adopted the *limited town meeting,* composed of delegates elected by the voters organized into town districts. This is a form of representative democracy rather than direct democracy.

The town meeting has retained its power to adopt the town budget, levy taxes, issue bonds, enact appropriations and ordinances, and elect town officers. In many towns where the annual meeting has proved cumbersome, a finance committee, elected or appointed for limited terms, has been established. It has responsibility for planning the town's future needs and for handling such complex affairs as land-use planning, public works, zoning, and financial administration. Because it violates the spirit of the secret ballot, because those who caucus beforehand tend to control it, and because many local problems are no longer simple, the town meeting is increasingly being viewed with skepticism as an efficient, responsible, and a democratic instrument of local government.

## The Town System

There is no chief executive in the town system, but administrative responsibility is centered in a board of selectmen, composed of three to nine members, and a town clerk. They are all chosen by members of the town meeting, generally for terms of one year. The selectmen serve as an executive committee of the town meeting. Their work is primarily administrative in character, and includes the granting of licenses, care of the poor, maintenance of streets and roads, and other community tasks. The town clerk, on the other hand, maintains town records; issues licenses for marriage, hunting, and other purposes; maintains voters' lists; registers deeds, mortgages, and other documents; and handles other rountine chores.

In addition to the selectmen and the clerk, the town meeting may also appoint other administrative officers:

| | |
|---|---|
| Constable | School committeeman |
| Highway supervisor | Tax assessor |
| Justice of the peace | Tax collector |
| Library trustee | Treasurer |
| Overseer of the poor | Tree warden |

In response to the need for more professionalized administration in town government, there has been a growing town-manager movement among New England towns.

While the New England town form of government represents only a small fraction of the units of local government and only a handful of the American people, it has been one of the most influential American experiments with democracy, even if parts of its operations have often been romanticized.


# TOWNSHIP GOVERNMENT

As pioneers from New England traveled westward, they carried their preference for the town form of government with them. New York, New Jersey, and Pennsylvania, for example, had been divided into counties by the Duke of Yorke's Laws in 1665, and by the end of that century county government prevailed. However, as the new settlers moved in, they further divided the counties into towns. Consequently, there is a band of states lying between the New England town and the southern county in which a combination of town and county has become the prevailing form of local government organization. In the state of New York the term "town" was adopted, while in New Jersey, Pennsylvania, and most of the states to the west, the word "township" was used.

As the lands of the old Northwest Territory were settled, the new states were divided into counties, and counties into square townships, 6 miles on a side and 36 square miles in area. The townships were not based on existing local communities; they were little more than arbitrary territories carved out of the plains by the surveyor. Tasks of local government were divided between county and township. This is generally the arrangement extending through Kansas, Nebraska, South Dakota, and North Dakota.

## Administration

Many township governments consist of a board, variously called a board of trustees or supervisors, composed of three elective members.

In practice, township affairs are frequently administered by a single elective officer called a town chairman, trustee, or supervisor. Generally, there is no assembly in the township comparable to the town meeting. A few states have established township meetings, but they are little more than paper organizations.

### Functions

In the early years, township government was responsible for public schools, poor relief, roads, bridges, and other functions, such as planting trees, disposing of dogs that killed sheep, and mediating disputes over fence lines. Over the years, however, most township functions have been transferred to the county and the state.

### Decline

Urban growth, which has in effect obliterated many township lines, has inevitably contributed to the decline of township government. The main task remaining to township government is supervision of township schools. In most other matters, the township is a hollow shell. While the New England town is based on an integrated community, the Middle West township generally has no organized public opinion or community to support it. Consequently, the town continues to thrive, while its western cousin has become a relic of America's frontier. The National Muncipal League has recommended that townships be abolished. They have already been completely eliminated in Iowa and Oklahoma.

# COUNTY GOVERNMENT

Outside New England the county emerged as the major unit of local government in the American colonial period. In Virginia, for example, the county was found more appropriate to Southern life than the town system. Land in the South was granted in vast tracts, and farming was conducted on the basis of great plantations rather than in small meadows and pastures. Furthermore, Southern people lived on scattered plantations, rather than in more concentrated towns. Southern life centered around the organization of the plantation, somewhat reminiscent of the medieval manorial system of Europe, and there was less intimacy and fewer personal contacts among the people of different plantations than there was among New England townspeople.

Today the population of counties ranges from about 300 in Loving County, Texas, to over 4,500,000 in Cook County, Illinois, containing the city of Chicago. Most counties have fewer than 40,000 people. Historically, the physical size of a county was generally determined by how far a remote settler could travel by horse to the county seat in one day. It was truly horse-and-buggy government. Today, however, counties range from 1 square mile in Clifton Forge, Virginia, to over 20,000 square miles in San Bernardino County, California, the largest in the country.

## The Evolution of Counties

The county—embracing a larger area than the New England town—emerged as the primary form of local government in the South. It was essentially an administrative unit rather than a policy-making government. Unlike the New England town, the Southern county developed no popular assembly like the annual town meeting. Tasks of local government were administered by county officials appointed by the colonial governor. Later, of course, under state constitutions, these county officials became subject to popular election by voters of the county.

This was the pattern that prevailed in the South. In time, as the great heartland of America was settled, the Southern stream of migration from Virginia, Maryland, and North Carolina crossed Kentucky into the Middle West, where the county system converged with the stream from New England. There the county-township system has developed.

Today, there are over 3,000 counties, located in all parts of the United States. (In Louisiana they are called parishes.) In most parts of the country, counties are both administrative subdivisions of the states and major units of local government. This is particularly true in rural areas, although as we shall see, there are significant urban counties within some of our giant metropolitan areas.

## County Powers and Functions

In terms of powers and functions, there are also sharp contrasts. In New England, for example, counties have so little to do that more than one state governor has seriously proposed their abolition. In the South, the mountain states of the West, and on the Pacific

During most of our history, the country store and the county courthouse have been the two centers of political discussion in rural America. Scenes such as this, however, are rapidly dying out. The auto, supermarkets, and television have radically changed the political habits of much of nonurban America.

Coast, however, counties are almost the exclusive form of local government in rural and semirural areas. In the Middle West, counties share their functions with many townships.

Legally, county governments do not rest on municipal charters. Instead, the details of most county governments are scattered in provisions of the state constitutions and in supplemental statutes. In a growing number of cases, county governments have been granted charters and a form of corporate existence. In 1939, for example, Westchester County, New York, was granted a charter under which its structure and operations were modernized and expanded. The boundaries of counties are determined by state legislatures, subject to state constitutional limitations.

There is much variation in the functions of county government. In those areas where county government is most active, their functions have traditionally included administration of the following:

Courts and jails
Election machinery
Law enforcement
Public schools
Recording of deeds, mortgages, wills, and other documents
Road and highway construction and maintenance
State laws
Taxation
Welfare and hospital services

With the progress of the last century, however, many new tasks have been assigned to county government. They include the following—not, of course, in all counties:

Aid to agriculture
Airports
Assistance to needy aged, the blind, and dependent children
Libraries
Parks and recreational facilities
Planning and zoning
Public health protection
Public markets
Public utilities
Rural housing

As cities have grown in the United States, hitherto rural counties have been surrounded by urban communities. Consequently, many county governments have assumed responsibility for functions usually associated with city governments. California counties, for example, may perform almost any function they choose to handle. In many cases in that state, counties are providing services for people living within cities and urban areas. The functions of Los Angeles County, for example, have expanded enormously in the past twenty years. In 1955, the Wisconsin legislature increased the scope of county government by broadening the interpretation of county powers and by granting more than a dozen new powers to most counties in that state. County government law in Wisconsin was also brought together and simplified.

At the same time, there has been a trend toward reduction of county tasks in the United States, as some county responsibilities are transferred to city, state, and federal governments. In many southern states, for example, responsibility for roads and highways has been transferred to the state, while elsewhere in the nation responsibilities for old-age assistance and aid to the blind and to dependent children have been transferred to state and federal governments.

## County Fiscal Practices

The fiscal powers of county governments are narrowly restricted. Counties may levy taxes for revenue purposes, but the power to do so is closely fixed by state law. Residents of the county pay taxes, but they have practically no voice in deciding how funds will be spent. This is a constant reminder to the taxpayer that legislative instruments of government, based on the principle of representation, have never fully developed in county government. Counties in most parts of the nation still practice taxation without representation.

## County Elective Boards

County government generally ignores the principle of separation of powers. There is no sovereign legislature, no chief executive with powers in his own right, no system of checks and balances. Instead, all powers are vested—theoretically at least—in the hands of an elective board, variously called a county board, board of commissioners, board of revenue, or board of supervisors. In most counties, the size of the board varies from three to seven members. In Westchester County, New York, there are forty-five members, while in Cook County, Illinois, there are only fifteen. In a few counties an executive is elected, but the practice is still an exception. The power of the county board to make general policy is narrowly restricted by state law.

Moreover, county government is not even unified in the county board. For one thing, the board generally must share its responsibilities with a number of other elective county officials such as the following:

Auditor
Clerk of the court
County attorney or solicitor
County clerk
Coroner
Recorder of deeds and other documents
Sheriff
Superintendent of schools
Surveyor or engineer
Tax assessor
Tax collector
Treasurer

## County Special-Purpose Boards

County government is even further diffused and divided by the practice of assigning many functions to special-purpose boards or commissions. Members of these special administrative bodies are generally appointed by the county board, but the board exercises little or no control over them. Thus in many counties tax assessment, finance, public health, highways, hospitals, personnel management, planning, schools, welfare, and other functions are administered by county officials who are effectively responsible to no one and who often do not even consult each other. The greatest need of county government, perhaps, is an executive system to bring order out of the chaos of diffusion of power and responsibility which presently exists. This combination of diffusion, bed-sheet ballots, ambiguities, and headlessness moved one county board member to remark recently, "Sometimes it appears like we have no county government at all here; and at other times it looks like we have fifteen county governments in this county."

## County Reform

There has been little progress in county reform. A few large and active counties have made efforts to unify their administrative machinery in the hands of single, elected executives, while others have appointed managers with broad administrative authority. Los Angeles County has made great strides by granting most of the administrative power to a "chief administrative officer." Proposals for incorporation of county governments, granting modern charters, shortening the ballot, unifying executive power, and reducing state control have recently been considered by many state legislatures.

County reform is often hard to sell. Only recently a proposed amendment to the Alameda County, California, government—recommended by specialists in local government—would have simplified the system and tightened administrative efficiency by making appointive the offices of county clerk, auditor, treasurer, tax collector, recorder, surveyor, superintendent of schools, sheriff, and coroner. However, the public defeated the proposal in a referendum.

Illustrative of the prevailing belief that county government is one of the great failures in the United States today, was the recent action of the Alaskan constitutional convention. Convinced of the weakness of this form of government, the convention avoided even the name "county" by providing specifically that "all local government power shall be vested in boroughs and cities." This negative attitude is unfortunate, for reorganized counties could perform vitally important functions in many parts of the United States—especially where populations have spilled over traditional city boundaries.

# CONCLUSION

## Synopsis

Once the dominant instruments of local government in America, towns, townships, and counties still perform important functions in our society—particularly in rural areas. The town, a product of early New England, is today the major form of rural government in the northeastern part of the country—just as the township is in the Middle West. County government is found everywhere in the United States, but is particularly active in the South and West. The county, although traditionally a rural government, is in some areas emerging as an important instrument of urban and even metropolitan government.

## Significance

Town meetings, selectmen, commissioners, and county boards make decisions which intimately touch the lives of people who live within their jurisdictions. The way these governments are organized, the powers they exercise, the way they make decisions, and the competence of their officials are key elements in determining whether the expectations of government held by rural and small-town Americans will become realities.

## Prospectus

But most Americans do not live in small towns or rural areas; they live in cities. It is in the cities that local governments presently face their greatest challenge. To the government of the cities of America we now turn.

## CHAPTER 24

# DIRECTORY

ANDREWS, ERIC A. COMM. PUBLIC WORKS ~302

BATES, ANDREW E. PLUMBING INSPECTOR 301
BRANDES, FRED C. PLAN. BOARD ENGINEER 201
BRENNER, COLIN M. DEP. COMM. FINANCE 102
BRENNER, WM. H. DEPUTY CORP. COUNSEL 204
BROCKING, HARRY A. COMM. PURCHASE ANNEX
BURGER, WM. H. 2ND. DEP. COMM. PUB. WORKS 302

COLE, THOMAS R. DEPUTY ASSESSOR 101
CONROY, EDW. J. 1ST. DEP. COMM. PUB. SAFETY 301
CRANE, CARL R. SUPT. FORESTRY AND PARKS 302

DARROVEN, E. ASST. ENG. STREET INSPEC. 302
DELTUFO, VINCENT ASST. CORP. COUNSEL 204
DOHERTY, ROBERT J. REAL ESTATE COM. 300

EBY, LILLIAN WELFARE SVCE. OFFICER B2

FARRINGTON, W. 2ND. DEP. COMM. PUB. SAFETY 301
FRIESE, JOHN H. SUPT. WATER 302

HOWARD A. SUPT. SEWER 302

LON, FRANK T. COMM. PUBLIC SAFETY 301
JAMES E. JR. DIRECTOR PERSONNEL 200
TEN, F. RUSSELL CHAIRMAN CIVIL B3
SERVICE COMMISSION
KENNETH ELECTRICAL INSPECTOR 301

ORATO, S. ASST. BLDG. INSPECTOR 301

KANE, MARJORIE M. CITY CLERK 100

MARRACH, JOHN ASSESSOR 101
MCKINLEY, WM. CORPORATION COUNSEL 204
MERCER, HAROLD EXEC. ASST. CIVIL DEFENSE B1
K, WM. ASST. PLANNING INSPEC. 301
AK, EDWIN G. MAYOR 202

E. COMM. FINANCE 102
M. SUPT. HIGHWAYS 302

SUPT. CITY OWNED BLDG. 302
SEC. CIVIL SVCE. COMM. B3
ET LIGHTING FOREMAN 302

WATER SUPT. 302
CORP. COUNSEL 204
SST. PURCH. AGENT ANNEX
REGISTRAR
M. PUB. WORKS 100

AMMUNITION, PERMITS
ASSESSOR
AUCTIONEER LICENSES
AWNING, PERMITS

BIRTH CERTIFICATES
BLASTING, PERMITS
BUILDINGS, INSPECTION, PERMITS
BUS LICENSES

CABARET LICENSES
CAMPING
CHRISTMAS TREE, STORAGE PERMITS
CITY CLERK, OFFICE OF
CITY COURT 279 HAMILTON AVE
CIVIL DEFENSE
CIVIL SERVICE COMMISSION
COMMON COUNCIL CHAMBERS
COMMON COUNCIL RECORDS
CONVALESCENT HOME LICENSES
CORPORATION COUNSEL, OFFICE
CURB CUTS, PERMITS

DEATH CERTIFICATES
DEMOLITION PERMITS
DOG LICENSES
DRIVEWAY PERMITS

ELECTION INFORMATION
ELECTRICAL, INSPECTION, ETC.
EMPLOYMENT OFFICE - PERSONNEL
ENGINEERING BUREAU
EVICTIONS
EXPLOSIVES, PURCH. OR POSSESSION
EXPLOSIVES, STORAGE, TRANS.
EXPRESS LICENSES

FINANCE, DEPT. OF
FISHING LICENSES
FLAMMABLE LIQUIDS, PERMITS
FORESTRY AND PARKS

GARBAGE COLLECTION
GOING _OUT_OF_BUS, SALES LICENSES

HEALTH DEPT.
MAIN OFFICE, COUNTY OFFICE BUILDING
WHITE PLAINS CENTER, 55 N. LEXINGTON AVE
BIRTH AND DEATH RECORDS
HIGHWAYS
HOISTING LICENSES
HOUSING LICENSES

301
101
100
301

100

301
301
100

301
B2
301
100

B1
B3
203
100
301
204
302

100
301
100
302

100
301
200
302
B2
301
301
100

102
100
301
302

302
100

OIL BURNER
OPERATING EN

PARKING AUT
PAWNBROKER
PEDDLER LICE
PERSONNEL, D
PLANNING BO
PLUMBING IN
POLICE HEADQU
PUBLIC ASSI
PUBLIC LIBR
PUBLIC SAFE
PUBLIC WOR
PURCHASE, D
PURCHASING,

REAL ESTATE
RECREATION,
REFRIGERATIO
ROOMING HOUSE

SCAFFOLD PER
SCHOOL DISTRIC
279 HAMILTO
SCHOOL TAX P
SEALER OF WEI
SECOND HAND D
SEWERS
SIDEWALK PER
SIGN PERMITS
SPECIAL EVEN
STREET LIGHTI
STREET OBSTR
STREET OPENI

TAX AND ASSE
TAXICAB LICE
THEATER LICE
TICKET AGENCY
TRAFFIC COMM

USED CAR DEA

VAULT PERMITS
VITAL STAT

# City Government

## THE VILLAGE: WAY-STATION OF LOCAL GOVERNMENT

VILLAGE GOVERNMENT marks the transition from a rural community to a city. Some communities outgrow their simple rural status, and yet are not sufficiently urbanized to be regarded as cities. Rather, they are frequently semiurban centers, located near or within the vast metropolises of the United States. Such communities, sometimes located within the town in New England, the township of the Middle West, or the county elsewhere may request incorporation by the state and the grant of a village charter. When this is done, the village becomes something of a miniature city, with most of the political and administrative paraphernalia of a full-fledged municipality. For example, there is the village of La Grange, Illinois, a suburb of Chicago, with a population of over 13,000, located in Lyons township. There are many other examples of such villages, particularly in the Middle West. Some states require that when a village reaches a certain population it be reclassified as a city. In other states the change is optional.

The village employs the principle of separation of powers. The local legislative or policy-making body is the village council, whose members are variously called trustees, burgesses, commissioners, aldermen, bailiffs, or councilmen. Membership varies from three to five in most villages. All top officials are popularly elected for short terms. Their primary task is to decide village policies and to enact local ordinances dealing with the usual local matters.

The primary executive official of the village is the mayor, also called the burgess, warden, or intendant. His functions vary widely. In some states he possesses almost full responsibility for administration of local affairs, while in other states he must share his authority with other administrative officers who are popularly elected in some villages and chosen by the council in others. The village mayor usually presides over sessions of the council.

# MUNICIPAL GOVERNMENT

Now that the United States has passed from a rural to an urban nation, and most Americans live in or near cities, the municipality has become the form of local government which affects most people in this country. As in the case of rural government, American inventiveness has produced a bewildering variety of city governments. There are three basic types: (1) council-mayor; (2) commission; and (3) council-manager. Of the approximately 2,500 cities in the United States with populations over 5,000, about 53 percent are council-mayor forms, about 14 percent are commissions, and about 33 percent are council-manager systems. Each basic form will be examined; but it should be remembered that the variations within each form are almost infinite.

# COUNCIL-MAYOR FORM

The oldest and most prevalent type of municipal government in the United States is a system with a separation of powers between a local legislature, usually called the common council, and a mayor, who serves as the local chief executive. This arrangement is particularly predominant in very large cities. Of the seventeen largest cities in the United States, only one—Cincinnati, Ohio—is not of the council-mayor form.

### The Council

The city council is a local legislature consisting of from nine to fifty members. Councilmen are usually popularly elected, either "at large," that is, by voters of the whole city, or geographically, by voters of city districts called wards. More than a third of the council-mayor cities elect all councilmen at large, while the remainder of the cities elect them by wards or by a combination of wards and at large. In South Bend, Indiana, for example, three of the nine city councilmen are elected at large, while in Syrcuse, New York, five are elected at large and five by wards.

Councilmanic terms range from two to four years. Salaries range widely—from nothing in Bridgeport, Connecticut, to $10,000 in Pittsburgh and $12,000 in Detroit.

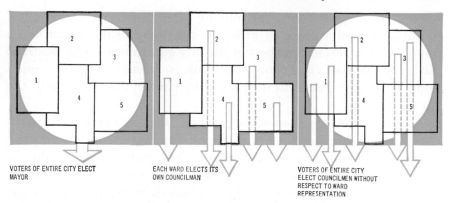

VOTERS OF ENTIRE CITY ELECT
MAYOR

EACH WARD ELECTS ITS
OWN COUNCILMAN

VOTERS OF ENTIRE CITY
ELECT COUNCILMEN WITHOUT
RESPECT TO WARD
REPRESENTATION

Election by wards, or election at-large? What should a councilman represent—
the interests of a section of the city or the interests of the entire city? How can
these two interests be distinguished? (Adapted from Sidney Baldwin and
Rolin P. Posey, *Civics for Young Americans,* White Plains, N. Y.: Row Peter-
son & Company, 1956, p. 63.)

Candidates for the city council run either under a political party
label or on a nonpartisan ticket. In about 55 percent of the council-
mayor cities, candidates for the council seek office under party ban-
ners. However, while candidates for the council in many cities run
on nonpartisan ballots, for all practical purposes many of them remain—in their behavior and in the mind of the voter—identified
with party organizations. Candidates for the city council of Chicago
run officially on a nonpartisan ballot, but there is no question as to
the Democratic party attachments of the majority. Similarly, election to the city council of Evanston, Illinois, on Chicago's northern
boundary, is nonpartisan in name, but there is never any doubt as
to the Republican party affiliation of its majority.

*Composition of Council.* The size of the council tends to increase
with the size of the city. At the same time many large cities have
increased the efficiency of their councils and centered responsibility
by *reducing* the council membership. Green Bay, Wisconsin, with a
population of less than 55,000, has a city council of 24 members,
while Los Angeles, with over two million people, has a council of
only 15, and San Francisco, with over 700,000, has a council of only
11 members. Chicago, however, still has the largest city council in
the United States: 50 aldermen, each elected from a city ward.

With only a few exceptions, city councils are composed of a single
house. Eight cities in the East, however, still have bicameral councils.
Springfield, Massachusetts, has a bicameral council consisting of
eighteen councilmen elected by wards and eight aldermen elected at

large. The city of New York, on the other hand, has a council of twenty-five, and a Board of Estimate, consisting of the mayor and a number of ex officio members of the city government. The Board of Estimate possesses crucial financial powers. A single, relatively small council, however, remains the prevailing pattern through most of the United States.

*Wards versus Elections-at-Large.* The issue of election by wards versus election-at-large, and the related question of the council's size remain on the agenda of those who seek to improve the quality of municipal government in the United States. On the one hand are those who favor the election of city councils by wards. They argue that neighborhood needs and interests can best be served by this arrangement, that the special needs of particular sections of a city do not get heard when councils are composed of members representing the entire community, and that minorities are underrepresented in at-large councils.

Those who favor elections by wards also maintain that the voter is confused by the long ballot that results from at-large elections. They believe that the voter can make a wise choice at the polls only when he votes for candidates who live in his neighborhood and with whom he has some familiarity. Those who favor the ward arrangement also argue that at-large elections give the advantage to political organizations with the most money, for a city-wide campaign is much more expensive than a ward campaign. At-large elections, they add, tend to deprive smaller localized parties and organizations in the community from representation, and to perpetuate the dominant party in power.

On the other hand, there are those who maintain that the abolition of ward lines in a city tends to free councilmen from having to serve as errand boys for dominant individuals and interests in the neighborhoods the councilmen represent. At-large elections, they point out, encourage city councils to tackle city-wide problems from a comprehensive point of view, to think about the needs of the whole city rather than their own wards. They argue that more qualified men are attracted to office, regardless of where they live in the city. In brief, the proponents of at-large elections believe that freedom from the parochialism of ward politics raises the status and prestige of the council.

*Size of Council.* Closely related to this dispute is the argument over the *size* of the council. Some reformers believe that large city councils are unwieldy, and that only by reduction in membership can they be adjusted to the needs of modern city life. Smaller councils, they believe, raise the prestige of councilmen and attract more qualified men to public office.

Opposed to this view are those who believe that city councils are legislatures rather than executive bodies, and thus they should serve as political arenas within which all interests and needs of the community can be fully expressed and studied. Larger councils, they believe, are more representative, even though they may be cumbersome. They provide greater opportunities for citizen participation in public office and help prevent special-interest organizations or individuals from dominating the council. A bank, a real-estate board, a labor union, a local business enterprise or a newspaper, they argue, can unduly influence a five-man council more easily than a twenty-five-man group.

Despite the heat and persistence of these arguments over size and mode of election, there is as yet no conclusive evidence to support one side or the other. Philadelphia, Los Angeles, and Denver, for example, have demonstrated that a city can have ward politics and good government while some at-large cities have municipal governments that are as representative as most ward cities. There is no automatic connection between "good government" and some magical number in council size.

*Work of Council.* The work of the council is generally of five kinds: (1) law-making, through passage of city ordinances; (2) fiscal planning and control, including establishment of tax rates, appropriation of funds, and planning for future financial needs and resources—although in some municipalities this function is complicated by the existence of independent, appointed boards of finance or estimates, often with enormous power; (3) improvement of the city's physical condition, through building and maintaining roads, bridges, parks, and the like; (4) supervision of or surveillance over the administrative work of the city; and (5) political leadership, through promotion of citizen interest, understanding, and participation.

These are admittedly broad functions. Exactly what does a city council do? Let us examine some of the problems that a large midwestern city council handled during a one-month period recently:

1. Smoke from many large industrial plants had begun to pollute the air of the city. A councilman introduced a resolution proposing

that the council's health committee investigate smoke-abatement methods.

2. Overloaded electric power lines and congestion of sewer facilities in one district of the city moved the council to order a survey of commercial launderettes to see whether washing machines should be limited to 10 pounds capacity.

3. The rate of automobile theft rose sharply. The council considered an ordinance, directing the city clerk to maintain records of motor vehicles: owner's name, make, horsepower, and amount of tax paid.

4. A series of flash-fires in flimsy "flophouses" along the city's "skid row" which took the lives of many sleeping derelicts moved the council to consider an ordinance requiring the certification and supervision of desk clerks in buildings that provide sleeping accommodations for twenty or more people.

5. Expansion of air travel and enlargement of the city's airport facilities induced one councilman to introduce a resolution directing the council's aviation committee to study the establishment of air passenger terminal facilities in the downtown business area.

6. Traffic congestion in the downtown business area induced the council to consider an order directing its traffic committee to conduct a survey aimed at a proposed one-way street system.

7. A great influx of Negroes from the South placed considerable strain on relations between the races in the city. In an effort to protect the rights of the growing minority, two council members introduced an ordinance to prohibit discrimination in hospital service on account of race, creed, or nationality.

Sometimes city ordinances are picayune and amusing. One council, for example, passed an ordinance prohibiting ladies from wearing hatpins that protrude more than half an inch. Another forbade placing flowerpots on window sills. In one city, movie-goers are prohibited from wearing anything on their heads in theaters but skull caps or beanies. In another there is an ordinance which specifically forbids baseball fans from throwing bottles or garbage on the baseball field or at the umpire. The city council of Cheboygan, Michigan, recently passed an ordinance imposing a five-dollar fine on any motorist found driving an automobile with a woman on his lap. The council of Riverside, California, finally voted to repeal an old ordinance prohibiting cheek-to-cheek dancing in public.

Much of the councilman's work has traditionally been concerned with helping people in need. This has been particularly true in

This is Dallas, Texas. One of the fastest-growing cities in North America, Dallas has tripled in population since 1920—from 150,000 to 450,000. Rapid change puts uncommon strains upon instruments of local government.

large cities containing recent foreign immigrants or people from other parts of the United States who have been strange to the language or the ways of the city. Boston, in the last century, with its people from Ireland; New York a generation ago with the Italians and Jews, and today with the Puerto Ricans; and Los Angeles with people from Mexico and numerous Negroes from the rural South are illustrative. The political role continues, even if its importance is somewhat diminished: a father needs a job; an elderly couple needs information about how to get government assistance; a teen-age son is in trouble with the law; a homeowner wants his street paved; a lonely widow wants more light on her street at night—these are some of the problems that consume the time of councilmen and of the political leaders behind them. Lincoln Steffens has not been the only one to defend this kind of political service in a confusing and impersonal urban environment.

## The Mayor

The council-mayor form of municipal government, as was pointed out, is based on a separation of powers. In theory, executive power is centered in a mayor, who is supposedly a partner of the city council. In practice, however, the power of the mayor varies sharply among cities. In some places he may be a "strong" mayor, and serve as a full-fledged chief executive—sometimes with the help of a professional administrator or manager. Elsewhere, he may be a "weak" mayor and have less part in city government than a silent partner has in business. Whether a mayor is a leader or a figurehead depends on a number of factors.

Some clues to his role may be found in the way he is chosen and in the privileges and emoluments of his office. About 95 percent of the mayors in the council-mayor cities are directly elected by the people. Frequently they seek office under a party label, although, as we have seen, many local elections—superficially, at least—are nonpartisan.

Terms of office range from one year in some smaller cities, particularly in New England, to six years in the larger municipalities. In the nation's largest cities, such as Chicago, New York, and San Francisco, the term is four years. Most commonly, the terms range from two to four years. Salaries vary from \$11,000 to \$40,000 in the larger cities, and in the smaller cities from a nominal \$50 or less to about \$15,000. In many of the largest cities the mayors receive salaries greater than those received by the governor.

*Powers of Mayor.* More important evidence of the power of a mayor can be discovered if we look at four other kinds of clues: (1) his legislative powers; (2) his executive powers; (3) the public prestige of his office; and (4) his personal political skill in exercising leadership.

Most mayors serve as the presiding officer in the city council. About one third have a right to vote in council, although in the majority of cities they may do so only when there is a tie in the council. The veto power, recognized as an important key to an executive's strength, varies sharply. Some mayors may veto any act of the council; others may veto ordinances or selected measures; others may veto only budget items. More than one third of the mayors have no veto power of any kind. In Chicago, for example, the mayor is empowered to vote only in case of tie, but may veto all measures. In Los Angeles, the mayor may not vote at any time, but may veto all issues; while in Gary, Indiana, the mayor has no voting power and no veto power. All mayors in mayor-council governments, of course, have informal powers of legislative initiative which if exercised with acumen (party support on the council helps) can be of enormous significance.

More important to the mayor than his power to vote in the council or veto the council's work is his capacity to rule his own executive house. Like the state executive, municipal government has an abundance of elective officials who sometimes act more as enemies than as teammates. Generally, the list includes the following:

    Attorney or corporation counsel
    Assessor
    Auditor

Clerk or recorder
Comptroller
Treasurer
Police chief
Public works director

There are often many others. Sometimes these separately elected officials have more political power than the mayor. Some of them even have their own political machines. Frequently, they compete with each other and with the mayor for political control. Like the state governor, the mayor may have to spend much time picking daggers from his back, thrown by his so-called teammates.

*Fragmentation.* The problem is aggravated by the existence under state law or local ordinance of special boards, commissions, and districts handling particular municipal functions, or of semi-public citizen organizations which have assumed public responsibilities. Instead of placing responsibility for all municipal functions in the hands of single department heads, appointed by and responsible to the municipal executive, legislatures—often under substantial outside pressures—have cut the fabric of government into tiny pieces. Schools are handled by school districts or school boards, libraries by library boards, and museums by museum boards, public health by a board of health, sanitation by a special sanitary district, land use by zoning boards and planning commissions and so on. Some specialized units are completely independent of the general government, are financed not by the city's general revenues but by special taxes, and are administered with little relation to the rest of the city's government.

There are many reasons for this splintering or fragmentation of local government. Partly, it is the result of the people's impatience or disgust with some kinds of local politics—their belief that museums, libraries, schools, fire services, urban planning, and the like should be "taken out of politics" and placed in the hands of nonpolitical "specialists." Partly it is because the taxing power of most city governments is narrowly limited by state law, and in order to escape the straitjacket of a restrictive debt limit or tax ceiling, special incorporated districts or authorities are set up, with independent taxing or borrowing powers. Another reason for splintered municipal government is the rigidity of state constitutions and municipal charters which prevent many cities from reorganizing their governments without painful and protracted charter-revision campaigns. Another factor is the effort by certain organized groups to place responsibility for certain functions in the hands of small groups of "specialists" who may be more "accessible." It is easier for an economy-minded taxpayers' league, for example, to make its influence felt in a separate finance board than in the city council or the mayor's office, where contrary interests may also have access. Government by special agency often becomes government by special interest.

*"Weak-Mayor" Government.* Diffusion and irresponsibility exist in most forms of local government, but the problem is particularly acute in "weak-mayor" cities. A recent report revealed the ordeal of a mayor who was seeking to coordinate more than fourteen boards, commissions, departments, districts, and other agencies involved in the planning and execution of an ambitious slum-clearance project. He had to deal with the following:

> City Planning Commission
> City Land Clearance Commission
> City Housing Authority
> City Dwellings Association
> Community Conservation Board
> Department of Buildings
> Fire Department
> Health Department
> Housing and Redevelopment Coordinator
> Law Department
> Municipal Courts
> Neighborhood Redevelopment Commission
> Neighborhood Redevelopment Corporations

No one questions that there must be a considerable amount of specialization in the work of modern city government just as modern business must operate on the principle of division of labor. Furthermore, there is always the need for new approaches to problems. Diversity of administrative instruments can sometimes improve the quality of local government. Furthermore, healthy self-government needs the initiative, skill, and interest of the citizen.

The evils flow from the absence of leadership, from the lack of effective instruments to relate and coordinate conflicting or contradictory proposals and viewpoints, and from a confusion between the desirable goals of citizen advice and participation on the one hand, and political responsibility on the other. The planning commission, for example, may design a slum-clearance project with little concern for the problems of human relocation. The health department may develop proposals for improved apartment-house sanitary arrangements, with little attention to construction difficulties. Neighborhood redevelopment corporations may spend time and funds improving neighborhoods that the planning commission proposes be torn down to make room for an industrial plant. Somewhere these conflicts and contradictions must be resolved, and responsibility must be placed. A weak-mayor form of government is not designed to provide co-ordinated or responsible leadership.

Here are the distinguishing features of the weak-mayor form— granted variations from locality to locality:

1. Council appoints and dismisses administrative officials.

2. The mayor lacks power to supervise administrative operations or to formulate the budget.

3. There is councilmanic involvement in the administrative de-tails of departmental and agency activity.

4. There is an absence of effective machinery for building agree-ment within the city government as a whole and among the people of the community. These conditions not only violate principles of sound administration; they often defeat or obstruct the achievement of the broader values of the community.

Perhaps the only thing that can be said in favor of a weak-mayor form of government is that it pushes the mayor into the pursuit of consent.

*Pursuit of Consent.* But the pursuit of consent is a constant in all forms of local government. A strong mayor may be armed with full authority over municipal operations, over the personnel of city hall, over the city's budget, and, through the veto, over the city council, but unless he acts with restraint—unless he, too, pursues consent—

The general lines of responsibility and authority in the three basic types of American city government are suggested in this diagram. Charts like this can be misleading, however. Power, influence, and legal authority do not always coin-cide in government.

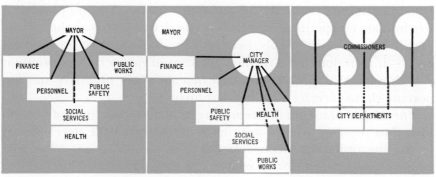

he may undermine the faith of his constituents and colleagues in democratic government and may find his formal power unusable.

*Politics and Ceremony.* The mayor, like the governor and the President of the United States at higher levels of government, must wear many hats. As chief executive, he serves as an administrator. As leader of a political party or a nonpartisan political organization or movement, he must take sides on controversial issues, and seek organized political support. He also serves as a local "chief of state"— attending church suppers, laying cornerstones, buying the first poppy on Veteran's Day, and performing the other ceremonial chores which dignify civic endeavors.

Many reformers have criticized combining management, politics, and ceremonial functions in the office of the mayor. They believe particularly that municipal government should be removed from partisan politics. There is, they claim, no Republican way of cleaning streets or Democratic way of fighting fires. They point to the bizarre examples of political bosses who at various times in our recent past have preyed upon the people: "Boss" Tweed of New York, "Big Bill" Thompson of Chicago, "Abe" Ruef of San Francisco, Thomas H. Pendergast of Kansas City, James M. Curley of Boston, and William S. Vare of Philadelphia.

Many municipal reformers have identified the mayor-council form of government and partisan politics as the root causes of bossism and corruption. They have campaigned for nonpartisan elections and a commission or council-manager form of government—often in the naive belief that municipal devils could be exorcised simply by the adoption of new institutional chants and charts. Sometimes devils actually have been rooted out by such campaigns—temporarily. But generally speaking the real evil has not been the form of government or the existence of competing parties; the evil has been the preoccupation, apathy, and self-righteousness of the "good" people who shunned partisan activities and municipal service and who failed to stimulate competition in one-party districts. Sometimes the "good" people stayed away simply because the council-mayor system was noisy—it is undoubtedly the noisiest form of municipal government —without realizing that noise and fuss are often necessary and important characteristics of self-government.

*The Mayor-Manager Concept.* The council-mayor form of government has recently taken a new lease on life with the development of the mayor-manager concept: the idea of having a professional administrator subordinate, not to the council, but to the mayor.

Cities like New York, Philadelphia, and New Haven, Connecticut, are experimenting with this device with considerable initial success. To its advocates, this form of municipal government combines the virtues of political leadership and responsibility of the council-mayor form of government with the virtues of administrative competence and professionalism of the council-manager form of government.

# THE COMMISSION FORM

Toward the end of the nineteenth century, dissatisfaction with municipal politics and administration led to many reform proposals. In 1900, as the reform movement picked up steam, a hurricane and tidal wave struck the city of Galveston, Texas. The existing city government was incapable of dealing with the emergency and lost the confidence of the people. The crisis provided an opportunity for the rise of a new form of city government—the commission plan.

What Galveston needed, the reformers believed, was a local government which might achieve the following: (1) more "business-like" operation; (2) centralization of all power and functions in the hands of a small group of men whom the public might hold unquestionably accountable; (3) encouragement of business and professional leaders of the community to serve in public office; and (4) the removal of government and public affairs from the hands of partisan politicians.

## Duties of Commissioners

The form of government which Galveston introduced and other cities refined and popularized is basically a repudiation of the principle of separation of powers. In brief, it consists of a popularly elected group of from three to seven commissioners who take the place of both the council and the mayor. All legislative and executive functions are combined in their hands. There is no separate chief executive. One member of the commission, either popularly elected or appointed by his fellow commissioners, serves as chairman, but exercises no greater power than the other commissioners. Each commissioner participates with the group in general policy-making, and at the same time is responsible for the operation of one or more municipal departments. Thus, one commissioner may be in charge of public finance and planning, another of streets and public works, another of public health and welfare, and so on. In theory, power is centralized in the hands of the commission, but in practice the administration of the city is completely diffused and divided, with no chief executive to put the pieces back together again.

By the 1920's, adoption of the plan reached its zenith, finding acceptance in almost 500 cities. It was most prevalent among small cities between 5,000 and 10,000 population, particularly in the Middle West. Baldwin, Pennsylvania; Benton, Illinois; Brookings, South Dakota; and Calexico, California, are present examples of commission cities of this size.

### Decline of Commission Plan Support

During the past few decades, however, the commission plan has declined in public support. Local business and professional men, serving for the first time as public officials with no prior training or preparation, were frequently inept in government affairs.

Furthermore, the processes of self-criticism and review tended to break down. Each commissioner, jealously guarding his own independent department, would take on a "live-and-let-live" attitude. In effect, commissioners would support each others' budget requests without question and would avoid criticism of each others' work. This was not the "businesslike" administration that had been promised.

Furthermore, the commission form of government did not always impede "bossism" and corruption. One-man political domination and party machines thrived in many commission cities, including "Boss" Frank Hague's Jersey City and "Boss" Crump's Memphis. These facts finally led to disillusionment with the commission plan.

Today, the form remains in less than 350 cities, located in several parts of the United States. St. Paul, Minnesota, Allentown, Pennsylvania, and Fresno, California are some of the more populous examples. The story of the commission plan demonstrates that there is no magic in any one form of city government.

## COUNCIL-MANAGER FORM

At the end of the nineteenth century, James Bryce, a penetrating English observer of America, wrote: "There is no denying that the government of cities is the one conspicuous failure of the United States." In the years that have intervened, the most significant innovation in city government has been the council-manager plan.

The plan was the outgrowth of several streams of reform. In 1908, Staunton, Virginia, unable to adopt the commission form because a state constitutional provision required the retention of a bicameral council, appointed a general manager of the city, with all administrative responsibility centered in his hands. A few years later, the South Carolina state legislature empowered the city of Sumter to establish a manager plan based on the ideas of Richard S. Childs, a man who has been called the "father of council-manager government."

Meanwhile, a group of reformers called the National Short Ballot Organization, headed by Woodrow Wilson, had been advocating the reduction of the number of elective officials in local government until they heard about the appointment of a manager in Staunton, Virginia. Wilson's organization then became an advocate of the council-manager plan.

Finally, in 1913 a flood in Dayton, Ohio, created a crisis in which the city fathers, in desperation, turned to the new experiment in local government. From these beginnings, the council-manager system has spread rapidly throughout the United States. Today, there are more than 1400 council-manager governments among all but the very largest cities. Almost half of the medium-sized cities (25,000 to 100,000 population) have adopted the plan.

## Principal Features

The principal features of the council-manager plan are: (1) unification of power; (2) separation of functions; and (3) professionalized administration. All power to decide policy questions is concentrated in the hands of a small council, generally consisting of from five to fifteen members, elected in most cases at large on a nonpartisan basis. The principle of separation of powers is ignored, but there is a separation of *functions*. That is, the Wilsonian distinction between "politics" and "administration" has become a hallmark of the council-manager plan. The theory of the system is as follows: a small council decides *what* the city will do, while a professional manager, appointed by and completely responsible to the council, simply carries out their policy decisions. Thus, there is no chief executive with policy-making power in his own right. There is only a chief administrator who is considered to be a technician rather than a politician.

There is usually a mayor, selected by the council from its own membership to serve as chairman, but usually he has no more power than other members. He presides over the council meetings, has a vote but no veto, and carries out the traditional ceremonial functions of the mayor, such as greeting prominent visitors, attending luncheons, or awarding diplomas to graduating school children.

One of the greatest contributions of the council-manager plan to the improvement of city government is the professionalization of municipal administration. That is, in place of the spoils system in many council-mayor governments, or the inexperience and incompetence of part-time administrators in the commission form, there is a full-time professional administrator, whose education and experience prepare him to handle the complex problems of the modern city.

## Status of City Manager

Under the leadership of the International City Managers' Association, the position of city manager has become a recognized profession. Managers receive specialized training in universities, they go through apprenticeships as assistants to city managers, they observe recognized standards of management operation, and they subscribe and contribute to professional journals, such as *American City, Public Management,* or the *National Municipal Review.* The International City Managers' Association has suggested the following professional code of ethics:

Loyalty to his employment recognizes that it is the council . . . who determine the municipal policies. . . .

Although he is a hired employee of the council, he is hired . . . to exercise his own judgment as an executive in accomplishing the policies formulated by the council, and to attain success in his employment he must decline to submit to dictation in matters for which the responsibility is solely his.

Power justifies responsibility, and responsibility demands power, and a city manager who becomes impotent to inspire support should resign.

The city manager is the administrator for all the people, and in performing his duty he should serve without discrimination.

To serve the people well, a city manager should strive to keep the community informed of the plans and purposes of the administration. . . .

A city manager should deal frankly with the council as a unit and not secretly with its individual members. . . .

No city manager should take an active part in politics.

## Relation between Manager and Council

In operation, the success of the system depends upon the relationship between the manager and the council. As chief administrator, the manager generally has complete control over all departments of the city government—police, fire, health, welfare, public works, and the rest. He hires and fires all administrative personnel, formulates the budget for council approval, and makes recommendations to the council with respect to basic policies. Interference by the council in the work of the manager may lead to his resignation, while efforts by the manager to resist or sabotage the council may lead to his dismissal. In the event of differences between council and manager over policy goals or administrative methods, the will of the council generally prevails.

The manager is especially forbidden to engage in political activity, but in practice he may emerge as an important community leader. His reputation as an impartial specialist in government and his skill in public relations may give him considerable support in the council and among the people of the city. The manager's threat to resign may even strengthen his hand in the council. He may not be a poli-

A modern city like New York, Chicago, or Los Angeles is something of a miracle: millions of people living and working together in terrifying proximity, and yet in reasonable harmony. The miracle, in large part, is a result of the protections and conveniences afforded by government.

The slum is to the city what cancer is to the human body. The war against the slum never ceases, for as one area is renewed, another area slips. But today the battle is at least joined.

tician in the usual partisan sense, but in advising and informing the council on policy questions, in mediating disputes between one city department and another, in promoting civic understanding, interest, and participation, the manager may become a politician in the larger sense. Carleton F. Sharpe of Hartford, Connecticut, L. P. Cookingham of Kansas City, Missouri, Sherwood Reeder of Richmond, Virginia, and other prominent city managers have demonstrated that in a successful council-manager system politics and administration need not—in fact, cannot—be divorced.

## Pros and Cons

But again, it must be pointed out that there are no miracles in any particular form of government. The council-manager system has raised the prestige of many city councils, has encouraged outstanding citizens to seek public office, has professionalized municipal administration, has attracted many promising young people to enter the city-manager profession, and has done much to raise the level of citizen interest and participation in their communities.

But this does not mean that the council-manager form is a miracle drug for diseases of the body politic. The strongest criticism of the system is its failure to establish an effective instrument for polit-

Here is the identical area shown on the opposite page—but after slum clearance. Through Federal Urban Renewal, and state, local, and private slum clearance projects, many of America's cities are being reborn.

ical leadership. The American people like to personalize their politics; they find it difficult to follow the lead of a congress, legislature, or council. Such collective bodies are poor substitutes for personal leadership. There must be someone to raise issues, dramatize them, and serve as a catalyst in securing action. If the council is divided, if the manager is restricted to a role of technician, then there is in effect no community leader. Some cities are in greater need of political leadership than others. Whether the council-manager form is appropriate depends on many political and social factors in the community: (1) the city's political history, (2) the nature and intensity of the city's problems, (3) the quality of its political parties, (4) the level of citizen interest and involvement in local government, and other factors.

The danger is that some citizens tend to see the council-manager plan as an automatic cure-all. They expect the system to run like a machine, failing to realize that good government demands political leadership as well as efficient management if the difficult issues of urban areas are to be solved.

## HOUSEKEEPING OR LEADERSHIP?

Underlying the failure of many experiments in local government has been a misunderstanding of what local governments are supposed to do. Local communities are too often treated simply as problems in administrative machinery. Like the human body, however, the local community is a living organism. It breathes, grows, and decays. It has hopes, fears and doubts. Its strength depends not only upon satisfactory functioning of the local economy, the government, and other institutions, but upon the character of the city's will and vision—upon community leadership. Technical questions of taxation, charter revision, police administration, personnel management, or partisan politics have little importance or meaning in themselves. They must be understood as part of the eternal struggle to make the local community a civilized environment for human life and freedom.

Housekeeping does not make a home. Good government is more than economy and efficiency. We can have all the latest IBM machines, all the best personnel systems, the best city charters and ordinances, the most efficient mayor or manager, and still not succeed in local government. Good local government is impossible unless we recognize goals, unless we know where we are going as a community. This is the task of political leadership. Certainly the greatest obligation of the leader, whether he is a moderator of a town meeting, a village trustee, a councilman, mayor, manager, or party politician, is vision—not just the anticipation of tomorrow but the creation of tomorrow.

It is not enough to want streets; we want streets lined with trees. It is not enough to have adequate schools; we want schools in which our children can get the best education possible. It is not enough to have sanitary jail cells; we want to avoid having to use them. It is not enough to contain our slums; we must destroy the slums and build new cities in their place.

Pittsburgh is a case in point—a city once described by Charles Dickens as "Hell with the lid off." The mayor, a leading banker, an industrial leader, a coal magnate, a prominent department-store owner, a labor leader, a newspaper editor, and others were brought together to plan one of the most comprehensive civic improvement programs in American history. The results of these efforts have been inspiring: industrial smoke has been almost completely eliminated, the central city has been transformed, civic pride has been reawakened, and the city's economy has been rejuvenated.

Formal instruments of government cannot solve all the problems of a great community. The task of leadership in local government is to identify all the possible resources—local, state, national, private, public—capable of being mobilized in a common struggle to build a more prosperous, more beautiful, and more humane local society.

The forms of local government, whether town, county, or city; whether council, mayor, or manager, are not ends in themselves. They are important and meaningful only as they help serve effectively the great purposes for which governments are instituted among men.

# CONCLUSION

### Synopsis

There are three basic forms of city government found in America —although the variations within these forms are almost infinite: the council-mayor system, the commission system, and the council-manager system. But no form of government can meet the strains of rapid social and economic transition without vigorous, creative, and courageous leadership, and without an informed, alert, and responsive public.

### Significance

The rise of vast urban areas has been accompanied by social, economic, and political problems which seem to defy man's capacity to govern himself. For more than half a century, Americans have sought to adapt inherited local instruments of government to the needs of a new age. The variety and ingenuity of these adaptations reflect the inventiveness of Americans; but they also reflect the capacity of the American people to create new problems faster than old ones can be solved.

### Prospectus

A discussion of American government in terms of levels, units, jurisdictions, institutions, or branches, tends to conceal the wholeness of our governmental system. The governments of our towns, townships, counties, villages, cities, states, and the nation itself are all interdependent strands of a single tapestry visible to each citizen in his local community. How these strands fit together is the subject of the following chapter.

# Intergovernmental
# Relations

IT SHOULD BE clear by now that each of us is a citizen of many governments—local, state, and national—which both serve and regulate us. We have, in other words, a variety of instruments at our disposal to help us fulfill our expectations of government.

It would be a serious mistake, however, to conclude that these many governments operate in separate, sealed compartments. A federal system is not "a pound cake or a layer cake," it is a marble cake. When the President and the Congress make policy in such fields as taxation, public health, education, or civil defense, there is not a state government or a local subdivision thereof in the nation which is not directly or indirectly affected. Similarly, the national government cannot help but be affected by many of the actions and activities of state and local governments.

These vertical interrelationships are further complicated by a series of lateral interrelationships. State legislatures and governors compete, conflict, cooperate, or collaborate with the legislatures and governors of other states in seeking to solve problems that cut across state boundaries. Furthermore, county commissioners, city councils, mayors, managers, village boards, and special districts, of necessity deal with each other in many of their daily operations.

It is the purpose of this chapter to examine some of these intergovernmental relations.

## THE NUMBERLESS PROBLEMS OF FEDERALISM

In creating a federal system, involving a constitutional division of power between two or more levels of government within a single area, the Founding Fathers established a form of government rich with the seeds of instability and complexity. Alexis de Tocqueville, for example, writing on democracy in America a century ago, declared: "I have never been more struck by the good sense and practical judgment of the Americans than in the manner in which they elude the numberless difficulties resulting from their Federal Constitution. . . ." It is through the web of intergovernmental relations that many of these difficulties are created, eluded, or solved.

Many difficulties are due to the lack of correspondence between the existing boundaries of state and local governments and the problems they are called upon to solve. That is, the jurisdiction of state, county, or city extends only to its legal boundaries, yet such problems as law enforcement, air and water pollution, or public health spread across legal lines, making it necessary for governments to cooperate in finding solutions, or to create special districts whose boundaries are coterminous with those of the problems requiring solutions.

### Origin of Existing Boundaries

Existing boundaries of state and local governments generally are not the result of rational design. Rather, they are the consequences of historical accident. Many state boundaries, for example, were inherited from colonial days, while others were determined by acts of Congress, compromises between states, or court orders. Similarly, boundaries of counties, cities, towns, townships, and villages have more frequently been determined by the computations of the surveyor than the nature or scope of the job at hand. At one time, for example, a village or town could satisfy its water needs at the pump in the public square, but as great cities have arisen, the capacity of local governments to provide for their water needs has declined. Today, water for some of the great metropolises of America must be brought from many miles away, and sometimes from reservoirs across state lines. Similarly, before the automobile, maintenance of roads was easily handled by counties and townships. Today, no local government can possibly satisfy its road and highway needs without state and federal assistance.

### Growth of Public Problems

As public problems have grown, it has been necessary for small governments to collaborate and for larger units of government to

**"Rest Assured That If We Find One Polio Germ Crossing A State Line—"**

assume greater responsibilities. Problems of industrial development, flood control, soil conservation, or crime and law enforcement defy the power and resources of individual state governments. The needs of public education, urban transportation, public health, and prevention of air and water pollution have outraced the capacity of local government to cope with them. Traffic congestion, urban blight, smog, and polio germs disregard municipal boundaries just as grasshoppers, flood-swollen rivers, and economic depressions ignore state lines.

The deceptively simple three-level compartmentalized approach to federal-state-local relations in government has been rendered obsolete by the automobile, rapid transit system, airplane, telephone, smog, suburb, and other features of modern life. Federal, state, and local governments have discovered that none of them can "go it alone."

## Proposals for Reform

In seeking to solve the numberless problems of federalism, extreme proposals have been made: abolition of the states, division of the United States into natural regions with separate governments, constitutional amendments which would permit the Federal government to assume the responsibilities of state and local governments, and measures which would seek to reduce the size of the Federal government and pour it back into its earlier mold.

In reality, these proposals ignore an important political fact of life: the states and the Federal government are with us and we must learn to live with them. If we are to solve our problems without upsetting the delicate balance of our system, techniques must be found which do not ignore the political and administrative facts of life. Such extreme proposals as those above are not realistic alternatives.

## Direct Federal Action

One attempted solution has been the expansion of direct federal action in the states and localities of the nation. Through exploitation of its various constitutional powers, the government in Washington, D. C., has directly administered programs through the federal administrative system, with lines of action extending from the nation's capital to the individual citizen. In agriculture, for example, the Department of Agriculture has set up agencies which work directly with the individual farmers of the nation. Programs in soil conservation, rural electrification, farm credit, and rural rehabilitation are illustrative.

While intergovernmental cooperation has been welcome in these direct action programs, they have been primarily national in character, with state and local governments on the sidelines.

Many of these programs have been controversial, of course, and their direct-action character has generated additional fear and opposition because they were administered directly by the national government rather than through intergovermental channels. While some of these programs have accomplished, and will continue to accomplish, their goals, it is doubtful that direct national action is a panacea for all our federal ills. Centralized control in a large, diverse, democratic society has dangers and administrative hazards which should not be ignored.

## Cooperative Federalism

A far more successful solution has been the development of effective cooperation among federal, state, and local governments. This arrangement has produced beneficial results for all without destroying the constitutional system. Variously called cooperative federalism, the new federalism, or functional federalism, this approach has emphasized not the division and conflict between levels of government, but rather the opportunities for cooperation among them.

A sense of common purpose has been developing among specialized governmental employees at all levels. For example, experts in public health, education, highway improvement, law enforcement, crime prevention, employment security, and soil and water conservation at federal, state, and local levels are learning to work together, despite the jurisdictional boundaries which legally divide them. They have, for many years, been building a sense of professional unity which bridges some of the gaps between governments, through the widespread use of such devices as grants-in-aid, the cooperative use of technical personnel, interstate compacts, the dovetailing of legislation making federal laws contingent on state participation, and the promotion of model state statutes.

## Grant-in-Aid Programs

The federal grant-in-aid program has been particularly significant. Briefly, a "grant-in-aid" is a fiscal device through which state and local governments receive federal funds for the support of some particular program. Sometimes they are "matching grants" in which the state or local governments contribute a matching amount to supplement the federal contribution. Grants-in-aid have been particularly useful in a wide variety of intergovernmental programs:

Airport construction and operation
Civil defense
Disaster assistance
Highway improvement

Public schools
Public health
Public housing
Public welfare
Tax relief in areas burdened by federal activity
Vocational training and rehabilitation

Today, federal grants constitute nearly 20 percent of all state revenues, and local governments received over a quarter of their revenues from state payments. Similarly, a third of all federal payments received by the states go to local governments. States, in other words, serve as the instruments through which some of the federal funds are transferred to local governments.

## Earmarked Funds

The practice in many states of "earmarking" funds for particular use, through administration of federal grants-in-aid and other devices, raises a serious problem for many governors who find the flexibility of their budgets has been destroyed. Special districts with their own exclusive tax bases also earmark funds for special projects and complicate intelligent budget procedure. These dedicated funds also tie the hands of local governments by denying them control over a large part of their annual revenue. Many state and local governments today have control over no more than 20 or 25 percent of their annual revenue, due largely to the necessity of matching federal grants-in-aid to specific programs, and also to the practice under many state constitutions of providing that certain taxes, such as those on gasoline and motor vehicles, be used only for highways. Similarly, state constitutions frequently provide that revenues derived from hunting and fishing licenses be spent only in conservation of fish and wildlife. There are many other examples.

Although policy controversies and many administrative difficulties remain, the system of federal grants-in-aid has generally helped state and local governments solve their fiscal problems without upsetting the delicate balance of federalism.

## Law-Enforcement Cooperation

In the area of law enforcement, federal-state-local cooperation has reached a high level of effectiveness. Congress, for example, has enacted many measures under its commerce and postal powers which provide federal penalties and punishment for offenses committed primarily against the states. Kidnapping, gambling, stealing

**Federal Financial Assistance to the States in 1955**

| | |
|---|---:|
| Public Welfare | $1,428,000,000 |
| Highways | 592,000,000 |
| Education | 299,000,000 |
| Employment Security Administrations | 208,000,000 |
| Health and Hospitals | 80,000,000 |
| Other | 154,000,000 |
| | |
| Total | $2,762,000,000 |

*Source:* United States Department of Commerce, Bureau of the Census, *State Government Finances in 1955* (Washington, D. C.: Government Printing Office, 1956, p. 6.)

automobiles, and drug peddling, for example, are some of the crimes which federal, state, and local police officers cooperate to solve. The Federal Bureau of Investigation, the Bureau of Narcotics, the Post Office Department's inspectors, the Secret Service, and the Immigration and Naturalization Service are some of the federal agencies that cooperate with state and local law-enforcement and crime-prevention officials.

Where many people are involved in joint endeavor, however, there is always danger that cooperation may deteriorate into confusion, that "many cooks may spoil the broth." In more than one case of murder or kidnapping in recent years, faulty coordination has defeated the advantages of cooperative federalism. The need for improvement remains.

# STATES' RIGHTS OR NATIONAL SUPREMACY?

Extension of federal action, through cooperation and direct action, may have solved many of the pressing problems of the day, but as students and citizens we should be concerned also with the underlying dispute which continues to punctuate discussion of intergovernmental relations.

## The States' Rights Argument

On the one hand are those who are more concerned with the dangers of governmental power than with its necessities. These are the people who belong to what William Anderson has called the "bring-government-back-home" school of thought. People of this temperament or persuasion tend to believe that government is a necessary evil, that centralization of power in the Federal government is automatically dangerous, that state governments should serve as brakes in the federal system. Government, they believe, should be rendered "safe and sound" by dividing power and authority into little pieces, and by surrounding the pieces with checks and balances.

This approach, which has deep Jeffersonian roots, tends to view the powers of the national government as particularly dangerous—to be used like a strong medicine only in emergencies when all other instruments or palliatives have failed.

Inherent in this argument, of course, is the assumption that smaller units of government, located closer to the people, are automatically more democratic, more efficient, and more clearly approved by the people. The Commission on Intergovernmental Relations reflected this position in 1955 when it declared:

. . . The local governments are in many instances the best governments for direct administration of programs affecting the daily lives of people. They are at "home base" where nonuniformities and special needs can best be weighed and understood.[1]

## The National Supremacy Argument

A contrary argument is advanced by those who believe in the doctrine of national supremacy rather than states' rights. They see the United States Constitution as a flexible blueprint of government rather than a strait jacket, and they believe that the national government may expand without doing so at the expense of state and local governments. They maintain that the growth of the Federal government has resulted from the failure of state and local governments to meet the people's needs. Unable to secure what they demanded from city halls and state capitals, the people turned to Washington, D. C.

According to this argument, the real dangers to society lie not in the Federal government's expansion, but rather in federal hesitation and inaction. Viewing with some alarm the problems of our times, they see no inherent dangers in national action so long as an alert public and press and a healthy two-party system are maintained. Many who subscribe to the doctrine of national supremacy believe that the problems of resource conservation, economic stability, education, and social welfare are too large and complicated to be handled adequately in town meetings, city councils, county commissions, or state capitals. The alternative to federal action, they believe, is inaction and chaos.

## Conflicts and Disputes

The conflicts and disputes of federalism tend to be fought out largely in terms of theories of government, but in reality most of the disagreements are over concrete interests. Desegregation of the schools in the South, for example, often appears to be a dispute over interpretation of the Constitution, but it is obviously more than that. Regional planning or the control of the nation's rivers have been discussed and debated in abstract terms, but as William E. Leuchtenberg has revealed, more is involved than political theory.

The main problem in developing a river valley is the resolution of conflicts between different water users. Shall farm land be flooded to permit the generation of power? Shall a reservoir be used for power or recreation? Shall a river be used as a sewer for industrial wastes or for fishing and swimming? [2]

*Pragmatic Solutions.* The common thread in American intergovernmental relations has been experience rather than logic, pragmatism rather than ideology. The record of the past 50 years reveals that whenever the majority of the articulate and politically effective people of any state or locality believe that they can best achieve their ends through Washington, D. C., they will seek to do so, regardless of their philosophic ideals. The history of "pork-barrel legislation" in Congress is illustrative.

In previous sections of this book, it has been argued that good government depends not only on the availability of administrative and political tools, and the skill in using them, but also on the *will* to use them. This argument is relevant here. It is an oversimplification to place all blame for the difficulties of federalism at the door of the United States Constitution. The existing legal and administrative arsenal is rich with tools for solving the problems. To some extent, they need only be tried.

The fault also lies with weaknesses in state and local government. Outworn state constitutions still look backward instead of ahead. Many state and local governments are still unable or unwilling to finance necessary programs. Men of competence are not attracted to state and local government in numbers proportional to the need. Many state and local governments seek to escape their responsibilities by turning to Washington, D. C., for easy solutions. The health of the federal-state relationship depends basically upon the health of state and local governments throughout the nation.

# INTERSTATE RELATIONS

The men who wrote the Constitution in Philadelphia fully realized that disputes between state governments would inevitably arise. They provided for the settlement of such disagreements by spelling out a pattern of interstate rights and obligations.

### Constitutional Framework

Article III, Section 2, for example, provides that the judicial power of the United States "shall extend . . . to controversies between two or more States; between a State and citizen of another State. . . . In all cases . . . in which a State shall be a party, the Supreme Court shall have original jurisdiction." As altered by the Eleventh Amendment in 1798, the Constitution provides that a state cannot be sued without its consent by a citizen of another state, by one of its own citizens, or by a citizen of any foreign power, but it can be sued by another state. The important point here is that a variety of disputes between states are subjected to the regular judicial process of the Federal government. So far the Supreme Court has rendered decisions in over 50 disputes between the states, involving such issues as interstate boundaries, the use of common bodies of water, construction of dams and power plants, and the payment of state debts.

The Founding Fathers also anticipated the rise of interstate conflicts when they wrote Article IV. The "full faith and credit" clause, for example, requires that each state accept or honor another state's laws, charters, deeds, judicial decisions, and court records. The "privileges and immunities" clause forbids unjust and arbitrary discrimination by the states against citizens of other states to the advantage of their own citizens. Similarly, the "interstate rendition" clause provides that fugitives from justice, found in another state, shall, on demand, be turned over to their own state for trial.

In writing these provisions, the authors of the Constitution were obviously not thinking about the problems of superhighways, interstate crime syndicates, regional valley authorities, or problems of racial desegregation, but they did create a legal framework within which these larger issues might be resolved.

## Modern Complexities

Complexities of modern life increase the opportunities for interstate competition and conflict. For instance, neighboring Arizona and California have been in conflict over use of scarce water and over construction of dams and power plants on the Colorado River. Southern state governments seek to attract the textile industry away from New England. Problems of reciprocity between the states in recognition of divorces, licensing of automobile drivers, enforcement of highway rules, regulation of business, and licensing of professions and trades emphasize the importance of interstate relations.

Over the years the states have learned to live together in considerable harmony. As Herman Finer has observed: "The Nation and the states are crisscrossed with lines of agreement and collaborative authority, designed to lave together what a Constitution has put asunder." [3]

## Interstate Compacts

An important—if tortuous—device is the interstate compact, provided for in the form of a prohibition in the federal Constitution (Article I, Section 10): "No State shall, without the Consent of Congress . . . enter into any Agreement or Compact with another State. . . ." An interstate compact is an agreement, approved by Congress, between two or more state governments. Over 50 compacts have been authorized by Congress and made effective through state ratification. They deal with a variety of interstate and regional problems: boundary disputes, conservation of natural resources, crime detection, establishment of regional educational institutions, flood control, and transportation. They often take years to negotiate. Some examples of interstate compacts are the following:

1. *Interstate Compact on Juveniles:* an agreement reached in 1955 and so far ratified by eleven states, providing for interstate cooperation in a broad area affecting juveniles.

2. *New England Pollution Compact:* an agreement among Connecticut, Massachusetts, and Rhode Island for control of pollution of interstate waters.

3. *New York Port Authority:* a compact between New York and New Jersey, providing for the planning and coordination of port and related facilities in the nation's leading harbor.

4. *Pacific Marine Fisheries Compact:* an agreement among California, Oregon, and Washington, setting up the Pacific Marine Fisheries Commission for the purpose of coordinating research and management of marine fisheries.

5. *Probation and Parole Compact:* an agreement among the forty-eight states for interstate supervision of exconvicts who have been paroled or placed on probation.

6. *Southern Regional Education Compact:* an agreement among fifteen southern and border states, dedicated to the promotion of higher learning and professional training in the educational institutions of the South.

7. *Western Interstate Compact for Higher Education:* an agreement among Arizona, Colorado, Idaho, Montana, New Mexico, Oregon, Utah, and Wyoming, designed to encourage efficient use of existing graduate, technical, and professional facilities in the West.

### Informal Agreements

In addition to the use of the interstate compact, considerable cooperation is achieved through more informal practices. Many state governors, for example, engage in agreements with neighboring governors, without the cumbersome legal requirements of an interstate compact. Governors of the same political party use the channels of communication and consultation within the Democratic and Republican party organizations for purposes of interstate agreement and collaboration. Correspondence, telephone calls, conferences, and meetings among governors, among state legislators, or among the heads of related state executive departments and agencies provide many opportunities to develop unity across state lines.

### Uniform State Laws

In order to escape the difficulties caused by diversity in state legislation on issues calling for uniformity, efforts have been made in

When Kansas completes a highway before Oklahoma can connect with it, the Kansas road ends at the state line in a cornfield. This is a dramatic indication of the necessity of interstate cooperation.

recent years to promote uniform state laws. Many states discourage divorces by making it difficult to secure such a legal action, while the state of Nevada, seeking to attract the nation's divorce business, simplifies divorce proceedings. Other states discriminate against the products of neighboring states by constructing trade barriers against them. Some years ago, for example, Florida sought to protect its own cement industry by requiring inspection and the payment of a charge on all cement from other states. Similarly, dairy states and poultry states seek to protect their own farmers from interstate competition by enforcing restrictive inspection standards. To discourage such practices, the National Conference of Commissioners on Uniform State Laws was established in 1892 by members of the American Bar Association. It is composed of commissioners appointed by the governors of the states, and promotes interstate cooperation by drafting and promoting model state laws in a number of important fields of state affairs. With no powers of enforcement, and forced to cope with deep-seated conflicts of interests between states, the Commission's progress has been disappointing. Most of the proposed laws have been largely ignored by state legislatures.

## Council of State Governments

Another semi-official agency dedicated to interstate cooperation is the Council of State Governments, established in 1925 and financed by contributions from state governments. It serves as the secretariat for the following professional organizations whose memberships are largely composed of state officials:

American Legislators Association
Governors Conference
Conference of Chief Justices
National Association of Attorneys General
National Association of Secretaries of State
National Association of State Budget Officers
Legislative Service Conference
National Association of State Purchasing Officers
Association of Administrators of the Interstate Compact for the
    Supervision of Parolees and Probationers
National Conference of Commissioners on Uniform State Laws

With a national headquarters in Chicago and regional offices in New York, San Francisco, and Washington, D. C., the Council seeks to serve as a clearing-house for information and research, and as an agent for the promotion of interstate cooperation. The Council also publishes a monthly magazine, *State Government,* devoted to the exchange of information about state and intergovernmental problems.

# STATE-LOCAL RELATIONS

The health of American government depends heavily upon the performance of the state-local partnership. In some states, where the federal principle of shared powers and responsibilities has been incorporated into the state constitution, and where local governments are permitted to control their own affairs, state-local relationships have been described as "little federalism." While some state constitutions do distribute power among state and local governments in a manner similar to the federal system of the national government, the analogy is not entirely sound. Legally, local governments are not the full partners of the states in the sense that the states are the constitutional partners of the national government.

### State Control of Local Government

Local governments are not sovereign units of government. Legally, they are the children of the state, the administrative and political agents through which many state functions are carried out. Cities, towns, and most villages, for example, are municipal corporations, created by act of the state legislature. Their organizational structure, powers, and functions are largely determined by the legislature. Furthermore, the legislature and the state executive exercise a large measure of supervision over their operations. Similarly, county governments, while not considered to be municipal corporations, are also created and controlled by the state.

## The "Dillon Rule"

The legal position of local governments has generally followed the picture described by the so-called Dillon Rule, a court decision handed down in 1868 by Judge J. F. Dillon, an eminent member of the state court of Iowa, and later sustained by the United States Supreme Court:

Municipal corporations owe their origin to, and derive their powers and rights wholly from the legislature. It breathes into them the breath of life, without which they cannot exist. As it creates, so it may destroy. If it may destroy, it may abridge and control. Unless there is some constitutional limitation on the right, the legislature might, by a single act, if we can suppose it capable of so great a folly and so great a wrong, sweep from existence all the municipal corporations in the State, and the corporation could not prevent it.[4]

In practice, however, state governments today do not treat their local subdivisions entirely as unwanted stepchildren. Rather, a form of "cooperative federalism," similar to that described at the federal-state level, has developed, as state and local governments have learned to cooperate and collaborate with each other.

## Local Fiscal Problems

Fiscal administration is such an area. Most local governments are faced with rising demands by their people for new and expensive municipal services. State governments, encouraged by the Federal government, have contributed to the pressure by inducing local governments to expand socially desirable functions. Most local governments, however, are unable to finance these new activities, let alone support the older traditional ones.

The property tax, long the major source of local revenue, yields an inadequate return, and it is extremely difficult and costly to collect. Furthermore, most states enforce restrictions on the *purposes* for which local governments might spend money, on the *sources* from which they can collect taxes, on the *methods* of levying taxes, and on the total *amount* of taxes which may be collected. In many areas, local communities have reached the saturation point on property taxes, but are restrained by state laws from tapping other sources of revenue.

## State Assistance

Unable to solve their fiscal dilemmas, local governments must depend on state assistance. In the state of New York, for example, 52 percent of the 1956–1957 state budget goes to direct state aid to localities. During the past few years, intergovernmental expenditures have accounted for over 45 percent of the total state expenditure in California, over 35 percent in Michigan, and over 28 percent in Texas. Among the states generally during recent years, about one third of the budgets represent intergovernmental assistance. All across the nation, the cities, towns, and villages have become dependent upon state aid.

The great bulk of state fiscal aid to local governments is for the local public schools and for public welfare programs. In the state of New York, 75 percent of the intergovernmental assistance in the 1956–1957 budget is for the schools.

## The Shared-Tax Plan

One particular form of state-local fiscal assistance is the shared-tax plan. The state levies taxes and then shares a portion of the proceeds with local governments. For example, many states levy a tax on gasoline and earmark a portion of the revenue for cities, towns, and counties, specifying that it must be used for streets, roads, and highways. The principal state-administered, locally shared taxes are on gasoline, motor vehicles, alcoholic beverages, income, sales, and business. About one third of the states use the gasoline tax. There are a variety of standards by which the revenues are allocated among local governments. The criteria include such factors as the physical size of the area, the number of miles of highway, the size of the population, the number of motor car registrations, and the assessed valuation of property in the community.

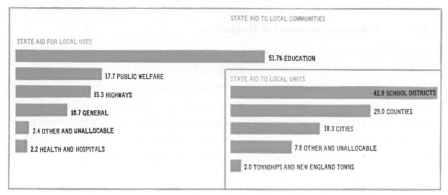

Just as the federal government gives grants-in-aid to the states, so the states pass part of their receipts along to local governments. Note once again the dominant places of education, welfare, and highways.

There are several difficulties involved in the shared-tax plan, however. For one thing, long-range local planning is made difficult, because the shared-tax revenues fluctuate according to changing economic conditions. Also, of greater importance, the earmarking of shared taxes for particular purposes tends to tie the hands of the state government as well as local officials. The plan also fails to distinguish adequately between the needs of one local government and another. Finally, as we have seen earlier, the allocation of the revenue is often determined by rural-dominated legislatures which tend to discriminate against urban communities.

## Grants-in-Aid

A somewhat more effective device has been the grant-in-aid, representing about three fourths of state fiscal assistance to local communities. Included in state grant-in-aid programs is the transfer function whereby national funds are transferred to local governments. The bulk of the grants go to the local public schools. Other major recipients of state assistance are public welfare programs and highway improvement.

## Other Forms of State Aid

In the past several years many state legislatures have relieved local governments by raising the ceiling on their permissible indebtedness. This has been done particularly in Georgia, Maine, Mississippi, Oklahoma, South Dakota, and Wyoming. Since World War II, twenty-four states have expanded the taxing powers of their local governments. State legislatures in Illinois and Mississippi have permitted sales taxes to be extended to all municipalities in those states, while

California has empowered all its counties to levy sales and use taxes. In other states, local governments have exercised their expanded taxing powers by adopting taxes on retail sales, admissions, income, alcoholic beverages, tobacco, gasoline, motor vehicles, private utilities, business licenses, hotel room rentals, and other activities and services. The property tax remains in use, although local governments are not so completely dependent upon it for their revenues.

### State Technical Assistance

While helping local governments financially, the states also provide technical assistance, such as information, advice, personnel services, and the use of state facilities. State departments of welfare, for example, assist their local counterparts in the administration of welfare programs. State departments of police help train local sheriffs and police officials in crime detection techniques. State departments of education assist local communities in teacher-training and recruitment programs, school construction plans, and curriculum design. State health officers assist their local counterparts in combating epidemics or outbreaks of contagious diseases.

### State Supervision

Some state activity is supervisory in character. Through the use of reports and inspections, for example, the states may require their local subdivisions to comply with certain standards of performance. Local health officials, police officers, school administrators, or welfare officials accept state help and in return are subjected to state supervision. Sometimes, in seeking to enforce local conformity, the states resort to compulsory methods. In Phenix City, Alabama, where the top municipal officials had failed to enforce the law, they were removed from office by order of the governor. In extreme cases, most states may suspend local self-government altogether.

### Effect of Party Politics

State-local intergovernmental relations are directly affected by party politics in the state. The governor whose political strength depends on the friendship of local officials in a particular community may hesitate to remove a recalcitrant local prosecutor or health officer who may be a hero to his community. Similarly, a governor may employ his supervisory powers to embarrass the opposition party in a local community. For example, a recent raid on gambling dens in Cook County, Illinois, by officers of the state police force was described by the local Democratic county sheriff as an attempt by the Republican governor to embarrass the local Democratic administration. Furthermore, the administration of shared taxes and grants-in-aid may reflect the domination of many state legislatures by rural Republicans. Many New England rural towns, for example, are favored by better schools and roads than their city cousins. The close relationship between politics and administration is evident in many aspects of state-local relations.

### Home Rule or State Rule?

Underlying these state-local relations is a dispute which resembles that between the states'-rights and national-supremacy arguments in federal-state relations. It is based on the contradiction between the legal subordination of most local governments to state authority, and the principle of local self-government. That is, in a country in which we subscribe to the principle of local self-government we also accept the practice of tight state supervision over local authorities.

The concern of local governments to operate unhampered by rigid and detailed constitutional and legislative restrictions has resulted in the "home-rule" movement. As its name implies, this movement is dedicated to the promotion of the right of local communities to frame, adopt, and change their own municipal charters by local action, and to enact their own local laws, providing only that they do not conflict with state laws. Since its beginning in Missouri in 1875, the movement has spread to more than half the states. Approximately twenty-nine states are recognized as having granted a large measure of freedom to their municipalities.

*The Case for Home Rule.* On the side of the home-rule movement are those who insist that the state legislature is not competent to exercise control over local community affairs. Government, they argue, should be kept close to home. Cities suffer at the hands of rural-dominated legislatures which do not understand urban problems or sympathize with city people. Purely local issues, such as the housekeeping functions of personnel management, should be determined by the local community. State legislatures are already burdened by state responsibilities and should not spend time and energy doing the things which county boards, city councils, or village boards could do. It is incongruous, they believe, for state legislatures to rule on such purely local issues as the salary of a town clerk, the promotion of a policeman, the construction of a new city hall, or the establishment of a parking authority. The proponents of greater home rule point to such cases as that of a town in North Carolina where local officials, in order to declare it a misdemeanor to use roller skates, bicycles, and scooters on the sidewalks, were required to go to the state legislature to secure a special statute authorizing such an ordinance.

*The Case for State Rule.* On the other hand, there is the contrary argument that most, if not all, municipal functions have an impact upon the whole state. The great problems of modern cities spread across municipal and county boundaries and can be handled adequately only by the states. Since the health and welfare of the whole state depends greatly on the condition of local communities, it would be dangerous, the argument holds, to allow counties, cities, towns, and villages to try to "go it alone." It would be unwise to permit them to spend themselves into bankruptcy; therefore, a debt limit must be imposed. It would be a mistake to allow a city or town to use a river for a sewer and thus jeopardize the interests and welfare of a neighboring community. It would be an error to permit a local community whose government has been captured by organized crime to decide for itself how much police protection it should have. Local governments are and should be the children of the state; they need the steadying hand of state guidance and supervision.

*The Middle Ground.* Like the dispute between states' rights and national supremacy, a realistic solution to the argument seems to lie in the middle ground. In the United States there has been a long-standing distinction between the strictly local services or functions of government and those generally regarded as nonlocal. The theory has been that a service or function which affects or benefits one geographic area should be paid for and controlled by the people of that area. Those which affect or benefit the people of the entire state should be considered statewide in character and should be financed and controlled by the people of the state, through the legislature and the executive. Similarly, services or functions which affect the whole nation should be considered national in character, and financed and controlled by the national government.

## Local-State Cooperation

However, such a distinction was more useful in the simpler days of the last century than today. As a consequence of modern life, the area of benefit and impact has been enlarged so greatly that the above distinction becomes somewhat meaningless. The education of the children of a particular community affects not only the people of that community, but the people of the state and nation. Should the local community be forced to pay the bill by itself? Similarly, the problem of smog in the city of Los Angeles is created by the lack of effective smoke-abatement practices in the Los Angeles metropolitan area, embracing many communities inhabited by over four million people. Should the taxpayers of the city of Los Angeles bear the whole burden for a solution? The streets and highways of every city and town in America are pounded by the automobile and truck tires of people living outside the municipal boundaries. Whose is the responsibility for street and highway maintenance? A new superhighway running the length of Alabama is as important to Chicagoans traveling to Florida as it is to most of the Alabamans who remain at home. Whose problem is it? Civil Defense for Detroit has a direct bearing on American national security. Is it entirely the responsibility of the people of Detroit?

Public education, water and air pollution, streets and highways, and civil defense are only a few of the issues that demonstrate the changing character of governmental problems. In all these, federal, state, and local governments have discovered that none of them can "go it alone."

It is indeed questionable whether such supposedly local matters as fire protection, highway improvement, crime detection and apprehension, traffic control, health and sanitation, slum clearance, or water and air pollution can be left entirely to municipal govern-

---

There may be those who think that what is happening to America in the metropolitan areas is an unmitigated calamity. But this is not a calamity, it is a challenge, the response to which will carry us to new levels of effective democratic life.

—Luther Gulick

ments. All of them affect a part or all of the state and may be solved, not by the local community alone, not by the state alone, but by cooperation between them.

In equating home rule with self-government, however, it has been forgotten that self-government is not an absolute principle. The states, we have already noted, cannot disengage themselves from the nation of which they are a part. Neither can the local community set itself apart from state and nation. Home rule is a relative concept.

# INTER-LOCAL RELATIONS: THE METROPOLITAN PROBLEM

The intergovernmental relations which affect the citizen's daily life most directly and intimately are those that occur within the local community. The child in the public school, the commuter on his way to work, the mother on her way to the suburban shopping center, the mailman on his rounds, the farmer on his way to the regional market—all are affected by a bewilderingly complex maze of local governments. While the tasks of government grow, the powers of local government seem to divide and redivide into smaller and smaller units of government: counties, towns, townships, cities, villages, boroughs, parking authorities, traffic authorities, airport authorities, slum clearance authorities, fire commissions, sewerage commissions, crime commissions, planning commissions, soil conservation districts, school districts, health boards, library boards, hospital boards, museum boards, cemetery boards, public works boards, and housing agencies. The relations among the many different local units of government have important administrative and political consequences which will be examined here.

## Problems of Urbanization

Within the memory of many men and women today, the majority of Americans were living on farms and in simple rural communities. Today, over 65 percent of our people live not only in cities, but in large urbanized metropolitan areas, composed generally of a large "core" city surrounded by many fringe or suburban communities.

About one fourth of all Americans today live in the twelve largest of these metropolitan areas. Thus, the problems of interlocal governmental relations in the United States are primarily urban problems. It should be pointed out, however, that the boundaries between urban and rural communities are hazy, and during past years cities have been growing outward into rural areas, so that today many people on farms and in rural towns feel the impact of city life and city problems.

The tide of urbanization has converted many of our cities into giant urban empires. In New York City alone, for example, there are over:

12,000 miles of power cables
4,000,000 miles of telephone wire
     25 miles of pneumatic tubes to carry the mail at more than 30 miles per hour
 1,200 miles of gas mains
   775 miles of water mains and tunnels to supply over 400 million gallons of water to the city daily
   560 miles of sewers to carry away the used water and refuse
    60 miles of subways

## Population Growth of the Nation's Largest Cities

| City | 1900 | 1950 |
|---|---|---|
| New York, N. Y. | 3,437,202 | 7,891,957 |
| Chicago, Illinois | 1,698,575 | 3,620,962 |
| Philadelphia, Pa. | 1,293,697 | 2,071,605 |
| Los Angeles, Cal. | 102,479 | 1,970,358 |
| Detroit, Michigan | 285,704 | 1,849,568 |
| Baltimore, Maryland | 508,957 | 949,708 |
| Cleveland, Ohio | 381,768 | 914,808 |
| St. Louis, Missouri | 575,238 | 856,796 |
| Washington, D. C. | 278,718 | 802,178 |
| Boston, Massachusetts | 560,892 | 801,444 |
| San Francisco, Cal. | 342,782 | 775,357 |
| Pittsburgh, Pa. | 451,512 | 676,806 |
| Milwaukee, Wisconsin | 285,315 | 637,392 |
| Houston, Texas | 44,633 | 596,163 |
| Buffalo, New York | 352,387 | 580,132 |
| New Orleans, La. | 287,104 | 570,445 |
| Minneapolis, Minn. | 202,718 | 521,718 |
| Cincinnati, Ohio | 325,902 | 503,998 |
| Seattle, Washington | 80,671 | 467,591 |
| Kansas City, Mo. | 163,752 | 456,622 |

## Population Growth in Selected American Cities, 1940–1950

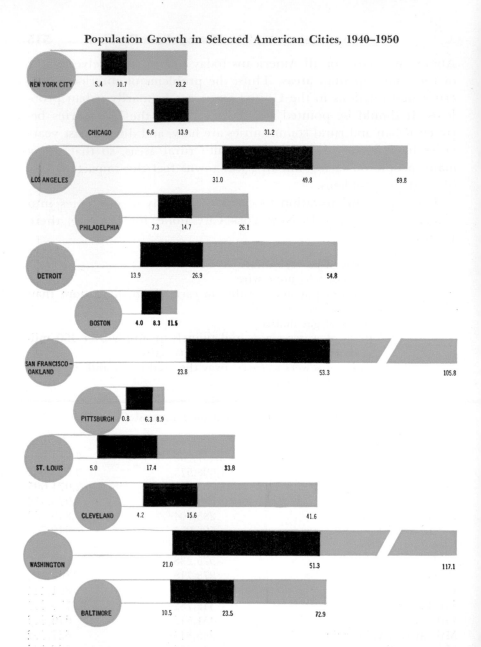

| | | | |
|---|---|---|---|
| NEW YORK CITY | 5.4 | 10.7 | 23.2 |
| CHICAGO | 6.6 | 13.9 | 31.2 |
| LOS ANGELES | 31.0 | 49.8 | 69.8 |
| PHILADELPHIA | 7.3 | 14.7 | 26.1 |
| DETROIT | 13.9 | 26.9 | 54.8 |
| BOSTON | 4.0 | 8.3 | 11.5 |
| SAN FRANCISCO–OAKLAND | 23.8 | 53.3 | 105.8 |
| PITTSBURGH | 0.8 | 6.3 8.9 | |
| ST. LOUIS | 5.0 | 17.4 | 33.8 |
| CLEVELAND | 4.2 | 15.6 | 41.6 |
| WASHINGTON | 21.0 | 51.3 | 117.1 |
| BALTIMORE | 10.5 | 23.5 | 72.9 |

White area: Percent growth of core city; Black area, percent growth in total area; Blue area, percent growth in suburbs.

In only ten years, from 1940 to 1950, the population of Los Angeles increased by 31 percent, while the surrounding communities grew by about 70 percent. During the same years, the population of the Chicago area grew by about 14 percent, Detroit by 27 percent, Baltimore by over 23 percent.

## Inroads of Urbanization

Nearby towns and villages find themselves swallowed up by the advancing wave of urban growth. A suburb of Chicago, for example, doubles its population in less than ten years as school enrollments and the demand for municipal services outrace the local government's capacity to expand facilities. Quiet towns and villages across the nation find themselves overrun by giant throughways or sprouting real-estate developments. A beautiful valley located over 30 miles from downtown Manhattan, New York, discovers that its area of meadows, forests, and rambling estates has been selected for the establishment of a 15-million-dollar headquarters of a large industrial corporation. Every day throughout the country the tranquillity of small towns and villages is being disturbed by the arrival of new people and new problems. Almost overnight, communities that have remained unchanged for a century are submerged by the swelling tide of urbanization.

## Problems of Metropolitan Government

Despite the growth of metropolitan area-wide problems, the metropolitan areas of the nation, as we have seen, do not have united, coordinated government. They have piecemeal government. As new problems have arisen, new administrative agencies, often independent of the general government, have been created to handle the new functions and activities. A recent count of local government units in Cook County, Illinois, embracing the city of Chicago and its suburbs, revealed the following:

```
  1 County
 30 Townships
102 Incorporated municipalities
179 School districts
 45 Park districts
  1 Forest preserve district
  4 Sanitary districts
  8 Drainage districts
  3 Mosquito abatement districts
  2 Public health districts
 30 Poor-relief districts
 25 Road and bridge districts
  1 Tuberculosis sanatorium district
 16 Fire-prevention districts
  1 Street lighting district
  1 Driveway-maintenance district
```

Problems which are metropolitan area-wide in character, however, cannot be solved piecemeal. Contagious diseases, for example, can be controlled only when they are recognized as area-wide and handled in a coordinated manner. Yet in many of our large cities more than a dozen different types of local government units are involved in administration of public health, with practically no coordination of their efforts.

Slums and urban blight, like human diseases, are contagious and spread across boundaries of government. Most local governments seek to protect land and other values by regulating the height, area, and use of buildings or lots through zoning—division of the community into areas where buildings may be restricted to manufacturing, commerce, residences, or other purposes. The best zoning plans of one community, however, cannot withstand the undermining effects of blight in neighboring territory. In a metropolitan area in the West, for example, a suburban city zoned its side of a street that served as the southern municipal boundary for expensive residences. The opposite side, lying within the central city, was at the time occupied by a natural woodland. Shortly afterward, the woodland was re-zoned as an industrial district, and a large unattractive manufacturing plant was constructed, to the chagrin of the surprised new homeowners.

The price of this diffusion of local government is sometimes high. In an eastern city recently a child died needlessly because the people of the community had voted in a public referendum against cooperating with their neighboring community in the joint use of special pulmotor equipment designed to revive drowning persons. Similarly, the delay and difficulty in securing adequate intergovernmental cooperation in apprehending the slayer of three boys in a large Middle Western metropolis is simply an additional dramatic example of the need for a metropolitan approach to metropolitan problems, and for governmental machinery with enough horsepower to do its job. Pasadena, California, cannot solve the problem of smog without the help of all other governments in the Los Angeles area; nor can Gary, Indiana, solve the problem of water pollution without the help of all governments in the area of Chicago.

### Inefficiencies of Local Government

The consequences of this multiplicity of governments are many. For one thing, the advantages of efficient administration, such as

These vast "look-alikes" meet a present need. But will they be tomorrow's slums? Home ownership may help to keep up standards, but in many areas courageous enforcement of building and occupancy codes will be necessary if rapid deterioration is not to set in.

rational planning, centralized purchasing, and budgeting are lost. Most local communities go their own way administratively; that is, they seek to provide their own water, fire and police protection, sewer systems, and so forth. "Going their own way" frequently means having to pay for their own separate municipal services, regardless of whether such separate facilities are economically justified. A study of the San Francisco–Oakland Bay area, for example, has revealed that if San Francisco and its neighbors were to establish a unified fire-fighting service, the city could eliminate approximately thirty-one fire-fighting companies, at considerable saving to the taxpayers, and with considerable improvement of the quality of protection for all. A separate fire service or a separate police force may boost a small community's sense of local pride, but it hurts the community's pocketbook and may also defeat the very purposes for which such agencies are established.

### Irresponsibility of Local Government

Another consequence is the diffusion and irresponsibility that may result. That is, when governmental power is broken up into little pieces, and decisions are made in a piecemeal fashion by many small, specialized, uncoordinated agencies, special interests may have a field day. It is easier to get favors from a small group of men in charge of single functions than it is to get such favors from a larger general unit of government, such as a city council or county board which must balance all interests in a community. "Divide and conquer" has been a useful principle of pressure politics.

Furthermore, where there is great diffusion of power, important decisions tend to get made, not with reference to the needs of the whole community, but on the basis of special issues and concerns. For example, highway experts may plan their routes without regard to historic landmarks, playgrounds, and parks; traffic experts may develop plans for solving the problems of congestion without regard to the interests of established business firms; and airport planners may neglect to consider the value of preserving scarce forests and wildlife. When all these activities are carried out by independent specialists, free from the control of general government, and without the necessity of having to secure popular approval for their work, the public interest inevitably suffers.

## Solutions of Intergovernmental Problems

The "Gordian knot" of intergovernmental relations will not be cut by a single stroke. Rather, progress lies in many directions. Some of the leading solutions include:

1. *Annexation and consolidation:* expansion of a city's legal boundaries by annexing nearby unincorporated territory or by consolidating neighboring municipalities, in order to keep pace with the actual urban growth. For example, in 1949 Houston, Texas, doubled its population by annexing 79 square miles of territory. In 1950, Baton Rouge, Louisiana, was consolidated with the adjoining parish (county), helping to increase the city's population from 33,719 for the city alone in 1940, to 123,954 for the enlarged area in 1950. In 1953, through annexation, Tampa, Florida, gained 95,000 new residents; Seattle, Washington, gained 56,347; and Long Beach, California, gained 32,000.

Annexation and consolidation are not entirely satisfactory solutions to the metropolitan problem. Annexation of unincorporated territory can be achieved in most states only after a favorable vote in a public referendum, in which the people of both the expanding city and the outlying area vote. The proposal is usually unpopular in the areas to be annexed. Opposition comes from residents, property owners, business firms, and local officials. Much of the opposition and fear is generated by lack of information or by misinformation. But the resistances are nonetheless real.

Consolidation of a city with surrounding incorporated territory requires difficult legal procedures and it may also rouse much opposition. In Pittsburgh, Pennsylvania, where considerable progress has been made in annexation and consolidation, strong opposition came from volunteer fire companies that had been subsidized by local governments, and from aldermen, justices of the peace, constables, and deputy constables in Allegheny County who feared losing both their jobs and their political status. Among the people of outlying communities generally, there is a fear of being "gobbled up" by the expanding city.

2. *Metropolitan districts:* consolidation of single governmental functions into large special districts, that is, the unification of all park facilities into a single metropolitan park district, all sewerage and sanitary services into a metropolitan sewerage or sanitary district, or all law enforcement activities into a metropolitan police force. Illinois and California are two states that have led in the use of this device. Examples are the Chicago Sanitary District, and the Metropolitan Water District of Southern California. In 1955 the legislature of Connecticut empowered cities, towns, and boroughs to establish metropolitan districts in order to provide certain municipal functions more equitably and economically.

While metropolitan districts have achieved much immediate prog ress, they are subject to some of the criticism that is leveled against special districts in general: they do not necessarily improve efficiency of operations, they do not necessarily unify the powers of government, they often increase the costs of operation, and they tend to take control over important activities out of the hands of the popularly elected officials of the city. Some experts believe, however, that the metropolitan district may offer a nucleus for a general metropolitan government in the future.

3. *Urban counties:* extension of the powers of urban county governments over urban areas, or consolidation of the city government with that of the county. There are many variations of city-county consolidation, but in general the plan calls for combination of city and county police, health, welfare, and other departments. The primary arguments in defense of the plan have been the anticipated dollar savings and the opportunities for area-wide planning and operation. The city-county consolidation approach has been tried in Denver, San Francisco, Philadelphia, St. Louis, Baton Rouge, and other cities. Only Baton Rouge has achieved substantial success. Since city-county consolidation requires state-wide approval in a referendum for amendment to the state constitution, the plan has been found politically difficult to achieve. Furthermore, many met-

ropolitan areas overlap more than one county. Others, like New York and Chicago, lie in more than one state.

The more significant trend, therefore, has been the emergence of the urban county as an appropriate unit of metropolitan government. While continuing to serve as agents of the state in administration of law enforcement, the conduct of elections, administration of the courts, and other functions, urban counties have been assuming responsibility for tasks which cities have been unable or unwilling to handle. Los Angeles County, for example, furnishes direct municipal services to unincorporated communities through its regular departments. Its county sheriff's department has become a form of municipal police department for many areas beyond the boundaries of Los Angeles. Similar developments have occurred in Erie County, Pennsylvania. Recently, the legislatures of California and North Carolina have permitted their counties to create urban districts for purposes of providing governmental services of a municipal character.

4. *Extraterritorial jurisdiction:* extension of a city's municipal functions and powers into neighboring territory. Under state law in many states a city may control the use of land outside of its municipal boundaries. Throughout the country, many cities, for example, have control over areas used for airports, cemeteries, reservoirs, refuse dumps, and other purposes, outside the city's legal boundaries. Chicago has recently been granted jurisdiction over the approaches to its new O'Hare Airport lying outside the city, while many cities in California operate camps and recreational areas in the Sierra Nevada Mountains. This practice, like annexation and consolidation, tends to generate considerable fear and opposition among the people in the affected areas. Effective public information programs and intergovernmental consultation can do much to reduce this political obstacle. Extraterritorial jurisdiction remains, however, only a partial solution. It is no substitute for broad metropolitan planning and coordination.

These are only some of the more prevalent solutions that are being proposed or tried. Others, involving more fundamental administrative and political reorganization and readjustment have been suggested. Much progress has been made through less ambitious forms of cooperation and consultation. Interlocal relations in government remain, however, one of the more important and complicated aspects of intergovernmental relations in the United States.

# CONCLUSION

## Synopsis

The central problem of intergovernmental relations is the lack of correspondence between existing boundaries of government and the issues these various governments are called upon to solve. Small units of government have proven incapable of handling large tasks. In order to escape resultant difficulties, many intergovernmental solutions have been tried, involving considerable experimentation in relationships among and between Federal, state, and local governments. Underlying this experimentation has been a long-standing philosophic and emotional paradox: a belief or feeling on the one hand that local and state governments are more democratic and responsive than a huge centralized bureaucracy—and, in the long run, possibly kinder to freedom; on the other hand, a recognition that only the central government has the taxing power, the fullness of authority, and the detachment needed to meet many of the crucial issues which today cut across local, state, and even national boundaries.

## Significance

One of the major tests of the next generation in American history will be its capacity to adjust old forms to meet new needs. Just as business, if it is to be successful, looks ahead, tries to anticipate new problems, and adjusts its organizational machinery to the size of its operation; so government in America must plan, anticipate, and reorganize. Acts of invention are needed in designing new instruments of intergovernmental relations; but equally needed are leaders and lay citizens who see the relatedness of things, and who are not afraid to reform in order to conserve.

## Prospectus

The next and final chapter is a Section all by itself. For all that has been described above stems ultimately from the individual citizen— his ways of looking at life and his sense of social responsibility. What we fondly call our "way of life" is preserved and constantly renewed by those among us who take seriously their obligations as citizens.

# SECTION VII

## CHAPTER 26

## Our Obligations as Citizens

*A*n Athenian citizen does not neglect the state because he takes care of his own household; and even those of us who are engaged in business have a very fair idea of politics. We alone regard a man who takes no interest in public affairs, not as a harmless, but as a useless character; and if few of us are originators, we are all sound judges of policy.

—Pericles

# Our Obligations as Citizens

WHATEVER FAULTS may be found with government in America, the fact remains that our political expectations—and the spiritual and moral values which underlie those expectations—have on the whole been well served by the democratic instruments at our disposal.

This is not happenstance. A lot of people have worked and thought and fought and sacrificed to this end. And it will not be happenstance if the future is as promising as the past. No "unseen hand" exists to ensure that our instruments of constitutional government will survive, let alone improve. No one stands guard if we sleep.

## THE MEANING OF GOOD CITIZENSHIP

The rights of a free people are the rich dividends of the willingness of men and women to invest time, energy, money, and sometimes life itself in meeting their obligations as citizens. Many of these obligations are not arduous, although we may occasionally grumble at having to pay taxes or serve on a jury. We make unnecessary trouble for ourselves by suggesting that most duties of citizenship are so complex and so time-consuming that active citizenship is always somebody else's business.

Good citizenship does not mean that we must know everything about everything; but it does mean that we must know something about something. Good citizenship does not mean that we have to become involved in every issue or campaign at every level of government; but it does mean that we must be concerned with some issue or campaign at some level. Good citizenship does not mean that we must embrace a particular catechism: liberal or conservative, radical or reactionary; but it does mean that whatever our social or economic goals, we must fight for them within the rules of the game set by the constitution and by our time-tested political habits of accommodation and compromise. Good citizenship does not mean that we must always forego personal interest; but it does mean that a sizable number of people at any one time must take the long view rather than the short view of personal interest, and that when sacrifice is necessary to maintain the values of our society, the overwhelming majority of people will, in Emerson's words, "recognize the terror of life and man themselves to face it."

This last must be said with particular emphasis because of the nature of the world we live in. The twentieth century is a century of unparalleled opportunity and of unparalleled terror. Our distant ancestors may have cowered in a cave during a thunderstorm, but we have no place to hide. If we are to survive physically, we must be willing to make whatever sacrifices responsible leadership indicates are necessary. If we are to go beyond the goal of physical survival to the goal of maintaining and improving the realities of freedom for ourselves and, in the New Testament sense, our neighbors, our obligations as citizens must be soberly and conscientiously understood and undertaken.

## LEGAL OBLIGATIONS

We are taught from childhood to "obey the law." This is certainly the first responsibility of citizenship. We may try through legal means to change the law, but until it is changed, our duty is to obey it. This needs saying over and over again because in spite of the fact that most Americans are law-abiding citizens, there is in our heritage an erratic and poisonous stream of lawlessness that has a tendency to burst its narrow banks under certain conditions of social strain. Frontier vigilantes, juvenile delinquents, white councils, goon squads, unethical businessmen, and mountaineer feuders have not been peculiar to America, but America has had her share.

Lawlessness cannot be wished away; but it can be recognized, isolated, and minimized if the public is alert, concerned, and dedicated to the principle of the rule of law which, as we have seen, is deep in our heritage. Katherine Lee Bates put the issue quite simply when she wrote in her hymn, *America the Beautiful:*

> Confirm thy soul in self-control,
> Thy Liberty in law.

Free discussion is the root of responsive and responsible government in America. Whether in the columns of newspapers, in letters to the President, or in civic meetings such as this, the willingness and right of American citizens to "sound off" when they are dissatisfied is the hallmark of our political system.

## Taxes

For nearly all citizens, most laws are not recognized as burdensome. There are thousands of statutes on the books—national, state, and local. In a lifetime, most citizens do not feel the direct coercive effect of more than a tiny fraction of them.

But some laws affect almost the entire adult population of the nation in a most personal way. This is certainly true of tax laws. Most people accept the inevitability of taxes, and like Justice Holmes understand that they "buy civilization." The homeowner, if he stops to think about it, knows that when he pays his local property taxes he is helping to build schools and pay teachers' salaries, to build highways and keep them plowed or sanded in the winter, to create and maintain parks and playgrounds, to pay the police and the firemen who protect lives and property, to pay officials to plan the orderly development of the area, and to provide many other services which make life in our American communities decent and reasonably equitable.

The housewife knows that the state sales tax on her nylon stockings helps maintain mental institutions, state parks, public health and welfare services, and a variety of other important activities, just as the state gasoline tax helps maintain state highways.

The husband struggling with his federal income-tax form knows, if he stops to think, that national security and the vast array of services presently provided by the national government to all segments of the population cannot be bought for nothing.

But two important issues of public policy are inevitably present in any discussion of taxes: first, what proportion of the total income of the American people should go for taxes; and second, where should the burden fall?

*How Much Taxes to Pay?* The first question is answered every year at every level of government in the decisions of school boards, town meetings, boards of finance, common councils, and county, state, and federal legislative bodies. The collective decisions of these policy-making bodies as to what governmental activities are essential determine the tax load of the country as a whole. The dilemma is always present: if the demanded service is not provided, society may suffer; if the service is provided, taxes will go up. Only the irresponsible politician promises something for nothing. Every activity of government costs somebody something; and this brings us to the second issue: where should the burden fall?

At the present time the total tax burden in the United States—national, state, and local—is upward of $80 billions a year. If evenly distributed, this would mean nearly $500 for every man, woman, and child in the country. The load is, of course, not evenly distributed. Through the graduated income tax, which is the principal source of revenue for the Federal government and for many state governments, those with higher incomes pay a considerably higher portion of their income in taxes than do those with low incomes. A movie star or a corporation president may pay an annual income tax in the hundreds of thousands of dollars. A sharecropper may pay no federal income tax at all. Roughly three quarters of all federal revenues are derived from personal or corporate income taxes, and these are levied on the principle of "ability to pay."

*The Equitable Distribution of Tax Burden.* This generally accepted maxim of justice in the tax field is not simple to apply. Originally, the very principle was fought through the Supreme

**National Debt of the United States Government**

| Year | |
|------|------|
| 1915 | $ 1,191,000,000 |
| 1920 | 24,298,000,000 |
| 1925 | 20,516,000,000 |
| 1930 | 16,185,000,000 |
| 1935 | 28,701,000,000 |
| 1940 | 42,971,000,000 |
| 1945 | 258,682,000,000 |
| 1950 | 257,357,000,000 |
| 1955 | 274,374,000,000 |
| 1956 (est.) | 275,000,000,000 |

The national debt has stayed high under both Democratic and Republican administrations. A product of depression and war, the national debt today costs the American taxpayers $7.0 billion in interest alone each year—the payment of which is a basic legal obligation.

Court. The first peacetime income tax was levied by Congress in 1894. A year later, the Supreme Court in the famous Pollock Case declared the tax to be unconstitutional. In a celebrated dictum, a majority of the Court held that such a tax was "communistic" and "socialistic." This decision delayed the introduction of a federal income tax until the passage of the Sixteenth Amendment in 1913. Although today the principle of a graduated income tax is generally accepted, there is no common agreement on just how graduated it should be. On one side are those who feel that hard work, success, initiative, and economic growth generally are unduly penalized by the present tax structure; on the other side are those who believe that the redistribution of income enforced by the graduated tax keeps consumer demand and consequently profit expectations high, and that most citizens, not just a few, gain.

The question of a just and equitable distribution of the tax burden is a perennial item on the legislative agenda of every level of government. Should citizens of Massachusetts be taxed to build dams in Idaho? Should the main source of revenue for local governments be restricted to the property tax? Should gasoline and cigarettes carry a larger or smaller share of the general tax burden? Should certain kinds of taxes be levied by only one level of government? Does a "soak the rich" policy deaden incentive in our society? Is a sales tax fair to the low-income breadwinner? On the other hand, if he pays *no* taxes, what kind of stake does he have in responsible government? How much of state and federal revenue should be returned to local government for expensive items like education, highways, and welfare? Should all charitable, religious, and educational institutions be tax exempt?

These are some of the toughest ethical, economic, and political questions on the policy agendas of American government. Regardless of how these questions are resolved, however, the citizen has the continuing legal obligation to pay whatever taxes are set by responsible representative instruments of government.

### Military Service

A second, frequently painful—or at least disruptive—legal obligation of the citizen is military service. Normally, the burden falls upon young, adult males—although no one can quite foresee what our manpower (and woman power) needs might be in case of another war, or how comprehensive and coercive manpower controls would then have to be.

It is possible, as Mr. Stevenson implied in the presidential campaign of 1956, that the continuing revolution in weapons systems may at some future time make the drafting of men for military service unnecessary. But until that day actually arrives, until, in other words, all our military manpower needs can be met by volunteers, young men in their late teens and early twenties must face the possibility of compulsory military service.

Presently administered by a large, highly decentralized Selective Service System, the draft is based upon the universal registration of males between the ages of eighteen and twenty-six. Such registration carries with it a liability for training and service in the military forces of the United States. Through a system of deferments and exemptions the government makes every attempt to see that lives are disrupted as little as possible, and that manpower is not foolishly utilized. But at best military service is hardly fun. It involves sacrifice —sometimes the supreme sacrifice of life itself. The romantic days of personal warfare have gone forever. Today military training is a tense exercise in relating complex men and complex machines to complex objectives.

America is fortunate in having a number of men who through family tradition or for other personal reasons are willing to dedicate their lives to the grim art of warfare. These professionals must, however, as the need arises be supported by civilians who accept with

One way a citizen can help discharge his civic obligations is to join a local Civil Defense organization. Here a group of volunteers train for a disaster that everyone hopes will never occur.

a sense of serious responsibility their obligation as citizens to defend their nation and the values for which it stands.

## Other Legal Obligations

In addition to taxes and military service there are, of course, a number of other legal obligations which affect most citizens at one time or another in their lives: jury duty; securing licenses or permits to drive, or fish, or build, or practice a profession; registering births and deaths. Many of these legal duties are necessary to the public safety and welfare; although the question may well be asked whether at the local and state level some licenses or permits are not set up to help a private guild maintain a monopoly rather than to protect the public interest.

But again, if we do not like a law, we may campaign to change it. Until it is changed, we are obliged—if we wish to maintain a civilized society—to obey.

# CIVIC OBLIGATIONS

Strict obedience to the law, important as it is, cannot by itself produce or sustain a free society. Beyond our legal obligations are civic and moral obligations; to ignore them would most certainly destroy the foundations of democracy.

## Keeping Informed

If, in order to keep our form of government working, citizens had to keep up to date on all issues before local, state, and national officials; if, in addition, citizens had to know something about all candidates for whom they have to vote; finally, if citizens had to conjure up an informed opinion on every public issue and communicate this opinion to relevant public officials, democracy would be impossible. Fortunately, modern, representative democracy does not require this impossible task of its citizens. It does require, however, that a sizable segment of the population will at any one time be reasonably informed about some of the important issues of the day, and about some candidates. Insofar as the public can hold political parties rather than individuals or amorphous groups responsible for what goes on in government, the presently impossible task of sorting out individual candidates is, of course, enormously simplified.

Those who have had the advantage of higher education have a special obligation to keep informed about as many issues of public policy as possible, since this group tends to move into leadership roles in public opinion formation. But how can a citizen become informed? How can he meet this particular obligation of citizenship —so necessary if he is to vote intelligently and participate effectively?

*Sources of Information.* First, of course, there are the obvious

"Now, if you'll excuse me, gentlemen, I have a very important meeting."

sources of news: newspapers, television, radio, and news magazines. The habit of reading or listening to the news for fifteen minutes a day is a necessary one for the conscientious citizen. Care must be taken, of course, to choose news sources well. Many newspapers devote very little space to news about government and about pending policy issues. Some newspapers and news magazines, and some radio and television commentators, give only one side of an issue; or worse, give both sides but one side unfairly. The conscientious citizen attempts to search for those media of communication which present issues and candidates fairly.

If, as is frequently the case, a citizen wishes to dig more deeply into a particular issue, governmental activity, or official performance there are a number of sources of reliable information available in libraries—particularly university or big city libraries. A trained reference librarian will be able to introduce the citizen to unusual local

## QUALIFICATIONS FOR VOTING*

| State | Minimum Age | U.S. Citizen | Residence in — State | County | District | Property | Literacy Test | Poll Tax(a) | Registration — Permanent — All Areas | Permanent — Some Areas | Periodic — All Areas | Periodic — Some Areas | Periodic — Frequency | Coverage — All Elections | Coverage — Some Elections |
|---|---|---|---|---|---|---|---|---|---|---|---|---|---|---|---|
| Alabama | 21 | ★ | 2 yrs. | 1 yr. | 3 mo. | — | ★ | (b) | (c) | — | — | — | — | ★ | — |
| Arizona | 21 | ★ | 1 yr. | 30 da. | 30 da. | — | ★ | — | (d) | — | — | — | — | (e) | — |
| Arkansas | 21 | ★ | 12 mo. | 6 mo. | 1 mo. | — | — | ★ | ★ | — | — | — | — | ★ | — |
| California | 21 | (f) | 1 yr. | 90 da. | 54 da. | — | ★ | — | ★ | — | — | — | — | — | (h) |
| Colorado | 21 | ★ | 1 yr. | 90 da. | 15 da.(g) | — | — | — | ★ | — | — | — | — | ★ | — |
| Connecticut | 21 | (i) | 1 yr. | — | 6 mo. | — | ★ | — | — | — | ★ | — | 4 years | ★ | — |
| Delaware | 21 | ★ | 1 yr. | 3 mo. | 30 da. | — | ★ | — | ★ | — | — | — | — | ★ | — |
| Florida | 21 | ★ | 1 yr. | 6 mo. | — | — | — | — | ★ | — | — | — | — | ★ | — |
| Georgia | 18 | ★ | 1 yr. | 6 mo.(e) | — | — | (j) | — | ★ | — | — | — | — | ★ | — |
| Idaho | 21 | ★ | 6 mo. | 30 da. | 30 da. | — | — | — | ★ | — | — | — | — | — | — |
| Illinois | 21 | ★ | 1 yr. | 90 da. | 30 da. | — | — | — | ★ | — | — | — | — | — | — |
| Indiana | 21 | ★ | 6 mo. | 60 da. (l) | 30 da. | — | — | — | — | — | ★ | — | 4 years | — | (k) |
| Iowa | 21 | ★ | 6 mo. | 60 da. | 10 da. | — | — | — | — | ★ | — | ★ | — | ★ | (h) |
| Kansas | 21 | ★ | 6 mo. | 30 da.(l) | 30 da. | — | — | — | — | ★ | — | ★ | — | ★ | (h) |
| Kentucky | 21 | ★ | 1 yr. | 6 mo. | 60 da. | — | — | — | — | — | ★ | — | 4 years | ★ | — |
| Louisiana | 21 | ★ | 2 yrs. | 1 yr. | 3 mo.(m) | — | (j)★ | — | ★ | — | — | — | — | ★ | — |
| Maine | 21 | ★ | 6 mo. | 3 mo. | 3 mo. | — | ★ | — | ★ | — | — | — | — | ★ | — |
| Maryland | 21 | ★ | 1 yr. | 6 mo. | 6 mo. | — | — | — | ★ | — | — | — | — | ★ | — |
| Massachusetts | 21 | ★ | 1 yr. | — | 6 mo.(n) | — | ★ | — | ★ | — | — | — | — | ★ | — |
| Michigan | 21 | ★ | 6 mo. | — | 30 da. | (o) | — | — | — | ★ | — | ★ | — | ★ | — |
| Minnesota | 21 | (f) | 6 mo. | — | 30 da. | — | — | — | — | ★ | — | ★ | — | ★ | — |
| Mississippi | 21 | ★ | 2 yrs. | 1 yr. | 1 yr.(p) | — | ★ | (q) | (c) | — | — | — | — | — | (r) |
| Missouri | 21 | ★ | 1 yr. | 60 da. | 60 da. | — | — | — | — | ★ | — | ★ | 4 years | ★ | — |
| Montana | 21 | ★ | 1 yr. | 30 da. | — | (o) | — | — | ★ | — | — | — | — | — | (h) |
| Nebraska | 21 | ★ | 6 mo. | 40 da. | 10 da. | (o) | — | — | — | ★ | — | ★ | — | — | (h) |
| Nevada | 21 | ★ | 6 mo. | 30 da. | 10 da. | — | ★ | — | — | — | ★ | — | 6 years | ★ | — |
| New Hampshire | 21 | ★ | 6 mo. | — | — | — | ★ | — | ★ | — | — | — | — | ★ | — |
| New Jersey | 21 | ★ | 1 yr. | 5 mo. | 6 mo. | — | — | — | ★ | — | — | — | — | ★ | — |

| State | Age | | State residence | County residence | Local residence | | | | Periodic registration | | |
|---|---|---|---|---|---|---|---|---|---|---|---|
| New Mexico | 21 | ★ | 12 mo. | 90 da. | 30 da. | (o) | | ★(s) | | | |
| New York | 21 | (f) | 1 yr. | 4 mo. | 30 da. | | | ★ | | Annual | ★ |
| North Carolina | 21 | ★ | 1 yr. | 90 da. | 4 mo. | | | | | | |
| North Dakota | 21 | ★ | 1 yr. | 40 da. | 30 da. | | | | | | ★ |
| Ohio | 21 | ★ | 1 yr. | 40 da. | 40 da. | | | ★ | ★ | | |
| Oklahoma | 21 | ★ | 1 yr. | 6 mo. | 30 da. | | | ★ | ★ | | ★ |
| Oregon | 21 | ★ | 6 mo. | — | — | | (t) | | | | |
| Pennsylvania | 21 | ★ | 1 yr.(u) | — | 2 mo. | | | | | | |
| Rhode Island | 21 | ★ | 1 yr. | — | 6 mo. | | | | | | ★ |
| South Carolina | 21 | ★ | 2 yrs.(p) | 1 yr. | 4 mo. | (v) | (v) | | | | ★ |
| South Dakota | 21 | ★ | 1 yr. | 90 da. | 30 da. | | | | | Decennial | ★ |
| Tennessee | 21 | ★ | 12 mo. | 6 mo. | | | | | | | ★ |
| Texas | 21 | ★ | 1 yr. | 6 mo. | 6 mo. | (o) | (w) | | | Annual | ★ |
| Utah | 21 | (f) | 1 yr. | 4 mo. | 60 da. | (o) | ★ | | | | ★ |
| Vermont | 21 | ★ | 1 yr. | — | 3 mo.(l) | | (z) | | | | ★ |
| Virginia | 21 | ★ | 1 yr. | 6 mo. | 30 da. | | (d) | | | | ★ |
| Washington | 21 | ★ | 1 yr. | 90 da. | 30 da. | | ★ | | | | ★ |
| West Virginia | 21 | ★ | 1 yr. | 60 da. | — | | | | | | |
| Wisconsin | 21 | ★ | 1 yr. | — | 10 da. | | | | | | |
| Wyoming | 21 | ★ | 1 yr. | 60 da. | 10 da. | ★ | | (w) | (w) | | ★ |
| Alaska | 21 | ★ | 12 mo. | — | 30 da.(aa) | ★ | ★ | | | Every gen. elec. | (h) |
| Guam | 21 | ★ | 2 yrs. | — | — | (ac) | (d) | | | | |
| Hawaii | 21 | ★ | 1 yr. | — | 3 mo. | | (ad) | | | | ★ |
| Puerto Rico | 21 | ★ | 1 yr. | — | 1 yr. | | ★ | | | | ★ |
| Virgin Islands | 21 | ★ | 1 yr. | — | 60 da. | ★ | | | | | |

* Reproduced by the courtesy of the Council of State Governments from *The Book of the States, 1954-55*, pp. 80-81.

(a) Poll or head taxes are levied in many other states. Those listed here, however, provide that payment of the poll tax is a prerequisite for voting.

(b) Must pay all poll taxes owed since 1901. Members of the armed forces are exempt from payment of poll taxes.

(c) Registration is permanent unless removed for cause.

(d) Conditioned upon voting and continued residence.

(e) Except for irrigation district elections.

(f) Must have been citizen ninety days.

(g) City or town, thirty days.

(h) All except certain minor elections.

(i) Must have been citizen five years.

(j) Under 1949 act, all voters must register and pass literacy test. Those failing test may qualify by answering 10 of 30 oral questions prescribed by law.

(k) For all state and federal elections.

(l) Township.

(m) Municipality, four months.

(n) In city or town.

(o) For vote on bond issues or special assessments only.

(p) Ministers of the Gospel and teachers in public schools may vote after six months' residence.

(q) Assessed upon citizens 21 to 60 years of age except those specifically exempted.

(r) Registration is for all elections of state and county, but voter must be registered in municipality also to vote in municipal elections.

(s) A person who became entitled to vote after January 1, 1922, must be able except for physical disability, to read and write English.

(t) Re-register in two years if not voting within that time.

(u) Six months if previously an elector or native of U.S.

(v) Ownership of property is an alternative to literacy.

(w) Constitution provides for registration in cities over 10,000, but no system exists. Poll tax receipts determine eligibility of voters aged 21 to 60 years; exemption certificates for those over 60 in cities over 10,000, and certain others.

(x) Must owe no past due taxes.

(y) Except in some cities.

(z) All elections except special elections.

(aa) Precinct.

(ab) Municipal election.

(ac) English or Hawaiian language.

(ad) Name subject to removal from registration list after failure to vote in a general election sources of information (for example, a local League of Women Voters may have drafted a "Know Your Candidates" sheet). Some of the more general guides to sources of information about government and politics are the following:*

1. *The New York Times Index* which summarizes and classifies news alphabetically by subjects, persons, and organizations. Once the student has located the exact date of a political decision by means of this Index, he can then go to any number of sources for further information.

2. *The Readers' Guide to Periodical Literature* and the *Bulletin of the Public Affairs Information Service* together constitute indispensable reference sources. The former covers all subjects; the latter, as its name implies, is limited to the public affairs area—but it has the advantage of covering books and monographs as well as magazine articles.

3. The surest guide to available information about the activities and policy-concerns of the national government is the *Monthly Catalogue of U. S. Government Publications* issued by the U. S. Government Printing Office. This lists, among other things, annual and special reports of departments and agencies, reports of special presidential and congressional commissions, presidential messages, reports and hearings of congressional committees, and special research and technical bulletins prepared for the benefit of the general public, or segments thereof. *The United States Government Organization Manual* is the most reliable up-to-date source of information about federal agencies and officials.

4. By far the most valuable reference source on the Congress is the *Congressional Quarterly* which, in addition to listing all roll-call votes, prepares a series of special features on legislative issues, lobbying activities, congressional campaigns, and the like. The *Congressional Quarterly* is privately owned, and it prides itself on its objectivity. Two important government publications dealing with Congress are of course the *Congressional Record* (the indexed verbatim record of floor deliberations and actions in both houses), and the *Congressional Directory* (a single volume, published annually, giving basic data about each session of Congress: committee assignments, thumbnail biographies of each member, the names of administrative assistants and committee staffs, accredited Capitol Hill newsmen, and so on).

* See Schattschneider, Jones, and Bailey, *A Guide to the Study of Public Affairs*, New York: the Dryden Press, 1952, for a more comprehensive listing.

5. At the state and local level, there are a wide variety of sources: public officials themselves, state and local annual reports, auditors' reports, legislative summaries, council minutes, and clipping files in state and local libraries. More general information cutting across the entire country can be found in the *Municipal Year Book* and in the *Book of the States*. The Public Administration  Service at 1313 E. 60th Street, Chicago, Illinois, maintains a Joint Reference Library which serves as a clearinghouse of information about public administration at all levels of government.

6. Finally, a post card dropped to government agencies or to private interest groups will usually bring prompt replies and a considerable amount of literature.

Actually, the tragedy in our democracy is not that we have too few sources of information about public affairs; the tragedy is that we as citizens use only a fraction of the sources available to us.

## Voting

But knowledge is not enough. Unless we use that knowledge we are not fulfilling our obligations as citizens. One level of participation is, of course, voting. It is one of the shames of our society that our national voting habits are so sloppy and intermittent. Voting is not compulsory in America, and no responsible person believes that it should be. But many of those who do not vote are parasitic. They are taking a free ride. They are shirking one of the elementary duties of citizenship. There is a right not to vote in America; but if most people exercised that negative right, our democracy would disappear. Voting is a solemn privilege. Upon settling in a new area, or upon arriving at voting age, each citizen should call the nearest town hall to find out the following information:

1. The dates on which he can register to vote
2. The length of time he must reside in the area in order to vote
3. The dates of primary as well as general elections
4. The location of the voting place

If the citizen has had no experience with a ballot or a voting machine, he should go to the registrar of voters or town clerk and ask for instructions in the simple mechanics of voting.

If the citizen knows he must be away from town on election day, he can easily make arrangements through his local election officials to receive an absentee ballot which he may mark and mail back in time to be counted.

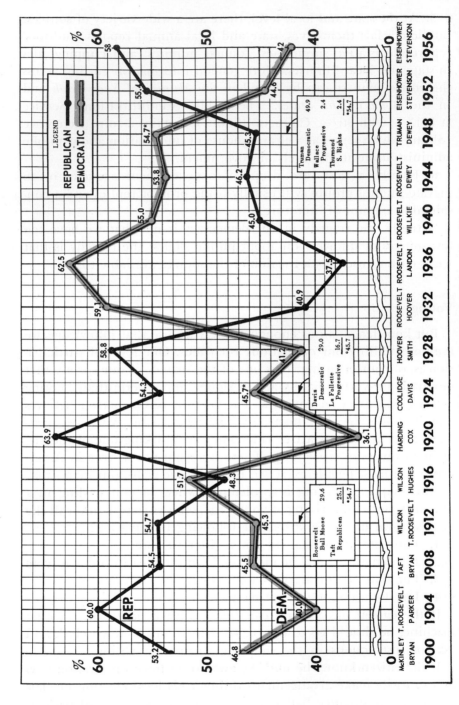

A relatively small change in the popular vote would have thrown many of these Presidential elections the other way. It pays to vote! (Gallup Poll.)

In most areas of the country, political party headquarters will be glad to provide transportation to the polls, and even baby-sitters. In short, there are very few legitimate excuses for not voting.

## Party Participation *

It is highly unfortunate that in the eyes of many Americans partisan politics is a sullen and dishonest trade. Deeply engrained in our constitutional tradition is the belief that parties are the enemies of constitutional government, or at least parasitic growths on an otherwise clean body politic. As we have seen, our Founding Fathers took a dim view of what they called factions. But as we have also seen, our Founding Fathers ensured the growth of parties by passing the First Amendment to the Constitution which guaranteed freedom of speech and press and association.

One hundred fifty years of perspective makes us realize that far from being parasitic enemies of democracy, parties have been and are among the most significant instruments of democracy.

For parties are the great mobilizers of majorities. Pressure groups may mobilize minorities for special privilege, but only political parties are set on mobilizing a majority of the voting population. If one is lukewarm to majorities, then he will be lukewarm to political parties; but if he believes with Franklin P. Adams that "the average man is above the average"—and that a majority of these above-average average men have a better right to control themselves than any minority has—no matter how smart—then he should have faith in, and respect for, our two-party system.

One of the most important comparisons that can be made between America and the Soviet Union is not between their constitutions (which compare quite favorably), but between their parties, which bear no resemblance to one another. In Russia there is a one-party system. In the United States there are two parties—the competition between which assumes, and helps to assure, our free way of life.

*Why Parties Are Viewed Critically.* If political parties are so good and so necessary, why do they have such a bad name? Why do we tend to look at parties as improbable conspiracies between schemers and dreamers? How does it happen as Professor Schattschneider once asked, that the date of Jefferson's resignation from Washing-

---

* The Citizenship Clearing House, c/o New York University Law School, New York, N. Y., is the outstanding instrument in America for getting student interest aroused in practical politics. Students are urged to write CCH for further information.

ton's cabinet (indicating the collapse of Washington's attempt to govern without parties) is not marked as a national holiday?

It is partly that, like Washington, none of us likes the opposition party and tries to discredit it. It is partly because our history has been written by political theorists and constitutional lawyers, not by practicing politicians; it is partly because many citizens have gotten the strange notion that politics in a democracy should involve all rights and no duties; it is partly because some political activity, like some business activity, is sleezy. We sometimes see insiders, many of them apparently interested in nothing but an extra "buck" or a judgeship, studiously working out ways and means of winning mass support without permitting mass participation in important party decisions. We see a few noisy self-seekers buffaloing citizens into believing that party politics is no enterprise for decent people. Politicians, so the myth runs, are too smart and too dishonest for well-meaning, honest folk to associate with.

*Who Controls Parties?* Political parties, like any other human organization, are run by a few. We would save ourselves a lot of grief if we made up our minds to accept this fact. We see churches and colleges and businesses run by a few people who have stayed around for some time and, on the basis of ability, effort, and seniority, deserve to run things. But we seem to think that a political party should be run from the ground up. The proper question is not how can we suddenly turn human nature upside down in a political organization, when we cannot do it anywhere else; the proper question is, How do we become a member of the small group which has influence *inside* the parties? For democracy lies primarily not within parties, but between them. It lies in the choices which party organizations provide for the electorate.

*Influential Activity.* Just how does one become an influential citizen in one of our two major parties? He does it through active participation in party affairs over a period of time: work on party committees, work checking caucus lists, ringing doorbells, doing research or speech-writing for candidates, and in a host of other ways. He must be regular enough to be recognized by fellow partisans as having a right to such influence; he must be independent enough to deserve ethical respect. This is a fine line. It involves intelligence, tact, and character. It takes time; it takes patience. Like everything else worthwhile in life, it takes work and courage.

Too many people take a single whiff of politics and run. All this does, of course, is to leave the game in the hands of the less scrupulous. Theodore Roosevelt faced this problem in the campaign of 1884 when James G. Blaine was the Republican candidate for President. Blaine had a very unsavory reputation—so unsavory, in fact, that T. R. wanted to stay out of the campaign entirely. Henry Cabot Lodge warned Roosevelt that unless the latter stuck around, held his nose, and campaigned for Blaine, that T. R.'s future in politics was dismal indeed. T. R. took Lodge's advice—and we know the rest of the story.

*Party Compromise.* George Bernard Shaw once heard that a labor candidate named Joseph Burgess had refused to compromise on some issue during a campaign and had, therefore, lost his seat in Parliament. Shaw commented bitterly,

When I think of my own unfortunate character, smirched with com-promise, rotted with opportunism, mildewed by expediency—dragged through the mud of Borough Council and Battersea elections, stretched out of shape with wirepulling, putrified by permeation, worn out by twenty-five years pushing to gain an inch here, or straining to stem a backrush, I do think Joe might have put up with just a speck or two on those white robes of his for the sake of the millions of poor devils who cannot afford any character at all because they have no friend in Parlia-ment. Oh, these moral dandies, these spiritual toffs, these superior per-sons. Who is Joe anyhow that he should not risk his soul occasionally like the rest of us? [1]

No one is going to pretend that there are no ethical storms in active, loyal, influential participation in political parties, although the number and incidence of these storms is nothing like what is generally pictured. But unless decent partisans face and weather these storms, the ship of state will be left in the hands of those who are in politics *only* for selfish gain.

And the stakes of active participation in partisan politics are the greatest in the world: vast influence in public affairs and perhaps a determining voice in the fate of the human enterprise. Lesser stakes are also present: political activity is fun.

## Civic Endeavors

Not everyone has the time or the temperament to indulge in regular partisan politics. But there are scores of ways in which citi-zens can contribute to our public life outside the partisan political field. As Paul Appleby has said,

Citizens vote by adding their names and energies to membership roles. They vote by swelling or failing to swell the circulation of particular newspapers or periodicals. They vote by contributing to the popularity of particular radio or newspaper commentators. They vote by writing letters to the editor. They vote much more potently than they know when they write or talk to members of legislative bodies and to administrative officials. They vote as they express themselves in labor unions, farm organizations, business and professional bodies. They vote in every contribution they make to the climate of opinion in a thoroughly political society. They vote more effectively in proportion to the persistence of their efforts, for persistence is an index to intensity of feeling.[2]

Anyone who has served as an official of a local government knows how valuable is the alert and creative individual citizen: the woman who sees a dangerous crossing near a school and brings this information to the attention of the common council; the businessman who notices the rubbish in back of a row of stores and stimulates a voluntary clean-up drive through the chamber of commerce; the worker who on the way home from work notices an abandoned town dump and thinks to call the mayor and ask why the dump could not be filled over and a playground created; the church worker who finds a number of local families in distress and is moved with others to organize a Community Chest campaign; the commander of the American Legion post or the head of the local Grange who starts a memorial swimming pool; the PTA member who works tirelessly for a new school or better teachers' salaries; the industrialist who in the course of remodeling his plant provides a screen of cypress trees to hide an ugly scrap-pile from public view.

Much of this activity does not involve government directly; but it most certainly involves government indirectly. For if citizenship did not include nongovernmental civic endeavors, government would move of necessity into many areas now covered by these volunteer activities.

And by and large those who are active in various private civic enterprises are the very ones who give freely of their time to government enterprises. They serve for nothing on boards and commissions

---

I am done with great things and big things, great institutions and big success, and I am for those tiny, invisible, molecular moral forces that work from individual to individual, creeping through the crannies of the world like so many sift rootlets, or like the capillary oozing of water, yet which, if you give them time, will rend the hardest monuments of men's pride.

—William James

of the city government. They give up the peace and quiet of their living rooms for the smoke-filled committee rooms where smoke-filled communities are scrubbed and cleaned. These are the men and women who see the world, not as it is, but as it might be—and who make their dreams into self-fulfilling prophecies. They are the most valuable resource any society has.

## MORAL OBLIGATION

The years ahead of us are fraught with uncertainties. Even if we were to be successful in maintaining for a number of generations a "balance of terror" so that a major war did not occur, vast problems will continue to confront the human race: problems created by rapid shifts in technology and population; by the lingering prejudices and hates of the human animal; by dwindling natural resources; by the inevitable clashes of customs, habits, and backgrounds among the various nations and cultures of mankind—now closely knit in a superficial sense by the magic of telecommunications and air travel.

Government will necessarily be involved in all these continuing and constantly changing issues; for in the final analysis government is simply one means by which we as a people attempt to resolve issues in the direction of our ultimate values. If our moral sense is blunted, democratic government will resolve issues at whatever level of self-interest and fear we set. But if our moral sense is not blunted, if we practice and insist upon free discussion, if we fight with intelligence every hysterical narrowing of the limits of debate, if we refuse to return to office public officials who attempt for selfish reasons to destroy our mutual trust, if we respect the laws and institutions which surround us, if we respect each other, the moral tone and moral authority of our society can be dramatically raised. If further, we keep informed; if we participate as time and ability permit in the common life of the local, state, national, and international communities of which we are a part; if in private as well as in public life we act in accordance with principles of human brotherhood without regard to race, color, creed, nationality background, or social or financial status; then we keep the options of freedom alive, not just for ourselves, but for everyone.

Only then have we fulfilled our true obligations as citizens—to each other and to our heritage. Only then have we as citizens made our supreme and necessary contribution to government in America.

# Appendix

# Footnotes

## Preface

[1] G. K. Chesterton, *Charles Dickens: A Critical Study*, New York: Dodd and Mead, 1906, p. 222.

## Chapter 2

[1] Ralph Barton Perry, *Puritanism and Democracy*, New York: the Vanguard Press, 1944, p. 92.

[2] George H. Sabine, *A History of Political Theory*, New York: Henry Holt and Company, 1937, p. 65.

[3] *Ibid*, p. 482.

[4] Quoted in Alpheus T. Mason, *Free Government in the Making*, New York: Oxford University Press, 1949, p. 12.

## Chapter 3

[1] Arthur M. Schlesinger, *New Viewpoints in American History*, New York: The Macmillan Company, 1922, pp. 80–81.

[2] *Ibid*, p. 81.

## Chapter 7

[1] *Britannica Book of the Year 1956*, p. 478.

[2] *United States Government Organization Manual 1956–1957*, Washington, D. C.: Government Printing Office, 1956, pp. 68–69.

## Chapter 9

[1] "The Roots of Liberty," an essay in Ruth Nanda Anshen, *Freedom: Its Meaning*. New York: Harcourt, Brace and Company, 1940, p. 31.

[2] Robert E. Cushman, *Civil Liberties in the United States*, Ithaca, New York: Cornell University Press, 1956, pp. 204–205.

[3] *United States Government Organization Manual 1954–1955*, Washington, D. C.: Government Printing Office, 1954, p. 204.

## Chapter 10

[1] T. Swan Harding, "The Marriage of Science to Government," *American Journal of Pharmacy* (October, 1944), reprinted in U. S. Congress, *Symposium on Congress by Members of Congress and Others*, Joint Committee Print, 79th Congress, 1st Session (Washington, D. C., 1945), p. 94.

[2] "National Q-&-A Game—The Polls," Robert Bendiner, in E. M. Kirkpatrick, and J. J. Kirkpatrick, *Elections—U. S. A.* New York: Henry Holt and Company, Inc., 1956, p. 118.

[3] Nathan B. Blumberg, *One Party Press?* Lincoln, Neb.: University of Nebraska Press, 1956.

[4] Leone Baxter, speech, quoted in Stanley Kelley, Jr., *Professional Public Relations and Political Power*, Baltimore: The Johns Hopkins Press, 1956, p. 44. On censorship, see Robert E. Cushman, *Civil Liberties in the United States*, Ithaca, N. Y.: Cornell University Press, 1956.

## Chapter 11

[1] Karl Schriftgiesser, *The Lobbyists*, Boston, Mass.: Little Brown and Company, 1951, p. 4.

[2] Rep. Clarence Cannon, quoted by Stuart Chase, *Democracy Under Pressure*, New York: The Twentieth Century Fund, 1945, p. 19.

[3] John Gunther, *Inside USA*, New York: Harper & Brothers, 1947, p. 221.

[4] Dayton D. McKean, "The Politics of the States," in *The Forty-eight States*, New York: The American Assembly, Columbia University, 1955.

## Chapter 12

[1] See B. R. Berelson, P. F. Lazarsfeld, and W. N. McPhee, *Voting—A Study of Opinion Formation in a Presidential Campaign*, Chicago: University of Chicago Press, 1954.

[2] "The Changing Party Pattern," *The Antioch Review*, Vol. XVI, No. 3 (Fall, 1956), p. 348.

[3] Cabell Phillips, "Party Chairman: Study in Feuds and Funds," *The New York Times Magazine*, July 1, 1956, p. 10.

[4] Duncan Norton-Taylor, "How to Give Money to Politicians," *Fortune Magazine* (May, 1956), p. 116.

[5] Dayton D. McKean, "The Politics of the States," in *The Forty-eight States*, New York: The American Assembly, Columbia University, 1955, p. 79.

[6] *How to Win, A Handbook for Political Action*, Washington, D. C.: Committee on Political Education, AFL-CIO, 1956, p. 65.

[7] See "Toward a More Responsible Two-Party System," a report by the Committee on Political Parties of the American Political Science Association, Washington, D. C., 1948.

## Chapter 13

[1] Charles E. and Robert E. Merriam, *The American Government*, Boston: Ginn & Company, 1954, p. 97.

[2] P. T. David and others, *Presidential Nominating Politics in 1952*, Baltimore: Johns Hopkins Press, 1954, Vol. I, p. 166.

[3] *Congressional Quarterly* (1956), pp. 16 ff.

[4] See Heinz Eulau, "Class Identification in Voting Behavior," *Western Political Quarterly*, September, 1955 vs. B. R. Berelson and others, *Voting—A Study of Opinion Formation in a Presidential Campaign*, Chicago: University of Chicago Press, 1954.

[5] Miami University, *Influence of Television on the Election of 1952*, Oxford, Ohio: Oxford Associates Inc., 1954.

[6] This tradition was violated in 1948 when one Democratic elector in Tennessee cast his ballot for a candidate of the States' Rights party; the same thing happened in Alabama in 1906.

## Chapter 14

[1] O. R. Altman, "Second and Third Sessions of the 75th Congress, 1937–38," *American Political Science Review*, XXXII (December, 1938), p. 1116, quoted in Robert K. Carr and others, *American Democracy in Theory and Practice*, New York: Rinehart & Company, 1955, p. 485.

[2] William Allen White, *Masks in a Pageant,* New York: The Macmillan Company, 1928, p. 156.

## Chapter 16

[1] Dean Acheson, "Legislative Executive Relations," *Yale Review* (Summer, 1956), p. 491.

[2] Edward S. Corwin and Louis W. Koenig, *The Presidency Today,* New York: New York University Press, 1956, p. 84.

[3] *Ibid.,* p. 88.

## Chapter 17

[1] We are indebted to Professor Clinton Rossiter for part of the classification of Presidential responsibilities which we have adopted. See his *The American Presidency,* New York: Harper & Brothers, 1956.

[2] *Ibid.,* p. 5.

[3] *Ibid.,* p. 23.

[4] *United States Government Organization Manual, 1955–1956,* Washington, D. C.: Government Printing Office, 1956, p. 66.

[5] *Ibid.,* p. 67.

[6] Quoted in Leonard White, *The Jacksonians,* New York: The Macmillan Company, 1954, p. 90.

## Chapter 18

[1] Commission on Organization of the Executive Branch of the Government, *Subcommittee Report on Special Personnel Problems in the Department of Defense,* Washington, D. C.: Government Printing Office, June, 1955.

[2] Morgan Thomas, *Atomic Energy and Congress,* Ann Arbor: University of Michigan Press, 1956, p. 4.

[3] *Ibid.,* p. 7.

## Chapter 19

[1] J. M. Burns and J. W. Peltason, *Government by the People,* New York: Prentice-Hall, Inc., 2d ed., 1955, p. 586.

## Chapter 20

[1] Lincoln Steffens, *Autobiography.* New York: Harcourt, Brace and Company, 1931, Vol. II, p. 466.

[2] Charles A. Beard, *American Government and Politics,* New York: The Macmillan Company, 10th ed., 1949.

## Chapter 22

[1] H. E. Barnes and N. K. Teeters, *New Horizons in Criminology,* New York: Prentice-Hall, Inc., 1945, pp. 292–293.

[2] Arthur T. Vanderbilt, *Traffic Enforcement and the Sixteen Resolutions of the Chief Justices and the Governors,* New York: Institute of Judicial Administration, 1953, p. 10.

[3] Carl L. Becker, *Freedom and Responsibility,* New York: Alfred A. Knopf, 1949, p. 82.

## Chapter 25

[1] United States Commission on Intergovernmental Relations, *An Advisory Committee Report on Local Government,* Washington, D. C.: Government Printing Office, June, 1955, pp. 7–8.

[2] William E. Leuchtenberg, *Flood Control Politics: The Connecticut River Valley, 1927–1950,* Cambridge: Harvard University Press, 1953, p. 253.

[3] Herman Finer, *Theory and Practice of Modern Government,* New York: Henry Holt and Co., 1949, p. 185.

[4] The City of Clinton *v.* Cedar Rapids and Missouri Railroad Company, 24 Iowa (1868).

# Quotation Sources

p. 1: Carl Becker, *New Liberties for Old*, New Haven: Yale University Press, 1941, p. 149 f.

p. 8: Carl Sandburg, "Upstream," quoted in William Rose Benét and Norman Cousins, *The Poetry of Freedom*, New York: The Modern Library, 1948, p. 474.

p. 28: Cicero, *De Republica*, quoted in George H. Sabine, *A History of Political Theory*, New York: Henry Holt and Company, 1937, p. 164.

p. 29: James Harrington, *Art of Lawgiving*, quoted in Sabine, *op. cit.*, p. 500.

p. 93: J. Edgar Hoover, quoted in Edwin S. Newman, *The Freedom Reader*, Vol. 2, Docket Series, New York: Oceana Publications, 1955, p. 194.

p. 113: Dwight D. Eisenhower, quoted in Robert J. Donovan, *The Eisenhower Story*, New York: Harper & Brothers, 1956, p. 183.

pp. 160–161:
Leviticus: *Holy Bible*, Revised Standard Edition, New York: Thomas Nelson and Sons, 1953, p. 130.
Pericles: Quoted in Sabine, *op. cit.*, p. 17.
John: *The Holy Bible*, King James Version, New York: James Pott and Company, p. 125 (New Test.).
Dante: *De Monarchia*, Book I, Chapter 12; quoted in *Introduction to Contemporary Civilization in the West, A Source Book*, Vol. I, New York: Columbia University Press, 1946, p. 198. (N.B. As quoted in the Columbia Source book, the word "disposed" is ambiguous out of context, and has been changed for this reason to "condition" with a necessary reordering of the sentence. The actual wording as quoted is, "And the human race when most free is best disposed.")
Milton: *The Areopagitica;* quoted in Finley M. K. Foster and Homer A. Watt, *Voices of Liberty*, New York: The Macmillan Company, 1941, p. 52.
Montesquieu: *The Spirit of the Laws*, Book XI, Sec. II; quoted in *Introduction to Contemporary Civilization in the West, op. cit.*, p. 936.
Jefferson: In a letter to James Madison, 20 December 1787; quoted in Alpheus T. Mason, *Free Government in the Making*, New York: Oxford University Press, 1949, pp. 248–249.
Mill: *On Liberty* in *Utilitarianism, Liberty, & Representative Government*, Everyman's Library, No. 482, London. J. M. Dent & Sons Ltd., 1931 Reprint, p. 111.
Holmes: The first section of the Holmes' quotation is from his dissent in *U. S.* v. *Schwimmer*, 279 U S 644 (1928); the second section of the quotation is from Holmes' dissenting opinion in *Abrams* v. *U. S.*, 250 U S 616 (1919).
Grenfell: Quoted in the *Cosmos Club Bulletin*, Vol. 9, No. 11 (November, 1956), p. 5.
Hand: Quoted in Newman, *op. cit.*, p. 26.

p. 164: Zechariah Chafee, Jr., quoted in Newman, *op. cit.*, p. 43.

p. 165: Justice William O. Douglas, quoted in Newman, *op. cit.*, p. 87.

p. 176: Charles S. Johnson, "A Southern Negro's View of the South," *The New York Times Magazine,* September 23, 1956, p. 67.

p. 181: James Madison, *The Federalist,* Number X, New York: Willey Book Company, rev. ed., 1901, p. 46.

p. 196: Neil Staebler, quoted in Stanley Kelley, Jr., *Professional Public Relations and Political Power,* Baltimore: The Johns Hopkins Press, 1956, p. 2.

p. 197: Edward L. Bernays, *The Engineering of Consent,* Norman, Okla.: University of Oklahoma Press, 1955, pp. 9, 10.

p. 236: Warren Moscow, "Exit the Boss, Enter the 'Leader,'" *The New York Times Magazine,* June 22, 1947, p. 48.

p. 244: *The* (London) *Economist,* quoted in Paul T. David, Malcolm Moos, and Ralph M. Goldman, *Presidential Nominating Politics in 1952,* Vol. I, *The National Story,* Baltimore: The Johns Hopkins Press, 1954, p. 232.

p. 245: Ivan Hinderaker, *Party Politics,* New York: Henry Holt and Company, 1956, p. 181.

p. 253: James Bryce, *The American Commonwealth,* quoted in David, Moos, and Goldman, *op. cit.,* p. 3.

p. 260: Wilfred E. Binkley, "The President as Chief Legislator," *The Annals,* Vol. 307 (September, 1956) , p. 101.

p. 265: John Jay, *The Federalist,* No. III, *op. cit.,* p. 10.

p. 268: U. S. Supreme Court, *McGrain* v. *Daugherty,* 273 U S 135 (1927) .

p. 312: Binkley, *op. cit.,* p. 95.

p. 313: Sidney Hyman, *The American President,* New York: Harper & Brothers, 1954, p. 101.

p. 321: Louis Brownlow, *The President and the Presidency,* Chicago: Public Administration Service, 1949, p. 75.

p. 332: Harlan Cleveland, "The Executive and the Public Interest," *The Annals,* Vol. 307 (September, 1956) , p. 7.

p. 333: Alexis de Tocqueville, quoted in Sidney Hyman, "The Art of the Presidency," *The Annals,* Vol. 307 (September, 1956) , p. 7.

p. 344: Sidney Hyman, *The American President,* New York: Harper & Brothers, 1954, pp. 317–318.

p. 345: Peter Frelinghuysen, Jr., "Presidential Disability," *The Annals,* Vol. 307 (September, 1956) , pp. 144, 155.

p. 387: James W. Fesler, "The Challenge to the States," *The Forty-eight States,* New York: The American Assembly, Columbia University, 1955, p. 7.

p. 405: Dayton D. McKean, "The Politics of the States," *The Forty-eight States,* New York: The American Assembly, Columbia University, 1955, p. 82.

p. 441: Jerome Frank, *Courts on Trial,* Princeton: Princeton University Press, 1950, p. 32 (fn) .

p. 453: Blaine E. Mercer, *The American Community,* New York: Random House, 1956, p. 295.

p. 513: Luther Gulick, *National Municipal Review* (January, 1957) , p. 13. From an address in Memphis, Tenn., November 13, 1956.

p. 523: Pericles' *Funeral Oration,* quoted in Sabine, *op. cit.,* p. 14.

p. 544: William James, quoted in O. E. Baker, Ralph Borsodi, and M. E. Wilson, *Agriculture and Modern Life,* New York: Harper & Brothers, 1939, p. 1.

## THE DECLARATION OF INDEPENDENCE

### In Congress, July 4, 1776

### THE UNANIMOUS DECLARATION OF THE THIRTEEN UNITED STATES OF AMERICA

When in the Course of human events, it becomes necessary for one people to dissolve the political bands which have connected them with another, and to assume among the Powers of the earth, the separate and equal station to which the Laws of Nature and of Nature's God entitle them, a decent respect to the opinions of mankind requires that they should declare the causes which impel them to the separation.

We hold these truths to be self-evident, that all men are created equal, that they are endowed by their Creator with certain unalienable Rights, that among these are Life, Liberty and the pursuit of Happiness. That to secure these rights, Governments are instituted among Men, deriving their just powers from the consent of the governed, That whenever any Form of Government becomes destructive of these ends, it is the Right of the People to alter or to abolish it, and to institute new Government, laying its foundation on such principles and organizing its powers in such form, as to them shall seem most likely to effect their Safety and Happiness. Prudence, indeed, will dictate that Governments long established should not be changed for light and transient causes; and accordingly all experience hath shown, that mankind are more disposed to suffer, while evils are sufferable, than to right themselves by abolishing the forms to which they are accustomed. But when a long train of abuses and usurpations, pursuing invariably the same Object evinces a design to reduce them under absolute Despotism, it is their right, it is their duty, to throw off such Government, and to provide new Guards for their future security.—Such has been the patient sufferance of these Colonies; and such is now the necessity which constrains them to alter their former Systems of Government. The history of the present King of Great Britain is a history of repeated injuries and usurpations, all having in direct object the establishment of an absolute Tyranny over these States. To prove this, let Facts be submitted to a candid world.

He has refused his Assent to Laws, the most wholesome and necessary for the public good.

He has forbidden his Governors to pass Laws of immediate and pressing importance, unless suspended in their operation till his Assent should be obtained; and when so suspended, he has utterly neglected to attend to them.

He has refused to pass other Laws for the accommodation of large districts of people, unless those people would relinquish the right of Representation in the Legislature, a right inestimable to them and formidable to tyrants only.

He has called together legislative bodies at places unusual, uncomfortable, and distant from the depository of their Public Records, for the sole purpose of fatiguing them into compliance with his measures.

He has dissolved Representative Houses repeatedly, for opposing with manly firmness his invasions on the rights of the people.

He has refused for a long time, after such dissolutions, to cause others to be elected; whereby the Legislative Powers, incapable of Annihilation, have returned to the People at large for their exercise; the State remaining in the mean time exposed to all the dangers of invasion from without, and convulsions within.

He has endeavoured to prevent the population of these States; for that purpose obstructing the Laws of Naturalization of Foreigners; refusing to pass others to encourage their migration hither, and raising the conditions of new Appropriations of Lands.

He has obstructed the Administration of Justice, by refusing his Assent to Laws for establishing Judiciary Powers.

He has made Judges dependent on his Will alone, for the tenure of their offices, and the amount and payment of their salaries.

He has erected a multitude of New Offices, and sent hither swarms of Officers to harass our People, and eat out their substance.

He has kept among us, in times of peace, Standing Armies without the Consent of our legislature.

He has affected to render the Military independent of and superior to the Civil Power.

He has combined with others to subject us to a jurisdiction foreign to our constitution, and unacknowledged by our laws; giving his Assent to their acts of pretended legislation:

For quartering large bodies of armed troops among us:

For protecting them, by a mock Trial, from Punishment for any Murders which they should commit on the Inhabitants of these States:

For cutting off our Trade with all parts of the world:

For imposing taxes on us without our Consent:

For depriving us in many cases, of the benefits of Trial by jury:

For transporting us beyond Seas to be tried for pretended offences:

For abolishing the free System of English Laws in a neighboring Province, establishing therein an Arbitrary government, and enlarging its Boundaries so as to render it at once an example and fit instrument for introducing the same absolute rule into these Colonies:

For taking away our Charters, abolishing our most valuable Laws, and altering fundamentally the Forms of our Governments:

For suspending our own Legislature, and declaring themselves invested with Power to legislate for us in all cases whatsoever.

He has abdicated Government here, by declaring us out of his Protection and waging War against us.

He has plundered our seas, ravaged our Coasts, burnt our towns, and destroyed the lives of our people.

He is at this time transporting large armies of foreign mercenaries to compleat the works of death, desolation and tyranny, already begun with circumstances of Cruelty & perfidy scarcely paralleled in the most barbarous ages, and totally unworthy the Head of a civilized nation.

He has constrained our fellow Citizens taken Captive on the high Seas to bear Arms against their Country, to become the executioners of their friends and Brethren, or to fall themselves by their Hands.

He has excited domestic insurrections amongst us, and has endeavoured to bring on the inhabitants of our frontiers, the merciless Indian Savages, whose known rule of warfare, is an undistinguished destruction of all ages, sexes and conditions.

In every stage of these Oppressions We have Petitioned for Redress in the most humble terms: Our repeated Petitions have been answered only by repeated injury.   A Prince, whose character is thus marked by every act which may define a Tyrant, is unfit to be the ruler of a free People.

Nor have We been wanting in attention to our British brethren.   We have warned them from time to time of attempts by their legislature to extend an unwarrantable jurisdiction over us.   We have reminded them of the circumstances of our emigration and settlement here.   We have appealed to their native justice and magnanimity, and we have conjured them by the ties of our common kindred to disavow these usurpations, which, would inevitably interrupt our connections and correspondence.   They too have been deaf to the voice of justice and of consanguinity.   We must, therefore, acquiesce in the necessity, which denounces our Separation, and hold them, as we hold the rest of mankind, Enemies in War, in Peace Friends.

We, therefore, the Representatives of the united States of America, in General Congress, Assembled, appealing to the Supreme Judge of the world for the rectitude of our intentions, do, in the Name, and by Authority of the good People of these Colonies, solemnly publish and declare, That these United Colonies are, and of Right ought to be Free and Independent States; that they are Absolved from all Allegiance to the British Crown, and that all political connection between them and the State of Great Britain, is and ought to be totally dissolved; and that as Free and Independent States, they have full Power to levy War, conclude Peace, contract Alliances, establish Commerce, and to do all other Acts and Things which Independent States may of right do.   And for the support of this Declaration, with a firm reliance on the Protection of Divine Providence, we mutually pledge to each other our Lives, our Fortunes and our sacred Honor.

JOHN HANCOCK [1]

---

[1] The remaining signatures are omitted.

## CONSTITUTION OF THE UNITED STATES OF AMERICA

We the people of the United States, in order to form a more perfect union, establish justice, insure domestic tranquility, provide for the common defense, promote the general welfare, and secure the blessings of liberty to ourselves and our posterity, do ordain and establish this Constitution for the United States of America.

### ARTICLE I

#### SECTION I

All legislative powers herein granted shall be vested in a Congress of the United States, which shall consist of a Senate and House of Representatives.

#### SECTION II

(1) The House of Representatives shall be composed of members chosen every second year by the people of the several States, and the electors in each State shall have the qualifications requisite for electors of the most numerous branch of the State legislature.

(2) No person shall be a Representative who shall not have attained to the age of twenty-five years, and been seven years a citizen of the United States, and who shall not, when elected, be an inhabitant of that State in which he shall be chosen.

(3) Representatives and *direct taxes* [1] shall be apportioned among the several States which may be included within this Union, according to their respective numbers, *which shall be determined by adding to the whole number of free persons, including those bound to service for a term of years, and excluding Indians not taxed, three fifths of all other persons.* [2]  The actual enumeration shall be made within three years after the first meeting of the Congress of the United States, and within every subsequent term of ten years, in such manner as they shall by law direct.  The number of Representatives shall not exceed one for every thirty thousand, but each State shall have at least one Representative; *and until such enumeration shall be made, the State of New Hampshire shall be entitled to choose three, Massachusetts eight, Rhode Island and Providence Plantations one, Connecticut five, New York six, New Jersey four, Pennsylvania eight, Delaware one, Maryland six, Virginia ten, North Carolina five, South Carolina five, and Georgia three.* [3]

(4) When vacancies happen in the representation from any State, the executive authority thereof shall issue writs of election to fill such vacancies.

(5) The House of Representatives shall choose their Speaker and other officers; and shall have the sole power of impeachment.

[1] Modified by Amendment XVI.
[2] Superseded by Amendment XIV.
[3] Temporary provision.

(1) *The Senate of the United States shall be composed of two Senators from each State, chosen by the legislature thereof, for six years; and each Senator shall have one vote.*[4]

(2) Immediately after they shall be assembled in consequence of the first election, they shall be divided as equally as may be into three classes. The seats of the Senators of the first class shall be vacated at the expiration of the second year, of the second class at the expiration of the fourth year, and of the third class at the expiration of the sixth year, so that one third may be chosen every second year; *and if vacancies happen by resignation, or otherwise, during the recess of the legislature of any State, the executive thereof may make temporary appointments until the next meeting of the legislature which shall then fill such vacancies.*[5]

(3) No person shall be a Senator who shall not have attained to the age of thirty years, and been nine years a citizen of the United States, and who shall not, when elected, be an inhabitant of that State for which he shall be chosen.

(4) The Vice President of the United States shall be president of the Senate, but shall have no vote, unless they be equally divided.

(5) The Senate shall choose their other officers, and also a president pro tempore, in the absence of the Vice President, or when he shall exercise the office of President of the United States.

(6) The Senate shall have the sole power to try all impeachments. When sitting for that purpose, they shall be on oath or affirmation. When the President of the United States is tried, the Chief Justice shall preside: and no person shall be convicted without the concurrence of two thirds of the members present.

(7) Judgment in cases of impeachment shall not extend further than to removal from office, and disqualification to hold and enjoy any office of honor, trust, or profit under the United States: but the party convicted shall nevertheless be liable and subject to indictment, trial, judgment, and punishment, according to law.

(1) The times, places, and manner of holding elections for Senators and Representatives shall be prescribed in each State by the legislature thereof; but the Congress may at any time by law make or alter such regulations, except as to the places of choosing Senators.

(2) *The Congress shall assemble at least once in every year, and such meeting shall be on the first Monday in December, unless they shall by law appoint a different day.*[6]

(1) Each House shall be the judge of the elections, returns, and qualifications of its own members, and a majority of each shall constitute a quorum to do business; but a smaller number may adjourn from day to day, and may be authorized to compel the attendance of absent members, in such manner, and under such penalties, as each House may provide.

[4] Superseded by Amendment XVII.
[5] Superseded by Amendment XVII.
[6] Superseded by Amendment XX.

(2) Each House may determine the rules of its proceedings, punish its members for disorderly behavior, and, with the concurrence of two thirds, expel a member.

(3) Each House shall keep a journal of its proceedings, and from time to time publish the same, excepting such parts as may in their judgment require secrecy; and the yeas and nays of the members of either House on any question shall, at the desire of one fifth of those present, be entered on the journal.

(4) Neither House, during the session of Congress, shall, without the consent of the other, adjourn for more than three days, nor to any other place than that in which the two Houses shall be sitting.

## SECTION VI

(1) The Senators and Representatives shall receive a compensation for their services, to be ascertained by law, and paid out of the Treasury of the United States. They shall in all cases, except treason, felony, and breach of the peace, be privileged from arrest during their attendance at the session of their respective Houses, and in going to and returning from the same; and for any speech or debate in either House, they shall not be questioned in any other place.

(2) No Senator or Representative shall, during the time for which he was elected, be appointed to any civil office under the authority of the United States, which shall have been created, or the emoluments whereof shall have been increased, during such time; and no person holding any office under the United States shall be a member of either House during his continuance in office.

## SECTION VII

(1) All bills for raising revenue shall originate in the House of Representatives; but the Senate may propose or concur with amendments as on other bills.

(2) Every bill which shall have passed the House of Representatives and the Senate, shall, before it become a law, be presented to the President of the United States; if he approve he shall sign it, but if not he shall return it, with his objections, to that House in which it shall have originated, who shall enter the objections at large on their journal, and proceed to reconsider it. If after such reconsideration two thirds of that House shall agree to pass the bill, it shall be sent, together with the objections, to the other House, by which it shall likewise be reconsidered, and if approved by two thirds of that House, it shall become a law. But in all such cases the votes of both Houses shall be determined by yeas and nays, and the names of the persons voting for and against the bill shall be entered on the journal of each House respectively. If any bill shall not be returned by the President within ten days (Sundays excepted) after it shall have been presented to him, the same shall be a law, in like manner as if he had signed it, unless the Congress by their adjournment prevent its return, in which case it shall not be a law.

(3) Every order, resolution, or vote to which the concurrence of the Senate and House of Representatives may be necessary (except on a question of adjournment) shall be presented to the President of the United States; and before the same shall take effect, shall be approved by him, or being disapproved by him, shall be repassed by two thirds of the Senate and House of Representatives, according to the rules and limitations prescribed in the case of a bill.

## SECTION VIII

(1) The Congress shall have power to lay and collect taxes, duties, imposts, and excises, to pay the debts and provide for the common defense and general welfare of the United States; but all duties, imposts, and excises shall be uniform throughout the United States;

(2) To borrow money on the credit of the United States;

(3) To regulate commerce with foreign nations, and among the several States, and with the Indian tribes;

(4) To establish an uniform rule of naturalization, and uniform laws on the subject of bankruptcies throughout the United States;

(5) To coin money, regulate the value thereof, and of foreign coin, and fix the standard of weights and measures;

(6) To provide for the punishment of counterfeiting the securities and current coin of the United States;

(7) To establish post offices and post roads;

(8) To promote the progress of science and useful arts, by securing for limited times to authors and inventors the exclusive right to their respective writings and discoveries;

(9) To constitute tribunals inferior to the Supreme Court;

(10) To define and punish piracies and felonies committed on the high seas, and offenses against the law of nations;

(11) To declare war, grant letters of marque and reprisal, and make rules concerning captures on land and water;

(12) To raise and support armies, but no appropriation of money to that use shall be for a longer term than two years;

(13) To provide and maintain a navy;

(14) To make rules for the government and regulation of the land and naval forces;

(15) To provide for calling forth the militia to execute the laws of the Union, suppress insurrections, and repel invasions;

(16) To provide for organizing, arming, and disciplining the militia, and for governing such part of them as may be employed in the service of the United States, reserving to the States respectively the appointment of the officers, and the authority of training the militia according to the discipline prescribed by Congress;

(17) To exercise exclusive legislation in all cases whatsoever, over such district (not exceeding ten miles square) as may, by cession of particular States, and the acceptance of Congress, become the seat of the government of the United States, and to exercise like authority over all places purchased by the consent of the legislature of the State in which the same shall be, for the erection of forts, magazines, arsenals, dock-yards, and other needful buildings; and

(18) To make all laws which shall be necessary and proper for carrying into execution the foregoing powers, and all other powers vested by this Constitution in the government of the United States, or in any department or officer thereof.

## SECTION IX

(1) *The migration or importation of such persons as any of the States now existing shall think proper to admit, shall not be prohibited by the Congress prior*

*to the year one thousand eight hundred and eight, but a tax or duty may be imposed on such importation, not exceeding ten dollars for each person.[7]*

(2) The privilege of the writ of habeas corpus shall not be suspended, unless when in cases of rebellion or invasion the public safety may require it.

(3) No bill of attainder or ex post facto law shall be passed.

(4) No capitation, or *other direct, tax* shall be laid, unless *in proportion to the census* or enumeration hereinbefore directed to be taken.[8]

(5) No tax or duty shall be laid on articles exported from any State.

(6) No preference shall be given by any regulation of commerce or revenue to the ports of one State over those of another: nor shall vessels bound to, or from, one State, be obliged to enter, clear, or pay duties in another.

(7) No money shall be drawn from the Treasury, but in consequence of appropriations made by law; and a regular statement and account of the receipts and expenditures of all public money shall be published from time to time.

(8) No title of nobility shall be granted by the United States: and no person holding any office of profit or trust under them, shall, without the consent of the Congress, accept of any present, emolument, office, or title, of any kind whatever, from any king, prince, or foreign State.

### SECTION X

(1) No State shall enter into any treaty, alliance, or confederation; grant letters of marque and reprisal; coin money; emit bills of credit; make anything but gold and silver coin a tender in payment of debts; pass any bill of attainder, ex post facto law, or law impairing the obligation of contracts, or grant any title of nobility.

(2) No State shall, without the consent of the Congress, lay any imposts or duties on imports or exports, except what may be absolutely necessary for executing its inspection laws: and the net produce of all duties and imposts, laid by any State on imports or exports, shall be for the use of the treasury of the United States; and all such laws shall be subject to the revision and control of the Congress.

(3) No State shall, without the consent of Congress, lay any duty of tonnage, keep troops, or ships of war in time of peace, enter into any agreement or compact with another State, or with a foreign power, or engage in war, unless actually invaded, or in such imminent danger as will not admit of delay.

## ARTICLE II

### SECTION I

(1) The executive power shall be vested in a President of the United States of America. He shall hold his office during the term of four years, and, together with the Vice President, chosen for the same term, be elected, as follows:

(2) Each State shall appoint, in such manner as the legislature thereof may direct, a number of electors, equal to the whole number of Senators and Representatives to which the State may be entitled in the Congress: but no Senator or Representative, or person holding an office of trust or profit under the United States, shall be appointed an elector.

---

[7] Obsolete provision.
[8] Modified by Amendment XVI.

*The electors shall meet in their respective States, and vote by ballot for two persons, of whom one at least shall not be an inhabitant of the same State with themselves. And they shall make a list of all the persons voted for, and of the number of votes for each; which list they shall sign and certify, and transmit sealed to the seat of the government of the United States, directed to the president of the Senate. The president of the Senate shall, in the presence of the Senate and House of Representatives, open all the certificates, and the votes shall then be counted. The person having the greatest number of votes shall be the President, if such number be a majority of the whole number of electors appointed; and if there be more than one who have such majority, and have an equal number of votes, then the House of Representatives shall immediately choose by ballot one of them for President; and if no person have a majority, then from the five highest on the list the said House shall in like manner choose the President. But in choosing the President, the votes shall be taken by States, the representation from each State having one vote; a quorum for this purpose shall consist of a member or members from two thirds of the States, and a majority of all the States shall be necessary to a choice. In every case, after the choice of the President, the person having the greatest number of votes of the electors shall be the Vice President. But if there should remain two or more who have equal votes, the Senate shall choose from them by ballot the Vice President.[9]*

(3) The Congress may determine the time of choosing the electors, and the day on which they shall give their votes; which day shall be the same throughout the United States.

(4) No person except a natural-born citizen, or a citizen of the United States, at the time of the adoption of this Constitution, shall be eligible to the office of President; neither shall any person be eligible to that office who shall not have attained to the age of thirty-five years, and been fourteen years a resident within the United States.

(5) In case of the removal of the President from office, or of his death, resignation, or inability to discharge the powers and duties of the said office, the same shall devolve on the Vice President, and the Congress may by law provide for the case of removal, death, resignation, or inability, both of the President and Vice President, declaring what officer shall then act as President, and such officer shall act accordingly, until the disability be removed, or a President shall be elected.

(6) The President shall, at stated times, receive for his services a compensation, which shall neither be increased nor diminished during the period for which he shall have been elected, and he shall not receive within that period any other emolument from the United States, or any of them.

(7) Before he enter on the execution of his office, he shall take the following oath or affirmation: "I do solemnly swear (or affirm) that I will faithfully execute the office of President of the United States, and will, to the best of my ability, preserve, protect, and defend the Constitution of the United States."

SECTION II

(1) The President shall be commander in chief of the army and navy of the United States, and of the militia of the several States, when called into the actual service of the United States; he may require the opinion, in writing, of the principal

[9] Superseded by Amendment XII.

officer in each of the executive departments, upon any subject relating to the duties of their respective offices, and he shall have power to grant reprieves and pardons for offenses against the United States, except in cases of impeachment.

(2) He shall have power, by and with the advice and consent of the Senate, to make treaties, provided two thirds of the Senators present concur; and he shall nominate, and by and with the advice and consent of the Senate, shall appoint ambassadors, other public ministers and consuls, judges of the Supreme Court, and all other officers of the United States, whose appointments are not herein otherwise provided for, and which shall be established by law: but the Congress may by law vest the appointment of such inferior officers, as they think proper, in the President alone, in the courts of law, or in the heads of departments.

(3) The President shall have power to fill up all vacancies that may happen during the recess of the Senate, by granting commissions which shall expire at the end of their next session.

### SECTION III

He shall from time to time give to the Congress information of the state of the Union, and recommend to their consideration such measures as he shall judge necessary and expedient; he may, on extraordinary occasions, convene both Houses, or either of them, and in case of disagreement between them, with respect to the time of adjournment, he may adjourn them to such time as he shall think proper; he shall receive ambassadors and other public ministers; he shall take care that the laws be faithfully executed, and shall commission all the officers of the United States.

### SECTION IV

The President, Vice President, and all civil officers of the United States, shall be removed from office on impeachment for, and conviction of, treason, bribery, or other high crimes and misdemeanors.

## ARTICLE III

### SECTION I

The judicial power of the United States shall be vested in one Supreme Court, and in such inferior courts as the Congress may from time to time ordain and establish. The judges, both of the Supreme and inferior courts, shall hold their offices during good behavior, and shall, at stated times, receive for their services a compensation, which shall not be diminished during their continuance in office.

### SECTION II

(1) The judicial power shall extend to all cases, in law and equity, arising under this Constitution, the laws of the United States, and treaties made, or which shall be made, under their authority;—to all cases affecting ambassadors, other public ministers, and consuls;—to all cases of admiralty and maritime jurisdiction;—to controversies to which the United States shall be a party;—to controversies between two or more States;—*between a State and citizens of another State;* [10]—between citizens of different States;—between citizens of the same State claiming lands

under grants of different States, and *between a State, or the citizens thereof, and foreign States, citizens, or subjects.*[10]

(2) In all cases affecting ambassadors, other public ministers, and consuls, and those in which a State shall be party, the Supreme Court shall have original jurisdiction. In all the other cases before mentioned, the Supreme Court shall have appellate jurisdiction, both as to law and fact, with such exceptions, and under such regulations, as the Congress shall make.

(3) The trial of all crimes, except in cases of impeachment, shall be by jury; and such trial shall be held in the State where the said crimes shall have been committed; but when not committed within any State, the trial shall be at such place or places as the Congress may by law have directed.

### SECTION III

(1) Treason against the United States shall consist only in levying war against them, or in adhering to their enemies, giving them aid and comfort. No person shall be convicted of treason unless on the testimony of two witnesses to the same overt act, or on confession in open court.

(2) The Congress shall have power to declare the punishment of treason, but no attainder of treason shall work corruption of blood, or forfeiture except during the life of the person attainted.

## ARTICLE IV

### SECTION I

Full faith and credit shall be given in each State to the public acts, records, and judicial proceedings of every other State. And the Congress may by general laws prescribe the manner in which such acts, records, and proceedings shall be proved, and the effect thereof.

### SECTION II

(1) The citizens of each State shall be entitled to all privileges and immunities of citizens in the several States.

(2) A person charged in any State with treason, felony, or other crime, who shall flee from justice, and be found in another State, shall, on demand of the executive authority of the State from which he fled, be delivered up, to be removed to the State having jurisdiction of the crime.

(3) *No person held to service or labor in one State, under the laws thereof, escaping into another, shall, in consequence of any law or regulation therein, be discharged from such service or labor, but shall be delivered up on claim of the party to whom such service or labor may be due.*[11]

### SECTION III

(1) New States may be admitted by the Congress into this Union; but no new State shall be formed or erected within the jurisdiction of any other State; nor any State be formed by the junction of two or more States, or parts of States, without the consent of the legislatures of the states concerned as well as of the Congress.

[10] Limited by Amendment XI.
[11] Superseded by Amendment XIII so far as pertains to slaves.

(2) The Congress shall have power to dispose of and make all needful rules and regulations respecting the territory or other property belonging to the United States; and nothing in this Constitution shall be so construed as to prejudice any claims of the United States, or of any particular State.

SECTION IV

The United States shall guarantee to every State in this Union a republican form of government, and shall protect each of them against invasion; and, on application of the legislature, or of the executive (when the legislature cannot be convened), against domestic violence.

## ARTICLE V

The Congress, whenever two thirds of both Houses shall deem it necessary, shall propose amendments to this Constitution, or, on the application of the legislatures of two thirds of the several States, shall call a convention for proposing amendments which, in either case, shall be valid to all intents and purposes, as part of this Constitution, when ratified by the legislatures of three fourths of the several States, or by conventions in three fourths thereof, as the one or the other mode of ratification may be proposed by the Congress; provided *that no amendment which may be made prior to the year one thousand eight hundred and eight shall in any manner affect the first and fourth clauses in the ninth section of the first article;* [12] and that no State, without its consent, shall be deprived of its equal suffrage in the Senate.

## ARTICLE VI

(1) All debts contracted and engagements entered into, before the adoption of this Constitution, shall be as valid against the United States under this Constitution, as under the Confederation.

(2) This Constitution, and the laws of the United States which shall be made in pursuance thereof; and all treaties made, or which shall be made, under the authority of the United States, shall be the supreme law of the land; and the judges in every State shall be bound thereby, anything in the constitution or laws of any State to the contrary notwithstanding.

(3) The Senators and Representatives before mentioned, and the members of the several State legislatures, and all executive and judicial officers, both of the United States and of the several States, shall be bound by oath or affirmation to support this Constitution; but no religious test shall ever be required as a qualification to any office or public trust under the United States.

## ARTICLE VII

The ratification of the conventions of nine States shall be sufficient for the establishment of this Constitution between the States so ratifying the same.

[12] Obsolete provision.

## AMENDMENTS

### AMENDMENT I [13]                                                   1791

Congress shall make no law respecting an establishment of religion, or prohibiting the free exercise thereof; or abridging the freedom of speech, or of the press; or the right of the people peaceably to assemble, and to petition the government for a redress of grievances.

### AMENDMENT II                                                      1791

A well regulated militia, being necessary to the security of a free State, the right of the people to keep and bear arms shall not be infringed.

### AMENDMENT III                                                     1791

No soldier shall, in time of peace, be quartered in any house, without the consent of the owner, nor in time of war, but in a manner to be prescribed by law.

### AMENDMENT IV                                                      1791

The right of the people to be secure in their persons, houses, papers, and effects, against unreasonable searches and seizures, shall not be violated, and no warrants shall issue, but upon probable cause, supported by oath or affirmation, and particularly describing the place to be searched, and the persons or things to be seized.

### AMENDMENT V                                                       1791

No person shall be held to answer for a capital or otherwise infamous crime, unless on a presentment or indictment of a grand jury, except in cases arising in the land or naval forces, or in the militia, when in actual service in time of war or public danger; nor shall any person be subject for the same offence to be twice put in jeopardy of life or limb; nor shall be compelled in any criminal case to be a witness against himself, nor be deprived of life, liberty, or property, without due process of law; nor shall private property be taken for public use, without just compensation.

### AMENDMENT VI                                                      1791

In all criminal prosecutions the accused shall enjoy the right to a speedy and public trial, by an impartial jury of the State and district wherein the crime shall have been committed, which district shall have been previously ascertained by law, and to be informed of the nature and cause of the accusation; to be confronted with the witnesses against him; to have compulsory process for obtaining witnesses in his favor, and to have the assistance of counsel for his defense.

### AMENDMENT VII                                                     1791

In suits at common law, where the value in controversy shall exceed twenty dollars, the right of trial by jury shall be preserved, and no fact tried by a jury shall be otherwise re-examined in any court of the United States than according to the rules of the common law.

[13] In strict legal language the Amendments are known as "Articles," but in order to avoid confusion with the Articles of the original Constitution and in conformance with general usage they are listed as "Amendments" here. The date is that of when they were declared ratified.

AMENDMENT VIII                                    1791

Excessive bail shall not be required, nor excessive fines imposed, nor cruel and unusual punishments inflicted.

AMENDMENT IX                                    1791

The enumeration in the Constitution of certain rights shall not be construed to deny or disparage others retained by the people.

AMENDMENT X                                    1791

The powers not delegated to the United States by the Constitution, nor prohibited by it to the States, are reserved to the States respectively, or to the people.

AMENDMENT XI                                    1798

The judicial power of the United States shall not be construed to extend to any suit in law or equity, commenced or prosecuted against one of the United States by citizens of another State, or by citizens or subjects of any foreign State.

AMENDMENT XII                                    1804

The electors shall meet in their respective States, and vote by ballot for President and Vice President, one of whom, at least, shall not be an inhabitant of the same State with themselves; they shall name in their ballots the persons voted for as President, and in distinct ballots the persons voted for as Vice President, and they shall make distinct lists of all persons voted for as President, and of all persons voted for as Vice President, and of the number of votes for each, which lists they shall sign and certify, and transmit sealed to the seat of the government of the United States, directed to the president of the Senate;—the president of the Senate shall, in the presence of the Senate and House of Representatives, open all the certificates, and the votes shall then be counted;—the person having the greatest number of votes for President, shall be the President, if such number be a majority of the whole number of electors appointed; and if no person have such majority, then from the persons having the highest numbers not exceeding three on the list of those voted for as President, the House of Representatives shall choose immediately, by ballot, the President.   But in choosing the President, the votes shall be taken by States, the representation from each State having one vote; a quorum for this purpose shall consist of a member or members from two thirds of the States, and a majority of all the States shall be necessary to a choice.   And if the House of Representatives shall not choose a President whenever the right of choice shall devolve upon them, before the fourth day of March next following, then the Vice President shall act as President, as in the case of the death or other constitutional disability of the President.—The person having the greatest number of votes as Vice President, shall be the Vice President, if such number be a majority of the whole number of electors appointed, and if no person have a majority, then from the two highest numbers on the list, the Senate shall choose the Vice President; a quorum for the purpose shall consist of two thirds of the whole number of Senators, and a majority of the whole number shall be necessary to a choice.   But no person constitutionally ineligible to the office of President shall be eligible to that of Vice President of the United States.[14]

[14] Modified by Amendment XX.

## Amendment XIII

*Section 1.* Neither slavery nor involuntary servitude, except as a punishment for crime whereof the party shall have been duly convicted, shall exist within the United States, or any place subject to their jurisdiction.

*Section 2.* Congress shall have power to enforce this article by appropriate legislation.

## Amendment XIV

*Section 1.* All persons born or naturalized in the United States, and subject to the jurisdiction thereof, are citizens of the United States and of the State wherein they reside. No State shall make or enforce any law which shall abridge the privileges or immunities of citizens of the United States; nor shall any State deprive any person of life, liberty, or property, without due process of law; nor deny to any person within its jurisdiction the equal protection of the laws.

*Section 2.* Representatives shall be apportioned among the several States according to their respective numbers, counting the whole number of persons in each State, excluding Indians not taxed. But when the right to vote at any election for the choice of electors for President and Vice President of the United States, Representatives in Congress, the executive and judicial officers of a State, or the members of the legislature thereof, is denied to any of the male inhabitants of such State, being twenty-one years of age, and citizens of the United States, or in any way abridged, except for participation in rebellion, or other crime, the basis of representation therein shall be reduced in the proportion which the number of such male citizens shall bear to the whole number of male citizens twenty-one years of age in such State.

*Section 3.* No person shall be a Senator or Representative in Congress, or elector of President and Vice President, or hold any office, civil or military, under the United States, or under any State, who, having previously taken an oath, as a member of Congress, or as an officer of the United States, or as a member of any State legislature, or as an executive or judicial officer of any State, to support the Constitution of the United States, shall have engaged in insurrection or rebellion against the same, or given aid or comfort to the enemies thereof. But Congress may by a vote of two thirds of each House, remove such disability.

*Section 4.* The validity of the public debt of the United States, authorized by law, including debts incurred for payment of pensions and bounties for services in suppressing insurrection or rebellion, shall not be questioned. But neither the United States nor any State shall assume or pay any debt or obligation incurred in aid of insurrection or rebellion against the United States, or any claim for the loss or emancipation of any slave; but all such debts, obligations, and claims shall be held illegal and void.

*Section 5.* The Congress shall have power to enforce, by appropriate legislation, the provisions of this article.

## Amendment XV

*Section 1.* The right of citizens of the United States to vote shall not be denied or abridged by the United States or by any State on account of race, color, or previous condition of servitude.

*Section 2.* The Congress shall have power to enforce this article by appropriate legislation.

## AMENDMENT XVI 1913

The Congress shall have power to lay and collect taxes on incomes, from whatever source derived, without apportionment among the several States, and without regard to any census or enumeration.

## AMENDMENT XVII 1913

The Senate of the United States shall be composed of two Senators from each State, elected by the people thereof, for six years; and each Senator shall have one vote. The electors in each State shall have the qualifications requisite for electors of the most numerous branch of the State legislature.

When vacancies happen in the representation of any State in the Senate, the executive authority of such State shall issue writs of election to fill such vacancies:

*Provided,* That the legislature of any State may empower the executive thereof to make temporary appointments until the people fill the vacancies by election as the legislature may direct.

This amendment shall not be so construed as to affect the election or term of any Senator chosen before it becomes valid as part of the Constitution.

## AMENDMENT XVIII 1919

*Section 1. After one year from the ratification of this article the manufacture, sale, or transportation of intoxicating liquors within, the importation thereof into, or the exportation thereof from the United States and all territory subject to the jurisdiction thereof for beverage purposes is hereby prohibited.*[15]

*Section 2.* The Congress and the several States shall have concurrent power to enforce this article by appropriate legislation.

*Section 3.* This article shall be inoperative unless it shall have been ratified as an amendment to the Constitution by the legislatures of the several States, as provided in the Constitution, within seven years from the date of the submission hereof to the States by the Congress.

## AMENDMENT XIX 1920

*Section 1.* The right of citizens of the United States to vote shall not be denied or abridged by the United States or by any State on account of sex.

*Section 2.* Congress shall have power, by appropriate legislation, to enforce the provisions of this article.

## AMENDMENT XX 1933

*Section 1.* The terms of the President and Vice President shall end at noon on the 20th day of January, and the terms of Senators and Representatives at noon on the 3rd day of January, of the years in which such terms would have ended if this article had not been ratified; and the terms of their successors shall then begin.

*Section 2.* The Congress shall assemble at least once in every year, and such meeting shall begin at noon on the 3rd day of January, unless they shall by law appoint a different day.

[15] Repealed by Amendment XXI.

*Section 3.* If, at the time fixed for the beginning of the term of the President, the President elect shall have died, the Vice President elect shall become President. If a President shall not have been chosen before the time fixed for the beginning of his term, or if the President elect shall have failed to qualify, then the Vice President elect shall act as President until a President shall have qualified; and the Congress may by law provide for the case wherein neither a President elect nor a Vice President elect shall have qualified, declaring who shall then act as President, or the manner in which one who is to act shall be selected, and such person shall act accordingly until a President or Vice President shall have qualified.

*Section 4.* The Congress may by law provide for the case of the death of any of the persons from whom the House of Representatives may choose a President whenever the right of choice shall have devolved upon them, and for the case of the death of any of the persons from whom the Senate may choose a Vice President whenever the right of choice shall have devolved upon them.

*Section 5.* Sections 1 and 2 shall take effect on the 15th day of October following the ratification of this article.

*Section 6.* This article shall be inoperative unless it shall have been ratified as an amendment to the Constitution by the legislatures of three fourths of the several States within seven years from the date of its submission.

## AMENDMENT XXI 1933

*Section 1.* The eighteenth article of amendment to the Constitution of the United States is hereby repealed.

*Section 2.* The transportation or importation into any State, Territory, or possession of the United States for delivery or use therein of intoxicating liquors, in violation of the laws thereof, is hereby prohibited.

*Section 3.* This article shall be inoperative unless it shall have been ratified as an amendment to the Constitution by conventions in the several States, as provided in the Constitution, within seven years from the date of submission hereof to the States by the Congress.

## AMENDMENT XXII 1951

*Section 1.* No person shall be elected to the office of the President more than twice, and no person who has held the office of President, or acted as President, for more than two years of a term to which some other person was elected President shall be elected to the office of the President more than once. But this Article shall not apply to any person holding the office of President when this Article was proposed by the Congress, and shall not prevent any person who may be holding the office of President, or acting as President, during the term within which this Article becomes operative from holding the office of President or acting as President during the remainder of such term.

*Section 2.* This article shall be inoperative unless it shall have been ratified as an amendment to the Constitution by the legislatures of three fourths of the several States within seven years from the date of its submission to the States by the Congress.

# Appendix III

## CHARTER OF THE UNITED NATIONS

*We the peoples of the United Nations determined to save succeeding generations from the scourge of war, which twice in our lifetime has brought untold sorrow to mankind, and*

to reaffirm faith in fundamental human rights, in the dignity and worth of the human person, in the equal rights of men and women and of nations large and small, and

to establish conditions under which justice and respect for the obligations arising from treaties and other sources of international law can be maintained, and

to promote social progress and better standards of life in larger freedom,

*And for these ends*

to practice tolerance and live together in peace with one another as good neighbors, and

to unite our strength to maintain international peace and security, and to ensure, by the acceptance of principles and the institution of methods, that armed force shall not be used, save in the common interest, and

to employ international machinery for the promotion of the economic and social advancement of all peoples,

*Have resolved to combine our efforts to accomplish these aims.*

Accordingly, our respective Governments, through representatives assembled in the city of San Francisco, who have exhibited their full powers found to be in good and due form, have agreed to the present Charter of the United Nations and do hereby establish an international organization to be known as the United Nations.

### Chapter I: PURPOSES AND PRINCIPLES

#### Article 1

The Purposes of the United Nations are:

1. To maintain international peace and security, and to that end: to take effective collective measures for the prevention and removal of threats to the peace, and for the suppression of acts of aggression or other breaches of the peace, and to bring about by peaceful means, and in conformity with the principles of justice and international law, adjustment or settlement of international disputes or situations which might lead to a breach of the peace;

2. To develop friendly relations among nations based on respect for the principle of equal rights and self-determination of peoples, and to take other appropriate measures to strengthen universal peace;

3. To achieve international co-operation in solving international problems of an economic, social, cultural, or humanitarian character, and in promoting and encouraging respect for human rights and for fundamental freedoms for all without distinction as to race, sex, language, or religion; and

4. To be a center for harmonizing the actions of nations in the attainment of these common ends.

### Article 2

The Organization and its Members, in pursuit of the Purposes stated in Article 1, shall act in accordance with the following Principles.

1. The Organization is based on the principle of the sovereign equality of all its Members.

2. All Members, in order to ensure to all of them the rights and benefits resulting from membership, shall fulfil in good faith the obligations assumed by them in accordance with the present Charter.

3. All Members shall settle their international disputes by peaceful means in such a manner that international peace and security, and justice, are not endangered.

4. All Members shall refrain in their international relations from the threat or use of force against the territorial integrity or political independence of any state, or in any other manner inconsistent with the Purposes of the United Nations.

5. All Members shall give the United Nations every assistance in any action it takes in accordance with the present Charter, and shall refrain from giving assistance to any state against which the United Nations is taking preventive or enforcement action.

6. The Organization shall ensure that states which are not Members of the United Nations act in accordance with these Principles so far as may be necessary for the maintenance of international peace and security.

7. Nothing contained in the present Charter shall authorize the United Nations to intervene in matters which are essentially within the domestic jurisdiction of any state or shall require the Members to submit such matters to settlement under the present Charter; but this principle shall not prejudice the application of enforcement measures under Chapter VII.

## Chapter II: MEMBERSHIP

### Article 3

The original Members of the United Nations shall be the states which, having participated in the United Nations Conference on International Organization at San Francisco, or having previously signed the Declaration by United Nations of January 1, 1942, sign the present Charter and ratify it in accordance with Article 110.

### Article 4

1. Membership in the United Nations is open to all other peace-loving states which accept the obligations contained in the present Charter and, in the judgment of the Organization, are able and willing to carry out these obligations.

2. The admission of any such state to membership in the United Nations will be effected by a decision of the General Assembly upon the recommendation of the Security Council.

## Article 5

A Member of the United Nations against which preventive or enforcement action has been taken by the Security Council may be suspended from the exercise of the rights and privileges of membership by the General Assembly upon the recommendation of the Security Council. The exercise of these rights and privileges may be restored by the Security Council.

## Article 6

A Member of the United Nations which has persistently violated the Principles contained in the present Charter may be expelled from the Organization by the General Assembly upon the recommendation of the Security Council.

## Chapter III: ORGANS

## Article 7

1. There are established as the principal organs of the United Nations; a General Assembly, a Security Council, an Economic and Social Council, a Trusteeship Council, an International Court of Justice, and a Secretariat.

2. Such subsidiary organs as may be found necessary may be established in accordance with the present Charter.

## Article 8

The United Nations shall place no restrictions on the eligibility of men and women to participate in any capacity and under conditions of equality in its principal and subsidiary organs.

# Index

# Index

573